Making the Most of Africa's Commodities:
Industrializing for Growth, Jobs and Economic Transformation

ECONOMIC REPORT ON AFRICA
2013

Ordering information

To order copies of *Making the Most of Africa's Commodities: Industrializing for Growth, Jobs and Economic Transformation* by the Economic Commission for Africa, please contact:

Publications:
Economic Commission for Africa
P.O. Box 3001
Addis Ababa, Ethiopia

Tel: +251 11 544-9900
Fax: +251 11 551-4416
E-mail: ecainfo@uneca.org
Web: www.uneca.org

Sales No.: E.13.II.K.1
ISBN-13: 978-92-1-125119-7
eISBN: 978-92-1-056076-4

Cover design: Carolina Rodriguez

Table of Contents

Foreword

Africa is at a critical juncture in its development trajectory. The global economic and geopolitical changes of the last two decades have shifted the global traditional power structures and witnessed the emergence of new powers from the South. This shift, driven largely by a revolution in information and communications technology, has led to substantial increases in cross-border capital flows and trade in intermediate goods, thus reflecting the rising importance of value chains. Changes in demography, rapid urbanization and a prolonged commodity-price boom have also made huge global changes, all of which present unprecedented opportunities for Africa to overcome its legacies and embark on a bold agenda that will see the continent emerge as a global economic power.

Given its remarkable growth since 2000, the continent has been hailed as the next frontier for opportunity and a potential global growth pole. Political conflicts have declined, economic growth is robust and economic management, governance and political stability have improved. All have contributed to a marked shift in global perception of the continent, from pessimism to enormous potential, with both traditional and new economic powers clamouring to offer their partnership.

Yet recent economic performance has not generated enough economic diversification, job growth or social development to create wealth and lift millions of Africans out of poverty. A key challenge, therefore, is how Africa can pursue more effective policies to accelerate and sustain high growth and make that growth more inclusive and equitable. African countries must use this global interest as springboard to achieving broad structural transformation based on the needs and priorities of Africans.

> *African countries have a real opportunity, individually and collectively, to promote economic transformation and to address poverty, inequality and youth unemployment. They can capitalize on their resource endowments and high international commodity prices as well as changes in how global production processes are organized.*

It is precisely because of these challenges that the theme of this year's *Economic Report on Africa 2013* is on "Making the most of Africa's commodities: industrializing for growth, jobs and economic transformation". This theme is important because commodity-based industrialization can provide an engine of growth for the continent, reducing its marginalization in the global economy and enhancing its resilience to shocks. African countries have a real opportunity, individually and collectively, to promote economic transformation and to address poverty, inequality and youth unemployment. They can capitalize on their resource endowments and high international commodity prices as well as changes in how global production processes are organized.

This report argues that the deindustrialization of many African economies over the last three decades, resulting in their increasing marginalization in the global economy, was mainly the result of inadequate policies and offers a policy framework for these countries to trigger resource-based industrialization. Key among the components of this framework is the need to design and implement effective development plans and industrial strategies to address constraints and tap opportunities for African countries to engage in value addition and commodity-based industrialization. For industrial policy to be effective there is a need for policy space. Many African countries saw notable improvements in policy space especially before the recent global financial crises thanks to prudent macroeconomic management. Successful industrial policy would assist African countries strengthen and sustain their policy space through higher and sustainable growth rates and tax revenue.

This report also underscores the need for African countries to develop appropriate local content policies, boost infrastructure, human skills and technological capabilities, and foster regional integration and intra-African trade. In this regard, the implementation of the Continental Free Trade Area (CFTA) and the regional and continental priorities of the Accelerated Industrial Development of Africa's (AIDA) Action Plan, for example, will be crucial.

This report is based on nine studies of African countries, which have helped to generate evidence-based policy recommendations. The studies show that African countries are adding value to their commodities and developing local backward and forward linkages to the soft, hard and energy commodity sectors. But the depth of linkages varies among countries and value addition remains generally limited, mainly because of country- or industry-specific constraints that require strategic and systematic industrial policies.

The need for Africa to industrialize to accelerate and sustain growth, create jobs for millions of its youth and achieve economic transformation makes this report timely. It is our belief that this report generates the kind of knowledge needed for the discourse on policy choices for Africa's transformative development.

Carlos Lopes
United Nations Under-Secretary-General
and Executive Secretary of UNECA

Nkosazana Clarice Dlamini Zuma
Chairperson
Africa Union Commission

Executive Summary

AFRICA'S IMPERATIVE TO INDUSTRIALIZE IN TODAY'S GLOBAL CONTEXT

The global economy has, since the turn of the century, seen vast shifts in production and trade patterns alongside the emergence of new growth poles in the South. The rapid rise of economic powers such as China, India and Brazil, the continuing financial and economic problems of industrialized countries, and ways of doing business revolutionized by advances in technology have taken the world into a new phase of globalization. This evolving order presents Africa with challenges as well as opportunities which, if met by effective policies, could lead to substantial socio-economic and political transformation, propelling the continent as a new pole of global growth.

Following two decades of near stagnation, Africa's growth performance has improved hugely since the start of the 21st century. Since 2000 the continent has seen a prolonged commodity boom and sustained growth trend. And although growth slowed from an average of 5.6 per cent in 2002–2008 to 2.2 per cent in 2009—hit by the global financial crisis and steep food and fuel price rises—Africa quickly recovered with growth of 4.6 per cent in 2010. The continent's growth slipped again in 2011 owing to political transition in North Africa, but rebounded strongly once more to 5.0 per cent in 2012, despite the global slowdown and uncertainty.

This remarkable performance—although largely commodity driven—is underpinned by a variety of factors, such as strengthening domestic demand associated with rising incomes and urbanization, increasing public spending (especially on infrastructure), bumper harvests in some regions (due to favourable weather), tightening trade and investment ties with emerging economies (linked to their investment in Africa's natural resource and extractive industries) and post-conflict economic recovery in several countries. Africa's medium-term growth prospects remain strong, too, at for example 4.8 per cent in 2013 and 5.1 per cent in 2014.

Yet this impressive growth story has not translated into economic diversification, commensurate jobs or faster social development: most African economies still depend heavily on commodity production and exports, with too little value addition and few forward and backward linkages to other sectors of the economy. Indeed, the pattern of social development in Africa has been mixed over recent years: changes for the better are still recorded in most areas (especially education, child and maternal mortality rates, and gender equality), but the pace is too slow for African countries to achieve their social development goals, especially some of the Millennium Development Goals by the end date of 2015.

The limited impact of commodity-driven growth on employment and social development has been aggravated by liberalizing reforms and globalization that, in the absence of serious government policies to promote economies' productive capacities and ability to compete in international markets, have left a legacy of inappropriate incentives and institutions that threaten economic and political stability as well as social cohesion. Major deficits in state and institutional capacities, in physical and policy infrastructure, as well as an inability to mitigate impacts of external shocks have contributed to the continent's "transformation challenge". African countries must therefore address the reasons why stronger growth and trade have not stimulated economic diversification, job creation and socio-economic development.

The key challenge for African countries today is how to design and implement effective policies to promote industrialization and economic transformation. Despite some gains in manufacturing over the last decade, the continent is yet to reverse the de-industrialization that has defined its structural change in recent decades: in 1980–2010, its share of manufacturing in aggregate output declined from more than 12 per cent to around 11 per cent, but remained at more than 31 per cent in East Asia, where labour-intensive industries induced high and sustained growth and helped lift hundreds of millions of citizens out of poverty.

Africa has also lagged behind East Asia on other measures. That region has seen not only surging per capita income but also a soaring share of global exports and income over the last four decades (table 1). Industrial policies were particularly successful in East Asia because of committed and visionary political leadership and institutions that designed and enforced strict performance criteria for industries that received subsidies and trade protection, supported by a capable bureaucracy largely insulated from political capture.

TABLE 1: AS AFRICA DE-INDUSTRIALIZED, EAST ASIA WAS FIRING ON ALL CYLINDERS

	1970	1980	1990	2000	2010
Africa					
Nominal GDP per capita (US$)	246	900	780	740	1,701
Share in world output (%)	2.75	3.65	2.22	1.85	2.73
Share in global exports (%)	4.99	5.99	3.02	2.31	3.33
East Asia					
Nominal GDP per capita (US$)	335	1,329	3,018	4,731	8,483
Share in world output (%)	9.83	12.94	18.14	21.53	20.69
Share in global exports (%)	2.25	3.74	8.06	12.02	17.8

Source: World Bank, World Development Indicators, 2012.

Africa's industrialization strategies have not, however, transformed its economies. The seeds of its woes were sown during the colonial period but the problem worsened after independence with the failure of often externally generated industrial policies.

The colonial legacy is the result of the extractive nature of African colonialism, which left behind structures, institutions, and infrastructure designed to benefit non-Africans. For instance, the roads and railways built in colonial times were primarily designed to transport minerals and other raw materials from the African interior to the continent's ports for shipping to Europe. They were not designed to join one part of the continent to another, and created a legacy that is still felt in the twenty-first century, with production and export of commodities geared towards the needs of the former colonial powers—not value addition.

Then comes the seesaw of policy failure after independence: first, import substitution policies under which African countries decided to industrialize, then structural adjustment programmes, which forced African countries to de-industrialize.

The continent's early state-led industrialization strategies that focused on import substitution were characterized by massive public investment and ownership of enterprises and financial institutions—and a range of policy measures including tariff and non-tariff barriers, credit controls and foreign exchange restrictions to protect infant industries. But most governments did not have the financial and managerial capacity to operate public enterprises and financial institutions, and the policies intended to direct investment towards industry distorted factor prices and rates of return. Thus, while import-substitution strategies succeeded elsewhere—especially in East Asia—they failed to ignite sustained industrialization in Africa, leading to mounting and unsustainable deficits, stagflation and debt crises in many countries by the end of the 1970s.

To help African countries deal with unfolding economic crises, the International Monetary Fund and the World Bank imposed structural adjustment programmes in the 1980s and 1990s. Their theoretical premise was that markets are efficient but government interventions are inefficient because they distort market signals. Hence, long-term development planning was abandoned and industrial policies neglected in most African countries. The market-led development model removed inefficient government interventions but did not create the conditions for development or address the numerous market failures in African economies, such as a severe shortage of technical skills and entrepreneurship and low rates of investment.

African governments focused on macroeconomic stability and institutional reforms to protect property rights and ensure contract enforcement—often on advice from donors and multilateral development institutions—but without coherent strategies to address market failures

and externalities that constrained investment, growth and economic diversification.

Thus, Africa's growth plummeted during the "lost decades" of the 1980s and 1990s while unemployment soared, and production and export bases became more concentrated. And without industrial policies to address policy and market failures (especially of information and coordination), African countries have been unable, until now, to diversify and parlay recent high growth and increased trade into social and economic development.

More recently, the structure of the global system has made it practically impossible for Africa to benefit from globalization or move up the value chain, which requires Africa to influence the global agenda in its favour.

TRIGGERING COMMODITY-BASED INDUSTRIALIZATION AS AN ENGINE OF GROWTH AND ECONOMIC TRANSFORMATION

Africa boasts significant human and natural resources that can be used to promote industrialization and structural economic transformation through value-addition strategies in all sectors (agriculture, industry and services), though not all African countries are rich in natural commodities—some are resource poor. As well as a growing, predominantly young and urbanizing population, the continent is endowed with many natural resources, including plentiful land and fertile soils, oil and minerals. Africa has about 12 per cent of the world's oil reserves, 42 per cent of its gold, 80–90 per cent of chromium and platinum group metals, and 60 per cent of arable land in addition to vast timber resources.

With such abundance and rising global demand for raw materials, African governments are forging new partnerships, boosting infrastructure investment and sharing skills and technology.

But Africa can do better. Primary commodity production and exports entail huge forgone income through lack of value addition, the export of jobs to countries that can add value, and exposure to high risks due to dependence on exhaustible commodities and fluctuations in commodity demand and prices. Instead of relying on exports of raw materials, the continent should add value to its commodities to promote sustained growth, jobs and economic transformation.

While African commodity-exporting economies have benefited greatly from recent sustained increases in the price of their primary commodity exports and an increase in resource rents, these rents cannot be relied on as an engine of growth and development. This is not only because commodities are exhaustible but also because adding value would help African countries to reduce exposure to the risk of commodity price fluctuation and at the same time move to higher-value and more diversified product- and end-markets where prices are more dependent on market fundamentals than speculation.

Indeed, the entry of financial agents on the spot and futures markets and the resulting financialization of commodity trading have frequently caused these markets to move from a price-taking environment to one of market power, partly because they are highly concentrated and often laced with information asymmetry. Financial agents have become key players in driving speculation and herd behaviour, and have distorted commodity markets including upward shifts in coffee and cocoa prices and all-time low prices for cotton.

This behaviour has left African countries more vulnerable to fluctuations in commodity markets, whereas artificially high prices for some commodities have reduced incentives for value addition. Promoting commodity-based industrialization could offer a powerful tool for African countries to tackle this "tyranny of financialization". Equally, production of many commodities is capital intensive, holding back employment and the distribution of their rents. A more sustainable, inclusive and equitable growth path in commodity-exporting economies lies in the possibilities of building backward and forward linkages for commodity production.

One upshot of the above factors is that, although Africa's growth exceeded the world average in the 2000s, it did not translate into commensurate poverty reduction at a time when poverty elsewhere fell heavily, skewing the global poverty reduction picture. Similarly, the global dispersion of production has led to unequal benefits, benefiting east and south-east Asian economies, especially China, the most.

So, how can Africa avoid marginalizing itself from the world economy and achieve inclusive economic growth? The 2013 edition of the Economic Report on Africa, themed "Making the most of Africa's commodities: Industrializing for growth, jobs and economic transformation", argues that one answer lies in effective industrial policies and commodity-based industrialization, strengthening industrial linkages to the commodity sector.

On top of offering short- to medium-term comparative advantages, commodity-based industrialization can, with the right industrial policies, serve as a launching pad for long-term diversification and competitiveness in new and non-commodity sectors in Africa's commodity-rich countries.

The conventional wisdom in the "resource curse" literature argues differently—that commodities are an undesirable form of economic specialization undermining the viability of industrial activity—although global economic dynamics now suggest that this trade-off between commodities and industry no longer holds. The shift in global economic gravity from high-income Northern to low-income Southern economies suggests a reversal in the long-term declining trend in the commodities–manufactures terms of trade. More important, on top of offering short- to medium-term comparative advantages, commodity-based industrialization can, with the right industrial policies, serve as a launching pad for long-term diversification and competitiveness in new and non-commodity sectors in Africa's commodity-rich countries.

9

Moreover, the past decade has seen a major shift in the structure of global value chains (GVCs) in many sectors, as major firms seek to outsource non-core competences, and thus promote linkages. This suggests that we may be entering a new era in the relationship between the exploitation of commodities and the growth of industry—if African governments put in place policies to facilitate and accelerate such dynamics. As firms that control GVCs cannot be relied on to promote linkages beyond their own interests, African governments need to make strategic interventions to empower indigenous firms to insert themselves and compete in regional and global value chains.

African governments need to put in place policies to facilitate linkage development. As firms that control GVCs cannot be relied on to promote linkages beyond their own interests, African governments need to make strategic interventions to empower indigenous firms to insert themselves and compete in regional and global value chains.

The desire by African governments to promote linkages from the commodity sector is not new and the continent offers many successful sector and country experiences. Mauritius provides a good example of a country that successfully developed visions and long-term strategies to move from a degree of high production and export concentration in 1980 to wide diversification three decades later. Changes in the nature of globalization in the current era have opened still-unrealized opportunities for increasing local industrialization linkages.

Against this backdrop, the report examines key constraints and opportunities for African countries to make the most of their commodities by adding value through linkage development. It then addresses how African countries can design and implement industrial and other development policies to promote value addition and economic transformation, and to reduce their dependence on producing and exporting unprocessed commodities.

The analysis uses desk research and country-specific background policy information, primary firm-level data and information from questionnaires and interviews to underpin evidence-based policy recommendations. The primary data were collected and country case studies prepared for nine African countries in the five subregions—Algeria, Cameroon, Egypt, Ethiopia, Ghana, Kenya, Nigeria, South Africa and Zambia.

As in previous years, the report begins by examining recent trends in Africa's economic and social development as well as selected issues, namely trade and financing for economic transformation and the question of how to translate growth into decent job creation, before focusing on "Making the most of Africa's commodities: Industrializing for growth, jobs and economic transformation"—a very brief synopsis of which is distilled into the following paragraphs.

MAKING THE MOST OF AFRICA'S COMMODITIES: CONSTRAINTS AND OPPORTUNITIES

Some of the nine countries show evidence of making progress in developing local linkages (backward and forward) from the hard, energy and soft commodity sectors. But value addition is still limited and the depth of linkages varies among countries, mainly because of country- or industry-specific constraints that cannot be overcome by market forces and that call for strategic and systematic industrial policies. Even today, up to 90 per cent of the total income from coffee goes to rich consuming countries—underscoring the benefits African countries are currently forgoing.

The following are the key findings of the report on value chain linkages.

THE BIG DIFFERENCES IN SOFT, HARD AND ENERGY COMMODITY SECTORS AFFECT HOW LINKAGES DEVELOP

Most soft commodities, as against hard commodities, have low technological content, lend themselves to small-scale production, are labour intensive, require a heterogeneous and diffused infrastructure and rarely stay fresh in their natural state, requiring early processing. Hard commodities generally embody more complex technologies and require intensive use of large infrastructure (such as roads, railways and ports) that can be used for developing other sectors. Energy commodities are mainly very technology, scale and capital intensive, requiring infrastructure of less use to other sectors.

ESTABLISHING MARKETING LINKS AND STAYING IN GVCS IS ESSENTIAL, BUT REQUIRES SYSTEMATIC INVESTMENT AND SUPPORT

Searching for buyers is a costly exercise for any firm, but a firm must be inserted in regional and global value chains. Building these linkages requires appropriate domestic strategic government support for firms to be globally competitive in "critical success factors" such as price, quality, lead times, dynamic capabilities and compliance with technical, private, health and environmental standards. Linkage development is thus a progressive and cumulative process, and requires continuous investment in technologies, research and development and skills, among other elements.

ALL LINKS IN THE VALUE CHAIN REQUIRE SUPPORT TO UPGRADE

Trade-offs between the links may, though, be needed. For example, because output from the food commodity sector can vary enormously in quality, price and technical specifications, adding value in agro-processing normally requires support at different stages, including production, marketing, storage and transport. To avoid unintended negative impacts on producers in other links, strategies that target processing industries must be integrated with interventions at the commodity-producing and primary-processing stages.

REGIONAL MARKETS MAY OFFER MORE OPPORTUNITIES THAN TRADITIONAL MARKETS

Such opportunities are more apparent when a firm enters a GVC. Regional markets may be initially less demanding and allow local firms to build the necessary production capabilities required to graduate into more demanding global chains, a point particularly important for countries without large domestic markets. The regional approach opens up space for ensuring that regional integration within Africa is fast-tracked and streamlined to provide local competitive advantage.

TRADE AGREEMENTS WITH TRADITIONAL INDUSTRIALIZED COUNTRIES AND EMERGING PARTNERS ARE IMPORTANT FOR ENTERING NEW MARKETS

African countries need to improve market access for their value-added products through agreements with traditional and emerging partners. Their strategies, based on a united framework for negotiation, should aim to maximize the development impact of partnerships and, specifically, to reduce high tariffs (on cocoa to India, for example) and remove tariff escalation (in the European Union, for instance).

MAKING THE MOST OF AFRICA'S COMMODITIES: A POLICY FRAMEWORK

The report identifies factors that influence linkage breadth and depth—technical features of the value chain, industry structure, lead-firm strategies for their critical success factors, location and infrastructure, a variety of constraints (trade restrictions, standards), and government industrial policy. The unevenness of development among countries is attributed to two primary sets of linkage drivers—structural and country-specific.

Structural drivers refer to the age of the commodity-exploiting sector and sectoral factors such as the requirement for just-in-time and flexible logistics, the characteristics of commodity deposits, and the sector's technological complexity. By their very nature, these drivers are difficult to influence through policy interventions. Country-specific drivers, on the other hand, are much easier to influence by government policy, and refer to factors dependent on national context, such as infrastructure and human resources.

There is no "one size fits all" policy approach for commodity-based industrialization in African countries, or anywhere for that matter, and government policy should be country specific and evidence based. It should also have clear priorities, designate institutional steps to ensure responsibility for implementation across ministries at central or local levels, and be backed by transparent budgets.

The key policy recommendations for adding value and industrializing in Africa follow.

ADOPT AND IMPLEMENT A COHERENT INDUSTRIAL POLICY

If African governments want to speed up and deepen value addition of local production linkages to the commodity sector, and to embark on a commodity-based industrialization path, they must adopt a strategic approach and work closely with all stakeholders to formulate and implement industrial policy. The policy should start by identifying value addition or linkage opportunities as well as medium- and long-term interventions.

CREATE APPROPRIATE INCLUSIVE AND TRANSPARENT INSTITUTIONAL INDUSTRIAL-POLICY MECHANISMS

It is critical for governments to develop prioritized country-specific, industrial-policy roadmaps for value addition, working closely with stakeholders including representatives of firms and of research and innovation institutions. They should set up a multi-stakeholder institutional council that focuses on developing linkages to the commodity sector, led by the most appropriate government department (usually the ministry of industry). This

council should be charged with developing a joint, strategic vision for industrialization—gathering the most reliable information and elaborating an appropriate step-by-step linkage strategy. The strategy should outline support mechanisms including responsibilities, activities, outputs and milestones.

DEVELOP AN APPROPRIATELY DIRECTED LOCAL CONTENT POLICY

Local content policies have probably been the single most important policy driver of linkages from the commodity sector. World Trade Organization rules provide some legal leeway to least-developed economies—and many countries anyway find real-world mechanisms to push through and sustain local content policies. Policies should focus on adding value locally (rather than satisfying special interest groups), removing red tape and streamlining regulations, as well as securing technical and financial assistance for developing linkages.

ADOPT STRATEGIC INTERVENTIONS TO INSERT INDIGENOUS FIRMS IN SUPPLY CHAINS

Following the dynamics of national, regional and global value chains, it is in the interests of major commodity firms to outsource many of their supplies and services. Industrial policy should cover customized supply-chain development programmes that help indigenous firms to insert themselves in these value chains and to remain competitive. Such policy may focus on upscale niche markets and quality certification—environmental sustainability, speciality products or fair trade—as well as on special funding mechanisms to build firms' capabilities in backward and forward linkages.

BOOSTING LOCAL SKILLS AND TECHNOLOGICAL CAPABILITIES

Skills shortages are often a binding constraint on developing industrial linkages in Africa.

They hamstring local suppliers in upgrading operational competitiveness, meeting technical requirements, innovating, adopting world-class manufacturing practices and running supply-chain and customer-management programmes. Backward linkage development to the hard commodity sector is particularly demanding of technological capabilities to compete with global suppliers. Building necessary skills requires coordinated support from other firms, the government and donors. Government support may include matching-grant programmes for skills development for local firms, creation of technical training institutions and staff hires.

ADDRESS INFRASTRUCTURE CONSTRAINTS AND BOTTLENECKS

Infrastructure deficits affect not only cross-border infrastructure but also feeder roads linking agricultural producers to processing centres. Infrastructure development helps to ease these bottlenecks, and has spin-offs for jobs for unskilled and semi-skilled workers as well as for training for those with higher artisanal skills. Industrial and development policy in Africa should include strategic investment in infrastructure and avoid "enclave" infrastructure projects and programmes aimed only at satisfying the needs of commodity producers. Governments should use commodity access to secure favourable financing (of infrastructure in bilateral agreements), to leverage public–private partnerships (to facilitate infrastructure provision) and to restructure institutions that provide soft infrastructure (to simplify and make the regulatory framework effective, efficient and business friendly).

IMPROVE POLICY IMPLEMENTATION THROUGH COORDINATION AMONG MINISTRIES

Value chains are cross-cutting, ministries are not. A commodity-based industrial strategy necessarily requires inter-departmental direction and implementation. Soft commodities tend to fall under the mandate of agriculture ministries and hard commodities under mining

and oil ministries; industrial policy requires the involvement and direction of ministries of industry, besides the budgetary allocations for implementation. Effective policy implementation therefore requires coordination across ministries and departments in the context of broader national development plans and frameworks that ensure participation of the private sector and other stakeholders.

NEGOTIATE REGIONAL TRADE ARRANGEMENTS AND FOSTER INTRA-AFRICAN TRADE

Regional markets can be important in facilitating local production linkages both within and between African countries. It is extremely difficult to export to high-income, industrialized-country markets as their critical success factors are often beyond the immediate reach of many domestic firms. Regional markets are often less demanding and provide learning opportunities for domestic firms to build their production capabilities step-by-step. They also allow them to build economies of scale, some degree of specialization between countries and functional upgrades through regional "country of origin" branding—hence greater returns. African countries should therefore fast-track implementation of the Continental Free Trade Area agreement and accelerate that of regional trade arrangements to reduce or eliminate non-tariff barriers, sanitary and phytosanitary measures, and technical barriers to trade. They should also improve regional infrastructure and harmonize customs procedures.

MAKING THE MOST OF REGIONAL POLICY FRAMEWORKS

To be effective and improve coordination at regional and continental levels, national industrial development frameworks in Africa should, as far as possible, be closely aligned with the priorities of the Accelerated Industrial Development of Africa Action Plan, endorsed by African Ministers of Industry in 2007. This identifies priorities for action at national, regional, continental and international levels, including product and export diversification policy, natural resource management and value addition in natural resources, infrastructure, human capital and technology, institutional frameworks and resource mobilization.

To cater to domestic and export markets, this report recommends that national value-adding strategies should also be closely coordinated to boost efforts by African countries to promote strategic commodities such as rice, legumes, maize, cotton, palm oil, beef as well as dairy, poultry and fishery products at continental level, and cassava, sorghum and millet subregionally.

... AND FINALLY

The findings and recommendations of this report strongly complement those of previous years that emphasized the need for African countries to pursue effective policy actions to address the factors constraining economic transformation. For example, the 2012 report pursued the theme that, to address the failures of state-and market-led development experiences and to unleash Africa's potential as a pole of global growth, the continent required developmental states that design and implement innovative and bold long-term actions.

This report underscores the point that commodity-based industrialization in Africa should not—and cannot—be the only way for African countries to industrialize. Not all African countries are rich in natural resources and, in the long-term, even resource-rich countries have to venture into innovative non-resource-based activities to sustain their industries when resources are exhausted.

Africa's industrialization is likely to take place in a changing globalized economy full of uncertainties. African governments should therefore work together to develop a united vision on how to influence the global economic agenda and, in so doing, shape the outcomes of globalization itself. The time has come for Africa to stop being a bystander to its own destiny.

Economic and Social Developments in Africa and Medium-term Prospects

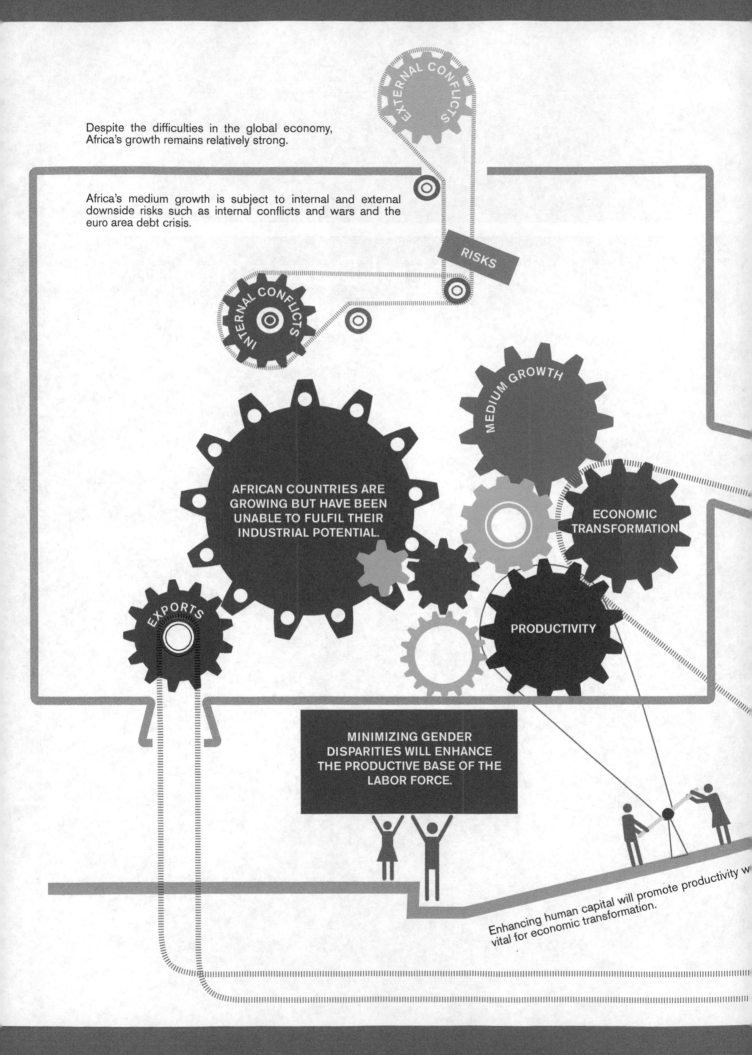

Despite the difficulties in the global economy, Africa's growth remains relatively strong.

Africa's medium growth is subject to internal and external downside risks such as internal conflicts and wars and the euro area debt crisis.

EXTERNAL CONFLICTS

RISKS

INTERNAL CONFLICTS

MEDIUM GROWTH

AFRICAN COUNTRIES ARE GROWING BUT HAVE BEEN UNABLE TO FULFIL THEIR INDUSTRIAL POTENTIAL.

ECONOMIC TRANSFORMATION

EXPORTS

PRODUCTIVITY

MINIMIZING GENDER DISPARITIES WILL ENHANCE THE PRODUCTIVE BASE OF THE LABOR FORCE.

Enhancing human capital will promote productivity w vital for economic transformation.

FRICAN COUNTRIES REQUIRE ROBUST, BROAD-BASED AND
NCLUSIVE ECONOMIC GROWTH FOR A LONG PERIOD.

HEY HAVE A REAL OPPORTUNITY, INDIVIDUALLY AND
OLLECTIVELY, TO PROMOTE ECONOMIC TRANSFORMATION
HROUGH COMMODITY-BASED INDUSTRIALIZATION AND TO
DDRESS POVERTY, INEQUALITY AND YOUTH UNEMPLOYMENT.

BROAD-BASED AND INCLUSIVE GROWTH

JOBS

OPPORTUNITIES

Economic transformation will create
job opportunities for the youth and
unleash Africa's growth potential.

JOBS

GROWTH POTENTIAL

OPPORTUNITIES

JOBS   JOBS

OPPORTUNITIES

JOBS

OPPORTUNITIES

JOBS   OPPORTUNITIES

RESOURCES

Africa's growth is heavily dependent on primary
commodity exports.

The world economy showed signs of decelerating in 2012, threatening the pace of the recovery from the global financial and economic crisis of 2008–2009. The euro area, Africa's biggest economic partner, headed for another recession with lingering worries over mounting sovereign debts and fiscal sustainability. Emerging economies, such as China and India, saw notably slower activity. Prospects of an early exit from the turmoil are clouded by uncertainty over the euro area sovereign debt crisis, fiscal consolidation in major world regions and the brinksmanship of negotiations over the "fiscal cliff" and debt ceiling in the United States (US). They have induced downside risks in an already fragile global economy.

Africa's economic growth picked up in 2012 to well above the worldwide average, despite these global headwinds. The recovery in many African countries was underpinned by a variety of factors, including high demand and prices for commodities on international markets, strengthening domestic demand associated with rising incomes and urbanization, increasing public spending (especially on infrastructure), bumper harvests in some regions (due to favourable weather), tightening trade and investment ties with emerging economies (linked to their investment in Africa's natural-resource and extractive industries), and post-conflict economic recovery in some conflict countries.

The continent's medium-term growth prospects are positive, although it faces risks such as reliance on traditional rain-fed agriculture, political instability and social unrest in some of its countries and uncertainty due to the global economic outlook.

Yet most African economies still depend heavily on commodity production and exports—despite diversifying into non-primary commodity sectors such as manufacturing and services—with limited value addition and few forward and backward linkages to other sectors of the economy. This structural weakness has prevented them from transforming growth into commensurate jobs and faster social development. Indeed, the pattern of social development trends in Africa has been mixed

over recent years: positive changes continue to be recorded in most areas but the pace of progress is slow and insufficient for African countries to achieve their social development goals—especially the Millennium Development Goals (MDGs) by the original date of 2015.

Value addition and structural transformation are, though, essential for these countries' economies to accelerate and then sustain broad growth; to improve social conditions by creating jobs, lowering inequality and cutting poverty; and to reduce their vulnerability to external shocks.

Boosting value addition appears to be an area of priority both in the development discourse and for stakeholders involved in consultations on the post-2015 development agenda organized by pan-African bodies, including the United Nations Economic Commission for Africa (ECA) and the African Union Commission (AUC). The preliminary findings of their consultations indicate a preference for an agenda that prioritizes structural transformation and inclusive growth, with a focus on promoting agriculture, manufacturing, technology and innovation, and human development.

1.1 AFRICA'S ECONOMIC PERFORMANCE IN 2012

The recovery strengthened as political tensions eased in North Africa

The economic recovery in Africa strengthened in 2012[1] to 5 per cent (figure 1.1), despite a slowing world economy. Political turmoil and tensions in North Africa began to ease—democratic elections were held and new leaders inaugurated in Egypt and Libya—and normal economic activity began to return. Africa's medium-term growth prospects remain strong at, for example, 4.8 per cent in 2013 and 5.1 per cent in 2014.

Commodity production and exports stayed essential for growth on the continent, although many countries are diversifying their economies and sources of growth. Thus in 2012 growth was

FIGURE 1.1: GDP GROWTH, 2008–2012

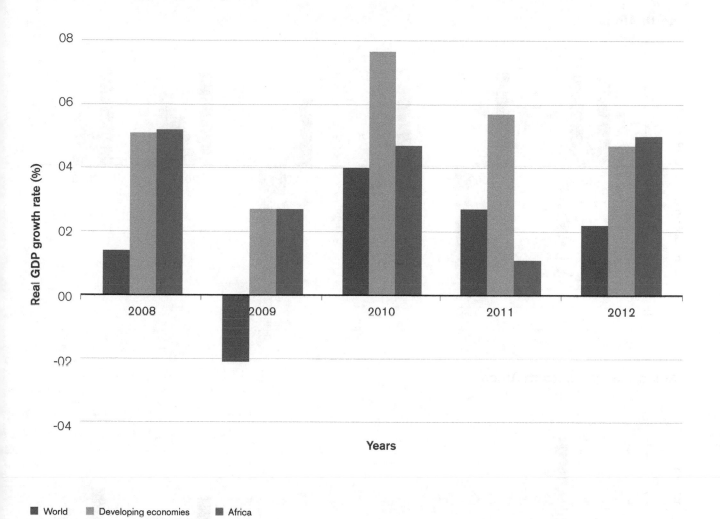

■ World ▪ Developing economies ■ Africa

Source: Calculations based on UN-DESA (2012).

strong in both commodity-rich and resource-poor countries, although of the two sets the oil-exporters saw growth rising slightly faster, thanks to increased oil production and high prices.

African growth also continued to benefit from improved macroeconomic management and prudential macroeconomic policies that underpinned strong public spending, especially on infrastructure and public services. Rising domestic consumption and investment demand, fuelled by rising incomes

and urbanization, accounted for more than half the growth in many African countries in 2012. Indeed, disaggregating the components of real gross domestic product (GDP) growth, private consumption was the key growth driver in Africa in 2012, followed by gross fixed investment and government consumption (figure 1.2). Gross fixed investment and exports recovered strongly in North Africa in 2012, but the contribution of gross fixed investment to real GDP growth declined in the rest of Africa as the external balance narrowed.

FIGURE 1.2: COMPONENTS OF REAL GDP GROWTH, 2008–2013

North Africa

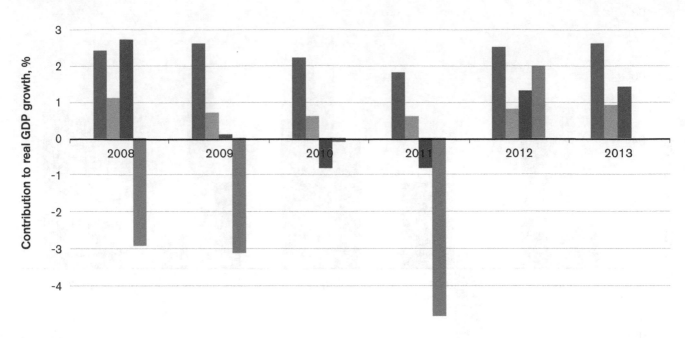

Africa, excluding North Africa

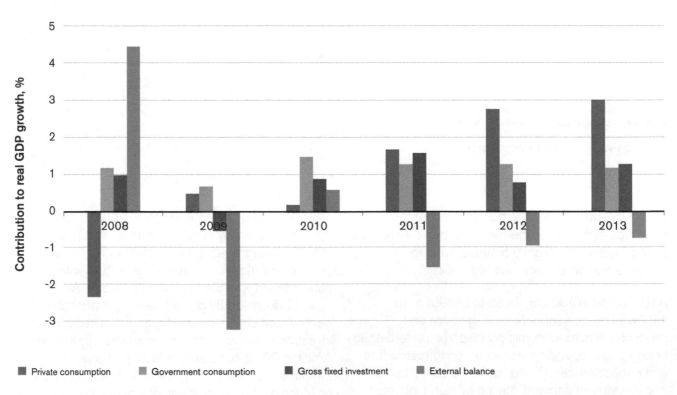

■ Private consumption ■ Government consumption ■ Gross fixed investment ■ External balance

Source: Calculations based on EIU (2012).

Growing importance of emerging economies

Although Africa's traditional partners from the "Global North" remain important, its increasing trade and investment ties with emerging economies have helped many of its countries not just to mitigate the impact of the recession in Europe but also to diversify exports by destination and composition. These ties are also helping African countries to diversify their sources of capital and to attract increased foreign direct investment (FDI) and official development assistance (ODA) for infrastructure and other non-commodity sectors. As political tensions declined, tourism receipts also rose in Africa, supporting growth in 2012.

Despite the slowdown in the global economy (box 1.1), many African countries benefited from foreign capital. ODA was almost unchanged despite the fiscal difficulties faced by major donor countries. Further, while overall FDI inflows declined, those originating from emerging economies actually increased and remittances remained high, supporting investment and demand in several African countries. Both FDI and remittances are projected to rise as the global economy recovers (see chapter 2).

BOX 1.1: KEY DEVELOPMENTS IN THE WORLD ECONOMY, 2012

The world economy grew by 2.2 per cent in 2012, slowing from 2.7 per cent in 2011, mainly owing to a decline in global demand, the euro area debt crisis and uncertainty over the fiscal cliff and debt ceiling in the US. The global recovery from the "triple crisis"—food, fuel and finance—is, however, expected to strengthen over the medium term.

Regional growth

Economic activity in the European Union (EU) contracted by 0.3 per cent in 2012 from 1.5 per cent in 2011 (UN-DESA, 2012). Germany's real GDP growth rate is expected to have contracted to 0.8 per cent in 2012 after 3.0 per cent growth in 2011, while France is estimated to have grown by only 0.1 per cent, down from 1.7 per cent. The US managed growth of 2.1 per cent in 2012, reflecting stronger private consumption and investment as well as a better credit environment. Japan's economy improved, largely on increased construction expenditure.

Economic growth decelerated in emerging economies owing to weak export demand and reduced investment growth, especially in China and India. Western Asia's economic growth rate fell to 3.3 per cent in 2012, from 6.7 per cent the previous year, owing to sluggish external demand and public spending cuts. The Latin America and the Caribbean region grew by 3.1 per cent in 2012, down from 4.3 per cent a year earlier, as export demand tailed off and commodity prices for non-food exports fell (UN-DESA, 2012).

The global job crisis persisted in 2012 despite governments' efforts to create employment and stimulate economic growth. World unemployment stood at 6 per cent in 2011 with joblessness at more than 8 per cent in developed economies as a group, down from 8.3 per cent the previous year. In 2012, unemployment reached over 25 per cent in countries such as Spain and Greece as austerity measures continued to take effect.

Prospects for the global economy hinge on an early exit from the euro area debt crisis, the success of bailout packages and the non-conventional monetary policies initiated to address fiscal and monetary integrity in major industrialized economies. Restoring fiscal integrity, coupled with measures aimed at reducing public indebtedness across the globe, still requires sound policy interventions.

With the global economy forecast to grow at 2.4 per cent in 2013 and 3.2 per cent in 2014, the worst of the sovereign debt crisis might be over, and most developed and emerging countries are expected to return to their growth trajectories in the medium term.

Inflation

World inflation declined from 3.6 per cent in 2011 to 2.8 per cent in 2012, and is expected to steadily decline to 2.6 per cent in 2013, mainly on sluggish aggregate demand, quantitative easing in the US, and ultra-low interest rates and extremely accommodative monetary policy stances in most countries. The combination of a weakened economic environment and falling inflation will enable governments in the US and euro area to allow further monetary easing, supporting the repair of private sector and bank balance sheets.

Fiscal trends

Fiscal balances improved in almost all major economies and regions, reflecting fiscal consolidation and austerity measures, although the pace may be derailed by economic and social pressures in many developed countries. Advanced economies cut their overall deficit from 6.5 per cent of GDP in 2011 to 5.9 per cent in 2012, with the US at 8.6 per cent and Japan at more than 10 per cent of GDP that year.

Fiscal positions for some developing regions such as the Latin America and the Caribbean strengthened as most countries continued their cautious fiscal policies while rebuilding fiscal buffers, aided by favourable export revenues.

Countries in the euro area are expected to reduce their overall fiscal deficit by only 0.8 per cent of GDP in 2013. In developing countries, fiscal deficits in 2013 are forecast to decrease, except in the Middle East and North Africa owing to reduced oil revenues caused by supply-side disruptions to oil production.

Commodities

The all-commodity price index increased in the first quarter of 2012, reaching a year-high of 202 in March 2012 as demand from developing countries rose. The world crude oil price remained high at around US$109.9 per barrel in 2012 compared to US$107.5 in 2011. The food price index surged after July as severe weather hit crops, especially in the US. Prices of sugar, cereals and rice rose the sharpest, while meat and dairy prices remained fairly flat. The index for agricultural raw materials and products such as coffee, rubber, cotton and beverages declined in 2012.

Most global commodity prices are expected to stay high in 2013, despite global economic growth below potential, owing to limited supply and weather risks stemming from global climate change.

External balances

World exports grew by only 5.0 per cent by value in 2012, much less than previous year's 17.3 per cent, as import demand from major developed countries sharply contracted. Current account balances for major economies and regions narrowed slightly in 2012, reflecting a decline in international trade and decelerating global demand, rather than any improvement in structural imbalances (UN-DESA, 2012).

The US dollar and Japanese yen appreciated in the first half of the year, as the euro area debt crisis drove up global investors' risk aversion and induced an appetite for safe-haven currencies. Global FDI moderated in 2012, while global remittance flows rose by 6.4 per cent (chapter 2).

Medium-term risks for the global economy

The greatest risks are difficulties in the euro area, uncertainty over tax reforms, spending cuts, the debt ceiling and high household indebtedness in the US, fiscal consolidation in most industrialized countries, economic slowdown in emerging countries and political instability, especially in the Middle East.

Policies to rectify global imbalances and ensure sound fiscal and monetary health in the global financial infrastructure remain crucial to restoring global health. The European Central Bank, for instance, has launched major policy interventions to calm the escalating crisis. These policies will, however, need to be accompanied by long-term structural reform to restore confidence in the financial sector and steer the global economy to long-term growth.

Such trade and investment ties and sources of growth will undoubtedly assist the continent to reduce vulnerability to external shocks and to expand opportunities for faster, sustainable and more equitable growth.

Largely stable, shared and robust growth

Growth has been widely shared and remained strong across the majority of African countries, despite the disruptive impact of the global economic and financial crisis, and the political turmoil in North Africa. More than a third of African countries grew at 5 per cent or more in 2012, with a large proportion achieving this rate over 2010–2012 (table 1.1). This underscores the growing potential of African countries to accelerate and then sustain growth in the foreseeable future.

TABLE 1.1: DISTRIBUTION OF GROWTH PERFORMANCE IN AFRICA, 2010–2012

Real GDP growth	2010		2011		2012	
	Oil exporters	*Oil importers*	*Oil exporters*	*Oil importers*	*Oil exporters*	*Oil importers*
Less than 3%	1	9	6	7	4	9
3–5%	7	8	4	16	3	17
5–7%	2	13	1	10	3	6
More than 7%	3	10	2	7	3	8
Total	**13**	**40**	**13**	**40**	**13**	**40**

Source: Calculations based on UN-DESA (2012).

Per capita GDP growth

Africa's population growth is estimated at above 2 per cent a year, but with projected increases in economic growth, per capita GDP is likely to rise over the medium term (AfDB et al., 2012). Indeed, in 2012 the continent's per capita GDP was estimated at around 3 per cent. However, while this suggests that the standard of living in African countries has on average been improving, the pace is very slow— gains in social conditions are failing to match the continent's robust economic performance.

Subregionally, West Africa and East Africa continued to register real per capita GDP growth of more than 3 per cent, followed by Central Africa and Southern Africa. North Africa (excluding Libya) was the only subregion experiencing a contraction because of the overall slow recovery from the civil war in Libya and political turmoil in other countries such as Egypt and Tunisia. Still, average per capita GDP has continued to grow in resource-exporting countries over the

last decade. With the right policy framework, this progress, if sustained, has the potential to reverse the "resource curse" that has blighted many African countries. Governments need to pursue policies that reduce inequality, promote job creation and increase social protection in order to make growth more conducive to social development (chapter 2).

Growth showed geographical variations

Real GDP growth varied among groupings, subregions and countries, but remained fairly strong in both oil-exporting and oil-importing countries.

Oil exporters and importers

Oil-exporting countries as a group recovered strongly in 2012 (6.1 per cent) as some countries' political situation improved (especially in North Africa), oil production increased (in many countries) and oil prices stayed high on international markets (figure 1.3).

FIGURE 1.3: AFRICAN GROWTH BY OIL EXPORTERS AND IMPORTERS, 2008–2012

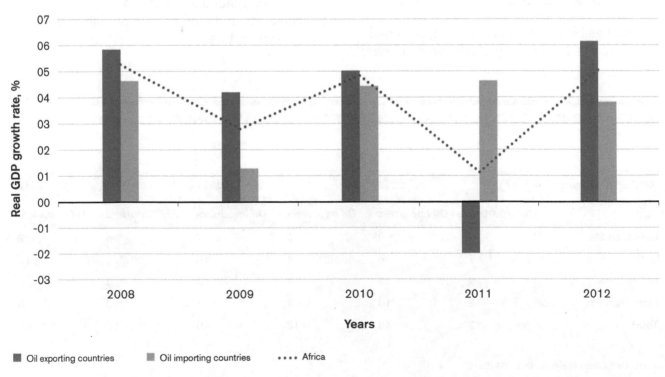

Source: Calculations based on UN-DESA (2012).

Oil-importing countries experienced a decline in growth to 3.7 per cent in 2012 from 4.5 per cent in 2011. Despite the reduction, the group maintained robust growth thanks to a variety of factors, including strong demand and high prices for non-oil commodities and improved performance in agriculture, services and other sectors. Strong non-oil based growth adds to the growing momentum of economic diversification in African countries. Countries like Kenya experienced strong recovery from the end of

drought, and post-conflict recovery in other countries contributed to the impressive growth rates experienced in this group.

Subregional trends

Growth rates also varied in 2012 by subregion, but remained robust in all of them (figure 1.4). West Africa registered the highest growth, followed by East Africa, North Africa including Libya,[2] Central Africa and Southern Africa.

FIGURE 1.4: GROWTH BY SUBREGION, 2008–2012

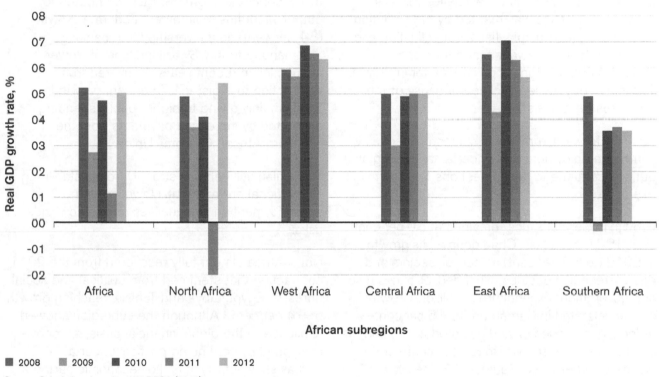

■ 2008 ■ 2009 ■ 2010 ■ 2011 ■ 2012

Source: Calculations based on UN-DESA (2012).

Economic performance in West Africa moderated to 6.3 per cent in 2012 from 6.5 per cent in 2011. Nigeria, the continent's second-largest economy, slowed to 6.4 per cent from 7.4 per cent, reflecting receding fiscal stimulus and slowing oil investments on security concerns across the Niger Delta. Ghana's economy, after a sharp increase in 2011 when the country launched commercial oil production, slowed from 15.1 per cent in 2011 to a more realistic 7.4 per cent in 2012.

Political instability in Guinea-Bissau and Mali affected subregional growth, and both countries saw growth decline by more than 4.4 percentage points, but this was balanced by growth in Sierra Leone of 26.5 per cent owing to the discovery of new oil deposits. Côte d'Ivoire posted 7 per cent post-conflict growth with a return to normal harvests. A growing pace of the extractive industry in oil supported Niger's 9.1 per cent expansion.

In East Africa, growth slipped to 5.6 per cent in 2012 from 6.3 per cent in 2011, although most countries performed well in 2012, marking a recovery in agriculture, vibrant domestic demand and expansion in services. Kenya's growth rose to 4.8 per cent in 2012 from 4.4 per cent, aided by robust domestic demand, strong services, increased government expenditure and sound monetary policies (which in fact brought inflation down in most East African countries).

Tanzania maintained strong growth (6.8 per cent) owing to prudent fiscal and monetary policies, increased tax collection and reduced non-recurrent spending. Growth also remained strong in Rwanda (7.9 per cent), Ethiopia (7 per cent), Eritrea (6.5 per cent) and Seychelles (3.6 per cent). Performance was marked by high inflation in, for example, Ethiopia, fiscal consolidation and aid dependency in Rwanda, and food security concerns and a stagnant private sector in Eritrea. Tourism in Seychelles declined because of the euro area debt crisis.

Looking forward, rural poverty, income inequality, youth unemployment and uncertainty in the global outlook continue to raise questions for growth in this subregion.

Growth in Central Africa remained at 5.0 per cent in 2012. Nonetheless, Chad doubled its growth in 2012 (to 6.2 per cent) as non-oil sectors and energy-related industries expanded, oil prices rose and government expenditure stabilized. Growth also accelerated in Cameroon (to 4.5 per cent—reflecting increased oil and gas production) and the Central African Republic (to 3.8 per cent—better harvests and exports). Equatorial Guinea saw a decrease, to 6.3 per cent. Strikes and interruptions in oil production took down Gabon's growth to 4.7 per cent, from 5.8 per cent in 2011, and the country continues to face high unemployment and low human development.

This region still relies heavily on output of primary commodities and extractive industries, making inclusive growth and job creation a major challenge.

Southern Africa's output stayed almost the same for the third consecutive year, at 3.5 per cent. South Africa's close integration with the world economy translated into a notable slowdown in growth from 3.1 per cent in 2011 to 2.5 per cent in 2012, exacerbated by mining strikes. Several other countries saw growth moderate. Growth in Botswana, Lesotho, Namibia and Zambia declined by more than 0.8 per cent of GDP because of lower government revenue from mining and weak global demand for copper, diamond and gold. Namibia pegged its dollar to the South African rand, exposing it to contagion from South Africa.

Angola registered the most robust growth, which nearly doubled to 7.5 per cent, on increased oil production and investment in natural gas. Mozambique, having become a coal exporter in 2011, also showed robust growth in 2012, of 7.5 per cent, as greater FDI contributed to output. Mauritius maintained moderate growth (3.1 per cent) as it diversified into banking and manufacturing. Swaziland, one of slower economies in recent years, recovered from contraction to register 1.7 per cent growth in 2012, mainly owing to higher public spending supported by increased payments from the Southern African Customs Union.

The region still benefits strongly from a stabilizing international environment. However, high unemployment and inequalities remain downside risks.

North Africa almost fully recovered from the 2011 contraction that stemmed from political and social unrest in Egypt, Libya and Tunisia, reaching growth of 5.4 per cent.[3] Although the subregion showed resilience to the global financial crisis, its recovery is plagued by continuing political uncertainty as well as slow activity in its key economic partners in the euro area. Egypt was particularly hit, as growth weakened to 1.1 per cent in 2012 from 1.8 per cent the previous year, mirroring uncertainty over parliamentary and presidential procedures as well as political tensions surrounding the country's new constitution, which hurt investment and services, notably tourism.

Morocco's GDP growth decelerated from 4.1 per cent to 2.8 per cent in 2012, also largely attributable to the European slowdown and its own poor performance in agriculture. In Libya, growth bounced back by 100.7 per cent as reconstruction investment stimulated the economy and oil production increased from 0.5 million barrels per day at end-2011 to 1.42 million by July 2012 (World Bank, 2012). Tunisia's economy switched from a 1.7 per cent contraction in 2011 to 2.6 per cent growth in 2012, reflecting a recovery in tourism, exports and FDI. Despite a partial shutdown of a key refinery, Algeria sustained its high level of oil production and expansionary fiscal policy, recording growth of 2.8 per cent. In Sudan, however, the economy contracted steeply by 11 per cent owing to the political environment, civil war, a sharp fall in oil production, exchange rate depreciation and escalating inflation. Mauritania saw growth slip to 4.8 per cent in 2012 from 5.1 per cent in 2011, though it was still robust thanks to investment in mining and strong public spending.

High youth unemployment remains an issue for the subregion. Reducing joblessness for all age groups requires structural labour market reforms, restoration of market confidence, inclusive growth, refurnished foreign exchange reserves and maintenance of political and social stability.

In 2008–2012, the top 11 growth performers in Africa reached the 7 per cent threshold estimated as a prerequisite for achieving the MDGs, with Ethiopia and Sierra Leone the top two (figure 1.5). Ethiopia's growth has been propelled by increased public and private investment, improved macroeconomic management and increasing role for manufacturing and services sectors among other factors, while growth in Sierra-Leone mainly reflects post–civil war recovery and natural resource discoveries and exploitation. The list of top performers underscores the centrality of commodity production and exports. The majority of these countries are heavily dependent on oil or minerals (or both).[4]

FIGURE 1.5: TOP 10 AND BOTTOM 5 PERFORMERS, 2008-2012 (AVERAGE % ANNUAL GROWTH)

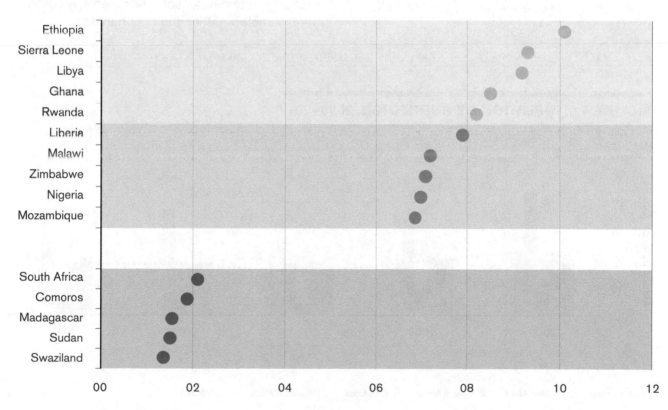

Source: Calculations based on UN-DESA (2012).

Swaziland, Sudan, Madagascar, Comoros and South Africa had the weakest performance during 2008-2012. The economy of Swaziland slowed down owing to a sustained declined in textile and clothing industry among other factors. Sudan's low average growth rate is largely due to a contraction of 11 per cent in 2012, caused by the political environment, continued civil war and the secession of South Sudan and related border tensions are contributing to its low average growth rates. However, given intensifying national and regional peace efforts, growth in the country is expected to rebound over the medium-term. South Africa's exposure to the global financial markets has played a significant role in its growth performance over the last 5 years.

Employment generation is still a major challenge

Strong growth across the continent has not been translated into the broad-based economic and social development needed to lift millions of Africans out of poverty and reduce the wide inequalities seen in most countries. This is because Africa's recent growth, driven by primary commodities, has low employment intensity—that is, the ability to generate jobs (ECA and AUC, 2010).

Thus the continent continues to suffer from high unemployment, particularly for youth and female populations, with too few opportunities to absorb new labour market entrants. North Africa is recovering from the Arab Spring of 2011 largely espoused by youth-led protests, but countries like South Africa are experiencing threats to political and economic stability, as seen in recent mining conflicts stemming from poor job quality in mining.

More than 70 per cent of Africans earn their living from vulnerable employment as economies continue to depend heavily on production and export of primary commodities. Investments remain concentrated in capital-intensive extractive industries, with few forward and backward linkages with the rest of the economy. Wider diversification from primary commodity production is therefore needed, as is intensified value addition in commodity sectors (discussed further in chapter 2).

Inflationary pressure waned in most countries

Average inflation for Africa, measured by the consumer price index, remained high at 9.2 per cent in 2012, a shade lower than the 9.3 per cent of the previous year (figure 1.6). Key factors included exchange rate devaluations, rising energy costs, unfavourable weather and poor harvests.

FIGURE 1.6: INFLATION BY SUBREGION, 2008–2012

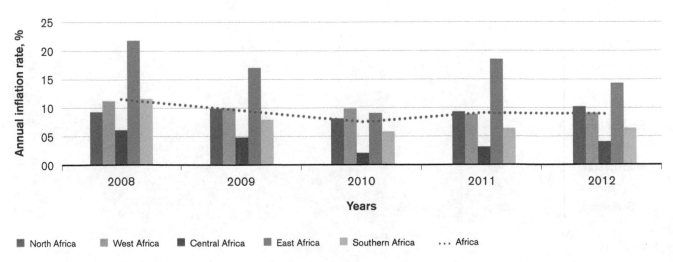

■ North Africa   ■ West Africa   ■ Central Africa   ■ East Africa   ■ Southern Africa   ••• Africa

Source: Calculations based on IMF (2012).

Inflation varied among African countries and subregions, and was 40 per cent in Sudan. Despite tightening its monetary policy, East Africa had the highest subregional rate (14.2 per cent) because of the effects of the previous year's severe drought on agricultural produce and uncertain weather. Ethiopia had the highest inflation (25 per cent) in the subregion. In Central and West Africa rates were mainly in single digits, apart from Sierra Leone (12.6 per cent) and Nigeria (12.5 per cent).

Inflation is expected to decline further, owing to tightening monetary policy and improving weather, especially in East Africa and the Horn of Africa.

Prudence ruled the macroeconomic policy stance

Owing to the adverse global economic environment and narrower macroeconomic space compared with the pre-crisis era, many African countries followed cautious macroeconomic policies in 2012. In response to inflationary pressures, Ethiopia, Kenya, Nigeria, Tanzania and Uganda tightened monetary policy in 2012, but others such as the Franc Zone countries—where average inflation of 3.9 per cent in 2012 was Africa's lowest—eased theirs. The pressure on central banks to tighten monetary policy

waned as non-oil commodity prices began to fall in some countries with improved rainfall and increased agricultural production. The central banks of South Africa and Morocco lowered interest rates to boost domestic demand and growth (EIU, 2012).

Most African countries continued their expansionary fiscal policies, supported by rising commodity revenue, with a strong focus on increasing public spending on infrastructure. As part of the drive to reduce dependence on external assistance and mobilize domestic resources, tax efforts picked up in many countries (see chapter 2). Supported by strong economic growth, many governments widened the tax base and improved tax collection and administration.

The average central government fiscal balance narrowed moderately from a deficit of 3.5 per cent of GDP in 2011 to a deficit of 3.0 per cent in 2012 (figure 1.7). It improved considerably for oil-exporting countries as a group, as oil production recovered with easing political tensions (and despite rising public spending on social security). The average worsened for oil-importing countries, however, as energy prices rose on the world market, demands for infrastructure investment increased and ODA declined or stagnated (on weak growth in developed economies).

FIGURE 1.7: AFRICAN CENTRAL GOVERNMENT FISCAL BALANCES BY COUNTRY GROUP, 2008–2012

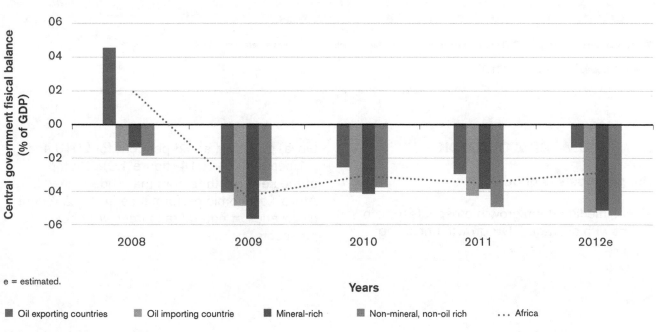

e = estimated.

■ Oil exporting countries   ■ Oil importing countrie   ■ Mineral-rich   ■ Non-mineral, non-oil rich   ··· Africa

Source: Calculations based on EIU (2012).

Many governments maintained accommodative fiscal policies owing to the significant requirement of public investments in areas of infrastructure and employment creation. Recent discoveries of minerals in several African countries are expected to further expand fiscal space as well as public spending in countries such as Ghana, Kenya, Mauritania and Uganda.

External positions continued diverging between oil exporters and importers

Africa's current account deficit widened from 1.2 per cent of GDP in 2011 to 1.6 per cent in 2012 (figure 1.8) owing to sluggish external demand for exports. A notable variation was

seen between oil-exporting and oil-importing countries. The former group's average current account surplus remained at 2.2 per cent, similar to 2011. Oil-importing countries, on the other hand, experienced expanding deficits (to 7.5 per cent) as world energy prices increased. For many oil-importers, the combination of rising and fairly inelastic import bills and declining export growth translated into higher current account deficits. Depreciation of domestic currencies against the US dollar and the effect of recession in Europe further contributed to wider deficits in this group. The socio-economic gap between these two groups may widen, as the oil-importing countries face the dual pressure of rising oil prices and falling external capital inflows (see chapter 2).

FIGURE 1.8: AFRICAN CURRENT ACCOUNT BALANCES BY COUNTRY GROUP, 2008–2012

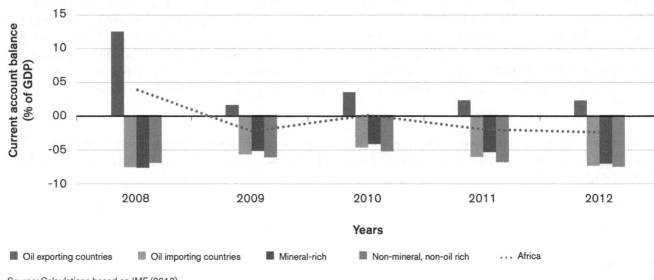

Source: Calculations based on IMF (2012).

1.2 MEDIUM-TERM OUTLOOK

The prognosis is good …

Africa's medium-term growth prospects remain robust with average GDP growth (including

Libya) projected at 4.8 per cent for 2013 and 5.1 per cent for 2014 (figure 1.9).[5] On top of the key growth factors that underpinned Africa's economic performance in 2012, recent discoveries of natural resources will boost prospects.

FIGURE 1.9: GROWTH PROSPECTS BY SUBREGION, 2008–2013 (%)

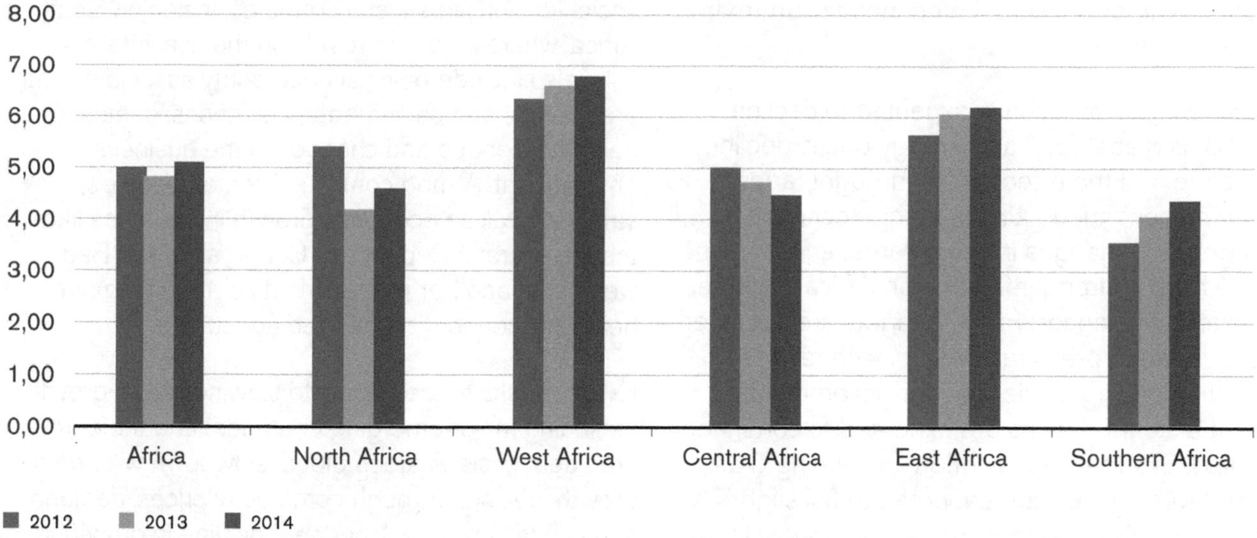

2012   2013   2014

Source: Calculations based on UN-DESA (2012).

Robust domestic demand, especially private consumption and buoyant fixed investment in infrastructure and extractive industries, as well as high government spending, remains a key driver of economic growth in Africa. Growth in many countries is expected to continue benefiting from expanding agricultural output and further moves to diversify into services—especially telecommunications, construction and banking—and manufacturing. Still, commodity production and exports are set to remain the key factors underpinning Africa's medium-term growth.

Among the five subregions, West and East Africa are still expected to be the fastest growing at 6.6 per cent and 6.0 per cent in 2013, followed by Central Africa, North Africa and Southern Africa.

West Africa will continue to gain from commodities—especially oil and minerals as Ghana, Niger and Sierra Leone exploit new discoveries—and from cemented peace and stability in Côte d'Ivoire.

Increasing economic diversity, rising agricultural output and exports, as well as new natural-

resource discoveries are expected to boost growth in East Africa, which has remained one of the top performing subregions. Consolidating peace and ensuring political stability in the Democratic Republic of Congo and Somalia will help to improve prospects in the subregion.

Central Africa is forecast to sustain moderate growth of 4.7 per cent in 2013 and 4.4 per cent in 2014, with strong commodity production and export demand, but the subregion is likely to be hit by an unfolding civil war in the Central African Republic.

Growth in North Africa (including Libya) is expected to remain strong at 4.2 per cent in 2013 and pick up to 4.6 per cent in 2014 as the political environment normalizes and economic activity gains momentum. The economy of Libya will recover to pre-crisis levels and those of Algeria and Sudan should benefit from better agricultural harvests.

Southern Africa is projected to grow at 4.0 per cent in 2013 and 4.3 per cent in 2014. The economy of South Africa is forecast to grow at 3.1 per cent, reflecting a stabilizing international environment and manufacturing.

Growth prospects for oil-exporting countries will remain robust (5.1 per cent) from sustained strong demand for oil and high prices. Non-oil activities will contribute strongly to the economic outturn in several countries.

Africa's average inflation is expected to decline in 2013 as global food and energy prices decline or stabilize and the effect of the drought fades. Assuming continued gains in macroeconomic management, changes in the external environment will still have a strong influence on Africa's internal and external balances. Fiscal budgets are expected to remain under pressure, though, with revenue generation posing challenges for governments. Current account deficits are expected to continue widening. External capital inflows, including ODA, FDI and remittances, are expected to fall slightly unless the global economy recovers strongly in 2013.

... and would be better still if Africa made up its structural shortfalls

Africa's growth outlook for 2013 faces several internal and external risks. Those on the internal side stem mainly from weak institutional capacity and huge infrastructure deficits. Also, high income-inequality and poverty rates are creating political and social tensions in several countries, including South Africa, where labour unrest is on the rise. Internal risks also include political uncertainty associated with presidential and parliamentary elections, domestic policy challenges and changes in the business environment. Armed conflicts threaten people's safety as well as economic growth in countries like the Democratic Republic of Congo and Mali. Bad weather is another risk, as most countries remain heavily dependent on rain-fed agriculture.

External risks relate largely to slowing global growth (including major emerging countries) and the euro area debt crisis. A steep global slowdown will affect growth in Africa through commodity prices, demand and capital flows—a 1 per cent decline in growth in the euro area is associated with a 0.5 per cent fall in growth in Africa (AfDB et al., 2012). Slowing activity in emerging economies might deepen such effects, but their likely continued strong growth would help Africa to mitigate the effects of recession in Europe, given Africa's increasing trade and investment ties with them (box 1.2).

BOX 1.2: EMERGING MARKETS AND AFRICA'S MEDIUM-TERM ECONOMIC PROSPECTS

The role of South–South cooperation in Africa's development process, as outlined in the Accra Agenda for Action, is becoming more evident and taking centre stage as the euro area debt crisis looms and some major developed countries flirt with recession.

Although economic growth in the top five emerging countries—China, India, Brazil, Republic of Korea and Turkey—cooled owing to the euro area crisis, optimism has returned. Growth in these markets is likely to boost commodity demand, supporting a positive outlook for African economies in 2013 and 2014, reflecting the fact that Africa is highly commodity dependent: the share of commodities in its merchandise exports is estimated at more than 65 per cent (UNCTAD, 2012). China has overtaken the US as Africa's major trading partner.

The rebound of emerging countries is also likely to boost capital flows, especially FDI and ODA to Africa, supporting government budgets and boosting investment, technology transfer and economic diversification.

Africa should, though, consider emerging countries as complements to traditional partners and export markets, rather than substitutes (AfDB et al., 2011). The heterogeneity of goods and services traded with emerging economies presents an opportunity for Africa to add value to its traditional commodity exports. This will require policymakers to adopt better engagement strategies and incorporate them in their development agenda, synchronizing them at both the regional and continental level in order to attain lower production costs, better bargaining power, and stronger terms of trade with both traditional and emerging partners.

Notwithstanding the positive outlook, Africa's over-dependence on commodities makes it vulnerable to commodity price shocks. The continent therefore needs structural transformation (chapter 2) and diversified products with value addition as a means of mitigating the impact of volatility and fluctuations linked to unprocessed commodity exports (chapter 3). Industrialization in Africa can help to cushion against these effects, although trade barriers (chapter 2), unsound investment policies and technological challenges—beyond institutional and infrastructure issues—will have to be resolved.

1.3 RECENT SOCIAL DEVELOPMENTS IN AFRICA

Improving the social conditions of a society is vital for achieving economic transformation in Africa, yet the continent's social development pattern has not changed much over recent years: positive changes are still recorded in most areas—poverty, hunger, education, health and equality for minorities—but progress is slow and not commensurate with the strides made in economic growth.[6] The achievement of most of the MDGs (by 2015 as initially set) is also unlikely. Africa's labour productivity remains low owing in part to poor levels of education and high prevalence of diseases. Low human capital is undermining structural transformation, and thus critical to transformation is enhanced labour force productivity, for which good health and quality education are critical.

Economic advances are not reducing poverty as much as they should

Recent data show some slight improvement in poverty reduction, even though the region will not be able to achieve the related MDGs. The proportion of people living in extreme poverty (below $1.25 a day) in Africa (excluding North Africa) has been projected to reach 35.8 per cent in 2015 against the previous forecasts of 38 per cent (UN, 2011). This slight, albeit slow, improvement is partly attributable to high and sustained economic growth since 2000.

Ethiopia, for example, which saw growth considerably above the required rate for eight years between 2000 and 2010, experienced a dramatic reduction in poverty, and the proportion of the population living on less than $1.25 a day fell from 55.6 per cent in 2000 to 39 per cent in 2005 (World Bank, 2010).

Poverty in Africa is still spatial, and highly prevalent in rural areas. The non-inclusive nature of economic growth and the more specific sectoral challenges—of poor rural infrastructure, failure to modernize rural livelihoods, little jobs diversification (for rural youth especially), limited access to education and pervasive child labour—are key drivers of rural poverty (FAO et al., 2010).

High inequality weakens the impact of growth on poverty (Ravallion, 2001; Fosu, 2011). Further, the restricted range of drivers of growth exacerbates inequalities (ECA and AUC, 2012). The world's widest urban–rural gaps are in Africa: for example in some countries, women in urban areas are almost twice as likely as those in rural areas to deliver their babies with a skilled health attendant (ECA et al., 2012).

Social protection programmes can help to reduce inequality by providing transfers (including through conditional cash transfers) to vulnerable groups and enabling people to become productive members of society, but in Africa at least most of them have worked through identified groups, rather than offering more transformative system-wide interventions. They are also fragmented in most countries, often donor funded and outside government systems.

The battle against hunger needs a further, determined push

The food situation has generally improved considerably in North Africa in recent years. For the rest of the continent, the Global Hunger Index of the International Food Policy Research Institute[7] improved by 18 per cent in 1990–2011 (somewhat less than 25 per cent in Southeast Asia and 39 per cent in North Africa). As with other indicators, the regional aggregate masks wide country divergence, as the Global Hunger Index in some countries worsened while picking up strongly in others. Hunger remains linked to poverty, reflecting fewer opportunities in rural areas.

The proportion of malnourished people in Africa (excluding North Africa) has stabilized at 16 per cent, as gains in nutritional levels no longer pace poverty reduction, partly owing to food prices, which are still higher than before the crisis (FAO et al., 2010; UN, 2011). This has an effect on income and other poverty correlates. Price volatility makes smallholder farmers and poor consumers increasingly vulnerable to poverty, because food represents a large share of the budget of poor consumers and smallholder farmers' income. Thus even short periods of high prices for consumers or low prices for farmers can lead to poverty traps, and farmers are less likely to invest in measures to raise productivity when price changes are unpredictable. Price hikes can also prompt coping mechanisms that defer educational and health spending by households, affecting overall welfare and long-term development.

Educational quality is a major drawback

Africa continues to make sustained progress towards ensuring that all children can complete a full course of primary schooling: aggregate net primary school enrolment in Africa rose from 64 per cent in 2000 to 84 per cent in 2009. But 18 countries are still more than 10 percentage points from achieving universal primary enrolment by the MDG target date of 2015.

The MDGs emphasize primary enrolment, and most African countries have done well. The quality of education, however, manifested by completion rates and access to educational facilities has deteriorated. Primary completion rates in Africa are low: only six countries recorded primary completion rates of 90 per cent or more in 2009. Also, many African countries have very high drop-out rates.

In secondary and tertiary enrolment, most countries are making slow progress. Vocational and technical training—reflecting a country's employment needs—also need to be prioritized by governments.

Health gains have to pick up pace

Health indicators remain the area in which African countries are making the slowest progress. Maternal and child health are a special concern for most of Africa, as are communicable diseases such as HIV/AIDS, malaria and tuberculosis (TB). Whereas communicable diseases are a large share of Africa's disease burden, as countries develop and lifestyles change, communicable diseases such as cancer, heart disease and diabetes become more prevalent. Thus African countries must take pre-emptive measures to mitigate the "double burden of disease", that is, the simultaneous burden of communicable and non-communicable diseases.

Child mortality

Most worryingly, of the 26 countries worldwide with under-five mortality above 100 deaths per 1,000 live births, 24 are in Africa. Yet encouragingly, Africa has doubled its average rate of reduction in child mortality from 1.2 per cent a year in 1990–2000 to 2.4 per cent in 2000–2010. But to accelerate progress in child health, African countries should expand interventions that target the main causes of child mortality, and intensify efforts to reduce neonatal mortality (deaths in the first 28 days of life). The decline in neonatal mortality is much slower than that among older children, perhaps due to lack of cost-effective interventions such as early post-natal home visits, and can be tackled if governments and health practitioners link neonatal and maternal health.

Maternal mortality

Maternal health is still a grave concern for most of Africa, yet even here the most recent data from the World Health Organization (WHO) show one of the steepest ever declines in Africa's maternal mortality ratio: from 590 deaths per 100,000 live births in 2008 to 578 in 2010—a 2 per cent fall in two years and the endpoint of a 46 per cent drop since 1990 (WHO et al., 2012).

Still, the fact remains that that of the 40 countries classified as having a "high maternal mortality ratio" in 2010, 36 are in Africa. Some of these countries are either experiencing or recovering from conflict, highlighting such countries' vulnerability and the need for health infrastructure.

To fast-track progress towards maternal health, African countries must look at the links between maternal health outcomes and other social and economic indicators, such as education, women's economic empowerment, key infrastructure such as roads, telecommunications and transport, and health systems. It is also necessary to look at cultural practices to improve contraceptive prevalence rates, the proportion of women making the WHO-recommended four antenatal care visits, the share of women delivering with a skilled birth attendant, and birth rates among adolescents.

HIV/AIDS

Africa's progress in the fight against HIV/AIDS is noteworthy. Although Africa (excluding North Africa) remains the region most heavily affected by HIV, the number of new HIV infections has dropped by more than 21 per cent, down to 1.8 million people newly infected in 2011, from an estimated 2.6 million at the epidemic's peak in 1997. The number of people dying from AIDS-related causes fell to 1.2 million in 2010 from a high of 1.8 million in 2005 (UNAIDS, 2012). These falls show that prevention efforts have greatly improved, as has treatment for people living with HIV/AIDS.

That said, Africa still holds an unbalanced burden of the global population living with HIV/AIDS: with

12 per cent of the world's population, the continent accounted for about 68 per cent of people living with HIV/AIDS and 70 per cent of new HIV infections in 2010. Women in Africa are particularly at risk—60 per cent of Africa's HIV-positive population are women. To accelerate efforts, African countries must continue to focus on prevention, especially among women and youth, and invest more resources into treating people living with HIV/AIDS.

Malaria and tuberculosis

The fight against malaria in Africa is seeing major advances. Increases in funding and attention to malaria control have led to a 33 per cent fall in malaria mortality from 2000 to 2010—much faster than the global rate of 25 per cent. Yet although malaria is preventable and curable, most of the world's 200 million cases and 650,000 deaths in 2010 were in Africa. Control strategies such as spraying and proper use of insecticide-treated mosquito nets, as well as funding, are crucial.

African countries must take pre-emptive measures to mitigate the "double burden of disease", that is, the simultaneous burden of communicable and non-communicable diseases.

In 2010, 27 countries in Africa adopted the WHO recommendation to provide insecticide-treated nets for all people at risk for malaria, especially children and pregnant women. The number of Africans protected this way rose from 10 million in 2005 to 78 million in 2010. A continuing focus on prevention and expansion of treatment will have profound benefits, economic as well as health, given that malaria has an economic burden of about 1.3 per cent of GDP in countries with high disease rates.

Incidence, prevalence and death rates associated with TB remain high and unchanging in most of Africa. Southern Africa has the highest prevalence, at more than 500 per 100,000 people, and this rate has in fact increased since 1990 owing to continued chronic poverty and malnutrition alongside inadequate medical attention, especially in conflict and drought-afflicted countries. TB is closely linked to HIV, and so tackling HIV has a positive impact on lowering TB infections.

TB infection rates also depend on institutional and socio-economic factors, such as crowded living and working conditions and poor sanitation. They are also driven by inadequate health care access as well as by, for example, malnutrition, diabetes mellitus, tobacco smoking, and alcohol and drug abuse. Thus TB's high and unchanging impact reflects numerous social and economic issues that must be addressed in the fight against the disease.

Programmes such as DOTS (directly observed treatment, short course)—the basis of the global Stop TB Strategy—have proved successful in diagnosing and treating TB patients. Properly implemented, DOTS has a success rate exceeding 95 per cent, and prevents further multi-drug-resistant strains of TB from emerging.

Women's empowerment is generally moving ahead but more jobs are needed for youth

Female gains in education, the economy and politics

Progress continues, slowly, in empowering women. Girls' enrolment in school is one pathway, building human capital, strengthening capacities and increasing productivity. African countries are making good strides on that front, with the gender parity index improving at all levels of education. In primary school, for instance, the index was higher than 0.9 in more than 40 countries in 2009 (90 girls enrolled for every 100 boys). At the secondary level, girls' improved access to school is coupled with fairly good performance in class, as girls tend to perform better than boys (ECA et al., 2012). In tertiary education, even though the gender parity gap is high, female enrolment has grown twice as fast a men's in the recent past.

Opportunities are increasing and diversifying on job markets—more African women have access to wage employment outside agriculture, for example. In 2009, 19 per cent of that category of workers was female in North Africa, but over 33 per cent in the rest of the continent.

In the political arena, in contrast, North Africa has impressed: representation of women in parliament has improved in most countries in the subregion, and the proportion in 2011 was seven times as high as in 1990. Factors included positive discriminatory actions such as legal frameworks guaranteeing seats for women in political spheres.

But efforts must continue, as some countries are stagnating or even regressing in some areas. Gender parity is held back by low living standards, and the gender parity index tends to be higher among children from rich than poor households. Equally, drop-out rates remain higher for girls, and cultural impediments reduce women's access to the labour market.

Youth employment

Africa's population is growing fast, but the remarkable economic growth of the past decade has not been fully inclusive and has failed to provide enough decent jobs, contributing to the Arab Spring—hence the urgent need of attention to youth employment. The bulk of African young people are still in school, but decent job opportunities remain few for those on the labour market, especially in poor countries. Indeed, in low-income countries only 17 per cent of working youth have full-time wage employment, against 39 per cent in lower middle-income countries and 52 per cent in upper middle-income countries. Youth employment issues also differ across countries, being more about quality in low-income countries, where underemployment, part-time jobs and self-employment are high, and more about quantity in middle-income countries, which have higher unemployment (AfDB et al., 2012). These problems have generated a large group more problematic than the purely unemployed, namely the discouraged—people who have stopped looking for a job and for opportunities to improve their skills (chapter 2).

> *Africa's youthful population provides potential for the continent to reap dividends, but this can only be achieved if the continent can create decent jobs, fast.*

Reasons for slow job growth are multifaceted: chronic, insufficient demand for labour; mismatches between training in schools and education centres and skills sought by employers; sources of growth primarily in capital-intensive industries such as minerals and oil and gas; and absence of backward and forward linkages between these productive sectors and other sectors. Recent work indicates that both the public and formal private sector will have to be supported substantively to be able to create decent jobs (chapter 2). The informal and rural sectors present the highest potential for job creation, and will require government support.

Africa's youthful population provides potential for the continent to reap dividends, but this can only be achieved if the continent can create decent jobs, fast.

1.4 CONCLUSIONS

Africa maintained well above global average growth in 2012, despite deceleration in the world economy. High commodity demand and prices, increased public spending and favourable weather conditions that led to good agricultural harvests are some of the factors that supported growth. Improved macroeconomic management and prudent macroeconomic policies also guided government expenditure across many countries. West Africa recorded the highest growth followed by East, North, Central and Southern Africa. Oil-importing countries saw their growth rate decline in 2012, while oil-exporting countries' growth improved significantly, largely due to political recovery of the North and increased oil production in many countries.

Medium-term prospects for the continent remain robust. Recent discoveries of natural resources offer the potential to boost economic growth, on top of the key growth factors of 2012. East and West Africa are expected to lead growth on the continent, followed by Central, North and Southern Africa. However, this positive growth outlook depends on the ability of the continent to mitigate several internal and external risks. Weak institutional capacities, huge infrastructure deficits, political uncertainties and high levels of poverty continue to pose internal threats. Externally, a major global slowdown will leave the continent exposed to volatility in commodity demand and prices and to uncertain capital flows.

Despite steady economic growth, African countries continue to make slow progress towards social development indicators, especially some MDG health indicators. And even though the continent has seen rapid enrolment in primary school, secondary and tertiary enrolment has been fairly slow. The quality of education also needs lifting, as the pace of enrolment has not been matched by investment in school infrastructure. In recent years, however, some countries have fast-tracked progress towards poverty, hunger, education, health and women's empowerment. Still, African countries need to do more to improve the quality of economic growth, and diversification into labour-intensive industries has the potential to induce inclusive growth, employment generation, poverty reduction and improved social conditions.

REFERENCES

AfDB (African Development Bank), OECD (Organisation for Economic Co-operation and Development), UNDP (United Nations Development Programme), and ECA (United Nations Economic Commission for Africa). 2011. *African Economic Outlook 2011: Africa and Its Emerging Partners*. Paris: OECD.

———. 2012. *African Economic Outlook 2012: Promoting Youth Employment*. Paris: OECD.

ECA and AUC (African Union Commission). 2010. *Economic Report on Africa 2010: Promoting High-level Sustainable Growth for Job Creation*. Addis Ababa: ECA.

———. 2012. *Economic Report on Africa 2012: Unleashing Africa's Potential as a Pole of Global Growth*. Addis Ababa: ECA.

ECA, AUC (African Union Commission), AfDB (African Development Bank), and UNDP (United Nations Development Programme). 2012. *Assessing Progress in Africa towards the Millennium Development Goals*. Addis Ababa: ECA.

EIU (Economist Intelligence Unit). 2012. Country data. (www.eiu.com, accessed 15 December 2012).

FAO (Food and Agriculture Organization), IFAD (International Fund for Agricultural Development), and ILO (International Labour Organization). 2010. "Food Prices in Africa: Quarterly Bulletin—December 2010." Regional Price Update and Responses, No. 7. Rome.

Fosu, Augustin Kwasi. 2011. "Growth, Inequality, and Poverty Reduction in Developing Countries: Recent Global Evidence." A paper presented at the UN-DESA/ILO Expert Group Meeting on poverty eradication, 20–22 June 2011, Geneva.

IMF (International Monetary Fund). 2012. *World Economic Outlook: Growth Resuming, Dangers Remain 2012*. Washington, DC.

Ravallion, Martin. 2001. "Growth, Inequality and Poverty: Looking Beyond Averages." *World Development* 29 (11): 1803–15.

UN (United Nations). 2011. *The Millennium Development Goals Report 2011*. New York.

UNAIDS (Joint United Nations Programme on HIV/AIDS). 2012. *UNAIDS Report on the Global AIDS Epidemic*. Geneva.

UNCTAD (United Nations Conference on Trade and Development). 2012. *Towards a New Generation of Investment Policies*. Geneva: United Nations.

UN-DESA (United Nations Department of Economic and Social Affairs). 2012. *LINK Global Economic Outlook*. New York.

World Bank. 2010. *Global Monitoring Report 2010: The MDGs after the Crisis*. Washington, DC.

———. 2011. *World Development Indicators 2011*. Washington, DC. (http://data.worldbank.org/data-catalog/worlddevelopment-indicators).

———. 2012. World Bank Country Briefs. (http://data.worldbank.org/data-catalog/countryprofiles, accessed 15 November 2012).

WHO (World Health Organization), UNICEF (United Nations Children's Fund), UNFPA (United Nations Population Fund), and World Bank. 2012. *Trends in Maternal Mortality: 1990 to 2010*. Geneva: WHO.

NOTES

[1] Libya saw a strong rebound at 100.7 per cent growth in 2012, after contracting by 61 per cent in 2011 owing to civil war. Africa's growth without Libya was 3.3 per cent in 2012 and is forecast to increase to 4.5 per cent in 2013 and 4.9 per cent in 2014.

[2] Excluding Libya, North Africa had the slowest growth (0.6 per cent).

[3] The subregion grew by 0.6 per cent in 2012, excluding Libya.

[4] Angola, Côte d'Ivoire, Ghana, Liberia, Libya, Niger, Mozambique and Sierra Leone.

[5] Excluding Libya, Africa's overall growth is forecast to sustain an upward trend: 3.3 per cent in 2012, 4.5 per cent in 2013 and 4.9 per cent in 2014.

[6] Many of the data in this section are derived from ECA et al. (2012).

[7] The index is a multidimensional statistical tool to measure progress and failures in the global fight against hunger. It combines three equally weighted indicators: proportion of the undernourished as a percentage of the population; prevalence of underweight children under five; and mortality rate of children under five.

Trade, Financing and Employment imperatives for Africa's Transformation

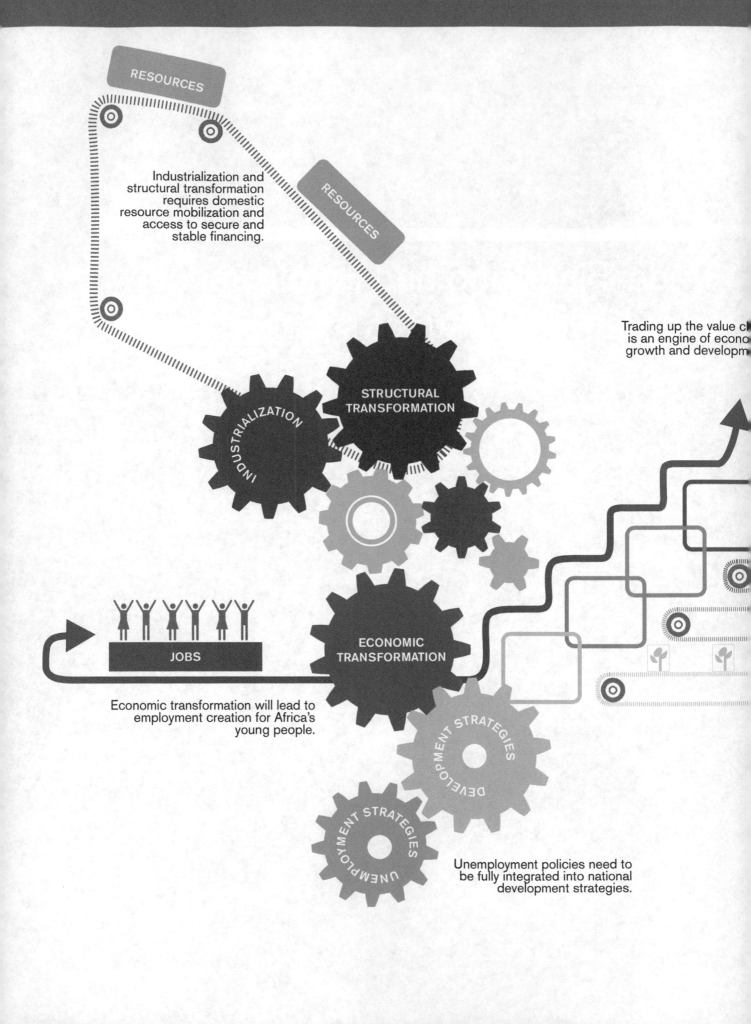

RESOURCES

Industrialization and structural transformation requires domestic resource mobilization and access to secure and stable financing.

RESOURCES

STRUCTURAL TRANSFORMATION

INDUSTRIALIZATION

Trading up the value ch is an engine of econo growth and developm

JOBS

ECONOMIC TRANSFORMATION

Economic transformation will lead to employment creation for Africa's young people.

DEVELOPMENT STRATEGIES

UNEMPLOYMENT STRATEGIES

Unemployment policies need to be fully integrated into national development strategies.

AFRICAN COUNTRIES NEED TO IMPROVE MARKET ACCESS FOR THEIR VALUE-ADDED PRODUCTS THROUGH AGREEMENTS WITH TRADITIONAL AND EMERGING PARTNERS.

THEIR STRATEGY SHOULD AIM TO REDUCE HIGH TARIFFS (ON COCOA TO INDIA, FOR EXAMPLE) AND REMOVE TARIFF ESCALATION (IN THE EU, FOR INSTANCE).

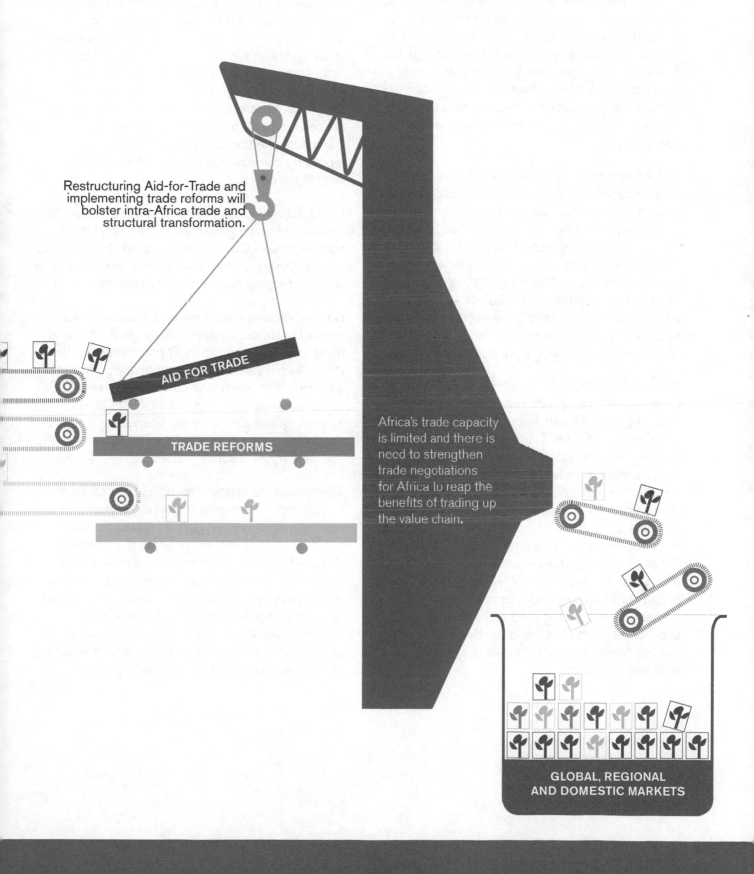

Restructuring Aid-for-Trade and implementing trade reforms will bolster intra-Africa trade and structural transformation.

AID FOR TRADE

TRADE REFORMS

Africa's trade capacity is limited and there is need to strengthen trade negotiations for Africa to reap the benefits of trading up the value chain.

GLOBAL, REGIONAL AND DOMESTIC MARKETS

For the higher economic growth seen in the last decade to create decent jobs, eradicate poverty and achieve broad-based, sustainable development, Africa needs to industrialize massively, transforming its economies structurally.

Yet its current trade relationships and composition offer only limited prospects for Africa to do that, and add value to its export products. Africa relies on imported capital and industrial inputs, and its exports are dominated by low-value primary products. (Intra-African trade is, though, dominated by industrial products, but such trade is still quite low—around 10–12 per cent[1]—as a share of total trade.)

Still, Africa's trade rebounded vigorously after the global economic and financial crisis. Exports and imports by value are now at all-time highs, thanks particularly to strong increases in trade between Africa and emerging economies in particular China and India. China has become a strategic trade partner to Africa, slightly reducing the influence of the traditional partners—the European Union and the United States. These three economies together take more than 60 per cent of Africa's exports and are the source of over 50 per cent of its imports.

The endorsement by African Heads of State and Government of an African Union Action Plan for Boosting Intra-African Trade and the Establishment of a Continental Free Trade Area (CFTA) in January 2012 in Addis Ababa may offer great opportunities for value addition and structural transformation. If the CFTA is accompanied by trade facilitation measures (primarily to accelerate customs procedures and port handling), the share of intra-African trade could more than double over the next 10 years (Mevel and Karingi, 2012). While the establishment of the CFTA could also support industrialization, key priorities are improving infrastructure, building productive capacity, exploiting opportunities to diversify exports and identifying sectors with value- and supply-chain potential in Africa.

Industrialization is costly to finance and Africa's economic transformation requires it to mobilize domestic resources to meet the associated financing costs given that external capital inflows, especially official development assistance (ODA), are likely to decline over time. As government revenues and private savings are the main domestic financial resources in most of the continent, governments need to improve their tax systems' efficiency, staunch the huge illicit capital flight abroad, better capture (or formalize) the informal sector, eliminate tax preferences, and improve transparency and fairness in negotiating concessions with multinational corporations. Deepening the financial system is critical for mobilizing domestic savings to finance Africa's investment needs.

Using natural resource wealth in oil-rich countries can help to boost government financing for the transformation. Governments should also continue progressively reducing their dependence on aid, as well as stopping the illicit flight of capital.

Beyond improving its trade and finance, Africa needs to provide job opportunities to a large and growing young population. These should be decent jobs, which it can achieve by enhancing productivity and competitiveness, strengthening domestic demand, diversifying into higher value added tradable goods and services, strengthening social capabilities, reforming labour market institutions and transforming social protection.

The continent's supply-side policy reforms must be backed by measures to support demand for domestically produced goods and labour, and should include improving education and training policies for skills development and broadening the social knowledge base, investing in research and development (R&D) and bringing in advanced technologies. Well-designed trade and export promotion measures will also serve to support productivity and knowledge gains, further widening options for diversifying and creating jobs.

2.1 ENHANCING THE ROLE OF TRADE IN ECONOMIC TRANSFORMATION

Trade rebounds as Africa strengthens ties with emerging economies

Latest data show that Africa's trade—hit hard by the global crisis—rebounded vigorously in 2011, exceeding pre-crisis volumes of 2008 (figure 2.1). The crisis worked through demand shocks and price movements, especially the free fall (and subsequent pick-up) of key commodities such as oil. Narrow export diversification in products[2] and destinations[3] renders the continent particularly vulnerable to external shocks, as epitomized by the collapse of export revenues suffered by oil exporters in 2009.

FIGURE 2.1: AFRICA'S EXPORTS AND IMPORTS, 2000–2011 ($ BILLION)

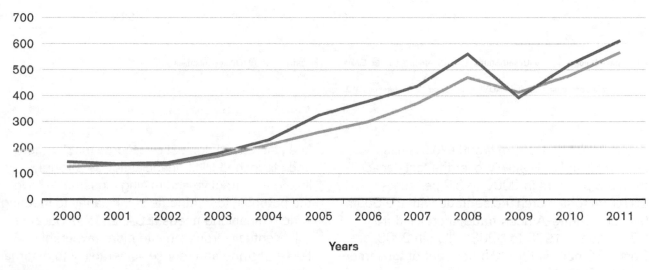

Source: Calculations based on UNCTADStat, accessed 18 September 2012.

Yet, thanks to the pick-up in primary commodity prices since the second half of 2009, and to strong demand for African products from China and other emerging economies, Africa's exports and imports increased in value terms by 28.3 per cent and 18.6 per cent, respectively, in 2010 and by 14.5 per cent and 19.5 per cent in 2011.These rates may well have fallen by at least half in 2012, owing to slower global activity (World Bank, 2012).

While the EU and the US together attracted about two thirds of African exports and sourced more than half of African imports just 10 years ago, their influence has been steadily declining over the last decade. Over that period, emerging partners, especially China and India, have passed from marginal to strategic partners as Africa continues to diversify its trade partners (figure 2.2), a trend reinforced after the global crisis through investment links, especially in commodities and infrastructure. Trade between Africa and its emerging partners has room to grow, given Africa's rich natural resource base and some of these partners' huge financial surpluses, notably China.

FIGURE 2.2: AFRICA'S MAIN EXPORT DESTINATION AND ORIGIN OF IMPORTS, 2001, 2008 AND 2011 (% SHARE)

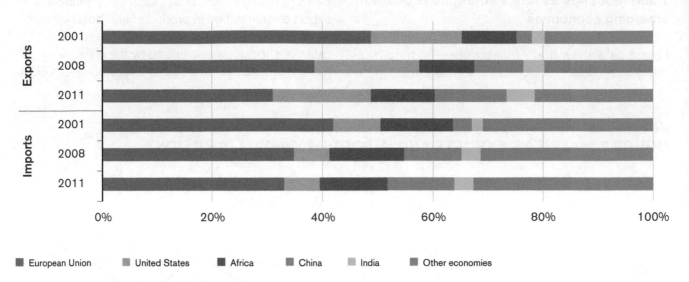

■ European Union   ■ United States   ■ Africa   ■ China   ■ India   ■ Other economies

Source: Calculations based on UNCTADStat, accessed 19 September 2012.

The continent's share of world exports has increased, but only slowly, over the last decade, from 2.3 per cent in 2000 to 3.2 per cent in 2010. Its total merchandise trade with the South (excluding intra-African trade) increased from $34 billion in 1995 to $283 billion in 2008, or from 19.6 per cent to 32.5 per cent of total trade (UNCTAD, 2010).

Africa needs better strategies and policies to promote transformation through trade

Most of Africa's exports towards outside partners—traditional and emerging—are fairly low-value products such as raw materials and primary commodities, while most of its imports are manufactured products. In that sense, emerging markets' burgeoning demand for primary commodities may not encourage Africa to diversify its export composition (and the continent cannot indefinitely rely on foreign capital and technology for its industrial needs, as discussed below).

Hence it must build required capacities to add value to the goods it produces. As elaborated

later, increased domestic resource mobilization and staunched illicit financial flows—strongly linked to extractive and mining industries—have the potential to contribute significantly to meeting Africa's financing needs (ECA, 2012a). Success will eventually translate into more favourable terms of trade and reduce vulnerability to external shocks.

It is equally important that African countries meet their commitments to promoting regional and intra-African integration. The share of intra-African trade is extremely low relative to other major regions, hovering around 10–12 per cent.[4] Yet, as intra-African trade is more diversified and favours manufactured goods than Africa's trade with external partners, increased trading among African countries has huge potential to support industrialization and structural transformation. The low share of intra-African trade also underscores the necessity to overcome the numerous trade-related constraints within the continent, such as tariff and non-tariff barriers, poor infrastructure, lack of exploitation of supply chain potential, paucity of productive capacity, governance issues and instability of security.

Continental Free Trade Area and trade facilitation

Steps have already been taken on this. African Heads of State and Government endorsed in January 2012 an African Union (AU) Action Plan for Boosting Intra-African Trade and Fast Tracking the Establishment of the CFTA (Assembly/AU/Dec.426 XIX) by 2017.[5] This decision is of utmost importance as it aims to reinforce trade relationships among African economies, focusing on a few activities for seven key priority clusters: trade policy, trade facilitation, productive capacity, trade-related infrastructure, trade finance, trade information and factor market integration.[6] AU member States hope that such measures will help to double the share of intra-African trade by 2022 (table 2.1), assuming trade facilitation measures; without the latter, the gain would be only half as large.

TABLE 2.1: TRADE REFORMS AND SHARE OF INTRA-AFRICAN TRADE IN TOTAL, 2012 AND 2022 (%)

2012		2022	
	Without trade reform	*After CFTA reform implemented*	*After CFTA reform implemented and complemented by Trade Facilitation measures*
10,2	10.6	15.5	21.9

Source: Mevel and Karingi (2012).

A quantitative assessment of the CFTA's economic effects reinforces this expectation, although some economies could see their real income decline (Mevel and Karingi, 2012). One of the reasons for this outcome is that tariff revenues often represent a major source of income for African governments, and so removing tariff barriers would inevitably entail revenue loss.

When specific trade facilitation measures are introduced, however—namely a halving of the time goods spend at African ports as well as a making twice as efficient customs procedures by 2017 relative to 2012—outcomes improve greatly. Potential real income loss would be offset for all African countries when trade facilitation measures are taken in parallel.

Intra-African trade of industrial goods particularly would benefit, as trading across borders improves. Indeed, if such trade sees progress in all main product categories (agriculture and food, primary and petroleum products, industrial products, and services), intra-African trade of industrial products would be stimulated the most, in relative and absolute terms (table 2.2).[7,8] The full removal of tariff barriers accompanied by trade facilitation measures would bring the share of industrial commodities in intra-African trade to about 70 per cent, offering greater opportunities for value addition.

TABLE 2.2: TRADE REFORMS AND INTRA-AFRICAN TRADE STRUCTURE BY MAIN PRODUCT CATEGORIES, 2012 AND 2022

Product category	2012	Measure		2022
	Without trade reform	After CFTA reform but no trade facilitation measures	After CFTA reform and trade facilitation measures	
Agricolture and food products	17,9	16,3	16,3	12,4
Primary and petroleum products	18,5	18,4	16,9	15,6
Industrial products	59,3	60,7	62,7	69,4
Services	4,3	4,7	4,1	2,7

Source: Mevel and Karingi (2012).

Although this analysis did not highlight services (owing to lack of data), these steps are critical in promoting value addition of intra-African trade. Arnold et al. (2006) found that improved access to reliable and affordable services such as telecommunications, financial services and energy was associated with "significant positive trends in manufacturing performance" in 10 African countries. Information and communications technology is crucial for rapid diffusion of knowledge (Hoekman and Mattoo, 2011) and for effective communication (Arnold et al., 2006). Therefore, the efficiency of that sector (and most other services sectors) through healthy competition and appropriate regulatory frameworks is important. Overall, though, much needs to be done for the CFTA and trade facilitation to bring the needed changes in volume and composition of intra-African trade, as now analysed in three areas.

Facilitating trade and upgrading infrastructure through Aid for Trade

Implementing trade facilitation measures and improving infrastructure are extremely costly. The Programme for Infrastructure Development in Africa, for example, has identified 51 priority projects for 2012–2020, estimated at $70 billion.[9]

Aid for Trade (AfT) can be instrumental in supporting Africa's efforts to secure funding in these areas. Africa has been the primary recipient of AfT with about $17.4 billion in commitments (42.2 per cent of total AfT commitments to the world) in 2010. However, the share of trade facilitation support in total AfT commitments remains marginal: in 2010, only 1.2 per cent of total AfT commitments to Africa were devoted to trade facilitation.[10] That share must increase, to boost intraregional trade.

At the same time, other sources of funding must also be explored, including public–private partnerships in infrastructure financing, as well as a special continental fund for such financing and for trade facilitation.

Diversifying exports

With exceptions, export diversification remains weak in most African countries, and the continent lags far behind other major regions (figure 2.3).[11] There is a strong positive correlation between intra-industry trade and export diversification by destination and product (Ofa et al., (2012). This suggests that export diversification could be achieved through increased exports of old products to new markets, through export of new products to old and new markets, and through increased trade of similar but differentiated products (products from the same industry but differentiated according to quality or final use) to both old and new destinations.

Increasingly diversified trade can help to transform African economies by shifting resources from low- to high-productivity activities and by exploring

new sectors with potential dynamic comparative advantage, instead of their continuing to rely on sectors with static comparative advantage, as old trade theory suggests. This will require effective industrial policy frameworks to allow countries to identify sectors with dynamic comparative advantage and supply chain potential, and thus support investment in new and differentiated products that meet quality standards.

FIGURE 2.3: EXPORT DIVERSIFICATION BY MAIN REGION, 1998–2009

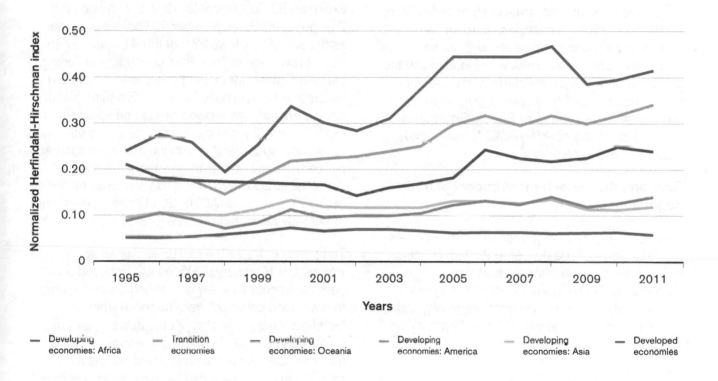

Source: Calculations based on UNCTADStat,http://unctadstat.unctad.org/ReportFolders/reportFolders.aspx, accessed 19 September 2012.

Note: The higher the normalized Herfindahl-Hirschman Index, the lower the export diversification.

Export diversification will also require investment in human capital, R&D, scientific and technological innovation and entrepreneurship. Concrete incentive mechanisms directly fostering higher-value output should be introduced. For instance, a clear policy on duty-exemption for capital machinery would facilitate access to imported capital goods and favour technological upgrading,

with beneficial effects on domestic production and value addition. A more specific example comes from Ethiopia, where the government provided incentives to floriculture exporters through export credit guarantees and foreign exchange retention schemes, making the country the world's fifth-biggest cut-flower exporter by 2007 (UNIDO and UNCTAD, 2011).

Enforcing regional and subregional decisions

All African countries should make concerted efforts to rapidly implement regional and subregional decisions aimed at overcoming trade-related constraints. These endeavours must be supported by specific measures including:[12] a comprehensive programme of capacity building to assist the eight AU-recognized regional economic communities that may be having difficulty in meeting the target date for concluding their free trade agreements (FTAs) to ensure that they can be ready for the CFTA;[13] measures to reduce border-crossing times towards international standards by setting up one-stop border-posts; a comprehensive industrial policy that includes industrial performance criteria, addresses structural changes, narrows the technological gaps of domestic with foreign firms and forges agricultural links with industry and the private sector; and establishment of an African Infrastructure Fund as a special-purpose vehicle co-guaranteed by member States. Governments should also found special banks for small and medium-sized enterprises.

Boosting the development impact of trade negotiations

Parallel to regional integration, African countries are negotiating trade agreements with countries outside the continent: the African Growth and Opportunity Act (AGOA), Economic Partnership Agreements and the multilateral trade negotiations under the aegis of the World Trade Organization (WTO).

African Growth and Opportunity Act

AGOA was enacted by the US President on 2 October 2000 for eight years, but was extended in 2004 until 30 September 2015. In principle, AGOA grants duty-free access for selected exports from African countries (excluding North Africa) to the US. More specifically it adds about 1,800 eligible product lines to the US Generalized System of Preferences, which already grants duty-free access for nearly 4,600 export products from developing countries to the US.[14]

In 2012, three developments stood out. First, South Sudan, which had proclaimed its independence in 2011, became the 41st AGOA-eligible country on 26 March.

Second, the third-country fabric provision, set to expire on 30 September 2012, was extended on 2 August until 30 September 2015. This is crucial as the provision allows 27[15] of the 41 countries to source raw material from third countries—including, critically, China—for making clothing that can then be exported duty-free to the US.[16] The third-country fabric provision has allowed textile and apparel exports from African countries to the US to be particularly successful, accounting for more than 48 per cent of total non-oil trade exports from AGOA countries in 2001–2011.[17] It has also created about 300,000 direct jobs (ACTIF, 2011) and indirect jobs of possibly twice that.

The trends in figure 2.4 can be explained as follows. On 1 January 2005, quotas imposed on developing countries' exports of textiles and apparel to developed countries were removed when the Multifibre Arrangement expired, offsetting part of the preference margin granted to African countries under AGOA, and resulting in fierce competition from Asian economies that were particularly efficient in textiles and apparel. Then in 2008–2010, the global crisis reduced US demand, which picked up as the crisis eased.

FIGURE 2.4: US IMPORTS OF TEXTILES AND APPAREL FROM AGOA COUNTRIES, 2001–2011 ($ BILLION)

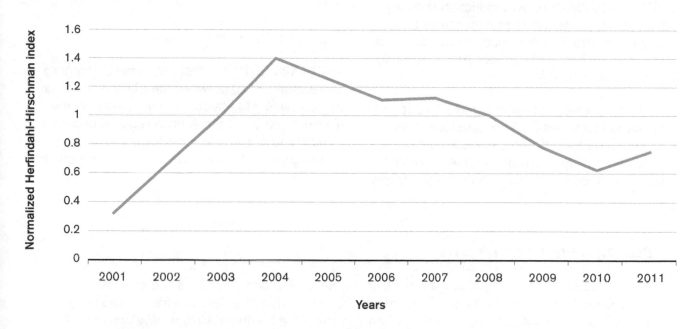

Source: Calculations based on US International Trade Commission, DataWeb, http://dataweb.usitc.gov/, accessed 20 September 2012.

Many argue that without the third-country fabric provision, textile and apparel exports from AGOA countries to the US could have simply disappeared after the Multifibre Arrangement expired, with potential devastating impacts on jobs across the continent. The recent extension is therefore a great relief to the countries that benefit.

Unfortunately, AGOA's benefits are concentrated in only a few countries and products, giving little impetus to export diversification, overall value addition or industrialization. In 2011, textiles and apparel accounted for only 4 per cent of exports from AGOA countries to the US, against 85 per cent for oil (table 2.3). Oil producers unsurprisingly head the list, while South Africa exports mainly motor vehicles and Lesotho textiles and apparel.

TABLE 2.3: SHARE OF TOP FIVE EXPORTING COUNTRIES AND TOP FIVE EXPORT PRODUCTS IN AFRICA'S EXPORTS TO THE US UNDER AGOA, 2011 (%)

Top five exported products		Top five exporting countries	
Oil	85,1	Nigeria	50,1
Motor Vehicles	7,1	Angola	29,8
Textile and apparel	4,3	South Africa	9,6
Iron and steel	1,2	Congo	2,4
Fruit and nuts	0,6	Lesotho	1,8
Total	**98,3**	**Total**	**93,7**

Source: Calculations based on the US International Trade Commission, DataWeb,http://dataweb.usitc.gov/, accessed 20 September 2012.

The third development came during AGOA's Annual Forum in June 2012, where African countries expressed their wish to see AGOA extended up to 2025 but with a broader product and country coverage. They also lobbied for measures to improve infrastructure development, as numerous trade-related constraints prevent Africa from fully benefiting from AGOA.

The US did not rule out extending AGOA but emphasized that it was not designed to run for ever and that other US–African trade relationships should be envisaged. Besides, AGOA is not WTO compatible (it does not comply with the reciprocity and non-discrimination clauses). Though AGOA currently enjoys a WTO waiver, it is uncertain whether WTO will extend it beyond 30 September 2015.

Economic Partnership Agreements

On 14 May 2012, the first Economic Partnership Agreement (EPA) between the EU and an African region came into effect: four countries from the Eastern and Southern African regional negotiating group (one of five) have started implementing their agreement. Other groups are still negotiating (box 2.1).

BOX 2.1: EPAs IN EARLY 2013

As of 21 January 2013 only Madagascar, Mauritius, Seychelles and Zimbabwe had an EPA in force. Côte d'Ivoire from the West African region; Cameroon from the Central African region; and Botswana, Lesotho, Mozambique and Swaziland from the Southern African Development Community had signed "stepping stone" or interim EPAs, although the agreements were not yet in effect.

Seven others—Ghana from the West African region; Burundi, Kenya, Rwanda, Uganda and Tanzania from the East African Community; and Namibia from the Southern African Development Community—have initialled EPAs but have not signed them. The remaining countries have not made any official commitments towards ratifying EPAs.

At least five outstanding issues deter African countries from officially engaging in or finalizing EPAs: the WTO's most-favoured-nation clause, which requires preferences granted outside EPAs also to be granted within the agreement; export taxes are prohibited in EPAs, but not by WTO; a non-execution clause in EPAs, which envisages unilateral trade sanctions for political violations (such as no respect of human rights or democratic principles); the notion of "economic development and cooperation" under EPAs, as this could potentially limit policy space for Africa's moves to industrialize and transform structurally; and potential conflicts over regional integration, because the five regional negotiating groups, which must establish regional FTAs, do not match the eight regional economic communities, which must also form regional FTAs and which are intended to be the building blocks for regionally integrating Africa.

To accelerate EPA negotiations, the European Commission announced towards the end of 2011 that all middle-income African countries not having ratified their EPAs by January 2014 would lose their Market Access Regulation preferences. This implies that exports from the countries that have not ratified their EPAs by the indicated deadline will face tariff barriers in the EU Generalized System of Preferences.

Africa's least developed countries(LDCs) will, however, continue enjoying preferences, owing to the Everything But Arms initiative: thus 33 of these countries will keep their preferential access to the EU even if they do not ratify their EPAs by 2014, while African non-LDCs that fail to ratify the EPAs by that date will experience a differential treatment as they compete with other developing countries under the EU Generalized System of Preferences.

World Trade Organization negotiations

WTO negotiations saw a change of focus in 2012 as trade facilitation came to the fore, relegating major topics such as agriculture and non-agriculture market access. Discussions on trade facilitation started at the Singapore Ministerial Conference in December 1996 and were integrated into the current, Doha Round in July 2004. Still, as negotiations were stalled by disagreement over the special safeguard mechanism (on special and differential treatment) between the US, China and India in July 2008, trade facilitation can be seen as a possible way out.[18]

Trade facilitation measures negotiated at WTO seem to require more support from developed countries than developing ones. Although technical assistance and capacity building are envisaged by WTO to help developing countries ease trade across borders, African countries—particularly least developed ones—have concerns over appropriate funding mechanisms (loans, grants and so on). They are also concerned that the strong focus on trade facilitation could divert WTO negotiations from other issues of importance to Africa, such as LDC packages, cotton, and special and differential treatment.

Trade negotiations on market access for LDCs received a boost when China recently indicated at the WTO that it would gradually expand its duty-free treatment for LDC exports, from the 60 per cent of tariff lines originally stipulated in 2010, to 95 per cent. A similar measure by India, gradually granting duty-free access to LDC exports for 85 per cent of its tariff lines, should become fully operational this year.

Coherence

To ensure a measure of coherence among the above initiatives and trade agreements, and their alignment with moves to foster structural transformation, African countries should ensure that the outcomes of the Doha Development Agenda and those of EPA and renewed AGOA negotiations are: mutually supportive; do not pre-empt them from engaging in regional trade agreements or from designing industrial policies that seek commodity-based industrialization and value addition on the continent; and help their economies to meet potential adjustment costs.

> *African countries should ensure that the outcomes of the Doha Development Agenda and those of EPA and renewed AGOA negotiations are: mutually supportive; do not pre-empt them from engaging in regional trade agreements or from designing industrial policies that seek commodity-based industrialization and value addition on the continent; and help their economies to meet potential adjustment costs.*

Preference erosion is one key issue. In the US, for example, African countries may see their preference margin shrink against those of Asian LDCs, in that the latter are allowed duty-free and quota-free access as part of a—so far hypothetical—"early harvest package" of the WTO negotiations, which may affect African textiles and clothing disproportionately. Rules of origin are another key issue. In AGOA and the EPAs, current rules of origin constrain countries from sourcing inputs from the region and from benefiting from value-chain creation across African borders. Also at issue are standards, sanitary and phytosanitary measures, and other technical barriers to trade, which are so restrictive and demanding that African countries cannot comply with them and therefore cannot access existing preferences under them.

Policy imperatives

National industrial policy and regional integration are critical. The discussion above underscores African countries' need to broaden their production base and diversify exports in products and markets—if they are to make trade an engine of growth and development. Diversifying in this way will support, and benefit from, efforts made by African countries and regional economic communities to implement the CFTA, boosting intra-African trade.

Indeed, the endorsement by the African Heads of State and Government of the CFTA may provide a vehicle for long-term growth and structural transformation through trade facilitation, allowing—on an optimistic scenario—the share of intra-African trade to double in 10 years, and raising the proportion of manufactured products in such trade significantly, on the assumption of adequate reforms and investment in infrastructure and productive capacity. Part of this investment could come from more AfT bankable projects that African countries should develop, refocusing existing AfT on trade facilitation.

For small African countries where domestic markets are limited, access of firms to international markets and establishing long-term trading relationships are important, as they allow countries to enhance economies of scale (ILO, 2011a).

Finally, African countries should continue to work together and commit to a unified framework to ensure that trade negotiations and agreements with traditional and emerging partners are consistent with their own development objectives; and that they are afforded adequate policy space as they design policies supportive of their economic transformation through commodity-based industrialization.

2.2 FINANCING AFRICA'S INDUSTRIALIZATION AND ECONOMIC TRANSFORMATION

To industrialize and structurally transform its economies, Africa has to ensure access to stable private and public financing. Even with good economic performance since the turn of the century, Africa's financing gap remains huge, caused by imbalances between exports and imports, between resource inflows and debt payments, and more important between domestic savings and domestic investment needs (ECA and AUC, 2012). Filling this gap has long been a preoccupation for African policymakers and their development partners, and they have taken several steps since the United Nations Financing for Development Conference in Monterrey in 2002 to enhance external and domestic resources (box 2.2).

BOX 2.2: THE MONTERREY CONSENSUS

This consensus identifies six core areas through which developing countries can mobilize development finance: international trade; international resources; sustainable debt financing and external debt relief; resolution of systemic issues such as enhancing the coherence and consistency of the international monetary, financial and trading systems; domestic financial resources; and international financial and technical cooperation.

The financing of Africa's industrialization and economic transformation has to be increasingly based on domestic public and private resources. Industrialization can, in turn, stimulate sustained domestic financing through increased income. Yet starting and sustaining a virtuous financing–industrialization circle require greater mobilization of savings and a deeper domestic financial system to ensure adequate access to long-term financing for new investment.

External finance is too unreliable, and misdirected

External financial flows, particularly foreign direct investment (FDI) and ODA, have generally risen during the last decade, but they are vulnerable to volatility in the commodity markets and to economic difficulties in donor countries. Little has gone outside extractive industries or into infrastructure and the productive sectors (manufacturing, communication, transport and construction), which largely explains these sources' minimal impact in Africa. Remittances, though, may offer increasingly important potential.

International resources

FDI flows are concentrated in extractive industries (especially oil). Given the weak links between extractive industries and the rest of the economy, this has induced little economic transformation (ECA and AUC, 2011).

Still, many African countries have policy incentives to attract FDI, but after attracting a decade-high of about $58 billion in 2008, they saw FDI inflows decline to a three-year low of $42.7 billion in 2011. This fall was largely due to the global crisis, exacerbated by continuing weak growth in developed countries.

ODA flows have been mainly directed to social sectors. Although their quantity and effectiveness have improved over the past decade, risks remain high in the current global environment.

Total ODA inflows to Africa, excluding debt relief, increased in nominal terms from $17.4 billion in 2002 to $50.0 billion in 2011, but they remain below international commitments under both the Monterrey Consensus and the Paris Declaration on Aid Effectiveness of 2005. Under the Monterrey Consensus, developed countries committed to increase ODA to 0.7 per cent of their GDP, with an additional 0.15–0.20 per cent to support the LDCs, yet by 2011 ODA from most of the developed countries had yet to reach this level.

Similarly, the Paris Declaration estimated ODA flows to Africa to increase to $64 billion by 2010, but Africa received only around half the increase implied by the 2005 commitments, partly owing to lower global ODA compared with commitments and partly to Africa's lower than expected share of the global increase. As with FDI, global uncertainties have raised legitimate concerns over the ability of donor countries to maintain their commitments.

Indeed, progress in delivering the Paris and Monterrey commitments has been slow, signalling the need to change the delivery of aid. Aware of this, the Fourth High Level Forum on Aid Effectiveness (Busan, Republic of Korea, 29 November–1 December 2011) adopted the Busan Partnership for Effective Development Cooperation, making a key shift from aid effectiveness to wider development effectiveness. The main argument is that, although ODA is one of the sources for financing Africa's development, it should be placed in the broader context to support capacity development and domestic resource mobilization.

Remittances present a different picture. They have surged over the past decade, and annual inflows to Africa are estimated to reach $60 billion by 2014, from $11.4 billion in 2000. Therefore, despite malaise in the developed countries—their major source—and the impact on migrants' jobs, remittances present an opportunity for many African countries to raise external capital. More serious policy efforts are needed, however, to maximize the potential gains (box 2.3).

BOX 2.3: AFRICAN UNION COMMISSION INITIATIVE ON REMITTANCES

Workers' remittances far exceed ODA for Africa, and for many individual African countries they exceed FDI as well. But with ODA and FDI flows under pressure from the crisis, remittances are a lifeline for tens of millions of African families. They have yet to reach their full development potential though, partly because they are not fully quantified. Remittances to and within the continent are still vastly undercounted, and transaction costs are the most expensive in the world by a wide margin.

The African Institute for Remittances (AIR) was conceived by the African Union Commission to help fill this knowledge gap. The Executive Council of the AU has acknowledged that the AIR will help to leverage remittances for Africa's social and economic development.

The 19th Ordinary Session of the AU Assembly of Heads of State and Government in July 2012endorsed the establishment of the AIR. Preparations have been finalized to set up the AIR with the aim of improving statistical measurement of remittance flows, lowering their transaction costs and leveraging their potential.

Debt relief

Africa's external debt has fallen since 2002, especially after the Heavily Indebted Poor Countries (HIPC) Initiative, the Multilateral Debt Relief Initiative and the Paris Club's Evian Approach for non-HIPC countries' debt relief.

As a share of gross national income (GNI), it fell from 53.5 per cent in 2000 to 20.6 per cent in 2011, or well below the 50 per cent sustainability threshold, an aggregate trend reflected in all five subregions (table 2.4). Improved macroeconomic management in many African countries also played a role.

TABLE 2.4: TRENDS IN EXTERNAL DEBT (% OF GNI)

Year	2000	2005	2008	2009	2010	2011
Africa	53.6	33.9	20.4	23.7	23.1	20.6
Central Africa	112.8	54.3	21.3	24.5	17.0	14.3
Eastern Africa	88.0	62.6	33.2	35.7	31.4	32.3
Northern Africa	41.8	29.0	16.9	20.0	20.8	15.6
Southern Africa	34.5	25.9	24.4	27.4	27.9	26.7
West Africa	94.3	41.3	16.7	19.9	16.9	16.2

Source: Calculations based on World Bank World Development Indicators (2012), http://data.worldbank.org/data-catalog/world-development-indicators, accessed 29 January 2013.

Systemic issues

The global crisis revealed weaknesses in the international financial architecture and prompted strident calls for reform. A key weakness in the system has been that, although developing countries in general—and African countries in particular—are increasingly affected by global shocks, they remain heavily underrepresented in global economic and financial institutions, including the International Monetary Fund, World Bank, WTO, Bank for International Settlements and G-20.

Mobilizing domestic resources is essential for Africa's industrialization

The above trends have put the spotlight on African countries' need to mobilize their domestic resources for industrialization, long-term economic growth and structural transformation. A domestic-oriented approach has long been recognized by African governments as effective to finance sustained growth and development, as it is less volatile and more stable than external financing. It also allows for country ownership of development policies and outcomes.

Massive increases in domestic savings needed to boost domestic investment and industrialization

Industrialization is costly and requires strong support from the financial system. Ever since the United Kingdom became the first industrialized country, characterized by the highest capital intensity and productivity in the world, heavy capital investments have been the common catch-up strategy for latecomers like the US, Germany and Japan (Wolff, 1991).

In the same vein, the experience of the newly industrialized economies in South-east Asia demonstrates an even stronger role of investment. Economies like the Republic of Korea, China, Indonesia, Malaysia and Thailand all experienced dramatic increases in their investment rates during their economic take-off: annual gross capital formation rose from around 20 per cent of GDP in the 1960s and 1970s—comparable to Africa's current saving rate—to nearly 40 per cent before the 1998 Asian financial crisis. China has sustained annual investment of close to 50 per cent of GDP.[19]

At present, gross capital formation in Africa is lower than in other regions and income groups (table 2.5). When one excludes the higher rate in Northern Africa, investment in the rest of the continent is around 21.0 per cent a year in 2006–2010. Clearly, African countries need to ramp up their domestic investment rates in order to diversify their economies and catch up—as many of them envisage—with emerging middle-income countries.

TABLE 2.5: GROSS CAPITAL FORMATION AND DOMESTIC SAVING RATES BY REGION AND INCOME GROUP (% OF GDP)

	Gross capital formation					Gross domestic saving				
	2006	2007	2008	2009	2010	2006	2007	2008	2009	2010
Africa	21.4	23.5	24.8	24.5	23.7	23.8	24.0	24.4	19.3	20.7
East Asia and the Pacific (developing countries)	37.7	36.8	38.8	41.1	42.1	44.8	44.7	45.3	46.0	46.1
Middle-income countries (average)	28.1	28.7	29.7	28.4	29.4	31.2	31.1	30.9	29.1	30.0

Source: World Bank World Development Indicators (2012), http://data.worldbank.org/data catalog/world-development-indicators, accessed 29 January 2013.

Africa's average domestic investment rate appears comparable with its domestic saving rate, but this average masks huge differences among countries and groups—the average saving rate is much lower when oil-rich African countries, especially Libya and Algeria, are excluded. This further illustrates the domestic resource gap that has led to dependence on external financing. Africa's domestic saving is very low compared with developing countries in East Asia and the Pacific and with middle-income countries. The financing gap is also huge when one compares actual with desired domestic saving, that is, the investment needed by African countries to achieve their socio-economic development goals (ECA and AUC, 2012).

Gross domestic savings in Africa reached a decade-high 24.4 per cent of GDP in 2008, but

declined to 20.7 per cent by 2010, and remained much lower than, say, developing Asia's 46.1 per cent (see table 2.5). This rather poor performance was heavily affected by global economic developments after 2007. Private saving remains low in the majority of African countries mainly because of low per capita incomes and inadequate incentives from the relatively few formal saving institutions, which offer very low or negative real rates of return on savings.

Efforts to boost Africa's low investment rates should go hand in hand with strategies to enhance total factor productivity and investment efficiency through, for example, innovation, R&D and the knowledge economy. Experiences in Africa and elsewhere show that the quality of investment is important and that the size of investment

To maximize domestic resource mobilization for industrialization and economic transformation, most African countries need to reform the domestic financial sector, address constraints to mobilizing private savings and tax revenue, explore innovative financing approaches, stem capital flight and make better use of natural resource revenue.

alone may not sustain industrialization. Indeed, although effective resource mobilization and massive investment in the former Soviet Union, for example, generated fast industrialization, lack of accompanying productivity and efficiency-enhancement measures resulted in subsequent deindustrialization (Krugman, 1994).

On the tax front, despite tax revenue standing at 27 per cent of GDP (well above the global average) for the continent in 2011, collection abilities vary greatly, so that for a quarter of African economies the figure still stands at less than 15 per cent of GDP, the threshold considered necessary for low-income countries(ECA and OECD, 2012).

Some of the factors affecting tax collection in African countries include low incomes that affect governments' direct taxation; cross-cutting structural bottlenecks, including high levels of informality; a lack of fiscal discipline and legitimacy; very tight administrative capacity constraints; excessive tax preferences; inefficient taxation of extractive activities; inability to fight abuse of transfer pricing by multinational enterprises; and excessive reliance on a narrow range of taxes for revenue (AfDB et al., 2010). The lack of urban cadastres and population censuses makes collecting urban property taxes particularly challenging for local administrations, on top of the difficulties they face in collecting taxes from higher income groups.

Need to deepen financial intermediation

Financial intermediation in Africa is far shallower and less developed than in the average middle-income economy (ECA, 2012b). Recent estimates suggest that the African average for domestic credit to the private sector is 52.7 percent of GDP, while money supply (M2) constitutes 48.4 percent of GDP. However, these figures are heavily influenced by South Africa and North Africa (ECA, 2012b). For example, excluding

them, domestic credit to the private sector drops to 22 per cent of GDP, slightly below the average of low-income economies (ECA, 2012b).North Africa and a few individual countries, however— Cape Verde, Mauritius and South Africa—are at a stage of financial intermediation comparable with that of Latin America's developing countries.

Markets for stocks and bonds can also play an important role in mobilizing resources and allocating them to productive investment. Part of a global trend over the last few decades, several stock markets have been set up in Africa since 1989. Today, the continent has 29 exchanges, but only three of them (in Egypt, Nigeria and South Africa) have listings of more than 100 companies; at least six have fewer than 10 listed companies.

The total value of stocks traded averaged 51 per cent of GDP in 2005–2010, compared with 20 per cent in the developing economies of Latin American and the Caribbean, 60 per cent in middle-income economies, and 124 per cent in developing economies of East Asia and the Pacific. In the same period, market capitalization of listed companies in Africa was double that of the average middle-income economy (140 per cent against 71 per cent), having expanded rapidly since the early 1990s.This figure is, though, largely driven by South Africa, with other countries exhibiting much smaller market capitalization (ECA, 2012b,c).

Policy options

To maximize domestic resource mobilization for industrialization and economic transformation, most African countries need to reform the domestic financial sector, address constraints to mobilizing private savings and tax revenue, explore innovative financing approaches, stem capital flight and make better use of natural resource revenue. Increased mobilization of resources should be accompanied by measures to ensure not only increased investment but also improve the quality of that investment. Steps to attract regional and international capital, especially market-seeking FDI, should also be considered.

Financial market development would facilitate the effective use of domestic resources (savings in particular) and their channelling towards productive sectors. On the supply side, most financial markets are still shallow—dominated by banks and thus short-term financial instruments—making it hard for the private and public sectors to tap their resources. On the demand side, many small enterprises and households still lack access to formal finance for a range of reasons, including cost and lack of collateral.

As government revenues are the main domestic financial resource for most African countries, governments should broaden the tax base and raise the efficiency of tax administration. Outsourced tax collection has gained popularity in Africa over the past two decades to overcome the inefficiencies and ineffectiveness of traditional models. It has involved semi-autonomous revenue authorities or privatized tax collection. Innovative financing schemes could include public–private partnerships, sovereign wealth funds, private equity funds and bonds targeted at the diaspora.

Stemming illicit capital flight is one of the top priorities. Illicit cross-border movement of financial resources in 1970–2008 totalled $854 billion, with another $945 billion due to other cross-border illegalities such as mis-invoicing and smuggling (ECA, 2012b,c). A particularly pernicious aspect is that in poor institutional environments, larger capital inflows actually facilitate external outflows of domestic resources, meaning that efforts to strengthen capital inflows might end up having little impact on structural transformation and development prospects as they may boost capital flight. Enhanced regulation and internationally mandated transparency for offshore bank accounts will be beneficial.

Better use of natural resource wealth in oil-rich countries can also help to close the financing gap. To do so, countries should put in place institutions and enforce the rules to allocate and manage resources better. The institutions should ensure transparency of the budget as to how the government produces and publishes information on revenue collection, of how the projections for the budget are formulated, and of budget accountability: "This requires making substantial changes in the political economy of public resource management, to address at core the structural weaknesses in domestic public resource mobilization" (ECA and AUC, 2012: 164).

African governments also need to look at regional solutions. Tremendous potential exists for creating and expanding access to finance through cross-border banking and regional financial markets, with protection for customers and the financial system. Facilitating cross-border movement of goods, capital and people is key in this regard. Remittances should also be tapped, and their role in financial intermediation enhanced through better use of post offices, mobile banking and microfinance.

Governments should also continue exploring external sources to complement domestic finance. FDI, when oriented towards manufacturing and beyond resource enclaves, has the potential to promote skill development, technology diffusion and much employment. It also provides substantial opportunities for backward linkages to the domestic economy, a prerequisite for economic transformation.

2.3 TRANSLATING GROWTH INTO DECENT JOBS FOR AFRICANS

Growth and employment trends

The strong growth witnessed in Africa since 2000 is catch-up for the lost decades of contraction or stagnation after the 1960s (ILO, 2011b). But it has not translated into meaningful job creation in most countries (see chapter 1), and may not mark the start of real structural transformation owing to severe shortfalls in the labour market and in the distribution of growth.

There is thus a strong case for placing greater emphasis on pro-employment economic and social policies and on private sector development to create productive employment and decent work, as well as to reduce poverty. Indeed, a consensus is emerging globally that attaining inclusive and pro-poor growth that translates into full and productive employment and decent work for all is one of the key means to achieve sustainable development, as recently emphasized by the Rio+20 summit held in Rio de Janeiro, 13–22 June 2012.

Africa's population of over 1 billion had a projected labour force of 419 million in 2012, with a participation rate of 65.5 per cent of the continent's working-age population, 1.4 percentage points higher than the global average (table 2.6). The participation rate for North Africa was low at 49.1 per cent, largely due to a raft of economic, social and cultural imperatives that resulted in a particularly low female participation rate (24.4 per cent). But the overall participation rate for the rest of the continent was very high at 70.4 per cent,

with female participation at 64.6 per cent. Yet this high supply of labour even during the global crisis reflects workers' vulnerability: they cannot afford to exit the labour market as they have no other means of survival, given the lack of social security and safety net programmes.

TABLE 2.6: LABOUR MARKET INDICATORS, 2000–2012 (%)

Africa		2000	2005	2008	2009	2010	2011[a]	2012[b]
Labour force participation rate	Total	64.6	64.9	65.2	65.2	65.2	65.3	65.5
	M	76.5	75.7	75.7	75.6	75.6	75.7	75.9
	F	53.0	54.2	54.8	54.8	54.9	55.1	55.3
Employment-to-population ratio	Total	58.3	59.4	59.9	59.8	59.9	59.9	60.0
	M	69.6	69.9	70.1	70.1	70.1	70.1	70.2
	F	47.3	49.0	49.8	49.8	49.9	49.9	50.0
Unemployment	Total	9.7	8.5	8.1	8.1	8.1	8.3	8.3
	M	9.0	7.7	7.4	7.4	7.3	7.5	7.5
	F	10.7	9.6	9.2	9.2	9.1	9.4	9.5
Youth unemployment	Total	16.0	14.5	13.6	13.7	13.5	14.0	14.0
	M	15.2	13.4	12.7	12.7	12.5	12.9	12.9
	F	16.9	15.8	14.8	14.8	14.7	15.2	15.2

Source: International Labour Organization, Trends Econometric Models database, accessed July 2012.

a = preliminary estimates; b = projection.

In 2000–2012, the aggregate employment-to-population ratio in Africa grew slightly from 58.3 per cent to 60 per cent.[20] A significant share of the working-age population is not recorded as part of the labour force—it is made up of those engaged in the care economy, students or discouraged workers. The challenge is to get more people into the labour market so that they can create—and receive—wealth.

Men and adults are more likely to join the labour market than women and youths. The catch-up process for women is too slow to bridge the gap to reasonable levels in the foreseeable future, unless states take drastic measures to increase their participation in economic activities.

Women's unemployment rates are more than double that for men in North Africa, but only slightly higher than men's in the rest of Africa. In many African countries, youth unemployment rates are about twice adult rates, and employment quality (underemployment, informality, vulnerability and working poverty) is a greater problem than quantity.

Young women are hit very hard, as female youth unemployment in North Africa, for example, was a staggering 41.7 per cent in 2012. Indeed, such lack of economic prospects for youths was one of the driving forces of the uprisings across North Africa and the Middle East in 2011. These events have catalysed policy reactions, with many governments taking steps to bring youths into the labour market through active labour market policies, including supply-side policies that focus on training and entrepreneurship development (AfDB et al., 2012). Temporary job creation

initiatives through public works programmes are also common.

Employment plays an intermediary role between growth and poverty if it is productive and increases returns to labour. Sustained poverty reduction therefore requires a rise in the labour productivity of men and women in wage and self-employment (Kanyenze et al., 2011). In many parts of Africa, however, labour productivity is very low, particularly in the informal economy where the majority of workers only eke out a living. In 2000–2012, continent-wide labour productivity is estimated to have grown by only 1.5 per cent a year (table 2.7). This slow growth in labour productivity needs to be reinforced by inclusive, pro-poor and employment-rich growth policies if it is to emulate earlier countries' success (box 2.4).

TABLE 2.7: OUTPUT PER WORKER AND SHARE OF VULNERABLE EMPLOYMENT AND WORKING POOR IN TOTAL EMPLOYMENT IN AFRICA, 2000–2012

		2000	2005	2008	2009	2010	2011[a]	2012[b]
Output per worker (constant 2000 US$) – African average		2,169.5	2,312.5	2,507.3	2,508.1	2,549.2	2,480.1	2,557.7
Share of vulnerable employment (% of total)	*Total*	73.9	71.9	70.2	70.5	70.1	69.9	69.7
	M	66.3	63.1	61.3	61.7	61.4	61.2	61.1
	F	84.9	84.2	82.5	82.7	82.0	82.0	81.8
Share of working poor (% of total)	*$1.25*	48.7	42.1	39.0	38.6	38.0	37.5	
	$2.00	68.3	63.2	59.7	59.3	58.6	58.3	

Source: International Labour Organization, Trends Econometric Models database, accessed July 2012; World Bank, World Development Indicators, http://databank.worldbank.org/ddp/home.do, accessed 10 December 2012.

a = preliminary estimates; b = projection.

BOX 2.4: SUCCESSFUL CATCH-UP

Empirical evidence from successful catch-up countries, such as the Republic of Korea, which sustained high growth during 1963–1995, and Costa Rica in the 1960 and 1970s, shows that educational transformation preceded accelerated productive transformation.

In particular, increasing shares of secondary and post-secondary education enhanced the "option space"— the feasible range of products and technologies into which countries may diversify but have not yet done so—for sustained diversification into low- and medium-technology manufacturing.

Industries are also important places of learning, where the deliberate and proactive promotion of technologically advanced and more complex sectors provides opportunities for workers and enterprises to enhance their capabilities to diversify.

Finally, labour market institutions, training systems and social protection embody the capabilities to translate employment into decent work, and they accelerate productive transformation because they provide incentives and pressures to invest in higher-productivity and learning-intensive economic activities.

Source: ILO (2012b)

Without sectoral labour-productivity data, it is hard to spot whether the growth in labour productivity is a result of the observed gradual structural shift of labour from low-productivity agriculture to services. In 1991–2012, the share of employment in agriculture fell from 67.1 per cent to 62.2 per cent and increased in services from 24.4 per cent to 29.3 per cent, while staying almost stagnant in industry at 8.6 per cent (ILO, 2012). Most economic activities in services in Africa are characterized by low-productivity informal enterprises, but their productivity could be higher than in subsistence agriculture. The entry of large foreign-owned consumer industries in Africa may also have pushed up overall labour productivity.

Consistent with low but improving labour productivity and the slow but steady structural shift of labour from agriculture to services (rather than to industry) are the high rates of vulnerable employment (defined as own-account and contributing family workers) observed over the past two decades (see table 2.7). The share of workers in such jobs in Africa stayed high at 69.7 per cent in 2012,and was only down slightly from 73.9 per cent in 2000 (the rate was globally comparable only with South Asia's). Thus the decline in vulnerability is too slow to lift the majority of workers into productive employment in the foreseeable future. Gender-wise, women have a much higher incidence of vulnerable employment than men, throughout Africa.

A further indicator of the low quality of employment and incomes is an estimate of the working poor— particularly useful given the paucity of wage data in the region. In 2000–2011, the working poor (those under the $1.25 a day poverty line) in Africa fell from 48.7 per cent to 37.5 per cent (see table 2.7). (But the fall was quite modest in low-income African countries, implying that if there was an increase in real wages in these countries, it was restricted to a very small proportion of employees.)

So, with slow growth in wages and employment, it seems that the benefits of the pick-up in growth in low-income countries since 2000 have largely gone to the profit share in income rather than the wage share. (In middle-income economies, however, the proportion of working poor under both poverty lines was much lower from the outset, and during a decade of high economic growth working poverty declined more rapidly than in low-income countries.).

Key policy options

Key policies for translating growth into decent jobs must include measures to raise productivity and reduce informality. Productivity can be increased by policies and institutions that stimulate technological upgrading and adoption of new work procedures through investment in R&D, transfer of advanced technologies, close collaboration between research institutes and the enterprise sector (to support adaptation of technologies to local needs and conditions), and skills development through investment in education and training(closely coordinated with technological change).

Diversifying—especially through manufacturing—production and exports into non-traditional, increasingly sophisticated goods can lift employment growth, as with investment in employment-intensive activities with strong backward and forward linkages to the rest of the economy. High value added and tradable services such as business services, finance and upmarket tourism can also create productive employment in some countries.

Education and training policies need to meet the specific human capital needs of labour markets, as well as support the economy more widely by developing social capabilities through increasing the breadth, diversity and complexity of the social knowledge base. But as countries differ in their social capabilities, they have different skills bases and options for transforming their economies (box 2.5).

BOX 2.5: SOCIAL CAPABILITIES

Social capabilities to diversify, reform and transform are embodied in the country-specific mix (nature and diversity) of the social knowledge base acquired in social networks, education and work experience, and in the "collective" procedures or "knowing how to do" that enterprises and societies have developed in past productive experience, and stored in their routines and institutions.

These capabilities are limited in many African countries and therefore restrict countries from entering a dynamic, sustained and employment-generating growth trajectory (Nübler, forthcoming).

In the short term, African countries need to design and set down transformative paths that are feasible for their own conditions. In the medium and long term, however, they need to accumulate social capabilities as part of their economic development process.

Further important supply-side measures relate to industrial policies enhancing competitiveness through promoting value addition, industrial policy and development of linkages (chapters 3–6).

These supply-side policies need to be accompanied by measures supporting demand for domestically produced goods. Macroeconomic policies have the potential to increase domestic demand, including for local production that, through improved productivity, is competitive against imports, underlining the need to boost productivity in the informal sector and agriculture.

Given the overwhelming predominance of the informal economy, therefore, governments should help to accelerate the transition from informality—characterized by huge decent work deficits—to formality across Africa. Policies should simultaneously promote formal employment; reduce informal employment by cutting the cost of the transition to formality, which would increase the benefits of being formal and increase the costs of being informal; and raise the volume of decent work in the informal economy, largely through providing better social protection.

The long-standing neglect of agriculture should also be reversed. Both Malawi and Rwanda have achieved record growth in recent years, driven primarily by agriculture. At the same time, intensification of agriculture needs to be complemented by an increase in productive non-farm wage employment and entrepreneurship development.

Extractive industries, which are capital intensive and so provide little direct employment, can only help to create jobs when revenues are invested in labour-intensive higher value added production. This challenges public and private investment. Yet resource-based industries can provide opportunities to diversify into higher value added activities, as illustrated by the diamond industry in Botswana where the government supported diversification into diamond cutting and polishing (see chapter 3). In essence, African countries need to formulate and implement productive transformation strategies that enhance, in a co-evolutionary way, productive capacity, employment and social capabilities.

REFERENCES

AfDB (African Development Bank), OECD (Organisation for Economic Co-operation and Development), UNDP (United Nations Development Programme), and ECA (United Nations Economic Commission for Africa). 2010. *African Economic Outlook 2010: Public Resource Mobilisation and Aid.* Paris: OECD.

———. 2012. African Economic Outlook 2012: Promoting Youth Employment. Paris: OECD.

ACTIF (African Cotton & Textile Industries Federation). 2011. "The AGOA Third-Country Fabric Provision Must Be Renewed Immediately To Prevent the Collapse of the AGOA Textile and Apparel Industry." Letter from Jaswinder Bedi, Chairman of ACTIF, to the United States Government, 5 May 2011.

Arnold, J.M., A. Mattoo, and G. Narciso. 2006. "Services Input and Firm Productivity in Sub-Saharan Africa: Evidence from Firm-Level Data." Policy Research Working Paper 4048, World Bank, Washington, DC.

ECA (United Nations Economic Commission for Africa). 2009. "Enhancing the Effectiveness of Fiscal Policy for Domestic Resource Mobilization: Issues Paper." Meeting of the Committee of Experts of the 2nd Joint Annual Meetings of the AU Conference of Ministers of Economy and Finance and ECA Conference of Ministers of Finance, Planning and Economic Development, 6–7 June 2009, Cairo.

_____. 2012a. "Illicit Financial Flows from Africa: Scale and Developmental Challenges." Third Meeting of the High Level Panel on Illicit Financial Flows from Africa, 14–15 August 2012, Nairobi.

———. 2012b. "Finance and Investment: Mobilizing Resources for Financing NEPAD/AU Projects." Addis Ababa.

———. 2012c. "An African Perspective on Illicit Financial Flows in Africa." Addis Ababa.

ECA (United Nations Economic Commission for Africa) and AUC (African Union Commission). 2011. *Economic Report on Africa 2011: Governing Development in Africa—The Role of the State in Economic Transformation.* Addis Ababa: ECA.

———.2012. *Economic Report on Africa 2012: Unleashing Africa's Potential as a Pole of Global Growth.* Addis Ababa: ECA.

ECA (United Nations Economic Commission for Africa) and OECD (Organisation for Economic Co-operation and Development). 2012. *The Mutual Review of Development Effectiveness in Africa 2012. A joint Report by ECA and OECD.* Paris: OECD.

Hoekman, B., and A. Mattoo. 2011. "Services Trade Liberalisation and Regulatory Reform: Re-invigorating International Cooperation." Policy Research Working Paper 5517, World Bank, Washington, DC.

ILO (International Labour Organization). 2011a. *Growth, Employment and Decent Work in the Least Developed Countries.* Report of the International Labour Office for the Fourth Conference on the Least Developed Countries, May, Istanbul.

_____. 2011b. *Efficient Growth, Employment and Decent Work in Africa: Time for a New Vision.* Geneva.

———. 2012. *Trends Econometric Models database.* Geneva.

Kanyenze, G., T. Kondo, P. Chitambara, and J. Martens, eds. 2011. *Beyond the Enclave: Towards a Pro-Poor and Inclusive Development Strategy for Zimbabwe.* Harare: African Books Collective.

Krugman, P. 1994. "The Myth of Asia's Miracle." *Foreign Affairs* 73(6):62–78.

Mevel, S., and S. Karingi. 2012. "Deepening Regional Integration in Africa: A Computable General Equilibrium

Assessment of the Establishment of a Continental Free Trade Area followed by a Continental Customs Union." Selected paper for the African Economic Conference 2012, 30 October–2 November 2012, Kigali.

Nübler, I. Forthcoming. *Capabilities, Productive Transformation and Development: A New Perspective on Industrial Policies.* Geneva: International Labour Organization.

Ofa, S.V., M. Spence, S. Mevel, and S. Karingi. 2012. "Export Diversification and Intra-Industry Trade in Africa." Selected paper for the African Economic Conference 2012, 30 October–2 November 2012, Kigali.

UNIDO (United Nations Industrial Development Organisation) and UNCTAD (United Nations Conference on Trade and Development). 2011. "Economic Development in Africa 2011-Fostering Industrial Development in Africa in the New Global Environment." United Nations, Geneva.

Wolff, E.N. 1991. "Capital Formation and Productivity Convergence Over the Long Term." *The American Economic Review* 81(3):565–79.

World Bank. 2012. Global Economic Prospects: *Managing Growth in a Volatile World. June 2012.* Washington, DC.

WTO (World Trade Organization). 2010. *International Trade Statistics 2010.* Geneva.

NOTES

[1] See UNCTADStat, http://unctadstat.unctad.org/ReportFolders/reportFolders.aspx, accessed 19 September 2012.

[2] About two thirds of Africa's exports were made up of primary commodities in 2011.

[3] In 2011, more than half Africa's total exports were still directed towards Europe and the United States (UNCTADStat).

[4] The share of intra-European trade is more than 70 per cent, while shares of intra-Asian and intra-North American trade are around 50 per cent, and the share of intra-South American trade is above 25 per cent (WTO, 2010).

[5] A full removal of tariff barriers on goods is assumed within the African continent.

[6] These activities are detailed in the Action Plan for Boosting Intra-African Trade of the African Union, 2012.

[7] As services are not subject to any tariff cuts in the analysis and would face severe competition from the other sectors in which tariff reductions are considered, intra-African trade for strictly services would increase comparatively less than intra-African trade for other sectors.

[8] Of Africa's exports to developed countries, 43.3 per cent are petroleum and other primary products; the corresponding ratio is still 53.8 per cent for Africa's exports to non-African developing countries (Mevel and Karingi, 2012).

[9] See "Programme for Infrastructure Development in Africa", www.afdb.org/en/topics-and-sectors/initiatives-partnerships/programme-for-infrastructure-development-in-africa-pida/, accessed 2012.

[10] Calculations based on OECD-DAC CRS, 2012, www.oecd.org/dac/aidstatistics/internationaldevelopmentstatisticsidsonlinedatabasesonaidandotherresourceflows.htm.

[11] Twelve African countries (Burundi, Central African Republic, Comoros, Democratic Republic of Congo, Egypt, Eritrea, Ethiopia, Gambia, Mali, Rwanda, Sierra Leone and Uganda) are slightly more export diversified today than in 1998 (Ofa et al., 2012).

[12] As agreed in the 2nd African Trade Forum, organized by the United Nations Economic Commission for Africa, African Union Commission and African Development Bank in Addis Ababa, 24–26 September 2012.

[13] The Common Market for Eastern and Southern Africa, East African Community, Southern African Development Community, Intergovernmental Authority on Development, Economic Community of West African States, Community of Sahel-Saharan States, Economic Community of Central African States and Arab Maghreb Union.

[14] These lines specifically relate to textiles and apparel, footwear, wine, certain motor vehicle components, chemicals, steels and a range of agricultural products.

[15] Twenty-seven African countries have established a visa system to prevent unlawful transshipment of clothing produced in non-AGOA countries, which complies with the standards of the US Customs Service.

[16] The extension of the third-country fabric provision may also act as an incentive for the growing engagement of China and other Southern partners in Africa, where foreign firms in special economic zones process inputs sourced in their own countries, while benefiting from the more favourable access of African countries to the US market.

[17] Computation based on US International Trade Commission, DataWeb, dataweb.usitc.gov, accessed 20 September 2012.

[18] The special safeguard mechanism aims to provide developing countries with special and differentiated treatment by allowing them to impose their own tariffs on a number of agricultural goods in case prices fall or if their imports rise enormously.

[19] See World Bank World Development Indicators (2012), http://data.worldbank.org/data-catalog/world-development-indicators,accessed 28 January 2013.

[20] The employment-to-population ratio is a measure of the proportion of the working-age population (15–64 years) that is employed.

State of Value Addition and Industrial Policy in Africa

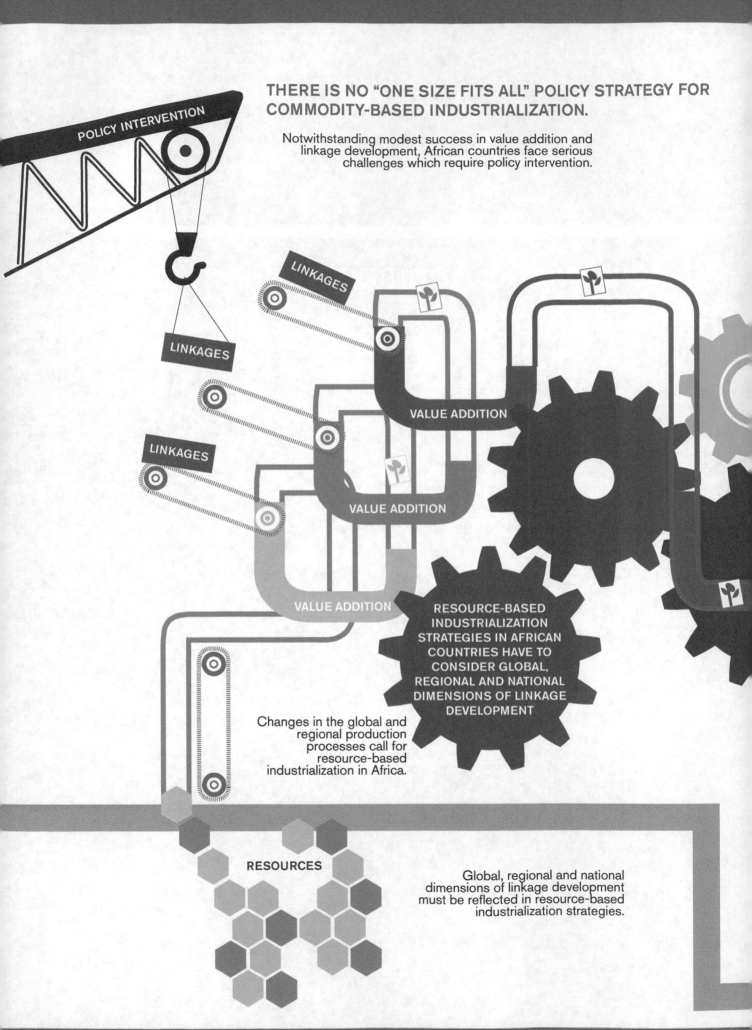

POLICY INTERVENTION

THERE IS NO "ONE SIZE FITS ALL" POLICY STRATEGY FOR COMMODITY-BASED INDUSTRIALIZATION.

Notwithstanding modest success in value addition and linkage development, African countries face serious challenges which require policy intervention.

LINKAGES

LINKAGES

LINKAGES

VALUE ADDITION

VALUE ADDITION

VALUE ADDITION

RESOURCE-BASED INDUSTRIALIZATION STRATEGIES IN AFRICAN COUNTRIES HAVE TO CONSIDER GLOBAL, REGIONAL AND NATIONAL DIMENSIONS OF LINKAGE DEVELOPMENT

Changes in the global and regional production processes call for resource-based industrialization in Africa.

RESOURCES

Global, regional and national dimensions of linkage development must be reflected in resource-based industrialization strategies.

INSTEAD THERE IS A CLEAR NECESSITY FOR EACH COUNTRY TO FOSTER LOCAL LINKAGE DEVELOPMENT AND ACCELERATE COMMODITY-BASED INDUSTRIALIZATION WITHIN THE DYNAMICS OF EACH COUNTRY, SECTOR AND DOMINANT VALUE CHAIN.

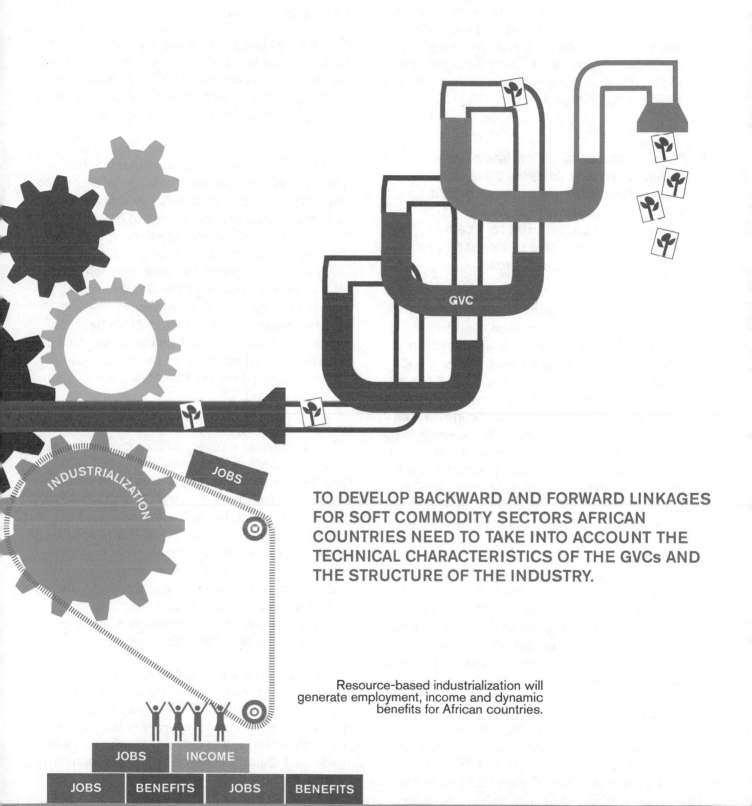

GVC

INDUSTRIALIZATION

JOBS

TO DEVELOP BACKWARD AND FORWARD LINKAGES FOR SOFT COMMODITY SECTORS AFRICAN COUNTRIES NEED TO TAKE INTO ACCOUNT THE TECHNICAL CHARACTERISTICS OF THE GVCs AND THE STRUCTURE OF THE INDUSTRY.

Resource-based industrialization will generate employment, income and dynamic benefits for African countries.

JOBS   INCOME

JOBS   BENEFITS   JOBS   BENEFITS

The need for African countries to make the most of commodities for industrialization, growth, jobs and economic transformation is the focus of this chapter. The chapter shows that Africa depends excessively on primary commodity exports, which makes it difficult to create decent jobs. Its average export concentration index has increased since 1995. Compared with both Asian least developed countries and Latin American commodity exporters, Africa shows significantly higher commodity dependence, obviously enhanced by the commodity price boom.

Africa's industrialization has been weak and inconsistent. In 1980–2009, the share of manufacturing value added to GDP increased marginally in North Africa, from 12.6 per cent to 13.6 per cent, but fell from 16.6 per cent to 12.7 per cent in the rest of Africa.

African economies depend heavily on natural resources, often a combination of soft, hard and energy commodities. The weights of these sectors vary among countries, but energy and hard commodities may hide the socio-economic importance of commodities, such as cotton in Egypt and sugar in Zambia. This export concentration on primary commodities reflects the weakness of Africa's industrial sector. Although the continent's export orientation and import penetration are high, exports are largely composed of raw materials and imports of final consumer goods. Imports of capital equipment and many intermediate goods are primarily destined for commodity extraction.

Another issue is that global industrialization has largely bypassed the continent. Africa's global trading links have not promoted the structural transformation of its economy towards industrial development. The gap with other developing countries is not only large, but also cumulative and path-dependent.

Africa's industrialization has been weak and inconsistent. In 1980–2009, the share of manufacturing value added to GDP increased marginally in North Africa, from 12.6 per cent to 13.6 per cent, but fell from 16.6 per cent to

12.7 per cent in the rest of Africa. Some African countries have managed to develop manufacturing activities on the back of preferences in third-country markets, but most of these have limited scope and size, and are vulnerable to erosion of trade preferences as trade liberalizes further in destination markets

Globalization has provided opportunities to Asia and Latin America to industrialize—and continues to do so—but in the 1980s and 1990s Africa suffered the most severe process of deindustrialization in the developing world. History—and policy failures—cast a long shadow.

There is strong evidence to show that the root causes of Africa's low levels of industrialization and dependence on primary commodity exports not only lie in the colonial extractive mode of production but also—and more important—the industrial policies executed from the 1950s to the 1990s. Judgement on import substitution industrialization (ISI) in developing countries is mixed, but it did not lead to massive industrialization in Africa. It is debatable whether ISI failed in Africa because many governments simply failed to pursue it, or whether they did not carry out the measures in the same methodical manner Latin American or Asian governments did.

In the mid-1980s, the economic situation of most African countries was very difficult, prompting the International Monetary Fund and World Bank to impose structural adjustment programmes (SAPs). It is now a shared view that the SAPs made African industry worse off. The SAPs in Africa failed in their aims: they did not raise productivity, boost manufacturing export performance or enhance value addition. But they did hurt technological capability and skills levels. Today, the weak African industrial structure has still to move out of the shadow of those interventions—a task made more onerous by the new international context.

Changes in global production systems present an opportunity for Africa. From the 1960s, the world economy witnessed a shift in how production processes were structured. Before then, they were organized within national boundaries, while trade was at arm's length between independent firms. Then, geographically dispersed activities were functionally integrated and organized in complex transnational production networks. Now known as global value chains (GVCs), they link the different value-added stages—composed of many activities—required to bring a product from conception and design to the final consumer and, finally, to its disposal. Developing countries in Asia, especially, have exploited globalization well and indeed benefited from the benign side by supplying intermediate and final products, engendering increasing relocation of the manufacturing stages of consumer goods to Asia and, to a much smaller degree, Latin America.

Africa must capitalize on its resource endowments and the commodity price boom. Since 2003, all commodity group prices have surged, except for a short-lived period from late 2008 to early 2009. So while in the past African development plans focused on diversifying from commodities, they now put them at centre stage. These plans are tackling issues of investment, labour, the environment as well as trade. Resource-rich countries are reforming their tax regimes to benefit from commodity export revenues, and must therefore tap the opportunities to pursue more diversified development paths, including commodity-based industrialization.

Thus while the booming resource sector carries the obvious risk of further deindustrializing Africa as it specializes in commodity production and export and provides revenues to pay for imports of consumer goods, its resource endowments also create opportunities, bolstered by the continent's increased leverage in negotiating with foreign investors over investment. They can also provide much-needed financing for capital investment, for example through infrastructure, as well as an opportunity to intensify knowledge transfer through backward and forward linkages to the wider economy.

Resource-based industrialization will yield employment, income and dynamic benefits. By moving up the value chain and developing backward and forward linkages to the commodity sector, countries can maximize direct and indirect job-creation effects. Provided their resource-processing industries are internationally competitive and well integrated in GVCs, exporting countries can move into higher-rent value-chain links and

extract the benefits of moving up value chains. For instance, up to 90 per cent of the total income from coffee, calculated as the average retail price of a pound of roasted and ground coffee, goes to consuming countries. This presents an opportunity that can be seized to improve incomes.

Forward integration confers other benefits. It can reduce the exposure of countries producing primary commodities to price fluctuations and thus yield dynamic skills-migration and cluster benefits of linkage development. By developing backward linkage supply firms to the commodity sectors and resource-processing industries, African countries can help to diversify their technological capabilities and skills base, deepening their industrial structure. Moreover, the natural resource sector's need for infrastructure (to extract and transport the commodities) enhances the potential for linkages.

Linkage development creates an opportunity to maximize positive externalities derived from clusters. Supplier and resource-processing industries' closeness to the extraction location generates agglomeration effects. Efficiency gains for firms in clusters include gaining access to a pool of specialist labour and networks of suppliers.

Yet critics argue that this resource-based industrialization is not feasible for Africa. Africa should ignore these criticisms. The experience of resource-rich countries shows the possibilities of commodity-based industrialization—despite all the criticisms, which run along three lines: that it is as hard as any other industrialization path; that commodity sectors are unlikely to promote linkages and externalities; and that resource-based industries do not match Africa's factor endowments. Yes, resource-based industrialization is as hard as any other path but still achievable with the right economic policies. Also, there are many exceptions to the argument that commodity sectors rarely promote linkages and externalities, as this chapter shows. Well-thought-out policies have catalysed resources in Argentina, Malaysia, Thailand and Venezuela. In other countries, good institutions and investment in human capital have paid off.

Africa's experience with linkage development has had modest success. Some African governments have not adopted linkage policies, forgoing potential opportunities to develop local manufacturing and services (Morris et al., 2012; see box 3.10). Others have adopted measures to promote linkages. However, export bans and taxes with local content regulations have rarely been accompanied by measures to support technological capabilities, skills development and entry into marketing/distribution networks.

The opportunities for linkage development to natural resource sectors are determined by the competitiveness of domestic firms and effectiveness of government policy. Domestic firms' competitiveness in price, quality, lead times and flexibility defines the extent to which they can seize the opportunity to supply commodity lead producers or move into resource-processing for domestic, regional and international markets, or even create domestic lead firms. Other factors also matter in defining linkage development opportunities, including GVCs' technical characteristics, industry structure, lead-firm strategies, location, trade barriers and other bottlenecks.

Continental policy initiatives present opportunities for regional industrialization and value addition. In 2007, the Conference of African Ministers of Industry endorsed the Accelerated Industrial Development of Africa (AIDA) Action Plan. The African Mining Vision, which foresees the mineral sector contributing to broader continental social and economic development, is another instrument that can change the situation. Other initiatives include the High-Level Conference on African Agribusiness and Agro-industries (3ADI), the Comprehensive African Agriculture Development Programme (CAADP), the Maputo Declaration and the African Union (AU) Summit on Boosting Intra-African Trade and Fast Tracking the Establishment of the Continental Free Trade Area.

African countries should consider designing strategies for linkage to GVCs but each African country must develop its own commodity-based industrialization within the specific dynamics pertaining to each country. A resource-based industrialization strategy should be grounded in the reality of each African country as well as the dynamics of the globalized world economy.

Although Africa has diversified its export markets in the past two decades, its export composition has changed little, and it remains highly dependent on primary commodity exports. And the commodity price boom can, under adequate regulatory frameworks, provide additional revenues for African treasuries and for much-needed capital investment.

However, if Africa is to achieve sustainable development and become a global growth pole, its strong economic growth has to be matched by structural transformation—essentially industrializing and raising agricultural productivity, moving from commodity dependence. So, although the commodity price boom is boosting Africa's economic growth, the continent has to embed industrialization into this trajectory, and developing backward, forward and horizontal links to the commodity sector is one platform for this.

3.1 COMMODITY DEPENDENCE

Africa depends excessively on primary commodity exports

Primary commodity exports have been the critical determinant of Africa's economic performance since it gained independence (ECA and AUC, 2012), even with increasing contributions to GDP from manufacturing, finance, telecoms and tourism. The continent's export profile has not moved far from the commodity dependence of colonial times, as discussed in chapter 2. Export dependence can be seen in export product concentration and diversification indices (table 3.1).

TABLE 3.1: EXPORT DEPENDENCE ON PRIMARY COMMODITIES, 2011

Export product concentration index				Export product diversification index			
Central Africa		**Southern Africa**		**Central Africa**		**Southern Africa**	
Central African Rep.	0.33	Angola	0.97	Central African Rep.	0.76	Angola	0.80
Cameroon	0.38	Botswana	0.79	Cameroon	0.71	Botswana	0.89
Chad	0.93	Lesotho	0.33	Chad	0.79	Lesotho	0.83
Congo, Rep.	0.79	Malawi	0.53	Congo, Rep.	0.81	Malawi	0.84
Equatorial Guinea	0.70	Mauritius	0.25	Equatorial Guinea	0.74	Mauritius	0.71
Gabon	0.75	Mozambique	0.51	Gabon	0.82	Mozambique	0.81
São Tomé and Príncipe	0.47	Namibia	0.22	São Tomé and Príncipe	0.56	Namibia	0.77
East Africa		South Africa	0.16	**East Africa**		South Africa	0.60
Burundi	0.54	Zambia	0.63	Burundi	0.75	Zambia	0.85
Comoros	0.51	Zimbabwe	0.20	Comoros	0.75	Zimbabwe	0.73
Congo, Dem. Rep.	0.43	Swaziland	0.28	Congo, Dem. Rep.	0.78	Swaziland	0.78
Djibouti	0.35	**West Africa**		Djibouti	0.61	**West Africa**	
Eritrea	0.65	Benin	0.28	Eritrea	0.83	Benin	0.77
Ethiopia	0.36	Burkina Faso	0.52	Ethiopia	0.79	Burkina Faso	0.81
Kenya	0.18	Cape Verde	0.48	Kenya	0.65	Cape Verde	0.72
Madagascar	0.21	Côte d'Ivoire	0.38	Madagascar	0.77	Côte d'Ivoire	0.70
Rwanda	0.40	Gambia	0.25	Rwanda	0.84	Gambia	0.75
Tanzania	0.19	Ghana	0.41	Tanzania	0.77	Ghana	0.75
Uganda	0.21	Guinea	0.45	Uganda	0.73	Guinea	0.74
Seychelles	0.51	Guinea-Bissau	0.89	Seychelles	0.83	Guinea-Bissau	0.75
Somalia	0.33	Liberia	0.50	Somalia	0.70	Liberia	0.72
North Africa		Mali	0.60	**North Africa**		Mali	0.81
Algeria	0.54	Niger	0.39	Algeria	0.72	Niger	0.84
Egypt	0.14	Nigeria	0.81	Egypt	0.55	Nigeria	0.78
Libya	0.78	Senegal	0.23	Libya	0.77	Senegal	0.73
Morocco	0.16	Sierra Leone	0.27	Morocco	0.70	Sierra Leone	0.71
Tunisia	0.16	Togo	0.24	Tunisia	0.54	Togo	0.73
Mauritania	0.52			Mauritania	0.82		
Sudan (…2011)	0.81			Sudan (…2011)	0.79		

Source: UNCTADStat, http://unctadstat.unctad.org, accessed 20 July 2012.

Note: For the export product concentration index, values closer to 1 indicate an economy more dependent on exports of one product. The export diversification index ranges from 1 (largest difference from world average) to 0 (alignment with world average). Data for South Sudan are not available.

The export product concentration index (or sectoral Hirschman index) measures the degree of export concentration within a country. Industrialized countries are characterized by values closer to zero, reflecting very diversified export sectors. More than half the 53 African countries, however, have an index equal to or higher than 0.40, and one quarter of them have an index equal to or higher than 0.60, marking dependence on a narrow range of products, such as hydrocarbons in Angola. In comparison, the average export concentration indices in 2011 were 0.12 for Asia and 0.13 for Latin America (table 3.2).

TABLE 3.2: COMPARATIVE EXPORT CONCENTRATION INDICES BY REGION, 1995 AND 2011

	Export concentration index	
	1995	2011
Africa	0.24	0.43
Africa excluding South Africa	0.34	0.51
Latin America	0.09	0.13
Asia	0.09	0.12
Low-income developing economies	0.14	0.25

Source: UNCTADStat, http://unctadstat.unctad.org/ReportFolders/reportFolders.aspx, accessed 20 July 2012.

The export diversification index measures the extent to which the structure of trade of a particular country differs from the world average. This index helps analysts to overcome a potential problem of the concentration index, namely that it is more susceptible to commodity price variations and so results in a higher concentration during such booms. All African countries have a diversification index of 0.5 or higher, meaning they have lower diversification levels than the world average. For almost a third of them, the diversification index is higher than 0.80, far higher than in other world regions (as supported by the analysis for figure 2.3 in chapter 2, which shows that the continent globally lags far behind in diversified trade).

Worse, Africa's average export concentration index has increased since 1995. Compared with both Asian least developed countries and Latin American commodity exporters, Africa shows significantly higher commodity dependence, obviously enhanced by the commodity price boom.

Africa's highly concentrated export structure is the result of a historical dependence on natural resource sectors. Disaggregating the export profile of 46 countries for which reasonably recent export data are available, we find that in three quarters of the countries, the share of primary commodities in total merchandise exports equals 50 per cent or more (annex table 3.1).[1] In a third of the countries, this share is 90 per cent or higher.

Considering the top three export products, by Standard International Trade Classification at the four-digit level, we find the extent of concentration high not only at sectoral level but also at product level (annex table 3.2). In more than half the listed African countries, the top three products represent more than 50 per cent of total merchandise exports; for a quarter of them this share rises to 80 per cent or more. In eight countries, one single product accounts for more than 70 per cent of total exports. Because products are identified at a fairly disaggregated level, sometimes two or three of the top products originate from the same commodity subsector—the top three export products of Zambia are copper-based, for example.

The relative share of agricultural raw commodities, ores and minerals (hard commodities) and fuel is further disaggregated in annex table 3.1. Historically, developing countries experienced the rising importance of food commodities and decreasing importance of agricultural raw materials (Yeats, 1991), although the latter group are still important for a small group of countries, mainly in West Africa, where it represents more than 10 per cent of total exports: cotton (Benin, Burkina Faso, Mali and Togo), wood (Cameroon, Central African Republic, the Republic of Congo, Gabon and Guinea-Bissau), rubber (Côte d'Ivoire) and tobacco (Malawi and Zimbabwe). While often dwarfed by minerals or oil in their relative contributions to total exports, these soft commodities remain important because of their labour intensity.

Hard commodities are the main source of foreign exchange in Zambia, Niger, Mozambique, Central African Republic and Guinea. Fuel is the main export for Algeria, Gabon, Sudan, and Nigeria. Notwithstanding some missing data, Angola and Libya also fit this profile. Diamonds are an important source of foreign exchange for Botswana and Namibia, and gold for Mali, Burkina Faso, Mauritania, Ghana and Guinea. Hard and energy commodities are generally capital and technology intensive, and are organized around large mines and production plants. These sectors are often considered enclave because of their disconnect from the rest of the economy and their closer links to global markets, generally at the lower end of the value chain.

In sum, African economies depend heavily on natural resources, often a combination of soft, hard and energy commodities. The weights of these sectors vary among countries, but energy and hard commodities may hide the socio-

economic importance of commodities. This export concentration in primary commodities reflects the weakness of Africa's industrial sector.

Global industrialization has largely bypassed the continent

Africa's global trading links have not promoted the structural transformation of its economy towards industrial development. The gap with other developing countries is not only large, but also cumulative and path-dependent (Lall, 2004)—in other words, countries in Asia and to a lesser extent Latin America, building on a competitive and dynamic industrial base, are moving faster than Africa to higher-technology and knowledge-intensive sectors. This, coupled with Africa's underdeveloped industrial base, makes it increasingly hard for the continent to catch up (box 3.1).

BOX 3.1: TIME TO CATCH UP

In addition to the legacy of the colonial extractive economic system, the weakness of Africa's industrial development is attributable to exogenous shocks, such as negative terms of trade and conflicts, as well as endogenous, policy-related ones (Lall and Wangwe, 1998). The following seem the most important.

The technological capabilities to begin industrializing and the financial resources to finance manufacturing development (see chapter 2) are often in short supply. Moreover, until the start of the new millennium, the political instability that characterized a number of African countries added costs that further reduced incentives to invest in manufacturing.

The increasing concentration of Africa's exports in primary commodities may adversely affect the potential for future growth in the region. Indeed, there is considerable evidence that the type of product that a country exports matters to long-run economic performance (Hausmann et al., 2007; Lall et al., 2006) although not all manufactures are better than all commodities (UNCTAD, 2002).

Manufactures, especially medium- and high-technology, have forward and backward linkages with other sectors that may generate positive benefits for the whole economy. Primary products, in contrast, have production structures that are capital intensive and often poorly linked to the rest of the econ¬omy. Moreover, primary product prices are set at the world level and are usually more volatile than those of manufactured products.

Africa's marginalization in manufacturing GVCs is evidenced by its trade patterns. Global trade flows have been increasingly characterized by intra-industry trade in intermediate goods, reflecting trade between lead firms—mainly transnational corporations (TNCs) and retail chains in developed countries—and their suppliers around the world. Although Africa's export orientation and import penetration are high, exports are largely composed of raw materials and imports of final consumer goods. Imports of capital equipment and many intermediate goods are primarily destined for commodity extraction.

Africa's industrialization has been weak and inconsistent. In 1980–2009, the share of manufacturing value added to GDP increased marginally in North Africa from 12.6 per cent to 13.6 per cent, but fell from 16.6 per cent to 12.7 per cent in the rest of Africa. Strikingly, by country (annex table 3.3), this share contracted by about 60 per cent in Chad, the Democratic Republic of Congo and Rwanda, by about 50 per cent in Zambia and by a third in Kenya, Malawi and South Africa (although a few countries such as Lesotho, Swaziland, Tunisia and Uganda showed positive trends).

Some African countries have managed to develop manufacturing activities on the back of preferences in third-country markets, but most of these have limited scope and size, and are vulnerable to erosion of trade preferences as trade liberalizes further in destination markets (Kaplinsky and Morris, 2008; Staritz, 2011). Even in their domestic markets, African manufacturers, which mainly concentrate on light consumer goods and agro-processing, are increasingly under pressure from some countries (box 3.2).

BOX 3.2: THE ASIAN GIANTS HELP, AND HINDER, AFRICA

Manufactured imports from some emerging countries, in particular China and India, are affecting local manufacturing in Africa.

In most cases, domestic producers suffer this competition and are obliged to leave the market. But in some, competition has prompted domestic firms to compete, as in the Ethiopian shoe sector, while in others it has offered some new opportunities. Indeed, as many emerging economies climb the GVC they leave space for other developing countries to produce some of their low-technology goods.

To help their firms exploit these new opportunities, governments need to design and effectively implement industrial policies that will, among other things, help to improve access to credit and address the problem of poor infrastructure and inadequate human capital, which currently constrain market-seeking, or "green", foreign direct investment flows into Africa.

History—and policy failures—cast a long shadow

Globalization has provided opportunities to Asia and Latin America to industrialize—and continues to do so—but in the 1980s and 1990s Africa suffered the most severe process of deindustrialization in the developing world (Lall and Wangwe, 1998). What went wrong?[2]

Import substitution industrialization

There is strong evidence to show that the root causes of Africa's low levels of industrialization and dependence on primary commodity exports not only lie in the colonial extractive mode of production but also—and more important—the industrial policies executed from the 1950s to the 1990s. As with most other developing economies in the 1960s and 1970s, African countries adopted ISI (Mkandawire, 2001; Galal, 2008).

Governments adopted this strategy largely in the belief that industrialization was necessary for development and that their infant industries had to be nurtured behind protective barriers, anxious lest free trade increased dependence on imported manufactured goods. They used a range of measures to maintain these barriers— tariffs as well as non-tariff barriers like quotas and licences.[3] It was very common, for instance, to grant export monopolies to particular firms, while foreign exchange restrictions frequently imposed large additional taxes on trade.[4]

As in all other developing countries, African governments were keen industrializers. Public ownership of industry was widespread, public investment was extensive and a number of firms were nationalized.[5] But unlike East Asia, most governments did not have the financial and managerial capacity to operate the enterprises efficiently (Nziramasanga, 1995). Moreover, the policies designed to direct investment towards industry had a negative impact on agriculture by distorting factor prices and rates of return. High tariff protection for final goods and subsidized import of foreign capital goods were incentives to expand production of consumer goods rather than of intermediate inputs.

In these circumstances, economies could not generate knowledge spillovers, which ironically were one of the main reasons to protect infant industries. Further, even when foreign firms were nationalized, technology transfer was virtually nil because the national technical capability to absorb it was still very low.[6] Relations between industry and research centres, as in Latin America, were very weak. In most cases, these centres were separate from industry and did not seek solutions to industry's technical problems.

In the African experience of ISI, state control of the financial sector was central (with variations among countries), often in the form of state ownership of banks and other financial institutions. State control was regarded as critical to ensure success of industrial and trade policies, because it provided the state with the power to influence private investment decisions and, more important, to discipline non-performers (Soludo et al., 2004).

Another issue was foreign direct investment (FDI), which was almost exclusively directed to primary and raw-material sectors.[7] Many countries granted monopolies in some areas to foreign firms, including exclusive exploration rights, sole-supplier contracts and domestic-market exclusivity (Stein, 1992), which had the perverse effect of blocking linkages to the domestic economy.

Judgement on ISI in developing countries is mixed, but the policy did not lead to massive industrialization in Africa. It is debatable whether ISI failed in Africa because many governments simply failed to pursue it, or whether they did not carry out the measures in the same methodical manner Latin American or Asian governments did (Riddell, 1990).

Structural adjustment

In the mid-1980s, the economic situation of most of African countries was very difficult, prompting the International Monetary Fund and World Bank to impose SAPs. The theoretical premises of SAPs were that markets are efficient, but government interventions are inefficient because they distort market signals; and that governments should manage the macro economy and improve general education and infrastructure, while the free market eliminated inefficient firms, releasing productive resources for other, more efficient, firms. The theory was that Africa would expand its agricultural and extractive mineral commodity sectors because those were the sectors with comparative advantages.

All the ISI apparatus was eliminated, as were the measures to protect the domestic market—tariffs and quantitative restrictions on imports, price controls and subsidies, and credit ceilings. SAPs were successful in liberalizing trade and the financial sector, privatizing public enterprises and inducing massive currency devaluations in most African countries (Ogbu et al., 1995). But there it stops.

It is now a shared view that the SAPs made African industry worse off. According to Lall (1995), industrial performance disappointed and many African countries suffered sustained deindustrialization in the 1980s and early 1990s, an impact confirmed for several African countries by Stein (1992), while Nziramasanga (1995) cites the difficulties of the sugar industry in Kenya and the textile industry in South Africa and Zimbabwe in the mid-1990s. All these sectors reduced output and employment owing to competition from imports in the domestic market. Ogbu et al. (1995) argue that growing dependence on imported goods eroded the weak industrial base of most African economies. According to Riddell (1990), SAPs were a major factor that prevented African countries from restructuring their industries away from primary commodity dependence.

The weakness of the African supply response was particularly marked in manufacturing production and export performance, and even when manufacturing showed an initial favourable response, it did not lead to sustained growth and diversification of production and exports (Jalilian et al., 2000). Stein (1996) concluded that economic reforms should have been based on transforming the economy, and not on retracting state institutions and policies in such a wholesale way. The SAP type of adjustment removed inefficient government interventions but did not create the conditions for development.

Nor did SAPs solve the numerous market failures of African economies, such as a weak tradition of industrial entrepreneurship and a severe shortage of technical skills. According to some, their main problem was that they ignored capability development (Grimm and Brüntrup, 2007, for example).

Moreover, African governments had, often on advice from donors and multilateral development institutions, focused on macroeconomic stability and institutional reforms to protect property rights and ensure contract enforcement, with no coherent strategies to address market failures and externalities that constrained economic activity. And while SAPs were intended to attract foreign capital and, through this, to ensure growth of a stable industrial sector, this did not happen except in the resource-extractive sectors (Elhiraika, 2008).

The SAPs had a particularly negative effect on technological accumulation (Chang, 2009).

Although innovation and growth during the ISI period were often poor, SAPs did not produce better outcomes—see Lall (1995) on Ghana, for example.

To sum up, the SAPs in Africa failed in their aims: they did not raise productivity, boost manufacturing export performance or enhance value addition. But they did hurt technological capability and skills. Today, the weak African industrial structure still has to move out of the shadow of those interventions—a task made more onerous by the new international context.

3.2 THE BIRTH OF GLOBAL VALUE CHAINS

Developing countries, in Asia especially, have exploited globalization well

From the 1960s, the world economy witnessed a shift in how production processes were structured. Geographically dispersed activities became functionally integrated and organized in complex transnational production networks (Dicken, 1998; Gereffi, 1994). Now known as global value chains (GVCs), they link the different value-added stages— composed of many activities—required to bring a product from conception and design to the final consumer and, finally, to its disposal (Kaplinsky and Morris, 2001).

The crucial aspect of globalization is outsourcing by developed-country lead firms of labour-intensive stages of production to countries with low costs. This was made possible by innovations in transport (commercial jets, container transport), communication systems (satellite, facsimile), and microelectronic technologies, which reduced the cost and time for communication and enabled flexible production systems.

By relocating these activities to outsourced firms, lead firms have moved from ownership of the production plants and the vertical integration of all production activities under their direct company control, but have retained control of the organization of such indirect manufacturing activities within the value chains that they drive. In other words, lead firms have focused on governing these value chains, that is, they are the drivers of these value chains and exercise power by requiring other firms lower in the chain to meet their requirements.

The lead firms decide which functions will be located in which countries, set the standards that supplier firms have to meet if they are to stay in the value chain (technical parameters such as costs, quality and lead times, or health, labour and environmental standards, and so forth), manage suppliers meeting these standards and decide on how to intervene when these parameters are infringed, all the while expanding or shrinking the number of suppliers. These activities can lead to developing-country producers receiving assistance to upgrade their capabilities to meet value chain requirements, and so staying globally integrated, or in their failing to meet these parameters and being excluded from the value chain.

Milanovic (2003) argues that globalization thus has two faces: a benign side accelerating the participation of developing countries into the world economy with positive impacts on industrialization and income levels, and a malign side increasing inequality and leading to major stress on workers and the environment.

Some developing countries indeed benefited from the benign side by supplying intermediate and final products, engendering increasing relocation of the manufacturing stages for consumer goods to Asia and, to a much smaller degree, Latin America. Since lead firms were outsourcing an increasing number of functions to firms in developing countries, they also became more interested in building some of the capabilities of selected supplier firms.

Lead firms kept control of the GVCs' most profitable stages—the intangible, knowledge-intensive activities such as product design, marketing and distribution, which had high entry barriers to competitors in developing countries. Their support to developing-country firms therefore tended not to encroach on their core business. US clothing and footwear manufacturers and distributing companies, for example, upgraded their Latin American suppliers' capacity to

manufacture complex products and manage the production process (Bair and Gereffi, 2001; Schmitz and Knorringa, 2000), but did not extend it to the spheres they regarded as their own core competence—design, product development, marketing and retailing.

"Lead firm" is therefore a political-economy term and not a normative concept implying benevolence. It refers to the power dimension that it exercises within a GVC, and the driving role it plays in setting the rules of the game and in governing the dynamics between the various links along these chains. This lead governance role means that the lead firms may sometimes act to foster the global dispersion of production to various countries and upgrade their suppliers, and sometimes to block upgrading and exclude suppliers from integrating in a GVC. It is a complex and contradictory dynamic, which if not understood and appropriately exploited by developing-country suppliers and governments, can have harsh consequences for countries seeking to industrialize.

> **Globalization thus has two faces: a benign side accelerating the participation of developing countries into the world economy with positive impacts on industrialization and income levels, and a malign side increasing inequality and leading to major stress on workers and the environment.**

Some developing-country governments, especially in Asia, did understand the dynamic, and adopted industrial and skills-development policies that enhanced their domestic firms' competitiveness and, in time, enabled these firms to take over more complex functions. As competition between low-cost developing countries became stiffer, profit margins on many types of manufacturing activities shrank. In order to escape this downward price trend, firms in some developing countries, applying various industrial policies, managed to move into more sustainable stages of GVCs. This was done by upgrading (table 3.3).

TABLE 3.3: UPGRADING TRAJECTORIES

Upgrading	Process	Product	Functional	Chain
	Increasing the efficiency of internal processes	Introducing new products or improving old products	Increasing value added by changing the mix of activities conducted within the firm or moving to different links in the value chain	Moving to a new value chain
Examples	Improving quality control processes in the plant	A beverage company introducing a new flavoured fizzy drink	Moving from manufacturing to design	Moving from manufacturing mobile phones to smart phones
Degree of intangible activities	Knowledge content of value added increases progressively ⟶			

Source: Adapted from Kaplinsky and Morris (2001).

Upgrading implies improvement in production systems (process upgrading), moving into more sophisticated product lines (product upgrading), moving into higher knowledge-content functions (functional upgrading), or moving into new production activities (inter-sectoral or chain upgrading). East Asia's industrial upgrading has been the result of a complex process shaped by private TNC strategies and local state industrial policies. It often involved domestic substitution of parts and components imported from more advanced economies (Japan, the Republic of Korea and Taiwan, China). The insertion of some Asian firms into dynamic GVCs in which lead firms outsourced increasing levels of value-added links created important opportunities to industrialize, which governments' industrial policies enabled the firms to seize. Although these GVCs were driven by Northern TNCs and retail chains, the result was growth in Southern firms' and economies' capabilities.

Africa must capitalize on its resource endowments and the commodity price boom

Africa's past dependence on primary commodity exports and lack of structural transformation must be seen in a context of declining or static commodity prices. Developing countries found it straightforward to adopt policy recommendations that urged them to diversify from natural resources to industrialize. This was, for example, the case of Latin American countries that followed the highly influential Prebish-Singer thesis of declining terms of trade (Prebish, 1950; Singer, 1950).

But since 2003, all commodity-group prices have surged, except for a short-lived period from late 2008 to early 2009 (figure 3.1). Prices for the metals group have done particularly well, before and after the global financial crisis. This was particularly the case after China shifted to investment-led growth after the crisis when its export markets in the North shrank considerably (Akyuz, 2012). Of 47 African countries in 2000–2005, the terms of trade improved for 25, worsened for 14 and remained almost unchanged for 8, according to World Bank data that estimate net barter terms of trade[8].

The key driver of the commodity price boom is China (Farooki and Kaplinsky, 2012). China is also becoming a key source of FDI in Africa's natural resource sectors, a major investment destination for Chinese state-owned enterprises and, increasingly, private firms. Until 2005, resource extraction was the second-largest sector for cumulative Chinese FDI (table 3.4).

FIGURE 3.1: COMMODITY PRICE INDEX, JANUARY 1980–JANUARY 2011

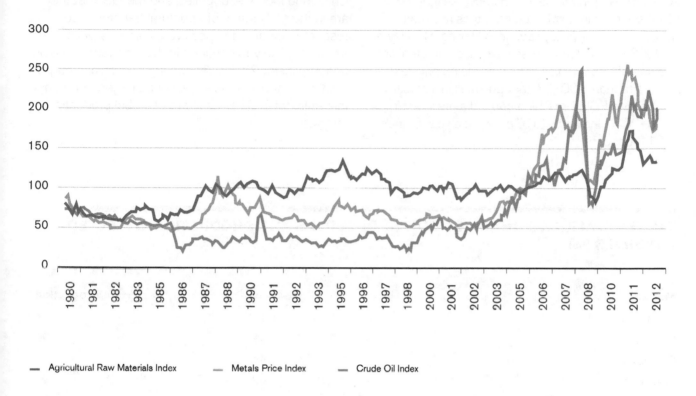

— Agricultural Raw Materials Index   — Metals Price Index   — Crude Oil Index

Source: International Monetary Fund, Primary Commodity Prices, www.imf.org/external/np/res/commod/faq/index.htm, accessed 20 October 2012.

Note: Indices based on 2005 (average of 2005 = 100). Group indices are weighted averages of individual commodity price indices

TABLE 3.4: SECTORAL DISTRIBUTION OF CHINA'S FDI STOCK IN AFRICA, 1979–2005

Sector/industry	Number of projects	Investment ($ million)
Manufacturing	230	316
Resource extraction	44	188
Services	200	125
Agriculture	22	48
Others	3	6
Total	**499**	**683**

Source: Adapted from UNCTAD (2007).

Note: Based on investment projects approved by China's Ministry of Commerce. The level of investment realized could be much larger as it includes, for example, projects that were not submitted for approval to government.

Since then, even larger FDI flows have targeted services and extractive industries (Cheng and Ma, 2010). These tend to be less risk-averse than FDI flows from industrialized countries and more influenced by the policy regime in Beijing (Buckley et al., 2007). Natural resources have also attracted large investments from Indian investors, mainly private (Pal, 2008; Pradhan, 2008). Although small in a global perspective, FDI from China and India grew fast in 2000–2010, India's by 26.6 per cent a year, China's by 91.7 per cent.[9]

The commodity price boom has implications for Africa's industrialization strategy. Given the size of China and India's economies, and the fact that they are in the early stage of structural transformation, resource demand and positive commodity price trends are likely to continue in the long term (Farooki and Kaplinsky, 2012). Yet although Africa has huge resource endowments—the world's largest for many minerals (table 3.5)—its share of global production is far lower.

TABLE 3.5: AFRICA'S SHARE OF GLOBAL RESERVES AND PRODUCTION, SELECTED MINERALS (%)

Mineral	Reserves	Production
Platinum group metals	60+	54
Gold	42	20
Chromium	44	40
Manganese	82	28
Vanadium	95	51
Cobalt	55+	18
Diamonds	88	78
Aluminium	45	4

Source: AfDB (2008).

So while in the past African development plans focused on diversifying from commodities, they now put them at centre stage. These plans are tackling issues of investment, labour, the environment as well as trade. Resource-rich countries are reforming their tax regimes to benefit from commodity export revenues (UNCTAD, 2007), and must therefore tap the opportunities to pursue more diversified development paths, including commodity-based industrialization.

Thus while the booming resource sector carries the obvious risk of further deindustrializing Africa as it specializes in commodity production and export and provides revenues to pay for imports of consumer goods, its resource endowments also create opportunities, bolstered by the continent's increased leverage in negotiating with foreign investors over investment (ECA and AUC, 2012). They can also provide much-needed financing for capital investment, for example through infrastructure, as well as an opportunity to intensify knowledge transfer through backward and forward linkages to the wider economy.

Resource-based industrialization yields employment, income and dynamic benefits

Employment gains

The last decade's higher GDP growth rates have not reduced poverty commensurately (see chapter 1), because they failed to translate into adequate job creation and social progress. Mining and energy—the source of much of the growth—are generally less labour intensive than other industries. Indeed, many African countries, particularly in Central and East Africa, have the lowest growth–poverty elasticity in the world (Fosu, 2011). And not only is unemployment high—the incidence of the working poor in total employment is also high (see chapter 2).

By moving up the value chain and developing backward and forward linkages to the commodity sector, countries can maximize direct and indirect job-creation effects. Manufacturing and services involved in input provision to the natural resource sector (backward linkages) and involved in resource processing (forward linkages) are characterized by varying levels of labour and skills intensity (box 3.3). This range and diversity of economic activities offer market opportunities to small and large businesses, and to many skilled and semi-skilled workers. Moreover, in soft commodity sectors, resource-processing industries can stimulate raw material supply, creating further employment in agriculture. China's remarkable success in reducing poverty provides a good example here.

BOX 3.3: A LINKAGE FRAMEWORK

A framework for linkage development was created some decades ago by one of the pioneers in studies of industrial development arising from commodities, Albert Hirschman. He characterized successful economic growth as an incremental (but not necessarily slow) unfolding of linkages between related economic activities and proposed three major types of linkage from the commodity sector (Hirschman, 1981).

The first are fiscal—the resource rents the government can harvest from the commodity sector in the form of corporate taxes, royalties and taxes on employees' incomes. These rents can be used to promote industrial development in sectors unrelated to commodities. Appropriate investment projects resulting from these fiscal linkages are essential if the rewards are to be reaped and the dangers of fiscal bubbles avoided. It therefore remains a priority for African countries to ensure that the natural resource sector provides much-needed financing, that such financing is allocated to productive investment projects, that risks associated with exchange rate appreciation and Dutch disease are effectively managed, and that corruption in misappropriating these fiscal rents is staunched.[1] The opportunities of an industrialization path based on natural resources do not therefore obviate the need for sound macroeconomic policies.

The second are consumption—the demand for the output of other sectors arising from the incomes earned in the commodity sector. The demand generated by employees in the sector has the potential to provide a major spur to industrial production as well as all incomes (whether salaries, wages or profits) earned in the resource sector are spent on products and services. However, Hirschman warned that, since most resource-rich developing economies had poorly developed manufacturing sectors, most consumption linkages would occur abroad as the needs of domestic consumers would be met through imports. The import liberalization of the past few decades has reinforced this trend for demand to "leak" abroad and for domestic manufacturing to be overwhelmed by imports.

The third are production—forward (processing commodities) and backward (producing inputs to be used in commodity production).[2] Hirschman argued that production linkages paved a path for industrial diversification, because he characterized the industrial development process "as essentially the record of *how one thing leads to another*" (1981:75, emphasis added). In other words, successful diversified industrial growth is inevitably an "incremental (but not necessarily slow) unfolding of linkages between related economic activities." It is this third set of production linkages arising from the commodities boom that this report focuses on.

[1] Fiscal linkages, as well as broader issues around environmental and social impact of mining, human rights, small-scale mining and corporate social responsibility, are comprehensively dealt with in ECA and AU (2011). See also Kaplinsky and Farooki (2012) for a detailed discussion of the relevance of fiscal and consumption linkages to Africa.

[2] Morris et al. (2012) add a further category of production linkages based on value chain analysis—"horizontal linkages"—which is a complex set of linkages made up of suppliers and users in the chain who develop capabilities to feed into other industrial and service chains. A variant of such horizontal linkages is value-adding production activities centred on using "by-products" or "waste" from commodity extraction processes.

Benefits of moving up the value chain

Provided their resource-processing industries are internationally competitive and well integrated in GVCs, exporting countries can move into higher-rent value-chain links. This is because GVCs have varying levels of value addition and, crucially, different entry barriers: the higher the entry barriers—usually created by skills, research and development (R&D) and technology—the more countries and firms can capture high rents because they have fewer competitors.

As an example, up to 90 per cent of the total income from coffee, calculated as the average retail price of a pound of roasted and ground coffee, goes to consuming countries (figure 3.2).

FIGURE 3.2: INTER-COUNTRY DISTRIBUTION OF INCOME (% SHARE OF FINAL RETAIL PRICE OF COFFEE)

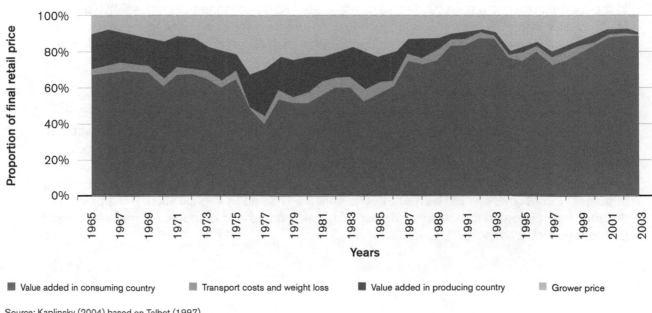

Source: Kaplinsky (2004) based on Talbot (1997).

Until the mid-1980s, the allocation of coffee income between producing and consuming countries was determined by two, mutually offsetting factors: fluctuations in world output, mainly from Brazil, and export restrictions under the International Coffee Agreement (Talbot, 1997). Except for a short period in 1976–1977, producing countries (growers and exporters) appropriated around half the total income. This changed in 1987–1992 when the world coffee price crashed due to the end of the agreement, but retail prices stayed the same or even increased, shrinking the income share of producing countries while lifting the share of consuming countries.

This reallocation was driven by the increased market power of the largest coffee TNCs, which controlled marketing and distribution links and were able to maintain high prices (Kaplinsky, 2004; Talbot, 1997). By the early 1990s, consuming countries already were already taking 90 per cent of income.

The diamond GVC provides another useful example. While much rent accrues at the extraction stage, the retail value of jewel manufactures is more than three times the value of the rough stone (table 3.6). Yet most African producers have traditionally been excluded from any value-adding, forward-processing links, including sorting, valuing and grading.

TABLE 3.6: VALUE ADDITION IN THE DIAMOND GVC

Stage	% of original value
Producer selling value	100
Sorting and valuing	115
Cutting and polishing	127
Polished dealing	133
Jewellery manufacturing	166
Retail	320

Source: Even-Zohar (2007).

Moving up the value chain can deliver benefits for income, but it requires competitive processing industries and access to marketing and distribution networks, as with coffee. Forward integration confers other benefits. It can reduce the exposure of countries producing primary commodities to price fluctuations (Roemer, 1979; Reinhardt, 2000), which can be very high. In 1965–1987, for example, volatility for unprocessed primary commodities was much higher than that for processed commodities (Yeats, 1991). This holds particularly true for the ore, minerals and metals group, with annual fluctuations of 23 per cent for unprocessed material against 13 per cent for processed products. Major gains in price stability for processed products versus raw materials are also associated with tin, tungsten, copper, cocoa and cotton (Yeats, 1991).

For commodity-producing countries, such price volatility has been more problematic than the long-term price decline (Cashin and McDermott, 2002). From the start of the 20th century, price volatility has involved yet larger price movements.

For African countries, price volatility has serious implications for consumption smoothing and investment planning. Indeed some have identified it, when coupled with capital market imperfections, as the key growth-reducing factor of resource-rich countries (Manzano and Rigobón, 2007). Some African countries for instance, have been managing the more recent boom better: some by paying off debt (Nigeria), others by building fiscal cushions against potential balance-of-payments shocks.

Dynamic benefits of linkage development—skills migration and clusters

Linkage development opens up opportunities for positive externalities that are difficult to quantify. By developing backward-linkage supply firms to the commodity sector and resource-processing industries, African countries can help to diversify their technological capabilities and skills base, deepening their industrial structure. The copper-mining value chain, for example, needs a wide array of inputs—and skills (see table 5.9 in chapter 5).

The variety of technological capabilities and skills fostered in linkages also opens up opportunities for lateral migration into other sectors, although some have more potential than others (Hidalgo et al., 2007). Engineering services and manufacturing competencies, for example, have general applicability across a wide variety of sectors. It is therefore crucial to invest in engineering skills, used in the broadest sense, encompassing basic technical vocational education up to tertiary education.

Although the migration of technologies and competences from the natural resource sector to other sectors is difficult, many developing countries show efforts in this direction (Lorentzen, 2008). Two examples come from South Africa: firms involved in maize starch production moved into biodegradable plastics, with successful commercial application to some basic products; and low dosage X-ray technology developed for the diamond sector was later used in the medical sector. Equally, oil and mineral supplier industries require, and sometimes help to create, engineering skills in the local economy, which are particularly susceptible to spilling over to other sectors.

Moreover, the natural resource sector's need for infrastructure (to extract and transport the commodities) enhances the potential for linkages, more often with high-volume mineral resources, which usually require roads and rail. As these

modes are built, it becomes easier to develop supplier and resource-processing activities, which increase the economies of scope for further infrastructure development. This positive externality is, however, rarer for commodities such as oil, gold and diamonds, which promote enclave-type infrastructure (Perkins and Robbins, 2011).

Linkage development creates an opportunity to maximize positive externalities derived from clusters. Closeness of supplier and resource-processing industries to the extraction location generates agglomeration effects. Efficiency gains for firms in clusters include gaining access to a pool of specialist labour and networks of suppliers. Knowledge and information flows are facilitated, promoting firms' ability to access information and adopt, adapt and innovate technology. Facilitating specialization and clustering lowers entry barriers for small and medium enterprises, which can enter the resource value chain by mobilizing limited financial and human capital for one activity, without having to invest in all the stages of the production process (Schmitz, 1997). This is particularly important for Africa: by promoting specialist supply networks, buyers accrue advantages in cutting costs, reducing stocks, shortening delivery times and increasing their flexibly to innovate.

The efficiency gains of clusters increase when firms cooperate. They may work together to establish training institutes or business organizations, for example, or when they engage in vertical supplier–buyer cooperation. These relationships are critical to promoting upgrading, because, as seen, supplier firms get access to knowledge and resources both to improve their production processes or products and to move into more technologically sophisticated functions. Clusters also allow governments to catalyse industrial policies, creating economies of scale for investment in skills, technologies, R&D and infrastructure. Chile's government, for one, managed to weave many of the above approaches to create a world-beating salmon industry from scratch (box 3.4).

BOX 3.4: REMARKABLE SUCCESS IN CHILE'S SALMON FARMING

In the 1970s, the government used Japanese technical assistance programmes to lay the foundations for the expansion of its salmon industry, buttressed in the 1980s by Fundación Chile, a government venture-capital foundation that transferred Norwegian and Scottish technology to local entrepreneurs and built local know-how.

In the early stages, the cluster was dominated by small, geographically dispersed domestic firms, but in the 1990s it attracted increasing FDI and became more concentrated. At the same time, firms cooperated on product quality, sustainability certification, branding and overseas marketing, while still receiving support from Fundación Chile, as well as university R&D and training.

Success has been remarkable. Exports were virtually zero in the 1980s, but by 2000 Chile had become the world's second-largest producer of Atlantic salmon, after Norway. Most of the exports are high value added fresh and frozen fillets, commanding a premium in the EU and US (Kjöllerström and Dallto, 2007).

The salmon industry has also fostered backward linkages: egg hatcheries, feed production, manufacturing of cages and nets, construction of floating warehouses, maintenance of refrigerated containers, and transport services. In 2004 around 300 local firms supplied capital goods and knowledge-intensive services worth $65 million, almost half the value of the supply chain (Torres-Fuchslocher, 2007). Some of the supply firms had already accumulated capital and capabilities in horticulture, and moved into the salmon-farming supply chain. Simultaneously, foreign feed producers integrated forward into farming (Perez-Aleman, 2005; Phyne and Mansilla, 2003).

Efficient supply industries are therefore critical not only in creating additional economic activity but also in achieving efficiency in the commodity sector (David and Wright, 1997). Natural resources are not a fixed asset—they depend on the efforts devoted to exploring, extracting and processing them (box 3.5).

BOX 3.5: EXPLOITING COPPER RESOURCES IN CHILE

Chile was the leading copper producer until the late 19th century. Between the 1870s and the 1900s the US overtook it through technological advances in drilling and blasting, and in concentrating and refining techniques, which allowed almost complete recovery of metal from the ore.

These innovations expanded the US resource base, at the same time as Chile grappled with declining ore quality.

Source: David and Wright (1997).

Today, countries with poorer natural resource endowments than Africa's are attracting large FDI in exploration and extraction. Although FDI is not necessarily the only way to go, African economies would become more attractive investment destinations if they developed systemic efficiency, as localized, efficient supply chains aligned with the outsourcing and production strategies of commodity-producing firms (Morris et al., 2012).

Africa should ignore the criticisms of resource-based industrialization

The experience of resource-rich countries shows the possibilities of commodity-based industrialization—despite all the criticisms, which run along three lines: that it is as hard as any other industrialization path; that commodity sectors are unlikely to promote linkages and externalities; and that resource-based industries do not match Africa's factor endowments.[10]

As hard as any other path? Yes, but still achievable with the right economic policies

The first line argues that resource-based industries encounter the same obstacles faced by any industry. Reviewing firm-level surveys conducted in many African countries from the 1990s, Bigsten and Söderbom (2006) found that the growth potential for Africa's manufacturing industries is critically constrained by high uncertainty and risks, which reduce firms' propensity to undertake capital investment, and by high entry barriers to export markets, which prevent firms from expanding beyond small domestic markets and accruing efficiency gains. Moreover, firms are burdened by high financing and indirect costs—physical and services infrastructure, inputs, etc. For many African countries—including Rwanda, which has ranked as one of the fastest reformers in the world—economic conditions have improved (see chapter 1), with macroeconomic stability, an improved business environment and more focus on developing infrastructure and human capital.

Proximity of a commodity often does not in itself confer sufficient cost advantages to enable an African country to develop competitive resource-based industries. Other factors, such as infrastructure, human capital and access to financial capital may be more important in determining final cost competitiveness. Access to skills has been found to be particularly critical in constraining Africa's resource-based industrial development (Owens and Wood, 1997).

Indeed, developing resource-based industries involves similar challenges to developing any other. Still, selective industrial policies are instrumental in catalysing resources in high-potential sectors rather than spreading them thinly across all sectors. The experiences of resource-rich Argentina, Malaysia, Thailand and Venezuela point to export success of resource-based industries stemming not so much from high levels of initial skills and capital, but from economic policies fostering their development (box 3.6).

BOX 3.6: WELL-THOUGHT-OUT POLICIES CATALYSE RESOURCES IN FOUR RESOURCE-RICH COUNTRIES

In Argentina and Venezuela, the export sector was led by two types of industry: resource-based industries, intensive in unskilled labour (especially for Argentina's agricultural resources); and manufacturing industries, intensive in semi- and high-skilled labour.

Argentina's agricultural resources led to the development of food, beverage and tobacco export industries, while Venezuela's mineral resources led to the development of basic chemicals and metal export industries. Resource-based industries enabled the accumulation of capital, skills and technological capabilities. This process, coupled with import-substitution policies, resulted in a deepening of the industrial base that advanced other manufacturing industries (Londero and Teitel, 1996).

Malaysia and Thailand were very successful in developing resource-based industries. In the 1970s and 1980s, these industries represented around a fifth of total exports in Malaysia, and a third in Thailand. Malaysia's selective policies targeted the expansion of rubber and palm oil production, while supporting domestic palm oil refineries and rubber semi-manufacturing. Thailand's export incentives targeted gems, tinned fish, dried and preserved fruit and preserved vegetables. Palm oil, rubber, leather, wood and fisheries are still important sectors in these countries' industrial development plans (Reinhardt, 2000).

In these countries, resource-based industries developed from initially low skills and capital by mobilizing domestic entrepreneurship and implementing effective industrial policies. Industrialization favoured skills and capital accumulation and facilitated the development of more sophisticated manufacturing capabilities.

Commodity sectors are unlikely to promote linkages and externalities? Indeed, they can

The second line is that commodity sectors have an enclave nature—offering few opportunities for backward or forward linkages and with weak positive externalities (Hirschman, 1958, 1981; Prebisch, 1950; Singer, 1950). According to this view, extractive industries are capital intensive and so provide few employment and skills-development opportunities. Moreover, they tend to require fewer supplier linkages than manufacturing, implying that technological externalities are lower and that incentives for

investment in supplier industries are weaker. As TNCs repatriate most revenues to their home countries, developing countries share few benefits. This enclave industry argument was espoused by dependency theorists in the 1970s (Girvan and Girvan, 1973).

The historical experience of many resource-rich countries nevertheless shows that commodity sectors foster productivity growth, technological innovation, as well as forward and backward linkages, if there are good institutions and investment in human capital and knowledge (de Ferranti et al., 2002), as shown in two Nordic countries and the US (box 3.7).

BOX 3.7: GOOD INSTITUTIONS AND INVESTMENT IN HUMAN CAPITAL PAID OFF

In the 19th century, Sweden relied on exports of cereals, sawn wood and, later, pulp, paper and iron ore, while Finland relied on wood pulp (Blomström and Kokko, 2007). Although access to foreign knowledge was important, the development of sophisticated processing industries was mainly the result of investments in skills and research from public and private institutions. These built the basis for sustained competitiveness and Swedish and Finnish processing industries were still competitive against low-cost producers. Moreover, successful backward linkage industries developed for specialized machinery, engineering products, transport services and equipment.

Similarly, US emergence as an industrial power at the turn of the past century was propelled by resource abundance: petroleum products, meat and poultry packing, primary copper products and steel works (Wright, 1990).

In recent times, the commodity sectors had a positive impact on broader economic development, including through promoting a diversified industrial structure, in developed economies (Australia, Norway and Scotland) and developing countries (Argentina and Malaysia, as seen; Raines et

al., 2001).With the right policies—for skills, technologies and linkages (Wright and Czelusta, 2004)—and under the right conditions, commodity production can therefore have a positive impact on broader development, including a more diversified industrial structure.

Resource-based industries do not match Africa's factor endowments

The final line is that Africa's industrial policies should be designed for unskilled labour–intensive sectors, such as light manufacturing. This is supported by arguments that resource-processing industries are generally capital or skills intensive, or both (Roemer, 1979). It has been estimated that manufacturing industries employ on average 26 per cent more labour per unit of output than resource-based manufacturing (Owens and Wood, 1997). Resource processing would therefore require two factors of production fairly scarce in Africa—capital and skilled labour.

This argument is increasingly challenged by the emerging dynamics of GVCs. Labour-intensive, export-oriented industrialization was the path followed by East Asia. Asia, however, relied on many measures that are prohibited, or at least discouraged, in today's multilateral trade arena. These include tariff protection and performance requirements, such as trade balancing and local content (Chang, 2002). As African countries negotiate trade agreements at multilateral and regional levels, they should push for the necessary policy space for their export oriented industrialization strategies. Further, given the political economy of trade negotiations, countries must work together in articulating regional strategies to have sufficient leverage when engaging with third parties, such as the EU, US or China. Regional integration is therefore an imperative to devise industrialization and value addition strategies which build the necessary

linkages between suppliers and producers within the continent, to overcome the constraints being faced by local production.

Moreover, policymakers need to remember that manufacturing is subject to downward price pressures when designing an industrial policy for Africa, as seen in the developed countries, whose high-cost consumer goods exports have largely been displaced by those from developing countries, mainly in Asia. Africa's manufacturing sector has to compete with these exports, where firms have better access to infrastructure, and to financial and human capital.

These downward price pressures are confirmed by an analysis of unit prices trends of EU imports of manufactured products in 1988–2002, which can be assumed to largely reflect global unit prices. Around a quarter of the EU's manufactured products imported from low-income countries and almost a third of those imported from China saw declining price trends, against less than a tenth of those imported from high-income countries (table 3.7). These declining price trends affected labour/resource–intensive sectors and low-skill/technology sectors the most, that is, those in which Africa competes with China and India. Africa's industrialization through export-oriented, light manufacturing would therefore take place in an environment of falling global prices and high competition. It is therefore arguable that resource-based industrialization will offer better opportunities for African countries to compete in global markets before they can eventually compete in other manufacturing activities.

TABLE 3.7: SHARE OF EU IMPORTS OF MANUFACTURED PRODUCTS WITH DECLINING UNIT PRICE TRENDS, 1988–2002 (%)

By region		By sector			
		UNCTAD classification		*Lall classification*	
Low-income	25.6	Labour/resource intensive	69	Resource-based	61
China	29.7	Low skill/tech/capital intensive	67	Low-technology	71
Lower middle-income	18.3	Medium skill/tech/capital intensive	64	Medium-technology	59
Upper middle-income	17.2	High skill/tech/capital intensive	59	High-technology	51
High-income	8.5				

Source: Adapted from Kaplinsky and Santos-Paulino (2006).

While opportunities still exist for some African countries to industrialize through light manufacturing exports, resource-rich countries need to seriously consider embarking on commodity-based industrialization where they have greater competitive advantage. China's hunger for natural resources is keeping commodity prices high (Kaplinsky, 2006), which provides a good opportunity to capitalize on.

The question then is not whether Africa can industrialize by "ignoring" its commodities, but rather how the latter can be used to promote value addition, new service industries and technological capabilities that span the subregions of the continent. In other words, how can African countries add more value to their commodities to reap larger benefits from them? Another key issue is how to move from resource-based industrialization to higher stages.

3.3 ADDING VALUE AND DEVELOPING LINKAGES

The world's number one, two, three and six cocoa bean exporters—Côte d'Ivoire, Ghana, Nigeria and Cameroon—show remarkably low levels of value addition: only Côte d'Ivoire and Ghana exported between a fifth and a quarter of their production in semi-processed form (figure 3.3). Yet 54 per cent of Indonesia's export value to the world was at the lower and higher end of the semi-processed stages (cocoa paste, butter and powder), and 94 per cent of Malaysia's export value to the world was at the higher end of the semi-processed stage (cocoa butter and powder). In Latin America, Brazil and especially Mexico have moved up the value chain: 31 per cent of Brazil's and 99 per cent of Mexico's cocoa exports consisted of chocolate products.

FIGURE 3.3: VALUE-ADDED CONTENT OF SELECTED DEVELOPING COUNTRIES' COCOA EXPORTS, 2011 (%)

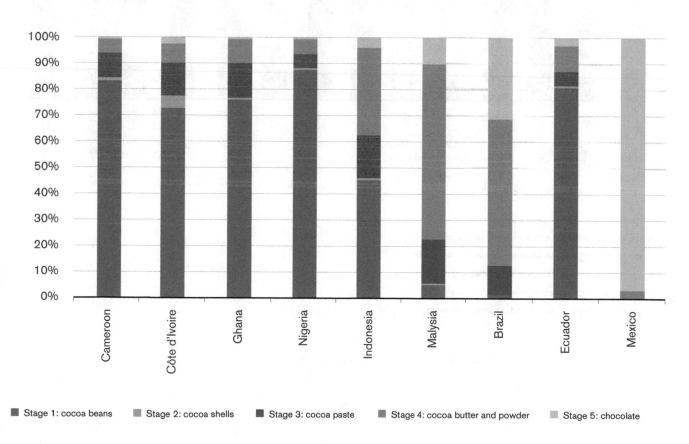

- Stage 1: cocoa beans
- Stage 2: cocoa shells
- Stage 3: cocoa paste
- Stage 4: cocoa butter and powder
- Stage 5: chocolate

Source: ITC Trademap, retrieved from http://www.trademap.org/, accessed 30 August 2012.

The timber GVC shows a similar interregional pattern. In Cameroon, the Republic of Congo, Mozambique and South Africa, between three quarters and all exports were logs or other basic processed forms (figure 3.4). Côte d'Ivoire, Gabon and Ghana export around a third of their production in higher value added form, including plywood and veneer sheets, in a move that Indonesia had made earlier (box 3.8). Other major Asian producers export 58–97 per cent of their timber in advanced processed stages, including China, the Republic of Korea and Sri Lanka, producing frames, tools and tableware, for example.[11]

FIGURE 3.4: VALUE-ADDED CONTENT OF SELECTED DEVELOPING COUNTRIES' TIMBER EXPORTS (EXCLUDING FURNITURE), 2011 (%)

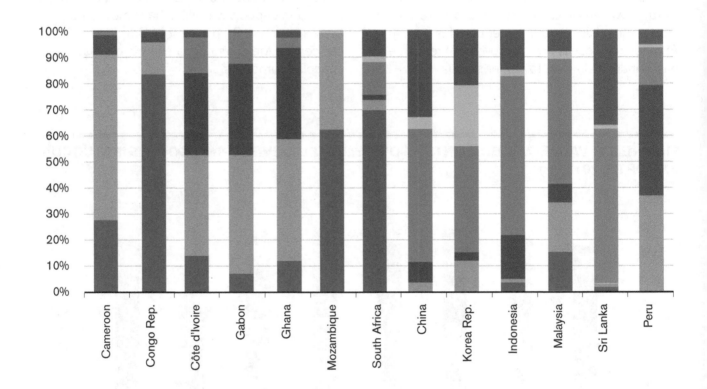

- Stage 1: wood in chips, in the rought
- Stage 2: hoopwood, split poles, railway sleepers, sawnwood
- Stage 3: veneer sheets, plywood, wood continously shaped
- Stage 4: particle board, fibre board, densified wood
- Stage 5: frames, packaging materials, casks, barrels
- Stage 6: tools, builders' joinery and carpentry, tableware

Source: ITC Trademap, retrieved from http://www.trademap.org/, accessed 30 August 2012.

BOX 3.8: CONTROL OF MARKETING CHANNELS ADD EXPORT VALUE IN INDONESIA

TThe critical feature of Indonesia's upgrading strategy was its control of domestic and international marketing channels (Gellert, 2003). A national marketing body, Apkindo, was established in 1976 and private firms were compelled to join, reflecting the government's objective of developing a national processing industry. Apkindo used its control of domestic channels to move into value-added, regional markets (Gellert, 2003).

Until then, it had largely been a "price-taker" for logs, and could not enter the plywood segment of its largest export market, Japan. Japan was protected by high tariff and non-tariff barriers, its plywood producers were highly efficient, and distribution was monopolized by eight trading houses interested in supplying cheap raw materials to their processors.

To break into this market, Apkindo obtained certification of compliance with Japanese agricultural standards for its timber processors and established an independent trading house in Japan, partnering with a minor local trader. This house assumed control of all Indonesian plywood imports, and sold to other trading houses and directly to construction firms. These imports were competitive as they were initially subsidized through the fees collected from Apkindo's members.

Indonesia's strategy paid off. Bypassing the Japanese trading houses competing with its own, it managed to become a "price-maker" for plywood in Japan. It raised the volume and price of its plywood exports: exports rose from $160 million in 1981 to $1 billion in 1986 and to $4 billion in 1992, making it the world's largest hardwood plywood exporter (Thee, 2009).The wood-processing industry also deepened its processing capabilities, investing in particle-board, woodworking, furniture and cement-bonded plants.

The cocoa and timber GVCs highlight a few issues. First, among some of the world's largest raw material producers, African producers are relegated to the bottom of the value chain. Second, intraregional variations emerge: Ecuador and Peru lagged behind other countries in their region, while Côte d'Ivoire and Ghana were ahead in theirs.

The stories of success and failure in creating backward and forward linkages in other developing countries (boxes 3.9–3.13) highlight that they are the result of, among other things, a straightforward combination of policies and domestic capabilities.

BOX 3.9: SUCCESSFULLY COMBINING POLICIES AND DOMESTIC CAPABILITIES, BRAZIL

Brazil's soybean industry took off in the 1970s. Initially, the government supported intensive soybean production in what had been coffee-producing areas such as Rio Grande do Sul. It did so by adopting price and input subsidies, a generous credit policy, and measures to modernize farming practices. Differential export taxes and quotas encouraged value-added exports. These measures were accompanied until the mid-1990s by a duty drawback system and price controls.

The soybean processing industry, increasingly owned by large, modern and often TNC-controlled enterprises, developed by supplying soybean oil to the domestic market, and soybean cake to the growing pig and poultry sector and to export markets. Upstream industries to soybean agricultural production and processing industries also developed (Fold, 2000).

Interventionist policies and high domestic capabilities boosted the cocoa industry, too. In the 1970s, incentives to local processing expanded domestic grinding capacity. When grinders could not access enough raw material, the government incentivized cocoa farming and set export quotas. A mix of Brazilian and transnational companies controls the processing industry (Talbot, 2002).

Africa's experience with linkage development has had modest success (ECA, 2011). In the past, efforts focused on state ownership but failed to build market competitiveness. Ghana's attempts to move into cocoa processing through state ownership performed poorly owing to a combination of mismanagement of firms and low supply of raw materials (Talbot, 2002). This outcome was common in resource-rich countries in the 1970s and 1980s, which pursued forward linkages through strong public participation, tariff protection and high subsidies.

Other strategies also found limited success: Côte d'Ivoire's forward integration relied on high producer prices to raise cocoa production and FDI (Talbot, 2002). It set up a cocoa-processing industry, largely controlled by foreign companies, but capacity stayed low.

Some governments have not adopted linkage policies (box 3.10), forgoing potential opportunities to develop local manufacturing and services (Morris et al., 2012). Others, adopting export bans and taxes as well as local content regulations, have rarely matched them with measures to support technological capabilities, skills development and entry into marketing/distribution networks (boxes 3.11 and 3.12).

BOX 3.10: MISSED OPPORTUNITIES IN GOLD MINING, TANZANIA

Tanzania's gold mining has, since the late 1990s, underpinned national economic growth. The objectives of the 1997 Mineral Policy and the 2012 Mineral Act include developing backward linkages, but the country has no definite target, incentives or penalty system, leaving linkage development largely to market forces. Legislation reserves primary prospecting and mining licensing to wholly owned Tanzanian companies, which can, however, sell these rights to foreign firms. In this way it has allowed some national companies to accrue rent from gold mining, but has not fostered value-added activities. In gold exploration, local content is limited to drilling services and logistics, while in gold mining, it is limited to fuel, equipment repair and maintenance, and basic services. Most services and goods are imported. One reason for the low value addition is the weak capability of local firms, which also suffer from poor competitiveness, partly owing to high production costs. Another is that tax exemptions for mining inputs apply to mines but not their suppliers, which therefore face higher import costs.

The gold-mines' remoteness is another more fundamental issue, but national infrastructure is poor, raising costs. To address them, Tanzania joined the project of a Central Development Corridor to connect Dar es Salaam port with the Great Lakes region and to stimulate broader economic activity centred on resources (Perkins and Robbins, 2011). The project is lagging behind, however, owing to lack of funding, weak political will and poor institutional capabilities. Skilled labour is also scarce, and industrial research institutes have largely ignored supply chains.

Source: Mjimba (2011).

BOX 3.11: ANGOLA'S LAWS ARE NOT ENOUGH ON THEIR OWN

Angola has an ambitious programme to increase local content in its oil and gas value chain. It is based on decrees of 1982 and 2003 and the 2004 Petroleum Activity Law, which required oil and gas companies to train and hire local labour, and to follow preferential procurement from Angolan companies for products that are not capital or knowledge intensive.

Yet despite comprehensive legislation, Angola has had little success in creating backward linkages. In 2010, the only value-added activities were the operations of two components of the subsea umbilicals, risers and flow lines subsector—assembly of flow lines and control lines (box table).

BOX TABLE: PROVENANCE OF INPUTS

Types of input	% of oper. exp	Description	Provenance	
			Imported	*Locally produced*
Production Machinery		Pipe pincers, loaders, rollers, stalk racks, cranes, amortization	✓	--
Raw Material	70–75	Metal, steel, copper	✓	--
Labour (skilled/ unskilled)	15–20	Engineers, managers, welders, etc.	✓	✓
Basic General Services	3–4	Health and Safety Executives, catering, cleaning, security, civil construction, recruitment, lease	--	✓
Basic General Goods	2	PPE, IT and electronic equipment, office furniture, stationery, etc.	✓	--

The local content policy helped to provide Angolan firms and joint ventures with access to the supply chain. Previously, oil and gas companies had outsourced supply links related to subsea umbilicals, risers and flow lines through engineering, procurement, construction and installation ("turnkey") contracts. These contracts outsourced the entire chain to overseas contractors, bypassing locally based suppliers. Through the local content policy, some local firms entered the supply chain, but their local content remained low because everything but labour and some services was imported.

Moreover, these firms were mostly joint ventures and were located in the oil terminal, which granted them access to good transport, electricity, water and telecom, insulating them from the national infrastructure. By contrast, the majority of local potential suppliers faced very poor infrastructure and lacked competitiveness. Moreover, while state ownership through Sonangol assured the linkage development vision, issues in implementation arose, such as lack of coordination with the private sector and with ministries and agencies responsible for industrial development.

Linkage development efforts have been more successful in employment, and the skills of the local labour force have risen steadily, largely owing to heavy investment in training by the oil and gas companies and the public sector.

Source: Teka (2011).

BOX 3.12: UNCOMPETITIVE TIMBER PROCESSING IN GABON

The 2001 Forestry Code provided a vision for the wood industry that encouraged sustainable farming and value addition (Terheggen, 2011). But as the export market shifted to China and timber was increasingly exported in unprocessed form, Gabon imposed an export ban on logs in 2010.

Although the ban forced domestic logging companies to increase local processing in exports, they remain uncompetitive internationally. Unprocessed wood has to be transported via water (road and rail are inadequate) keeping transport costs high at 14–25 per cent of total production costs, but water is unsuitable for moving processed wood. Labour is also an issue: processing companies have to import not only skilled and semi-skilled labour, but also some of their unskilled workers.

Botswana's beneficiation policy (establishing resource-processing industries) is generally meeting its targets (Mbayi, 2011). The country has been very successful in using natural resources—especially its huge diamond reserves (box 3.13)—to promote economic growth and reduce poverty through value addition and job creation.

BOX 3.13: DIVERSIFYING THE ECONOMY THROUGH DIAMOND BENEFICIATION, BOTSWANA

Botswana stands out as Africa's success story in expanding its economy. Growth averaged around 9–10 per cent a year, transforming the country from one of the poorest countries at independence in 1966 with GDP per capita of $77 to a middle-income country with a per capita GDP of $5,716 in 2005. This growth was driven by diamond mining, which accounts for half of government revenues, two thirds of exports and a third of GDP.

Yet Botswana's growth model—rooted in the neo-liberal orthodox macroeconomic framework—delivered growth that was neither pro-poor nor inclusive, and failed to diversify the economy from almost total dependence on mining. Unemployment, poverty and inequality have remained high relative to comparator middle-income countries: in 2010, unemployment was estimated at 17.8 per cent, poverty at 20 per cent.

As part of its economic diversification strategy, the government started to beneficiate diamonds to create jobs. The ultimate objective is to transform Botswana into a world-class diamond centre and sustain revenues from the industry beyond the life span of the diamond deposits by creating downstream skills in cutting and polishing, jewellery manufacturing, diamond trading and ancillary businesses.

The immediate aims are to increase skilled jobs through labour-intensive cutting and polishing and to diversify the economy by stimulating local economic development and promoting linkages with the rest of the economy. Local communities are to benefit from value addition through employment as well as technical knowledge and skills, which also enrich the social knowledge base, creating capabilities and options for firms to diversify into related goods and services.

The diamond cutting and polishing industry employs around 3,000 workers (about a third of mining jobs) but its jobs are very susceptible to global shocks: the number fell from 3,267 in 2008 to 2,183 in 2009, subsequently recovering to 3,262 in 2011 (Statistics Botswana, 2012). Downstream activities are likely to create more jobs as the sales function of the international branch of the Diamond Trading Company, established in 2008 by the government and De Beers mining company, relocates to Botswana.

Botswana has successfully used its resource intensity to help diversify its economy and create jobs, but it still has to resolve incoherence between social and economic policies and duplication of institutions and functions, as well as weak skills development, especially given the demand for specialist skills under the beneficiation strategy.

Source: Mbayi (2011).

Too few of Africa's linkage development strategies have been matched by efforts to improve the supply of raw materials. Mozambique's cashew-nut processing industry is one example (Cramer, 1999). Previously state owned, it was in prolonged crisis owing to mismanagement and civil war. After privatization, there was policy uncertainty between the objective of exporting high-value raw kernels and encouraging local processing through export duties, making it hard to define strategy. However, the key constraints were related to technology, skills, infrastructure, standards, marketing, branding, and, most of all, access to raw materials. By contrast, Brazil, India, Indonesia and Vietnam promoted cashew-nut processing through industrial policies, export taxes and bans over the last 4 decades.

3.4 FACTORS IN LINKAGE DEVELOPMENT

The opportunities for developing linkages to natural resource sectors are determined by the capabilities of domestic firms and effectiveness of government policy. Domestic firms' competitiveness in price, quality, lead times and flexibility define the extent to which they can seize the opportunity to supply commodity lead producers or move into resource-processing for domestic, regional and international markets or even create domestic lead firms. Other factors also matter, as now discussed.

Technical characteristics of GVCs

GVCs have different technical characteristics for processing commodities. Some commodities have to be processed shortly after extraction because the intermediate products are not storable, especially soft commodities such as tea, rubber and palm oil, which need immediate post-harvest processing to preserve their essential qualities. Tea processing from the leaf into "made tea" has to be quick, and customarily has been carried out in producing countries (Talbot, 2002).

By contrast, coffee roasting and grinding have to be done near the consumption stage, to preserve the flavour. Traditionally, forward linkages in producing countries have been limited to processing into parchment coffee (coffee seeds are separated, rinsed and dried) and green beans. Green beans are the most common form of trading because they can be stored for years (Talbot, 2002). Forward linkages have increased in a few producing countries that process coffee into instant coffee or vacuum pack coffee for roasting, which increases durability but also transport costs (Roemer, 1979).[12]

Forward integration by commodity-producing countries is facilitated when there are many discrete stages of production of storable products within a GVC. This is because lead firms could find it profitable to outsource the processing of intermediate products to producing countries, while retaining control of the higher value added stages. The large food TNCs have outsourced the intermediate processing stages of the value chain to international trading houses, because this has not infringed on their core business (Talbot, 2002). From the 1980s, some cocoa processing activities partly relocated to cocoa producing countries, including West Africa (Fold, 2002).

The technical characteristics of the value chain also determine the breadth and type of backward linkages. Ore extraction, for example, is a large-scale activity that requires a raft of suppliers, from low-skilled, labour-intensive to capital-intensive providers, while sugar production requires a narrower range and lower value of capital inputs.

The opportunities for linkage development are also shaped by relative factor intensity and the varying requirements of firms' capabilities. Mineral processing is generally more skills and capital intensive than soft-commodity processing, but wood, rubber and non-basic metal semi-fabricates production are more labour intensive than steel-making or alumina smelting (Londero and Teitel, 1996; Roemer, 1979).

In backward linkages, service-based supply firms are more knowledge intensive and require smaller economies of scale than capital-intensive machinery suppliers, which require larger amounts of capital and R&D and have greater economies of scale.

They are usually controlled by TNCs, although in knowledge-intensive economies like Germany, small and medium-sized producers (*the Mittelstand*) are successful.

Different value chain characteristics affect the capabilities that firms need. The technological distance between stages of the value chain determines how firms can move into backward and forward linkages (Hirschman, 1958). For example, the capabilities required to process wood into sawn wood, plywood and veneer sheets are different from those required for furniture making. In order to undertake this non-linear upgrading, local firms require new capabilities in product design and marketing. Forward and backward integration is facilitated when firms require capabilities similar to their existing ones.

While transport costs do not automatically create an advantage in local processing, in some value chains, processing heavily reduces weight or volume (or both), which is critical with high fuel prices. Copper refining, for instance, cuts the weight of ores by two thirds (Radetzki, 2008). Steep reductions come from processing timber into board products. Rubber processing, by contrast, increases weight and volume, and processing sulphur into acid adds to transport costs because it raises handling risks.

Some processing activities, such as aluminium smelting or steel production, depend critically on cost-effective access to complementary inputs like energy. This factor explains the competitiveness in processing of some developed countries with no endowment of alumina or iron ore.

Lastly, technological change is important. The timber value chain saw sweeping changes when flat-packed furniture arrived in the 1980s, which enabled lower value added activities to be outsourced to low-cost countries (Morris et al., 2012).

Industry structure

Metal and oil refining present high economies of scale, as do their intermediate product manufacturing (ECA, 2011). This has two implications: the natural resource sector must generate enough output to make processing viable; and manufacture into intermediate or final goods requires large domestic markets or must be internationally competitive for the export market. Nonetheless, if the continent could eliminate barriers and constraints to regional trade, regional markets might well be instrumental in exploiting economies of scale and in selling the intermediate and final goods that have value added locally and regionally.

Highly concentrated markets can result in captive supplier networks, that is, where suppliers are transactionally dependent on their large buyers (Gereffi et al., 2005). As these networks tend to support local upgrading where industrial capabilities are weak, such market-structure and supplier-network arrangements could benefit Africa's industrialization.

They can also induce firms to forward integrate. As well as the cocoa value chain (discussed above), many larger oil companies are involved in upstream and downstream activities. Forward integration by dominant firms raises entry barriers to potential competitors, a particular problem when the capital and skills requirements are not prohibitive for local processing firms.

It follows that governments have to take account of the market dominance of lead firms in their linkage development strategies, as Botswana did when designing its forward linkage policy (see box 3.13). In the diamond GVC, as De Beers controls much global production as well as marketing and distribution, Botswana's beneficiation policy was designed around

the company, setting restrictions on its marketing of raw diamonds (Mbayi, 2011). When the government renewed the company's mining licence, it established that a set amount of raw diamonds had to be locally marketed, cut and polished. (It is too early to assess the success of this strategy, but many processing firms have now relocated to Botswana and are training local workers.)

Lead-firm strategies

The strategies of lead firms have a large impact on linkage development. In the clothing value chain for example, US retailers and marketers encouraged their suppliers to upgrade to "full-package" production, while branded manufactures only required basic assembly from their suppliers (Gereffi, 1999). High concentration and the financialization of companies (i.e. the entry of banks and other financial institutions into commodity markets and the development of a range of commodity-based financial instruments) in the United Kingdom led buyers there to rationalize their supply chains, which increased entry barriers and constrained upgrading opportunities for developing-country suppliers (Palpacuer et al., 2005).

In the timber and cassava GVCs, when African and Asian producers widened their export markets to China, they also reduced their processing capabilities as these went to China (Kaplinsky et al., 2010). Gabon exemplifies the downgrade (box 3.14).

BOX 3.14: LOSING ITS PROCESSING PROWESS, GABON

The timber industry used to export veneer sheet and plywood products to the EU and to adhere to strict environmental sustainability regulations. But in the 2000s, much of the market shifted to China, which is more interested in large volumes and cheap supplies.

From the 1960s to the 1990s, wood exports averaged around 80,000 cubic metres a year, around 70 per cent of which was exported in semi-processed form (plywood). The shift to China saw, after 2004, an almost fivefold increase in export volumes, but a downgrade to sawn wood and, less so, to veneer sheet (both with less value added than plywood).

In 1997–2007, export volumes of sawn wood—the least processed form—rose 770 per cent.

Source: Terheggen (2011).

Zambia's copper value chain has been shaped by the various strategies of mining companies, often reflecting their country of origin (Fessehaie, 2012). Since 2008, industrial-country mining companies, for example, have increasingly rationalized their supply chains, focusing on value-adding supply firms and raising entry barriers to entry. They cooperate with local suppliers to enhance their processes and competitiveness. Although the largest Chinese copper mining company, NFCA, grants more market opportunities than Western companies to many local suppliers, it offers no cooperation to upgrade local processing. The Indian mining company, KCM, reduces both market opportunities and upgrading processes, through poor supply-chain management.

Location and infrastructure

Geographical distribution and access to infrastructure play a key role in shaping agglomeration configurations around the commodity sector. Africa's infrastructure has largely been inherited from colonial times, and tends to be designed to link plantations, as well as oil and mining facilities, to ports.

When infrastructure is poor and commodity extraction is based in remote locations, local supply firms face high marketing and distribution barriers, having either to relocate their business or to travel when meeting buyers and to arrange transport of supplies and services. Knowledge and information flows are also curtailed. Moreover, local supply or processing firms find it costly to relocate where there are no second-tier suppliers or other specialist suppliers.

The commodity itself considerably influences the potential for infrastructure to promote linkages (Morris et al., 2012). For example, oil extraction is supported by pipelines, which have very few spillover benefits. Conversely, roads or railways are a public good: they can be used by different users and they generate network effects. This type of infrastructure is particularly beneficial to developing backward linkages because it reduces costs for local suppliers.

Through infrastructure development, the resource sector can promote supply clusters. Geographical agglomerations reduce marketing and networking costs for suppliers or processing firms, and favour technological spillovers and knowledge flows. They also facilitate just-in-time deliveries and close inter-firm relationships that encourage customized solutions.

Africa's infrastructure deficiencies are therefore a major impediment to linkage development, and regional integration could catapult the continent's ability to enter GVCs. Several initiatives promoting "corridors" across Africa or focusing on infrastructure (such as roads and power pools that span several countries) are examples of how the continent could tackle these deficiencies.

Trade barriers

Tariff escalation is one major barrier to commodity-based GVCs (alongside rules of origin, product or process standards, and sanitary and phytosanitary measures, which are seldom explicit and are often argued as being non-intentional "technical barriers to trade"). It occurs when import tariffs increase according to the degree of processing of imported products. Raw materials face lower duties to provide processing companies in the importing country with cheap materials, while semi-processed and processed products face increasingly higher duties to protect firms in the importing country from competition. Tariff escalation thus discourages natural resource–rich countries from moving up their commodity-based GVCs.

Tariff escalation is significant not only between raw and semi-finished products but also between semi-finished and finished products (Cernat et al., 2002). It is present in the markets of developed and developing countries (even with various multilateral and bilateral trade initiatives), and it may affect some African countries more seriously in the future.

Both the US African Growth and Opportunity Act (AGOA) and the EU's Economic Partnership Agreements (EPAs) contain trade barriers affecting Africa's move up the commodity-based value chain (see chapter 2). The rules of origin under AGOA impede African beneficiaries from sourcing inputs from African countries that are not beneficiaries to the agreement (Karingi et al., 2011). In the EPA negotiations, pressure from the EU to obtain MFN treatment would wash down the preference margins of existing and future bilateral and regional agreements between African partners, a prerequisite to shift the sourcing structure to inputs within the continent and foster the creation of regional value chains.

Equally, sanitary and phytosanitary measures, as well as requirements for standards, have impeded countries such as Namibia from exporting table grapes or Botswana from entering the EU beef sector, which would have brought opportunities to highly segmented markets.

It is these aspects that are holding back African countries from fully realizing preferential treatment and using liberalization as a launch pad to industrialize and transform their economies.

Technology and Skills Bottlenecks

African firms face tight bottlenecks in technological capabilities (box 3.15) and skills, among other areas. In 2002, for example, the number of engineers enrolled in tertiary institutions in Africa (excluding North Africa) was only 12 per cent of the number enrolled in the Republic of Korea (Lall and Pietrobelli, 2005).

BOX 3.15: TECHNOLOGY'S GATES HAVE YET TO SWING OPEN

In 2002, Africa's per capita imports of capital equipment (embodied technology) ranged from very low (Uganda, $7) to quite high (South Africa, $165). Yet these pale in comparison with the Republic of Korea ($1,032) and Thailand ($403). Regionally, the per capita figures for Africa (excluding North Africa) were $8 compared with $242 for East Asia and $198 for Latin America. Africa (excluding North Africa) attracted much less FDI in manufacturing, and represented a tiny 1.5 per cent of the licence fees for imported technology paid by developing countries.

Total R&D, as a share of gross national product, stood at 0.28 per cent in Africa (excluding North Africa), compared with an average of 0.39 per cent for developing countries and 0.72 per cent for Asia. Most R&D in Africa targets agriculture rather than manufacturing or services.

Source: Lall and Pietrobelli (2005).

Technological efforts are critical for upgrading, but they are not cost-free or risk-less. In Africa, most efforts focus on searching, buying and experimenting with technologies, and adapting them to local conditions. Knowledge needs to be acquired and updated to keep up with

innovation, but most local technology institutions are very poorly resourced (Lall and Pietrobelli, 2005). Africa's industrial-policy weakness is thus hampering local firms' capabilities to be globally competitive in resource processing.

3.5 CONTINENTAL POLICY INITIATIVES PRESENT OPPORTUNITIES FOR REGIONAL INDUSTRIALIZATION AND VALUE ADDITION

Africa-wide policy moves are a chance to address challenges. In spite of these disappointing experiences with industrialization, African governments have always included such moves among the highest policy priorities at the continental level, as evidenced by the large number of initiatives calling for action to spur industrialization.

Indeed, the Lagos Plan of Action considered industrialization as a means of attaining self-reliance and self-sustainability. This was strongly reflected in subsequent proposals for Industrial Development Decades for Africa (IDDA) I and II. However, despite isolated successes, IDDA I and II were deemed disappointing by most African countries, as they were hampered by an absence of mechanisms for implementation, coordination and monitoring. In furthering the objectives of the New Partnership for Africa's Development (NEPAD), the African Productive Capacity Initiative was adopted by the AU and NEPAD in 2004 to be the overarching framework for sustainable industrial development in Africa.

In 2007, the Conference of African Ministers of Industry endorsed the Action Plan for Accelerated Industrial Development of Africa (AIDA) (AU, 2007). The plan identifies priorities for action at national, regional, continental and international levels on product and export diversification; natural resource management; infrastructure; human capital, science and technology; standards compliance; institutional frameworks; and resource mobilization. It also recommends national industrial strategies to target value addition of natural resources; national and continental mining codes to support local processing; and revenues from resource sectors to be invested in industrialization.

The Action Plan was endorsed by Heads of State and Government in 2008. They requested the AU and the United Nations Industrial Development Organization (UNIDO) to develop an implementation strategy with relevant regional economic communities and international bodies such as ECA and the World Bank, which led to the following Strategy.

Strategy for the Implementation of the Action Plan for AIDA

This is a key document in continental action on industrial policies (AU, 2008). Among its objectives are insertion of African companies into GVCs, and development of forward linkages to commodity sectors and backward linkages to local small and medium-sized enterprises. The Strategy recognizes the scope for increased participation by Africa in commodity-based GVCs. It also proposes investing in the first stages of resource-based processing, in the context of increasing FDI into Africa's natural resources from economies like China and India. If complemented by preferential trade agreements to ensure access to these markets, Africa could tap into other emerging economies' capital and technological endowments to foster local industrialization.

The Strategy is composed of seven programme clusters—to be undertaken in the immediate, medium and long term—on industrial policy and institutional direction; upgrading production and trade capacities; promoting infrastructure and energy for industrial development; human resources development for industry; industrial innovation systems, R&D and technology development; financing and resource mobilization; and sustainable development.

Recognizing the role of industrial policies in correcting market failures and of the state as facilitator, its priority sectors for industrial upgrading include resource-processing industries such as agro-food, minerals, textiles and garments, leather and forestry. It recommends that skills training should be aligned with the priority sectors, particularly infrastructure and beneficiation industries. It targets measures to increase the role of the private sector in upskilling workers, as well as technological development and R&D capabilities.

The Strategy envisages several channels to access investment capital. For resource-rich countries, it aims to establish national sovereign wealth funds for industrialization. By establishing a Supplier Benchmarking and Partnership Exchange, countries could assist local enterprises to enter TNCs' supply chains. This project aims to identify and match suppliers and buyers; it also recognizes the need to build the competitiveness of local firms.

The last cluster specifically aims at promoting local content and beneficiation in extractive industries as an avenue for sustainable development.

Part of a wider approach to supranational policy and strategy formulation, the Strategy includes the AU's Vision Paper on African Industrial Development; the road maps adopted by the regional economic communities (RECs), Economic Community of West African States, Common Market for Eastern and Southern Africa, Southern African Development Community (SADC), and Economic Community for Central Africa; and the UNIDO-assisted African Productive Capacity Initiative.

African Mining Vision

The African Mining Vision foresees the mineral sector contributing to broader continental social and economic development. Integral to this vision is the development of upstream, downstream and horizontal linkages (infrastructure, skills and R&D) with the mining sector.

The Vision is informed by initiatives at subregional, continental and global levels. These include the Yaoundé Vision on Artisanal and Small-scale Mining; the Africa Mining Partnership's Sustainable Development Charter and Mining Policy Framework; the SADC's Framework and Implementation Plan for Harmonisation of Mining Policies, Standards, Legislative and Regulatory Frameworks; and the Common Mining Policy and Code Minière Communautaire of the Union Economique et Monétaire Ouest Africaine.

The Vision proceeds from an understanding that companies have an important role. The corporate world, according to the Vision, has now accepted that its success will be assessed on a triple bottom line: financial success, contribution to social and economic development, and environmental stewardship. The Global Reporting Initiative (GRI) was developed to assist corporations to include this supplement in their reporting guidelines. The 2004 GRI guidelines contain social, environmental and economic indicators such as revenue management; compensation payments to local communities; employee benefits beyond those legally mandated; and equal opportunity policies or programmes. The Vision states, however, that the GRI did not incorporate linkage development.

In 2007, the Conference of African Ministers of Industry endorsed the Action Plan for Accelerated Industrial Development of Africa (AIDA) (AU, 2007). The plan identifies priorities for action at national, regional, continental and international levels on product and export diversification; natural resource management; infrastructure; human capital, science and technology; standards compliance; institutional frameworks; and resource mobilization

To maximize the impact of the commodity price boom on linkage development, the Vision identifies the following strategies:

*   Channelling resource rents to improve the basic physical and knowledge infrastructure;

*   Collateral use of the high-rent resource infrastructure to open up other economic activities (such as agriculture, forestry and tourism);

*   Establishing resource-processing industries (beneficiation);

*   Use of the fairly large resources sector market to develop the resource supply/inputs sector (capital goods, consumables, services);

*   Development of niche technological competencies in the resource inputs sector. Opportunities for these are open by the fact that resource exploitation technologies generally need adaptation to local conditions (climate, mineralogy, terrain). These competencies could later migrate to non-resource industries.

So far, these strategies have not been fully pursued because of poor governance in managing resource rents, poor management of feeder infrastructure linking to the resource infrastructure, and real exchange rate appreciation, which hampers local firms' competitiveness. Downstream beneficiation has been hindered by lack of complementary inputs, large economies of scale, and strategies of TNCs. Upstream linkage and local technological development are often prevented by low local capabilities and TNCs' central procurement and R&D strategies.

The Agribusiness and Agro-industry Development Initiative was endorsed by the High-Level Conference on Development of Agribusiness and Agro-industries in Africa, held in Abuja, Nigeria, in March 2010. The goal of the initiative is to have an agriculture sector in Africa that, by 2020, is made up of highly productive and profitable agricultural value chains. The initiative aims to accelerate development of agribusiness and agro-industrial sectors that ensure value addition to agricultural products. Four key areas of support will focus on: enabling policies and public goods; value-chain skills and technologies; post-production institutions and services; and reinforced financing and risk-mitigation mechanisms.

The relevance of value chain analysis and linkage development was endorsed at the Eighth African Development Forum held in Addis Ababa on 23–25 October 2012, convened by the AU, ECA and African Development Bank. The Consensus Statement adopted at the conference said that the "full potentiality of [Africa's] mineral wealth endowment remains largely untapped owing to structural and institutional challenges [including] the lack of forward and backward linkages" (AU et al., 2012: 2).

Among the recommendations, African countries should undertake to "enhance the contribution of mining activities to various backward and forward linkages in the local economy throughout the entire mineral value chain and overcome the phenomenon of enclave economies" and "urgently invest in tackling the institutional and human capacity challenges faced by stakeholders along the mineral value chain" (AU et al., 2012: 3–4).

The High-Level Conference on 3ADI, CAADP and the Maputo Declaration

Following African leaders' vision of a food-secure Africa and the establishment of a Common Food and Agricultural Market, the 2010 High-Level Conference on African Agribusiness and Agro-industries (3ADI) aimed to trigger the structural transformation of African agriculture through promoting public-private partnerships (PPPs). AU member States are to establish the requisite legal, regulatory and institutional framework

to support agribusiness and agro-industry development and to put in place programmes to accelerate development of the value of strategic food commodities, build competitive food supply systems and reduce reliance on food imports.

In support of this initiative, the AUC and ECA have set up a multi-institutional platform, to promote and assist in the development of regional value chains especially for designated strategic food and agricultural commodities. It is expected that this will contribute to the achievement of the ultimate objective of Pillar II of the CAADP framework, which is to accelerate growth in the agricultural sector by raising the capacities of private entrepreneurs, including commercial and smallholder farmers, to meet the increasingly complex cost, quality and logistical requirements of domestic, regional and international markets. The 2003 Maputo Declaration had earlier committed member States to increase their public spending on agriculture to 10 per cent of their budget allocation in the context of CAADP.

An example of the work undertaken for value chain creation in agricultural commodities relates to the launch of a pilot scheme in two RECs (COMESA and ECOWAS) that focuses on three of the strategic food and agricultural commodities identified at the 2006 Abuja Summit (livestock, maize and rice). Baseline studies with a regional perspective on livestock in these two regions have determined that intra-REC exports of livestock registered average growth of 15 per cent, compared with overall growth in intra-Africa exports of 25 per cent in 2005. This suggests that trade confined to RECs is less optimal than Africa-wide trade, which would argue for redoubling efforts to harmonize community markets to create a larger Africa-wide marketplace, such as the Continental Free Trade Area (CFTA), given that countries' trading interests are not confined within their REC borders.

AU Summit on Boosting Intra-African Trade and Fast Tracking the Establishment of the CFTA

African Heads of State and Government recently took decisive steps to move the regional integration agenda forward (see chapter 2), adopting a

Decision on Boosting Intra-African Trade and Fast-Tracking the Establishment of the CFTA during the 18th AU Summit in January 2012. They agreed to operationalize the CFTA by 2017. The Decision and Declaration contain an Action Plan for Boosting Intra-African Trade (BIAT), which is being implemented. The Action Plan has seven critical clusters for development, two of which deal with elements at the heart of industrialization and linkage development, namely productive capacity and factor market integration. The Action Plan has short, medium and long-term periods to deliver concrete outputs and targets pertaining to the clusters, with responsibilities shared between the RECs, member States and the AU, among others.

These regional initiatives are important for industrialization in Africa. They require major coordination efforts from member States, regional bodies and development partners. If taken seriously, their implementation has the potential to support Africa's transformation through resource-based industrialization and value addition.

African countries should consider designing strategies for linkage to GVCs

A resource-based industrialization strategy A resource-based industrialization strategy should be grounded in the reality of each African country as well as the dynamics of the globalized world economy. Unlike the past, Africa has to design linkages for a world in which goods and services move across borders with ease and speed, and GVCs are governed by multinational lead firms that set parameters and have access to consumer markets and for whom Africa's interests may not be a priority.

To be economically sustainable, African countries could, as a first step, look for ways of inserting themselves into these value chains and to continually upgrade their position. Thereafter, they should seek ways of developing their own lead firms. State industrial policies and strategies by lead firms will ultimately define the success of any linkage development strategy.

The global mining industries have similarly moved away from a high level of vertical integration towards outsourcing various stages in the mining process, ranging from the provision of capital goods and intermediate inputs such as chemicals to low-tech and more basic labour-intensive services to independent firms. What they have not done in many African countries, South Africa for example, is to support beneficiation efforts.

Supplier firms have responded to these opportunities and global mining companies are also involved in building capabilities among their suppliers. The same logic of unfolding outsourcing, initially to the lowest-cost global supplier and then, wherever possible, to low-cost close suppliers, is being observed in many commodity sectors, including Africa's.

Finding efficient local suppliers is particularly attractive in Africa, because transport and logistics are poorly developed (goods from outside may be greatly delayed) and because government policies have often mandated the deepening of local value addition (Morris et al., 2012). Also, large commodity firms have come to realize that unless their activities are associated with broader local development, they are likely to face hostility both from government and locals. Many such firms have therefore signed agreements to support local development.

Although the expansion of local linkages is thus largely fostered by the growing trend towards outsourcing by the core lead firms, it is not the only driver of localized production. Many inputs into the commodity sector in low-income economies were previously imported by independent suppliers and processors, for example foodstuffs for mineworkers or the cutting of timber from logs into sawn wood. When local capabilities are adequate, these activities can be undertaken domestically and, where possible, close to the point of commodity extraction.

Morris et al. (2012) created a general model of the trajectory of backward linkage development and the impact of industrial policy on it, taking account the growing trend towards outsourcing by lead commodity firms (figure 3.5).

FIGURE 3.5: DIFFERENT TRAJECTORIES OF LINKAGE DEVELOPMENT OVER TIME

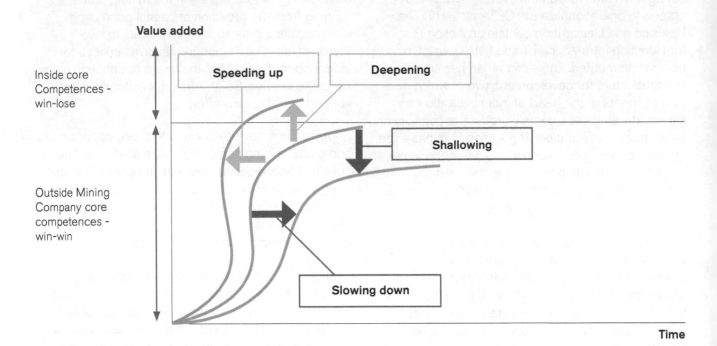

Source: Morris et al. (2012).

The horizontal axis reflects time. The vertical axis represents value added in provision of inputs for production of a commodity. The curve shows that, as a general consequence of the outsourcing of non-core competences, there is a market-driven process of linkage development in which the lead firm relinquishes the production of those inputs that embody the least rent and that are thus least profitable for them to produce.

Initially, the pace of outsourcing is low. With the accretion of technological capacities by suppliers, the pace of outsourcing speeds up. However, as technological and scale requirements become very demanding and as suppliers begin to stray into the core competencies of the lead firm, the easy hits are exhausted and the degree of outsourcing tails off. Countries and suppliers with weak capabilities will be located towards the bottom of this industry curve and those with strong capabilities towards the top of the curve.

We can therefore distinguish win-win and win-lose linkages. Inputs that the lead commodity producers have no interest in maintaining in house as they do not reflect their core competences, and that they wish to outsource to suppliers in their value chain, are win-win linkages. Lead producers and local suppliers and customers have a potential common interest in developing efficient local linkages. For example, lead commodity extraction companies may want auditing, office provisions and utilities to be provided by outsiders, and in the best of all cases, by reliable and low-cost suppliers based as close to their operations as possible.

Win-lose linkages are the range of inputs that are central to a firm's competitiveness and that it is reluctant to see undertaken by a competitor or outsourced. There may even be a conflict of interest between lead firms and potential suppliers and users. For example, in diamond extraction lead firms are very reluctant—indeed, have had to be forced—to allow local firms to cut and polish or to be involved in the logistics that guarantee their control over diamond supplies. These are their core competences, and the factors determining their profitability over time.

Contrary to the conventional wisdom of the "resource curse", therefore, it has now been argued (see e.g. Morris et al., 2012), following Hirschman, that linkage development in the resource sector is possible. But these "linkage effects need time to unfold" (Hirschman, 1981: 63). The older and more established a particular resource sector, the more likely that local linkages will have developed. Moreover, the unfolding of linkages will vary by sector, with the soft commodities at the one extreme and deep-sea energy at the other (Morris et al., 2012).

These linkage relationships are not immutable, in pace or form. Depending on a variety of determinants they can be altered by purposive state and institutional policy intervention. In other words, the curve in figure 3.5 can be deepened or made shallower, and the process can be accelerated or retarded as a result of effective, ineffective or indeed absence of country-specific policy implementation.[13]

For example, local content policies can move the curve to the left, accelerating the development of backward linkages, as in Angola where basic goods and services are increasingly imported through local firms. The breadth of linkages has increased, but not the depth (Teka, 2011).

However, local content policies need to be matched by industrial and business development policies as well as high domestic capabilities in order not only to speed linkage development, but to increase the local value-added content of such linkages. This is seen in Nigeria (chapter 5), where both the breadth and the depth of local linkages have improved (Oyejide and Adewuyi, 2011).

The lack of any local content policy and weak industrial policy, in contrast, tend to slow development of linkages for the range of supplies sourced locally and local value addition. The gold-mining value chain in Tanzania (see box 3.10) is characterized by such dynamics, where mines largely rely on imports and local businesses are not supported in entering the supply chain (Mjimba, 2011).

Forward linkage development is subject to similar dynamics. Beneficiation policies such as Botswana's (see box 3.13) can move the curve to

the left, speeding and deepening the development of local value-added activities (Mbayi, 2011). Likewise, Ethiopia's export taxes combined with local upgrading processes have shifted the composition of the country's exports from raw hides into intermediate and final leather products (chapter 4).

> *The lack of any local content policy and weak industrial policy, in contrast, tend to slow development of linkages for the range of supplies sourced locally and local value addition.*

Each African country must develop its own commodity-based industrialization strategy

Given the diversity of resource endowments, social and economic backgrounds, and geographical locations in Africa, the continent cannot be shoehorned into a "one size fits all" industrialization strategy. On the contrary, it has a raft of potential strategies: development of a modern service economy (tourism, information technology, transport), low- and medium-tech manufacturing development in countries endowed with large domestic markets, and resource-based industrialization in countries rich in natural resources. Indeed, each country is likely to have a multifaceted approach to industrializing and to pursue more than one strategy. What links them all is the necessity for African governments to take action to overcome market failure.

Along this perspective, three different strategies for resource-based industrialization can be pursued.

The first is to avoid competing simply on price and, instead, to increase revenues from unprocessed or semi-processed commodities by raising entry barriers to other competitors. This can be done by targeting the high end of the export market through process upgrading and certification (Page, 2010). This strategy can be effective for products such as fresh vegetables and fruits, and speciality products such as coffee and cocoa. The GVCs require efficient service industries (for quality control, transport and storage) and technologies. Among commodity groups, fresh produce is the only one that has experienced both price stability and long-term positive price trends. Ethiopia (chapter 4), Kenya and Zambia are following this strategy.

Given the diversity of resource endowments, social and economic backgrounds, and geographical locations in Africa, the continent cannot be shoehorned into a "one size fits all" industrialization strategy.

The second strategy is to develop backward linkages to commodity sectors. Booming investment in the extractive industries is creating large demand for goods and services. Oil and mine companies prefer to focus on their core business and outsource all non-core activities. Outsourcing is facilitated when undertaken though local rather than foreign suppliers, because it reduces transaction costs and lead times (Morris et al., 2012).

The advantage of this strategy is that it can be easily anchored on lead firms, because they have a commercial interest in developing efficient local supply clusters. However, this is often not possible because oil and mining companies are not familiar with local suppliers, or because local suppliers cannot meet their market parameters or because of the long-standing policy of multinationals. While with time, oil and mining companies will tend to increase outsourcing to competent local suppliers, African countries can intervene strategically to both accelerate this process and increase the value-added content of the local supply chain. The African Mining Vision offers a framework for greater engagement of lead firms in the extractive minerals industry and can help to set the modalities and conditions for mineral beneficiation and establishment of local supply clusters.

The third strategy consists of boosting industries that process natural resources. These industries represent on average half the manufacturing activity in lower-middle income countries (Owens and Wood, 1997). A few factors can facilitate this strategy: lead firms in consuming markets who want to relocate their manufacturing; rising fuel costs, which can generate weight or volume savings from processing; and growing regional markets. For example, in the context of relations with emerging economies such as China and India and the need to establish a strategy for engaging with them, it is important to ensure no resource flight to them, by requiring local

content as well as technology and skills transfer to the local workforce.

While much attention has traditionally focused on the final stages of commodity-based GVCs, African countries have considerable room to advance into intermediate manufacturing stages in the short term, as for sawn lumber, cellulose, fishmeal and preserved fruits. Building on their natural resource endowments, countries will find these industries easier to reach than the final stages of beneficiation; these industries will also provide opportunities for learning, technological capabilities, economies of scale and positive externalities (Reinhardt, 2000).

3.6 CONCLUSIONS

A discussion of linkage development cannot be conducted in abstract or aggregate terms, but must be country specific, as no single policy has proven to be successful in promoting linkages. The experiences reviewed in this and subsequent chapters highlight that a combination of policies and factors have played a key role in influencing the pace of value addition in Africa.

First, policies to promote value addition were implemented with policies to raise productivity and product quality in the natural resource sector. Raising the output of the sector enabled processing industries to reach economies of scale and governments to sustain investment in ancillary research and technological upgrading.

Second, in the early stages, processing industries exported final products to developing countries and intermediate products to industrialized countries. Only at later stages was it possible to export final products to meet the stringent requirements of Northern markets. Such exports usually require a global market presence acquired through GVCs' brand distribution networks. This implies that there is an opportunity for greater regional and subregional market integration at pan-African level. If African countries can facilitate such integration, this would be equivalent to creating large domestic markets that can help firms to build their competitiveness in final products before they attempt to penetrate industrial-country markets.

Third, domestic firms' capabilities facilitated linkage development. In the early stages, industrialization policies targeted domestic firms and built on existing capabilities. However, the role of foreign investors was also important and tended to increase with the success of the industry, as more FDI was attracted to the supply chain and to processing activities. Further research is required on whether it is possible to rely exclusively on FDI for this type of linkage-based industrialization. Countries such as Brazil, India, Indonesia and Malaysia depended on domestically mobilized capital to targeted sectors.

Finally, the right mix and sequencing of policies were equally important. Export restrictions at times helped to increase value-added content of exports and domestic production. Sectoral policies that selectively allocated resources and created incentives to shift domestic capital and entrepreneurship to targeted industries were also important, as were efforts to build technology and skills, which enabled domestic firms to absorb foreign technologies, partner with TNCs, catch up with competitors and then stay competitive.

REFERENCES

AfDB (African Development Bank). 2008. *African Development Report 2007*. Abidjan.

AU (African Union). 2007. "Action Plan for Accelerated Industrial Development of Africa." AU Conference of Ministers of Industry 1st Extraordinary Session, 24–27 September, Midrand, South Africa.

———. 2008. *Strategy for the Implementation of the Action Plan for Accelerated Industrial Development of Africa.* Report of the Conference of African Ministers of Industry (CAMI) 18th Ordinary Session, 24–28 October, Durban, South Africa.

AU (African Union), AfDB (African Development Bank), and ECA (United Nations Economic Commission for Africa). 2012. "Consensus Statement." Eighth African Development Forum (ADF-VIII), "Governing and Harnessing Natural Resources for Africa's Development", 23–25 October 2012, Addis Ababa.

Bair, J., and G. Gereffi. 2001. "Local Clusters in Global Chains: The Causes and Consequences of Export Dynamism in Torreon's Blue Jeans Industry." *World Development* 29(11): 1885–903.

Bigsten, A., and M. Söderbom. 2006. "What Have We Learned from a Decade of Manufacturing Enterprise Surveys in Africa?" *The World Bank Research Observer* 21(2): 241–65.

Blomström, M., and A. Kokko. 2007. "From Natural Resources to High-tech Production: The Evolution of Industrial Competitiveness in Sweden and Finland." In *Natural Resources, neither Curse nor Destiny*, ed. D. Lederman and W. F. Maloney, 213–56. Washington, DC: World Bank.

Buckley, P. J., L. J. Clegg, A. R. Cross, X. Liu, H. Voss, and P. Zheng. 2007. "The Determinants of Chinese outward Foreign Direct Investment." *Journal of International Business Studies* 38(4): 499–518.

Cashin, P., and C. J. McDermott. 2002. "The Long-run Behavior of Commodity Prices: Small Trends and Big Variability." IMF *Staff Papers* 49(2): 175–99.

Cernat, L., S. Laird, and A. Turrini. 2002. *Back to Basics: Market Access Issues in the Doha Agenda*. Geneva: United Nations Conference on Trade and Development, Division on International Trade in Goods and Services, and Commodities.

Chang, H. J. 2002. *Kicking Away the Ladder*. London: Anthem Press.

———. 2009. "Economic History of the Developed World: Lessons for Africa" In *Eminent Speakers Series Volume II—Sharing Visions of Africa's Development*, ed. S. Tapsoba & G. Oluremi Archer-Davies. Tunis: African Development Bank.

Cheng, L. K., and Z. Ma. 2010. "China's Outward Foreign Direct Investment." In *China's Growing Role in World Trade*, ed. R. C. Feenstra and S. J. Wei, 545–78. University of Chicago Press.

Cramer, C. 1999. "Can Africa Industrialize by Processing Primary Commodities? The Case of Mozambican Cashew Nuts." *World Development* 27(7): 1247–66.

David, P. A., and G. Wright. 1997. "Increasing Returns and the Genesis of American Resource Abundance." *Industrial and Corporate Change* 6(2): 203–45.

de Ferranti, D., G. E. Perry, D. Lederman, and W. E. Maloney. 2002. *From Natural Resources to the Knowledge Economy: Trade and Job Quality*. World Bank Latin American and Caribbean Studies 23440. Washington, DC: World Bank.

Dicken, P. 1998. *Global shift: Transforming the World Economy*, 3rd ed. London: P. Chapman.

ECA (United Nations Economic Commission for Africa). 2011. "Industrial Policies for the Structural Transformation of African Economies: Options and Best Practices." Policy Research Paper 2, Addis Ababa.

ECA (United Nations Economic Commission for Africa) and AU (African Union). 2011. *Minerals and Africa's Development: The International Study Group Report on Africa' Mineral Regimes*. Addis Ababa: ECA.

ECA (United Nations Economic Commission for Africa) and AUC (African Union Commission). 2012. *Economic Report on Africa 2012: Unleashing Africa's Potential as a Pole of Global Growth*. Addis Ababa: ECA.

Elhiraika, A. 2008. "Promoting Manufacturing to Accelerate Economic Growth and Reduce Volatility in Africa." Paper prepared at the African Economic Conference, jointly organized by the African Development Bank and ECA, November, Tunis.

Even-Zohar, C. 2007. *From Mine to Mistress: Corporate Strategies and Government Policies in the International Diamond Industry*. London: Mining Communications.

Farooki, M., and R. Kaplinsky. 2012. *The Impact of China on Global Commodity Prices: The Global Reshaping of the Resource Sector*. London: Routledge.

Fessehaie, J. 2012. "What Determines the Breadth and Depth of Zambia's Backward Linkages to Copper Mining? The Role of Public Policy and Value Chain Dynamics." *Resources Policy* 37(4): 443–51.

Fold, N. 2000. "Globalisation, State Regulation and Industrial Upgrading of the Oil Seed Industries in Malaysia and Brazil." *Singapore Journal of Tropical Geography* 21(3): 263–78.

———. 2002. "Lead Firms and Competition in 'Bi-polar' Commodity Chains. Grinders and Branders in the Global Cocoa-Chocolate Industry." *Journal of Agrarian Change* 2(2): 228–47.

Fosu, A. K. 2011. "Growth, Inequality, and Poverty Reduction in Developing Countries: Recent Global Evidence." Working Paper 2011/01, United Nations University World Institute for Development Economics Research, Helsinki.

Galal, A. 2008. "Comparative Assessment of Industrial Policy in Selected MENA Countries." In *Industrial Policy in the Middle East and North Africa: Rethinking the Role of the State*, ed. A. Galal, 1–10. Cairo: American University in Cairo Press.

Gellert, P. K. 2003. "Renegotiating a Timber Commodity Chain: Lessons from Indonesia on the Political Construction of Global Commodity Chains." *Sociological Forum* 18(1): 53–84.

Gereffi, G. 1994. "The Organization of Buyer-driven Global Commodity Chains: How U.S. Retailers Shape Overseas Production Networks." In *Commodity Chains and Global Capitalism*, ed. G. Gereffi, and M. Korzeniewicz, 95–122. Westport, CT: Praeger.

———. 1999. "International Trade and Industrial Upgrading in the Apparel Commodity Chain." *Journal of International Economics* 48(1): 37–70.

Gereffi, G., J. Humphrey, and T. Sturgeon. 2005. "The Governance of Global Value Chains." *Review of International Political Economy* 12(1): 78–104.

Girvan, N., and C. Girvan. 1973. "The Development of Dependency Economics in the Caribbean and Latin America: Review and Comparison." *Social and Economic Studies* 22(1, Dependence and Underdevelopment in the New World and the Old): 1–33.

Grimm, S., and M. Brüntrup. 2006. "EU Economic Partnership Agreements (EPAs) with ACP Regions." In Africa Agenda for 2007: *Suggestions for the German G8 and EU Council Presidencies*, ed. S. Klingebiel. Bonn: German Development Institute.

Hidalgo, C. A., B. Klinger, A.-L. Barabasi, and R, Hausmann. 2007. "The Product Space Conditions the Development of Nations." *Science* 317: 482–87.

Hirschman, A. O. 1958. *The Strategy of Economic Development*. New Haven, CT: Yale University Press.

———. 1981. Essays in *Trespassing: Economics to Politics and Beyond*. New York: Cambridge University Press.

Jalilian, H., M. A. Tribe, and J. Weiss. 2000. *Industrial Development and Policy in Africa*. Cheltenham, UK: Edward Elgar.

Kaplinsky, R. 2004. *Competitions Policy and the Global Coffee and Cocoa Value Chains*. Geneva: United Nations Conference on Trade and Development.

———. 2006. "Revisiting the Revisited Terms of Trade: Will China Make a Difference?" *World Development* 34(6): 981–95.

Kaplinsky, R., and M. Farooki. 2012. *Promoting Industrial Diversification in Resource Intensive Economies—The Examples of sub-Saharan Africa and Central Asia Regions*. Vienna: United Nations Industrial Development Organization.

Kaplinsky, R., and M. Morris. 2001. *A Handbook for Value Chain Research*. Ottawa: International Development Research Centre.

———. 2008. "Do the Asian Drivers Undermine Export-oriented Industrialization in SSA." *World Development* 36(2): 254–73.

Kaplinsky, R., and A. U. Santos-Paulino. 2006. "A Disaggregated Analysis of EU imports: The Implications for the Study of Patterns of Trade and Technology." *Cambridge Journal of Economics* 30(4): 587–611.

Kaplinsky, R., A. Terheggen, and J. Tijaja. 2010. "What Happens When the Market Shifts to China: The Gabon Timber and Thai Cassava Value Chains." Policy Research Working Paper 5260, World Bank, Washington, DC.

Karingi, S., L. Páez, and D. Degefa. 2011. *Report on a Survey of AGOA's Past, Present and Future Prospects: The Experiences and Expectations of Sub-Saharan Africa*. Addis Ababa: African Trade Policy Centre.

Kjöllerström, M., and K. Dallto. 2007. "Natural Resource-based Industries: Prospects for Africa's Agriculture." In *Industrial development for the 21st Century: Sustainable Development Perspectives*, ed. United Nations Department of Economic and Social Affairs, 119–81. New York: United Nations.

Lall, S. 2004. "Industrial Success and Failure in a Globalizing World." *International Journal of Technology Management and Sustainable Development* 3(3): 189–213.

Lall, S., and C. Pietrobelli. 2005. "National Technology Systems in sub-Saharan Africa." *International Journal of Technology and Globalisation* 1(3/4): 311–42.

Lall, S., and S. Wangwe. 1998. "Industrial Policy and Industrialisation in sub-Saharan Africa." Journal of African Economies 7(suppl 1): 70–107.

Lall, S., J. Weiss, and J. Zhang. 2006. "The 'Sophistication" of Exports: A New Trade Measure." *World Development* 34(2): 222–37.

Londero, E., and S. Teitel. 1996. "Industrialisation and the Factor Content of Latin American Exports of Manufactures." *The Journal of Development Studies* 32(4): 581–601.

Lorentzen, J. 2008. "Knowledge Intensification in Resource-based Economies." In *Resource Intensity, Knowledge and Development: Insights from Africa and South America*, ed. J. Lorentzen, 1–48. Cape Town, South Africa: HSRC Press.

Manzano, O., and R. Rigobón. 2007. "Resource Curse or Debt Overhang?" In *Natural Resources, neither Curse nor*

Destiny, ed. D. Lederman and W. F. Maloney, 41–70. Washington, DC: World Bank.

Mbayi, L. 2011. "Linkages in Botswana's Diamond Cutting and Polishing Industry." MMCP Discussion Paper 6, Open University, Milton Keynes, UK.

Milanovic, B. 2003. "The Two Faces of Globalisation: Against Globalisation as We Know It?" *World Development* 31(4): 667–83.

Mjimba, V. 2011. "The Nature and Determinants of Linkages in Emerging Minerals Commodity Sectors: A Case Study of Gold Mining in Tanzania." MMCP Discussion Paper 7, Open University, Milton Keynes, UK.

Mkandawire, T. 2001. "Thinking about Developmental State in Africa." *Cambridge Journal of Economics* 25(3): 289–313.

Morris, M., R. Kaplinsky, and D. Kaplan. 2012. *One Thing Leads to Another: Promoting Industrialisation by Making the Most of the Commodity Boom in sub-Saharan Africa.* Published online by M. Morris, R. Kaplinsky, and D. Kaplan.

Morris, M., and G. Robbins. 2007. "Government Support and Enabling Environment for Inter-firm Cluster Cooperation: Policy Lessons from South Africa." In *Industrial Clusters and Innovation Systems in Africa. Institutions, Markets and Policy,* ed. B. Oyelaran-Oyeyinka and D. McCormick, 243–62. New York: United Nations University Press.

Nziramasanga, M. 1995. *Formulating Industrial Policy in Africa: 2000 and Beyond.* Geneva: United Nations Industrial Development Organization.

Ogbu, O. M., B. Oyeyinka, and H. M. Mlawa, eds.. 1995. *Technology Policy and Practise in Africa.* Ottawa: International Development Research Centre.

Owens, T., and A. Wood. 1997. "Export-oriented Industrialization through Primary Processing?" *World Development* 25(9): 1453–70.

Oyejide, T. A., and A. O. Adewuyi. 2011. "Enhancing Linkages of Oil and Gas Industry in the Nigerian Economy." MMCP Discussion Paper 8, Open University, Milton Keynes, UK.

Page, J. 2012. "Can Africa Industrialise?" *Journal of African Economies* 21(suppl 2): ii86–ii124.

Pal, P. 2008. "Surge in Indian Outbound FDI to Africa: An Emerging Pattern in Globalization?" http://e-server.iimcal.ac.in/research/download/OFDI_Partha-pal.pdf.

Palpacuer, F., P. Gibbon, and L. Thomsen. 2005. "New Challenges for Developing Country Suppliers In Global Clothing Chains: A Comparative European Perspective." *World Development* 33(3): 409–30.

Perez-Aleman, P. 2005. "Cluster Formation, Institutions and Learning: The Emergence of Clusters and Development in Chile." *Industrial and Corporate Change* 14(4): 651–77.

Perkins, D., and G. Robbins. 2011. "The Contribution to Local Enterprise Development of Infrastructure for Commodity Extraction Projects: Tanzania's Central Corridor and Mozambique's Zambezi Valley." MMCP Discussion Paper 9, Open University, Milton Keynes, UK.

Phyne, J., and J. Mansilla. 2003. "Forging Linkages in the Commodity Chain: The Case of the Chilean Salmon Farming Industry, 1987–2001." *Sociologia Ruralis* 43(2): 108–27.

Pradhan, J. P. 2008. *Indian Direct Investment in Developing Countries: Emerging Trends and Development Impacts.* Paper No. 12323. Munich University.

Prebisch, R. 1950. *The Economic Development of Latin America and Its Principal Problems.* Economic Bulletin for Latin America 7. New York: United Nations Department of Economic and Social Affairs.

Radetzki, M. 2008. *A Handbook of Primary Commodities in the Global Economy*, Cambridge, Cambridge UP.

Raines, P., I. Turok, and R. Brown. 2001. "Growing Global: Foreign Direct Investment and the Internationalization of Local Suppliers in Scotland." *European Planning Studies* 9(8): 965–78.

Reinhardt, N. 2000. "Back to basics in Malaysia and Thailand: The role of resource-based exports in their export-led growth." *World Development* 28(1): 57–77.

Riddell, R. 1990. *Manufacturing Africa*. London: James Currey.

Roemer, M. 1979. "Resource-based Industrialization in the Developing Countries: A survey." *Journal of Development Economics* 6(2): 163–202.

Schmitz, H. 1997. "Collective Efficiency and Increasing Returns." IDS Working Paper 50, University of Sussex, Institute of Development Studies, Brighton, UK.

Schmitz, H., and P. Knorringa. 2000. "Learning from Global Buyers." *Journal of Development Studies* 37(2): 177–205.

Singer, H. W. 1950. "The Distribution of Gains between Investing and Borrowing Countries." *The American Economic Review* 40(2): 473–85.

Soludo, C., Ogbu, O. and Chang, H.J (Eds.). 2004. *The Politics of Trade and Industrial Policy in Africa: Forced Consensus?* Africa World Press/IDRC.

Staritz, C. 2011. *Making the Cut? Low-income Countries and the Global Clothing Value Chain in a Post-quota and Post-crisis World*. Washington, DC: World Bank.

Statistics Botswana. 2012. *March 2011 Formal Sector Employment*. Stats Brief No. 2012/01. Gabrone: Central Statistics Office, Ministry of Finance and Development Planning.

Stein, H. 1992. "Deindustrialization, Adjustment, the World Bank and the IMF in Africa." *World Development* 20(1): 83–95.

Stein, H., ed. 1996. *Asian Industrialization and Africa*. London: Palgrave Macmillan.

Talbot, J. M. 1997. "Where Does Your Coffee Dollar Go?: The Division of Income and Surplus along the Coffee Commodity Chain." *Studies in Comparative International Development (SCID)* 32(1): 56–91.

———. 2002. "Tropical Commodity Chains, Forward Integration Strategies and International Inequality: Coffee, Cocoa and Tea." *Review of International Political Economy* 9(4): 701–34.

Teka, Z. 2011. "Backward Linkages in the Manufacturing Sector in the Oil and Gas Value Chain in Angola." MMCP Discussion Paper 11, Open University, Milton Keynes, UK.

Terheggen, A. 2011. "The Tropical Timber Industry in Gabon: A Forward Linkages Approach to Industrialisation." MMCP Discussion Paper 10. Open University, Milton Keynes, UK.

Thee, K. W. 2009. "The Indonesian Wood Products Industry." Journal of the Asia Pacific Economy14(2): 138–49.

Torres-Fuchslocher, C. 2007. "Desarrollo de proveedores en la salmonicultura chilena." *Journal of Technology Management & Innovation* 2(1): 92–107.

UNCTAD (United Nations Conference on Trade and Development). 2002. *Trade and Development Report 2002*. New York: United Nations.

———. 2007. *World Investment Report 2007: Transnational Corporations, Extractive Industries and Development*. New York: United Nations.

Wood, A., and J. Mayer. 2001. "Africa's Export Structure in a Comparative Perspective." *Cambridge Journal of Economics* 25 (3): 369–94.

Wright, G. 1990. "The Origins of American Industrial Success, 1879–1940." *The American Economic Review* 80(4): 651–68.

Wright, G., and J. Czelusta. 2004. "Why Economies Slow: The Myth of the Resource Curse." *Challenge* 47(2): 6–38.

Yeats, A. J. 1991. "Do Natural Resource-based Industrialization Strategies Convey Important (Unrecognized) Price Benefits for Commodity-exporting Developing Countries?" Working Papers in International Trade WPS 580, World Bank, Washington, DC.

ANNEX TABLES

ANNEX TABLE 3.1 COMPOSITION AND SHARE OF AFRICA'S MERCHANDISE EXPORTS, BY COUNTRY (LATEST AVAILABLE YEAR)

	Primary commodities (%)	Of which (excluding precious stones and gold/food commodities; %)		
		Agricultural raw materials	Ores and Minerals	Fuel
Central Africa				
Central African Republic (2009)	97	11	62	0
Cameroon (2010)	80	15	40	0
Congo, Rep. (2010)	69	2	0	67
Gabon (2009)	94	9	3	81
São Tomé and Príncipe (2010)	95	1	0	0
East Africa				
Burundi (2010)	92	4	5	0
Comoros (2007)	14	0	0	0
Djibouti (2009)	24	0	0	0
Eritrea (2003)	68	7	3	0
Ethiopia (2011)	90	8	1	0
Kenya (2010)	62	11	0	2
Madagascar (2010)	35	2	8	0
Rwanda (2011)	81	4	40	0
Tanzania (2011)	84	3	22	1
Uganda (2010)	64	5	1	1
Seychelles (2008)	42	0	0	0
North Africa				
Algeria (2011)	88	0	0	87
Egypt (2011)	46	3	6	18
Morocco (2010)	35	2	12	2
Tunisia (2010)	23	1	2	13
Mauritania (2010)	92	0	20	0
Sudan (2009)	97	1	0	77
Southern Africa				
Botswana (2011)	88	0	8	0
Lesotho (2009)	15	3	0	0
Malawi (2011)	90	5	9	0
Mauritius (2011)	39	1	1	0
Mozambique (2010)	91	4	53	18
Namibia (2008)	71	0	31	0
South Africa (2011)	61	2	32	9
Zambia (2010)	91	1	83	0
Zimbabwe (2010)	70	6	32	1
Swaziland (2007)	30	7	1	1

West Africa

Benin (2010)	85	24	1	0
Burkina Faso (2010)	97	18	1	0
Cape Verde (2011)	85	0	1	0
Côte d'Ivoire (2011)	79	13	0	13
Gambia (2011)	41	6	1	0
Ghana (2011)	91	4	1	39
Guinea (2008)	89	3	52	0
Guinea-Bissau (2005)	100	0	1	0
Mali (2010)	93	8	0	0
Niger (2011)	93	2	69	0
Nigeria (2010)	82	2	1	76
Senegal (2011)	46	1	3	0
Sierra Leone (2002)	93	1	0	0
Togo (2011)	51	31	6	0

Source: Comtrade, retrieved from http://comtrade.un.org/, accessed 30 July 2012. Some countries have been excluded because data were older than 2000.

Note: For many countries, the sum of columns 2, 3 and 4, does not equal column 1. This is because column 1 includes food commodities (such as cocoa and coffee), precious stones and gold, which are not represented in columns 2, 3 and 4.

ANNEX TABLE 3.2: AFRICA'S COMPOSITION AND SHARE OF TOP THREE EXPORTS, BY COUNTRY (LATEST AVAILABLE YEAR)

	Top three export products (% of total merchandise exports by product)	% of total merchandise export of top three export products
Central Africa		
Central African Republic (2009)	S3-2771 Industrial diamonds (62%) S3-2475 Wood, non-conif, rough, unt (20%) S3-2484 Wood of non-coniferous species, sawn or chipped lengthwise, sliced or pee (11%)	93
Cameroon (2010)	S3-3330 Crude petroleum (37%) S3-0721 Cocoa beans, whole or broken, raw or roasted (16%) S3-2484 Wood of non-coniferous species, sawn or chipped lengthwise, sliced or peeled (6%)	59
Congo, Rep. (2010)	S3-3330 Crude petroleum (65%) S3-3425 Butanes, liquefied (2%) S3-2475 Wood, non-conif, rough,unt (1%)	68
Gabon (2009)	S3-3330 Crude petroleum (81%) S3-2475 Wood, non-conif, rough, unt (7%) S3-2877 Manganese ores and concentrates (including manganiferous iron ores and co (3%)	91
São Tomé and Príncipe (2010)	S3-0721 Cocoa beans, whole or broken, raw or roasted (85%) S3-4211 Soya bean oil, fractions (4%) S3-0739 Food preparations containing cocoa, n.e.s. (3%)	91

East Africa

Burundi (2010)	S3-0711 Coffee, not roasted (59%) S3-9710 Gold, non-monetary excl. ores (11%) S3-0741 Tea (9%)	79
Comoros (2007)	S3-0752 Spices, ex. pepper, pimento (14%)	14
Djibouti (2009)	S3-0222 Milk concentrated or sweetened (8%) S3-0989 Food preparations, nes (7%) S3-4222 Palm oil, fractions (3%)	18
Eritrea (2003)	S3-0345 Fish fillets, frsh, child (13%) S3-2911 Bone,horn,ivor.coral,etc. (9%) S3-0341 Fish,fresh,chilled,whole (5%)	27
Ethiopia (2011)	S3-0711 Coffee, not roasted (32%) S3-2225 Sesame (Sesamum) seeds (13%) S3-0545 Oth.frsh,chll.vegetables (10%)	55
Kenya (2010)	S3-0741 Tea (23%) S3-2927 Cut flowers and foliage (8%) S3-0545 Oth.frsh,chll.vegetables (4%)	35
Madagascar (2010)	S3-0361 Crustaceans, frozen (6%) S3-0752 Spices,ex.pepper,pimento (5%) S3-2878 Ore etc. molybdn. niob. etc. (4%)	15
Rwanda (2011)	S3-2876 Tin ores and concentrates (24%) S3-0711 Coffee, not roasted (18%) S3-0741 Tea (13%)	55
Tanzania (2011)	S3-9710 Gold, non-monetary excl. ores (36%) S3-2891 Prec.mtl.ore,concentrats (11%) S3-2877 Manganese ores and concentrates (including manganiferous iron ores and co (10%)	58
Uganda (2010)	S3-0711 Coffee, not roasted (17%) S3-0345 Fish fillets,frsh,child (6%) S3-0741 Tea (4%)	27
Seychelles (2008)	S3-0371 Fish,prepard,presrvd,nes (27%) S3-0352 Fish salted or in brine (13%) S3-4111 Fat,oil,fish,mar.mammals (1%)	41

North Africa

Algeria (2011)	S3-3330 Crude petroleum (49%) S3-3432 Natural gas, in the gaseous state (18%) S3-3431 Natural gas, liquefied (9%)	76
Egypt (2011)	S3-3330 Crude petroleum (10%) S3-3431 Natural gas, liquefied (6%) S3-9710 Gold, non-monetary excl. ores (6%)	21
Morocco (2010)	S3-2723 Natural calc.phosphates (6%) S3-0371 Fish,prepard,presrvd,nes (3%) S3-3352 Mineral tars and product (2%)	12
Tunisia (2010)	S3-3330 Crude petroleum (13%) S3-4214 Olive oil etc. (2%) S3-0579 Fruit,fresh,dried, nes (1%)	16
Mauritania (2010)	S3-9710 Gold, non-monetary excl. ores (34%) S3-2831 Copper ores and concentrates (17%) S3-0342 Fish,frozenex.fillets (17%)	67

Sudan (2009)	S3-3330 Crude petroleum (77%) S3-9710 Gold, non-monetary excl. ores (14%) S3-0012 Sheep and goats, live (2%)	93

Southern Africa

Botswana (2011)	S3-6672 Diamonds excl. industrial (75%) S3-2842 Nickel mattes,sintrs.etc. (6%) S3-9710 Gold, non-monetary excl. ores (1%)	83
Lesotho (2009)	S3-1110 Non-alcohol.beverage,nes (5%) S3-2681 Wool, greasy (2%) S3-6672 Diamonds, excl.industrial (2%)	10
Malawi (2011)	S3-1212 Tobacco, wholly or partly stemmed/stripped (25%) S3-1211 Tobacco, not stemmed/stripped (14%) S3-0611 Sugars,beet or cane, raw (13%)	53
Mauritius (2011)	S3-0371 Fish,prepard,presrvd,nes (12%) S3-0612 Other beet,cane sugar (10%) S3-0611 Sugars,beet or cane, raw (4%)	26
Mozambique (2010)	S3-6841 Alum.,alum.alloy,unwrght (52%) S3-3510 Electric current (12%) S3-3431 Natural gas, liquefied (6%)	70
Namibia (2008)	S3-6672 Diamonds excl.industrial (16%) S3-2861 Uranium ores and concentrates (16%) S3-0342 Fish,frozenex.fillets (7%)	39
South Africa (2011)	S3-6812 Platinum (12%) S3-3212 Oth.coal,notagglomeratd (8%) S3-9710 Gold, non-monetary excl. ores (8%)	27
Zambia (2010)	S3-6821 Copper, anodes, alloys (64%) S3-6825 Copper plate,etc.15mm+th (9%) S3-2831 Copper ores and concentrates (3%)	76
Zimbabwe (2010)	S3-2842 Nickel mattes,sintrs.etc. (14%) S3-1212 Tobacco, wholly or partly stemmed/stripped (13%) S3-9710 Gold, non-monetary excl. ores (9%)	36
Swaziland (2007)	S3-0611 Sugars,beet or cane, raw (14%) S3-2514 Chem.woodpulp,soda,unbl (3%) S3-2484 Wood of non-coniferous species, sawn or chipped lengthwise, sliced or pee (2%)	18

West Africa

Benin (2010)	S3-2631 Cotton (other than linters), not carded or combed (22%) S3-0123 Poultry, meat and offal (21%) S3-0423 Rice,milled,semi-milled (21%)	65
Burkina Faso (2010)	S3-9710 Gold, non-monetary excl. ores (69%) S3-2631 Cotton (other than linters), not carded or combed (17%) S3-2225 Sesame (Sesamum) seeds (4%)	90
Cape Verde (2011)	S3-0371 Fish,prepard,presrvd,nes (44%) S3-0342 Fish,frozenex.fillets (36%) S3-0362 Crustaceans, other than frozen, including flours, meals and pellets of cr (1%)	82

Côte d'Ivoire (2011)	S3-0721 Cocoa beans, whole or broken, raw or roasted (27%) S3-3330 Crude petroleum (12%) S3-2312 Natural rubber exc.latex (10%)	49
Gambia (2011)	S3-2690 Worn clothing,textls,rag (5%) S3-0612 Other beet,cane sugar (3%) S3-0371 Fish,prepard,presrvd,nes (3%)	11
Ghana (2011)	S3-9710 Gold, non-monetary excl. ores (26%) S3-3425 Butanes, liquefied (24%) S3-3330 Crude petroleum (16%)	65
Guinea (2008)	S3-2851 Aluminium ores and concentrates (40%) S3-9710 Gold, non-monetary excl. ores (32%) S3-2852 Alumina (aluminium oxide), other than artificial corundum (11%)	83
Guinea-Bissau (2005)	S3-0577 Edible nuts fresh,dried (99%) S3-2821 Waste and scrap of cast iron (<1%) S3-2475 Wood,non-conif,rough,unt (<1%)	100
Mali (2010)	S3-9710 Gold, non-monetary excl. ores (79%) S3-2634 Cotton, carded or combed (7%) S3-0011 Bovine animals, live (2%)	89
Niger (2011)	S3-2861 Uranium ores and concentrates (69%) S3-9710 Gold, non-monetary excl. ores (9%) S3-0545 Oth.frsh,chll.vegetables (3%)	81
Nigeria (2010)	S3-3330 Crude petroleum (70%) S3-3431 Natural gas, liquefied (3%) S3-3425 Butanes, liquefied (2%)	75
Senegal (2011)	S3-9710 Gold, non-monetary excl. ores (10%) S3-0342 Fish,frozenex.fillets (4%) S3-0341 Fish,fresh,chilled,whole (3%)	17
Sierra Leone (2002)	S3-0711 Coffee, not roasted (87%) S3-0721 Cocoa beans, whole or broken, raw or roasted (3%) S3-0459 Buckwheat etc. unmilled (1%)	91
Togo (2011)	S3-2631 Cotton (other than linters), not carded or combed (31%) S3-2723 Natural calc.phosphates (5%) S3-9710 Gold, non-monetary excl. ores (4%)	40

Source: Comtrade, retrieved from http://comtrade.un.org/ (accessed 30 July 2012).

ANNEX TABLE 3.3: AFRICA'S MANUFACTURING VALUE ADDED, BY COUNTRY (% OF GDP, SELECTED YEARS)

	1970	1980	1990	2000	2005	2009
Central Africa						
Central African Republic	6.8	7.2	11.3	7.0	7.4	
Cameroon	10.2	9.6	14.5	20.8	17.7	
Chad	11.1		14.4	8.9	5.3	
Congo, Rep.		7.5	8.3	3.5	4.0	4.5
Equatorial Guinea				1.4	6.2	18.2
Gabon	6.8	4.6	5.6	3.7	4.1	4.3
São Tomé and Príncipe					6.4	
East Africa						
Burundi	7.3	7.4	12.9	8.7	8.8	
Comoros		3.9	4.2	4.5	4.4	4.3
Congo, Dem. Rep.		15.2	11.3	4.8	6.6	5.5
Djibouti			3.6	2.6	2.6	
Eritrea				11.2	6.8	5.6
Ethiopia			4.8	5.5	4.8	4.0
Kenya	12.0	12.8	11.7	11.6	11.8	8.7
Madagascar			11.2	12.2	14.0	14.1
Rwanda	3.6	15.3	18.3	7.0	7.0	6.4
Tanzania			9.3	9.4	8.7	9.5
Uganda	9.2	4.3	5.7	7.6	7.5	8.0
Seychelles		7.4	10.1	19.2	13.1	11.8
Somalia	9.3	4.7	4.6			
North Africa						
Algeria	17.2	10.6	11.4	7.5	5.9	6.1
Egypt, Arab Rep.		12.2	17.8	19.4	17.0	16.0
Libya					4.7	
Morocco		16.9	19.0	17.5	16.3	15.9
Tunisia	8.4	11.8	16.9	18.2	17.1	16.5
Mauritania			10.3	9.0	5.0	4.1
Sudan	7.8	7.5	8.7	8.6	6.9	6.8
Southern Africa						
Angola			5.0	2.9	3.5	6.1
Botswana		5.1	5.1	4.5	3.7	4.2
Lesotho	4.7	8.4	14.6	14.0	20.5	17.0
Malawi		13.7	19.5	12.9	9.2	10.0
Mauritius		15.8	24.4	23.5	19.8	19.4
Mozambique			10.2	12.2	15.5	13.6
Namibia		9.2	13.8	12.8	13.6	14.7

South Africa	**22.8**	**21.6**	**23.6**	**19.0**	**18.5**	**15.1**
Zambia	11.0	18.3	36.1	11.4	11.9	9.6
Zimbabwe	17.9	21.6	22.8	15.8	16.9	17.0
Swaziland	12.5	20.9	36.8	39.5	40.0	44.4
West Africa						
Benin		8.0	7.8	8.8	7.5	
Burkina Faso	17.1	15.2	15.2	16.2	14.6	
Cape Verde			8.2	9.3	7.6	6.7
Côte d'Ivoire	10.3	12.8	20.9	21.7	19.3	18.0
Gambia	3.3	5.6	6.6	5.4	5.0	5.0
Ghana	13.2	8.1	9.8	10.1	9.5	6.9
Guinea			4.6	4.0	4.1	5.3
Guinea-Bissau	21.2		8.4	10.5		
Liberia	4.0	7.7		9.5	12.4	
Mali	7.9	6.5	8.5	3.8	3.2	
Niger	4.6	3.7	6.6	6.8		
Nigeria					2.8	
Senegal		13.5	15.3	14.7	15.2	12.7
Sierra Leone	6.3	5.3	4.6	3.5		
Togo	10.0	7.8	9.9	8.4	10.1	

Source: African Development Indicators, http://data.worldbank.org/data-catalog/africa-development-indicators, accessed 30 June 2012. Empty cells denote missing data.

NOTES

[1] Primary commodities are categorized according to the broadest United Nations Conference on Trade and Development definition—that is, including not only food commodities, agricultural raw materials, minerals and fuel, but also precious stones and gold.

[2] This section relies heavily on ECA (2011).

[3] The use of non-tariff barriers creates serious problems owing to the difficulties associated with its management as well as its opacity in terms of the effect on beneficiaries.

[4] The effect of foreign exchange restrictions on the current account is an overvalued official exchange rate, coupled with some form of secondary market exchange rate.

[5] In some case, such as Ghana and Zambia, governments even announced five-year plans and very ambitious targets. In Algeria almost the whole economy was nationalized in 1966.

[6] As an example, Nziramasanga (1995) cites the Zambian case: nationalizing the copper mining industry induced a larger use of local inputs but it had no effect on the domestic process of technological knowledge accumulation, because the latter was embodied in expatriate management.

[7] On the strategy of FDI in developing countries, see Amsden (2001).

[8] World Bank African Development Indicators, http://data.worldbank.org/data-catalog/africa-development-indicators, accessed 30 June 2012.

[9] Retrieved from http://uncladstat.unctad.org/ReportFolders/reportFolders.aspx, accessed 30 July 2012.

[10] In this section, we refer in particular to resource-based manufacturing rather than primary processing. The latter is often already undertaken in resource-rich African countries in hard commodities in the form of smelting and refining, and in soft commodities in the form of post-harvest processing. Also, existing research has focused largely on resource-based manufacturing.

[11] See www.trademap.org/, accessed 30 August 2012.

[12] Also the technical characteristics of the cocoa value chain facilitate trade in intermediate products rather than the final one, as chocolate tends to deteriorate when transported (Roemer, 1979).

[13] These processes, with concomitant forms of policy intervention, are discussed in detail in chapters 4, 5 and 6 for some value chains and African countries; Morris et al. (2012) discuss other cases.

Making the Most of Linkages
in Soft (Food) Commodities

PROCESSING PRIMARY SOFT COMMODITIES OPENS UP MAJOR POSSIBILITIES FOR VALUE ADDITION AND COMMODITY-BASED INDUSTRIALIZATION IN AFRICA. HOWEVER, IT REQUIRES LARGE AND RESOURCE-INTENSIVE INTERVENTIONS TO EXPAND AND UPGRADE AGRICULTURAL PRODUCTION.

Agro-processing is one of the most developed manufacturing sectors in Africa. Most countries have agro-processing industries, although with significant variations among countries in size, international competitiveness, breadth of processing capabilities (range of products), depth of local value added, extent of backward linkages to agriculture, and extent of forward linkages to domestic, regional and international markets.

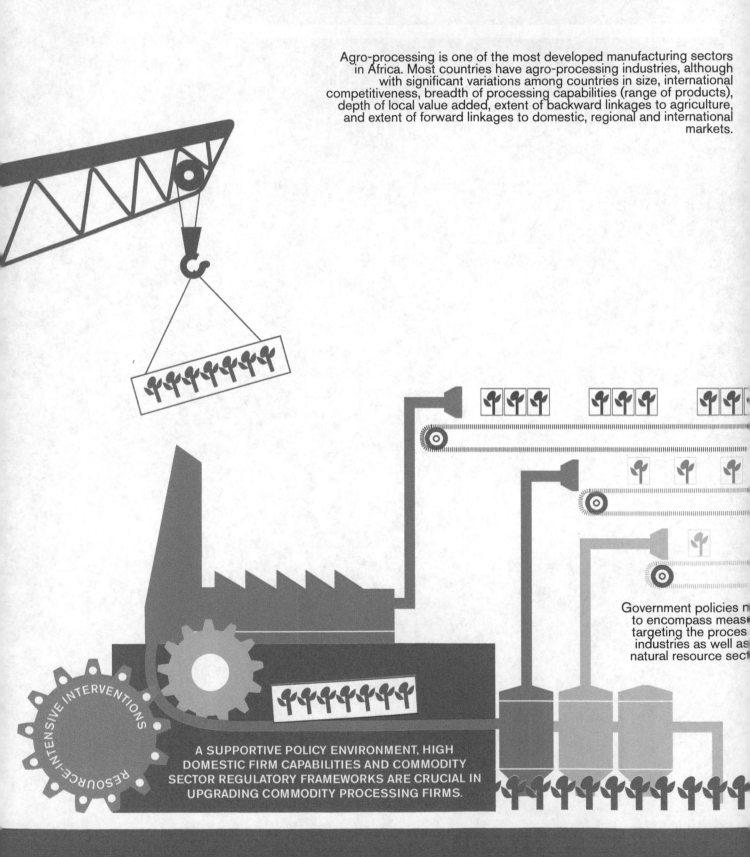

Government policies n to encompass meas targeting the proces industries as well as natural resource sect

RESOURCE-INTENSIVE INTERVENTIONS

A SUPPORTIVE POLICY ENVIRONMENT, HIGH DOMESTIC FIRM CAPABILITIES AND COMMODITY SECTOR REGULATORY FRAMEWORKS ARE CRUCIAL IN UPGRADING COMMODITY PROCESSING FIRMS.

INTERVENTIONIST STATE POLICIES ARE CRUCIAL TO MAKE THE MOST OF SOFT COMMODITIES.

These include export restrictions, important to increase the value-added content of exports (in Indonesia and Malaysia) and of exports and domestic production (Brazil). Sectoral policies that selectively allocated resources and created incentives to shift domestic capital and entrepreneurship to targeted industries were also important. Substantial efforts in building technology and skills enabled domestic firms to absorb foreign technologies, partner with multinational corporations, catch up with competitors and maintain their long-term competitiveness.

Despite intra-country variations, most African countries face challenges such as market requirements and stiff international competition in their efforts to integrate forward into higher value added activities.

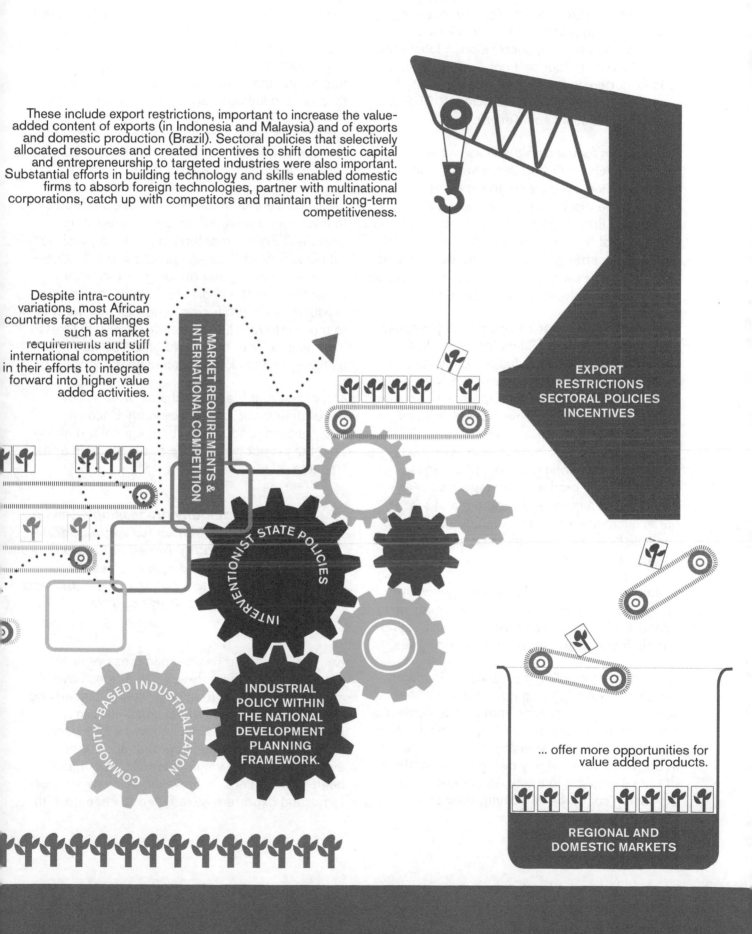

MARKET REQUIREMENTS & INTERNATIONAL COMPETITION

EXPORT
RESTRICTIONS
SECTORAL POLICIES
INCENTIVES

INTERVENTIONIST STATE POLICIES

COMMODITY-BASED INDUSTRIALIZATION

INDUSTRIAL POLICY WITHIN THE NATIONAL DEVELOPMENT PLANNING FRAMEWORK.

... offer more opportunities for value added products.

REGIONAL AND DOMESTIC MARKETS

This chapter focuses on the extent to which Africa is making the most of linkages in soft commodities to drive a new process of industrialization. Through case studies, it deals with forward linkages (semi-processing, processing and marketing) and backward linkages (to farmer suppliers) along global value chains (GVCs) in four soft-commodity sectors (cocoa, coffee, tea and agro-products) with examples from five countries (Nigeria, Ghana, Cameroon, Ethiopia and Kenya).

The analysis focuses on the links within the various GVCs driving these sectors and connecting local producers to export end markets. The discussion shows how the lead commodity firms facilitate or obstruct the breadth and depth of forward linkages, the factors that constrain a shift by local firms into value-added activities, and how government industrial policies can influence domestic industrialization.[1]

The chapter finds that soft-commodity processing opens up major possibilities for value addition and commodity-based industrialization, but it requires large and resource-intensive interventions to expand and upgrade agricultural output. By expanding domestic and regional markets for inputs, these interventions will create multiple opportunities and economies of scale for developing backward linkages, related to local production of inputs such as fertilizers, small capital equipment and spare parts, maintenance and repair, and so on—and specialist service providers such as certification bodies, laboratories and business support.

The countries in this chapter have generally struggled to integrate forward into higher value added activities such as processing, marketing and distribution, to greater or lesser degrees.

The cocoa-processing industries in Ghana and Nigeria are growing (though from a low base) as seen in rising investment from private domestic and foreign sources and, in Nigeria, public listed companies. Public ownership remains important in both countries, largely owing to the strategy of global grinders to integrate backward into producing countries, relocating their processing and purchasing facilities and working closely with local partners. Such integration helps them to secure supplies and allows them to adjust to changes in global chocolate manufacturers' specifications on quality and price very fast. It is also encouraged by policies to incentivize local processing, in Nigeria for example. In Cameroon by contrast, the weakness of the policy framework and of domestic capabilities mean that forward linkages are struggling to develop.

In Ethiopia's coffee sector and Kenya's tea sector, the lack of government policy has hampered linkage development, as has the fact that few global coffee roasters and tea manufacturers—the key drivers of these GVCs—have strategies to relocate value-added stages to producing countries. Coffee roasters, in particular, wish to retain control of their key processing activities—blending, roasting and grinding—which may be justified by the short shelf life of roasted products. Thus producing countries that want to move into roasting coffee for export markets must ensure very short lead times, as well as blending and packaging capabilities.

The cocoa and tea value chains offer more opportunities for local processing. Cocoa intermediate products (but not chocolate) and final tea products are more easily storable and tradable.

> *Soft-commodity processing opens up major possibilities for value addition and commodity-based industrialization, but it requires large and resource intensive interventions to expand and upgrade agricultural output.*

Kenya's upgrading has been impressive in agro-products, as fresh-vegetable firms have moved into high value added exports. Underlying this are very high domestic capabilities to meet exacting standards, coupled with a very supportive policy framework that addresses every stage of the value chain. Success has been highly selective, however, as many smaller farms and exporters have failed to keep up with global market requirements and have exited the value chain.

Ethiopia's case suggests that the upgrading trajectory of commodity-producing countries should be viewed within a framework that goes beyond processing. Indeed, for producing countries to reap higher revenues, an appropriate strategy could be to target fast-growing, speciality-coffee niche markets in a strategy that requires moving further downstream into marketing and distribution. It would also require highly sophisticated capabilities for cultivating consumer tastes, promoting products, and managing brands and distribution networks— while taking some ideas from how the wine industry denominates its products

The experiences suggest that links to international buyers are very important. For a firm, searching buyers for its products is costly but vital if it wishes to enter a GVC. Kenya's fresh vegetable exporters and Ghana's cocoa-processing firms have been fairly successful. Their insertion into the value chains dates back many decades, and they rely on relationships that took a long time to build. This implies that building these linkages is not easy or quick. For Ethiopia's coffee exporters or Cameroon's cocoa-processing firms, for example, it is very difficult to find buyers interested in higher value added products.

Once firms are inserted into a GVC, they have to meet very demanding market requirements— price, quality and lead times. Technical standards are also crucial when the markets are Europe, the US or Japan. "Private standards" based on social and environmental sustainability apply to cocoa, coffee and tea as much as to less traditional agro-processed products.

Assistance from the firms driving these GVCs therefore becomes very important to support local upgrading. Kenya's fresh vegetable exporters and Ghana's cocoa processors receive support from their global buyers in technical and non-technical areas, yet this is the exception rather than the rule. Other exporters operate at arm's length, which is particularly problematic

Regional and domestic markets offer opportunities for value-added products.

when they have to meet private standards that are becoming general-market rather than niche-market requirements. By becoming general requirements, these standards do not attract a price premium, but still create compliance costs.

A key finding of these case studies is that regional and domestic markets offer opportunities for value-added products. Nigerian cocoa-processing firms have found regional and domestic markets for confectionaries and beverages. Cameroon's chocolate manufacturers and Ethiopian roasted-coffee firms supply domestic retailers. Being inserted into regional value chains therefore offers the opportunity to build firms' capabilities in final-product manufacturing, marketing (including brand management) and distribution. This is particularly important for countries that (unlike Nigeria for chocolate and Ethiopia for coffee) do not have large domestic markets. Indeed, an illustrative example is provided by Ghana's intermediate cocoa producers that struggle to enter regional markets, because these markets demand final products—they are also seeing stiffer competition from Asia, which could be problematic if this trend curtails opportunities for African agro-processing industries.

High domestic firm capabilities and a supportive policy environment are essential in upgrading. A large domestic market is not always necessary, as seen with Kenya's fresh vegetable exporters. What is critical is that the competitiveness of the natural resource sector affects possibilities of developing forward linkages.[2]

Indeed, supply chain bottlenecks for local commodities are hampering the competitiveness of Africa's processing industries. The opportunity for processing firms to position themselves in quality-driven GVCs is constrained by the low quality of coffee or cocoa beans and poor post-harvest practices (such as cold chains, handling and transport) in Cameroon, Ethiopia and Nigeria, and by poor fresh vegetable farming practices in Kenya. High quality attracts a price premium in Ghana and Nigeria.

The regulatory frameworks therefore play an important role, and the demise of marketing boards has led to quality problems in most countries. But even in the few countries that retained institutional control over the commodity sectors (Ethiopia and Ghana) quality problems persist, particularly in Ethiopia, where such control discourages buyer–supplier links from upgrading growers' capabilities. Such links have proved to be important between cocoa growers and processing firms in Ghana and Nigeria, and between farmers and tea and fresh vegetable exporters in Kenya. Indeed in Ethiopia, the only coffee farmers' cooperative included in the case study is managing to address quality issues primarily because it can work with growers.

Supply chain bottlenecks are not the only issue. Costly access to finance and poor infrastructure cut across all case studies, and other issues include limited access to external markets, high-cost environments, high import tariffs on inputs, shortage of skills, corruption and security. These areas affect the quality, cost competitiveness and lead times of African processing firms. The policy implications of these findings are addressed in chapter 6.

4.1 COCOA

The global value chain

A few countries in West Africa have traditionally been key global suppliers of high-quality cocoa beans (figure 4.1). Production is dominated by small farmers. In Ghana alone, 720,000 small farmers are involved in cocoa farming (Barrientos and Asenso-Okyere, 2008). From the 1980s, the cocoa sector has suffered from the twin challenges of declining world prices and deteriorating quality.

The first stems from the entry of new producing countries, especially in Asia—Malaysia, India and Indonesia—which base production around plantations as well as commercial and small farms. The second stems from the removal of national marketing boards as recommended by structural adjustment programmes, and the fact that traditional countries (Côte d'Ivoire, Cameroon and Nigeria) began exporting previously restricted inferior cocoa (Fold, 2002). Trade in poorer cocoa was facilitated by automation, allowing grinders to process cocoa beans of lower or inconsistent quality into standardized intermediate products that met the requirements of chocolate manufacturers.

FIGURE 4.1: COCOA PRODUCTION IN 2009/10 (THOUSAND METRIC TONS)

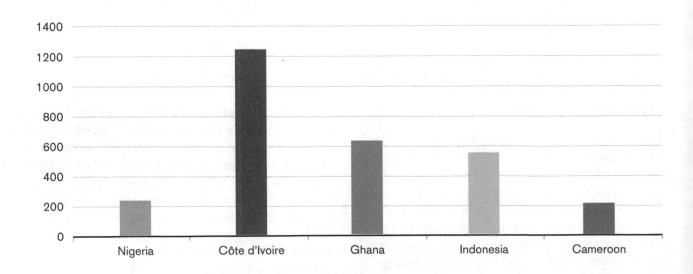

Source: ICCO (2012).

In the world market, where cocoa prices have increased (figure 4.2), the price surge has been partly influenced by political instability in the world's largest producer, Côte d'Ivoire (box 4.1).

BOX 4.1: SOFT-COMMODITY PRICE MOVEMENTS

Since 2002, world prices for agricultural commodities, including coffee, cocoa and tea, have generally grown steeply. Record oil prices have led to higher production costs, which, with environmental concerns, have led to land reallocated to biofuel production and from food commodities. World supplies have been further eroded by adverse weather conditions and declining investment, aid, research and development (R&D) and productivity in developing-country agriculture since the 1990s. At the same time, a growing middle class in China, India and other emerging markets has raised global demand for food commodities.

Lastly, the financialization of commodity markets—that is the entry of banks and other financial institutions into commodities markets and the development of a range of financial instruments, some highly volatile and short term—has increased speculative movements, allowing prices to go far beyond levels dictated by market fundamentals (FAO, 2009; Farooki and Kaplinsky, 2012).

The price increases in nominal terms for coffee, cocoa and tea have been less dramatic than for other food products (cereals, oilseeds) but also less vulnerable to the global economic downturn (FAO, 2011).

FIGURE 4.2: WORLD COCOA PRICE, JANUARY 1980–SEPTEMBER 2012($ PER METRIC TON)

Source: IMF Primary Commodity Price monthly data, retrieved from www.imf.org/external/np/res/commod/index.aspx (accessed 20 October 2012).

Processing

Broadly, there are three types of cocoa—
Forastero, Criollo and Trinitario (a hybrid of the
first two). These types have several varieties.
The Forastero variety is the most widely grown in
West Africa and Brazil. Primary processing starts
with harvesting (figure 4.3). Once cocoa beans are
extracted from fully ripened pods, they are left to
ferment for six to eight days. Next, fermented beans
are dried in sunlight or in artificial driers. Gradual
drying is preferred for preparing high-quality beans.
Great care must be taken in fermentation and
drying because any defect in these stages cannot
be subsequently rectified without affecting the
quality of the final product. The shelling nature,
colour, aroma and flavour of the dried beans
show whether they are well fermented or not.

FIGURE 4.3: COCOA–CHOCOLATE GLOBAL VALUE CHAIN

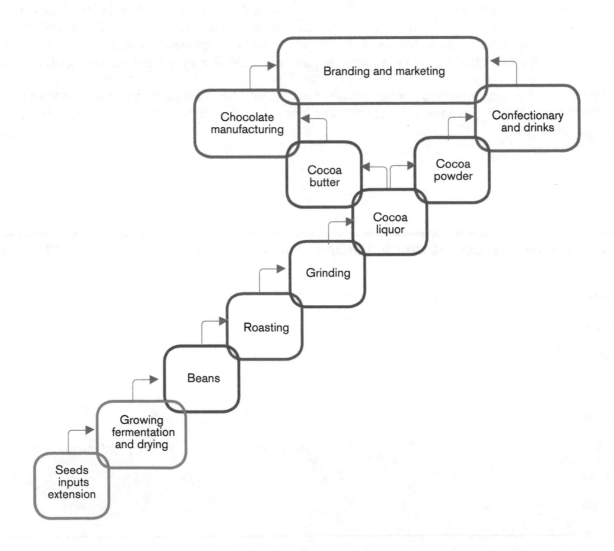

Source: ECA and AUC.

The intermediate stage of the cocoa value chain starts after the beans are cleaned and roasted, and is capital intensive. After roasting, the beans are cracked to extract the nibs. The nibs are ground between heated grindstones or disc crushers, resulting in a thick, fluid, cocoa liquor (or paste).

Cocoa liquor solidifies into hard brown blocks, lumps or tablets after cooling. In this state it can be used by confectionaries (chocolate manufacturers). However, it is normally further processed into cocoa butter (which results in a by-product called cocoa cake) and into cocoa powder (box 4.2).

BOX 4.2: COCOA BUTTER AND COCOA POWDER

Cocoa butter is one of the best-known stable fats, containing natural antioxidants that prevent rancidity and give it a storage life of two to five years. It is used in food products (white chocolate) and non-food goods (pharmaceuticals, cosmetics, soaps and lotions).

Cocoa powder, the solid product resulting from processing cocoa liquor, can be used alone (cocoa drinks) or recomposed with other ingredients (biscuits, sweets and chocolates).

Cocoa intermediate products such as cocoa paste, butter, powder and cake are easily storable and tradable, two characteristics that have made it possible to relocate processing facilities in producing countries (Talbot, 2002).

Market concentration

Two types of lead firms dominate forward linkages in the cocoa GVC: grinders and chocolate manufacturers. They control the links characterized by the highest value added and profitability: trading and marketing (Barrientos and Asenso-Okyere, 2008). Supermarkets, which account for an estimated 54 per cent of the global chocolate retail sector, are trying to appropriate a larger share of the value added by selling their own-brand products.

Increasing market concentration through mergers and acquisitions has characterized both grinders and chocolate manufacturers. Since the 2000s, a handful of grinders have dominated the intermediate stages of the cocoa GVC: Cargill, Archer Daniels Midland and Barry Callebaut. They control R&D and technologies in food processing, and bulk logistics. This has created very high knowledge and capital barriers to entry. In order to manage large logistical systems, grinders

have vertically integrated backward, relocating purchasing, grading and shipping functions to producing countries. Their purchasing arrangements vary: they deal with local traders and cooperatives in Cameroon and Côte d'Ivoire, purchase on the open market in Nigeria and buy from the marketing board in Ghana. The competitiveness of large grinders' operations has sidelined international traders and warehouses.

Chocolate manufacturing is dominated by a few European and US transnational corporations (TNCs), such as Nestlé, Mars and Ferrero (Fold, 2002). During the 1990s, these outsourced intermediate manufacturing stages, in some cases even standard chocolate production, to grinders. This enabled them to focus on their core business of product development, marketing and distribution, as well as on high value added products and markets differentiated by product quality and by social and environmental standards (Barrientos, 2011). The only exceptions are smaller manufacturers like Ferrero and Lindt & Sprüngli, which remain vertically integrated to preserve commercial secrecy and tight quality control systems.

To supply intermediate products on a just-in-time basis and to comply with national standards, grinders have invested in technological and logistical capabilities, increasing their market power along the GVC. Chocolate manufacturers nevertheless are interested in maintaining some competition in the intermediate stages of the value chain, to avoid grinders encroaching on their core businesses and profits.

FIGURE 4.4: SALIENT ELEMENTS OF THE COCOA VALUE CHAIN

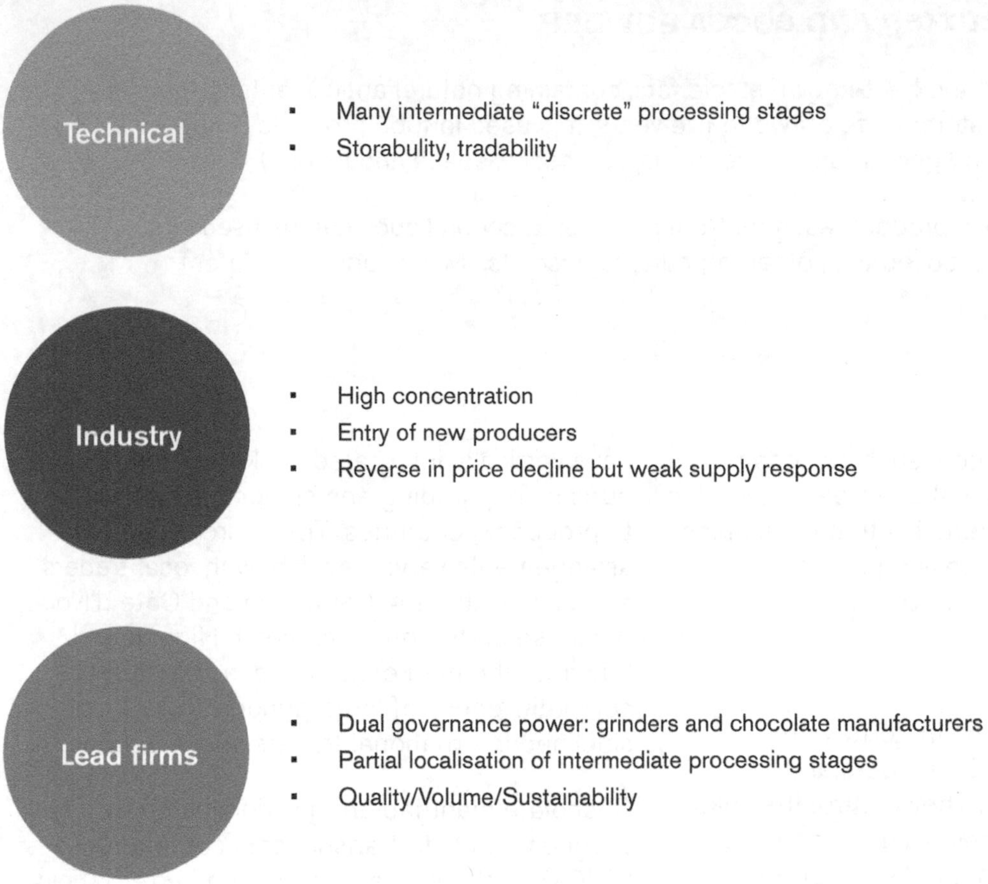

Technical
- Many intermediate "discrete" processing stages
- Storabulity, tradability

Industry
- High concentration
- Entry of new producers
- Reverse in price decline but weak supply response

Lead firms
- Dual governance power: grinders and chocolate manufacturers
- Partial localisation of intermediate processing stages
- Quality/Volume/Sustainability

Source: ECA and AUC

Challenges for producers and manufacturers

The global market for chocolate can be divided into three segments: high-volume, low-value bulk chocolate; mainstream standard-quality chocolate; and high-quality niche markets, such as single origin, Fair Trade and organic (Barrientos, 2011). Global consumption is driven by demand growth for low-value chocolate in emerging economies. Niche product markets have grown far faster than low-value and conventional product markets, although from a low base, which is why quality, diversification and brands are key for manufacturers.

Developing countries' contribution to value added in the GVC fell by half between the early 1970s and the end of the 1990s (World Bank, 2008). In Africa, producing countries are excluded from control over global logistics and marketing, and from intermediate and final product manufacturing.

Moreover, the supply response of cocoa bean production to the price surge in the 2000s has been very slow (Barrientos, 2011). This is not only attributable to long time lags (five years between planting and first harvesting) but also to low farm-gate prices over two decades, deterring farmers.

Chocolate manufacturers need to respond to the twofold challenge of increasing the volume of production, and the quality of cocoa beans. Moreover, growing consumer concern for sustainable development, has led, for example, to the Netherlands market committing to 100 per cent certified sustainable cocoa by 2025. For these reasons, chocolate manufacturers are becoming involved in initiatives with growers in producing countries. The International Cocoa Initiative brings together companies, politicians, civil society and workers to fight child trafficking and illicit labour practices. The Sustainable Trade Initiative cocoa programme brings together more than 40 per cent of the worldwide cocoa-processing industry and 30 per cent of worldwide chocolate manufacturing businesses to support sustainable production of cocoa in Brazil, Cameroon, Côte d'Ivoire, Ecuador, Ghana, Indonesia, Nigeria and Vietnam.

Processing links are weak in all three cocoa case study countries (figure 4.5). In Ghana, the largest producer by far and exporting more than $3.5 billion of cocoa, raw bean exports represent 76 per cent of the total, Nigeria 83 per cent (of $1 billion)and Cameroon 87 per cent (of almost $0.7 billion).

FIGURE 4.5: VALUE-ADDED CONTENT OF COCOA EXPORTS, GHANA, NIGERIA AND CAMEROON 2011 ($ THOUSAND)

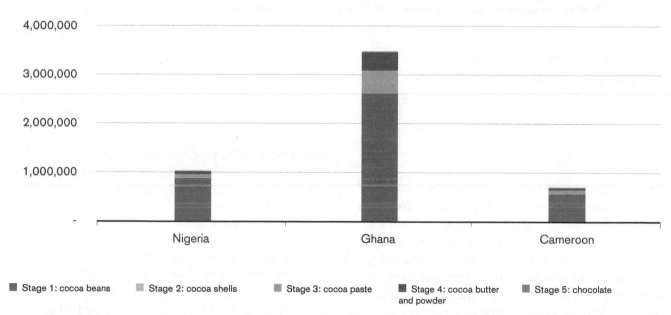

Source: ITC Trademap, retrieved from www.trademap.org/SelectionMenu.aspx (accessed 30 August 2012).

Nigeria's cocoa industry

Nigeria is the world fourth-largest cocoa producer. Cocoa has been the largest non-oil export since 2007 (figure 4.6). In 2006–2010, cocoa exports rose by 47 per cent to $822.8 million. But only about 20 per cent of the cocoa output is processed locally, with the rest exported as raw beans (Mwanma, 2011). Chocolate, however, is heavily imported into Nigeria from Europe and the US.

FIGURE 4.6: NIGERIAN FEDERAL GOVERNMENT REVENUES FROM NON-OIL EXPORTS, 2006–2010 ($ MILLION)

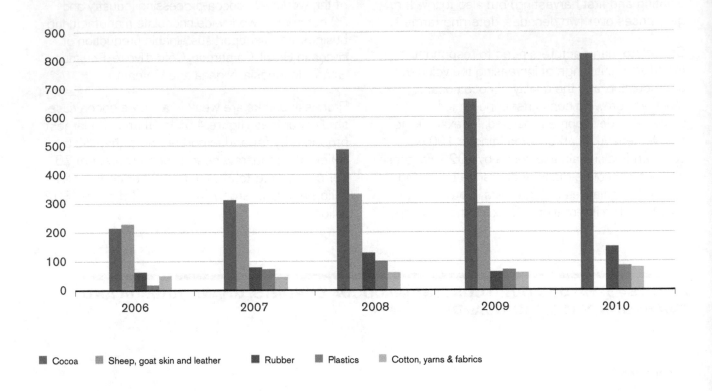

Source: Nigerian Export Promotion Council data.

Note: Sheep, goatskin and leather data are unavailable for 2010.

Background

Nigeria's cocoa-processing industry was established between the 1960s and the 1970s, with three factories set up in the south-west (Iyama, 2007). In the following decades, more factories were set up in the western states. Most processing companies, national and international, are private, and some are listed on the Nigerian Stock Exchange.[3] Processors are organized under the umbrella of the Cocoa Processors Association of Nigeria (COPAN). They are fairly important for income, with each factory employing about 200 workers and providing up to 1,000 indirect jobs.

Nigerian processing companies are involved in both intermediate and final stages of the cocoa–chocolate value chain. Companies such as Multitrex Integrated Foods Plc, Tulip Cocoa Processing Ltd and Stanmark Cocoa Processing Company Ltd

produce cocoa butter, cake, liquor and powder. TNCs such as Cadbury Plc and Nestlé produce beverages (Bournvita and Milo) and confectionaries.

Five firms' perceptions

Five medium to large processing firms were selected for this case study. Three out of the five are state owned, two of which have foreign minority ownership. Some of these companies are part of conglomerates, and directly control other subsidiaries in Nigeria. All but one are listed on the Nigerian Stock Exchange. According to information collected through face-to-face interviews in 2012, the firms' core businesses are manufacturing intermediate products, confectionaries and beverages, and trading cocoa and other agro-products.

Europe represents the bulk of their export market, absorbing as much as 97 per cent of one company's output. New export markets are China, India and North America. Major buyers include local and international traders, wholesalers and retailers. Two firms producing beverages and confectionaries export 35–55 per cent of their output to regional markets, highlighting that regional markets open opportunities for higher value added products, unlike developed-country markets where TNCs tightly control the final stages of the cocoa GVC.

The five firms were asked to rate the weight attached by their buyers to six market parameters, or critical success factors (CSFs), on a Likert scale of 1 to 10 (10 being very important, 1

unimportant),[4] which are represented on radar charts.

According to the firms, key critical success factors are good quality, trust and lead times (figure 4.7). Different markets have different expectations of price and quality. Domestic markets are easier to supply because of low trade barriers, but foreign markets offer a price premium for high-quality cocoa. Relations with buyers tend to be at arm's length—when cocoa-processing firms fail to meet CSFs, foreign buyers do not assist them but rather sanction them by excluding them from the supply chain.

FIGURE 4.7: BUYERS' CRITICAL SUCCESS FACTORS IN NIGERIA'S COCOA INDUSTRY

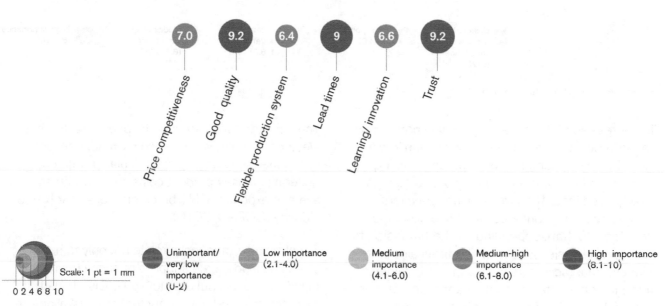

Source: Interviews with five processing firms, 2012.

The cocoa-processing firms identify opportunities for upgrading by moving further up the cocoa–chocolate value chain (by producing ready-to-drink chocolate, for example, but they need to resolve challenges first) and diversifying horizontally (by producing such products as palm kernel oil, palm kernel cake, sesame, cotton, cashew and ginger).

Consistent with their own international buyers, cocoa-processing firms place heavy emphasis on good quality, trust and lead times when dealing with their suppliers (figure 4.8). Again, price

competitiveness is not the most important CSF. Based on their experience, firms rated local suppliers as underperforming compared with foreign suppliers. Preference for foreign suppliers over local suppliers was more marked in trust and in learning/innovation. (The firms noted some improvement in suppliers' capability in price competitiveness and quality.)

Supplier performance is very important for the firms' competitiveness. Over time, Nigeria's weak extension services have resulted in poor quality of cocoa bean supplies.

FIGURE 4.8: RATING OF LOCAL AND FOREIGN SUPPLIERS RELATIVE TO LEAD-FIRM EXPECTATIONS IN NIGERIA'S COCOA-PROCESSING INDUSTRY

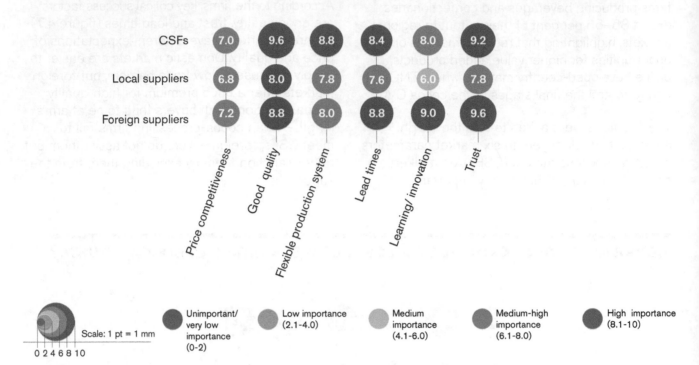

Source: Interviews with five processing firms, 2012.

To address some of these supply chain bottlenecks, cocoa-processing firms often assist suppliers to meet technical standards by imparting training on farming best practices and by providing high-quality seedlings. The firms monitor suppliers' compliance with standards, and have allocated from 2 to 30 staff, depending on the firm's size, to monitor and assist suppliers. The firms also work with external facilitators such as the Sustainable Trade Initiative, International Finance Corporation and United States Agency for International Development (USAID) in training, finance and input support services.

Other constraints affect the cocoa-processing industry (figure 4.9). Access to finance is marginally the worst. A medium-sized factory requires about 3 billion in capital to operate profitably, plus working capital to purchase thousands of tons of beans. Borrowing costs are as high as 20–23 per cent a year for working capital. At the same time, capacity utilization is low, which makes it difficult to absorb fixed operating costs. The capital market therefore discourages investment in value-added activities for both new and existing firms.

The industry is also affected by poor infrastructure—electricity supply, water, telecoms, road/transport networks—and security. In particular, private energy generation raises product costs steeply, with an average expense of N1 billion on fuel a year by the industry (COPAN, 2010).

Supply chain bottlenecks relate not only to high costs and inadequate supplies of cocoa beans to local factories, but also to high costs of spare parts for imported machinery that are unavailable in Nigeria (COPAN, 2010).

Access to external markets is problematic because of tariff escalation (see Factors in linkage development, chapter 3). Under the EU tariff regime, raw cocoa beans are duty free. But as Nigeria has not signed an Economic Partnership Agreement with the EU, the country cannot benefit from trade preference margins of 4.2 per cent for cocoa butter and 6.1 per cent for liquor/cake, which loses the processing industry about $30 million a year. The impact of the tariff structure on value-added products is compounded by the cost difference between processing companies, which have high overheads and labour costs, and cocoa bean traders.

FIGURE 4.9: RATING OF FACTORS AFFECTING LINKAGE DEVELOPMENT IN NIGERIA'S COCOA INDUSTRY

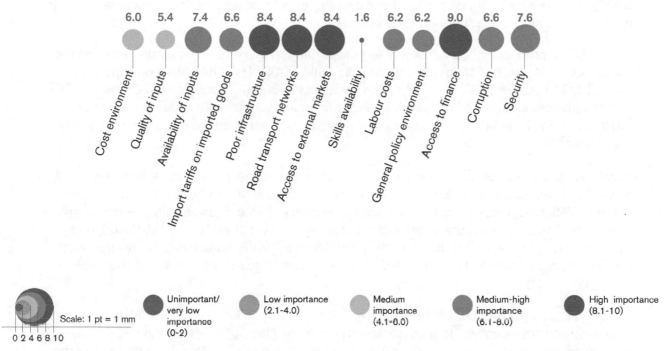

Source: Interviews with five processing firms, 2012.

Nigeria does not have an industrial policy for cocoa processing, but provides incentives for manufacturers and processors in general, the most important of which for cocoa exporters is the Export Expansion Grant (EEG).[5] Given that cocoa-processing firms are involved in exporting, they are entitled to these incentives.

The EEG is the most relevant for forward linkages to the cocoa sector. An employment quota for processing firms to be eligible for EEG is another indirect incentive to increase local skills. The EEG has encouraged cocoa-exporting companies to embark on forward integration and undertake heavy investment in plant and machinery, although implementation is often problematic. Surveyed firms noted cumbersome application procedures and delays in processing and paying grants: the 2008/09 EEG, for example, had yet to be disbursed in 2012, and COPAN in 2009 had

to petition the federal government to urgently release EEG funds as firms faced a liquidity crisis. Similarly, equipment and spare parts are meant to be free of import duty under the New Manufacture in Bond Scheme but cocoa-processing firms are almost always forced to pay duty. They are too vulnerable to argue for duty-free treatment when importing because they need the inputs urgently, and any clearance delays would invariably cause them production losses.

One of the severest constraints for developing forward linkages is that, while the processing stages of the cocoa value chain have incentives, cocoa bean production has none. The deregulation of the domestic cocoa market in the 1990s, in the absence of an overall sector strategy, have created problems for cocoa bean quality and incentives to value addition. Policy synergy is essential for the success of linkage industries (box 4.3).

BOX 4.3: AGRICULTURAL, INDUSTRIAL AND TRADE POLICIES WORKING TOGETHER FOR MALAYSIA'S PALM OIL INDUSTRY

Malaysia is the world's largest producer and exporter of palm oil. The industry's success rests on a range of agricultural, industrial and trade policies.

In the 1970s, production of palm oil was expanded through a resettlement programme and the conversion of plantations from rubber to oil palm (Fold, 2002). Palm oil cultivation expanded from 55,000 hectares in 1960 to 3.4 million hectares in 2000 (Kjöllerström and Dallto, 2007). The government established regulatory agencies in areas such as quality control and contract registration, and invested in R&D in agricultural productivity, value-added industries and quality improvements.

Local capital, sometimes in joint ventures with Indian and Japanese companies, invested in milling and refining industries, which became increasingly competitive in developing countries' export markets. With time, these companies became more concentrated and vertically integrated, and state capital became more prominent in plantations and milling operations (Fold, 2002). A key role was played by the export duty system which from the 1960s systematically favoured local processing into semi-processed oil products, final consumer goods and advanced chemical products.

In later years, as palm oil became a traditional industry, Malaysia targeted diversification into new industries and set incentives to produce and export cocoa (Talbot, 2002). By the mid-1990s, it had become the world's largest cocoa butter exporter, before slipping to second place after the Netherlands.

Nigeria lacks an industrial skills training programme for cocoa processing. The state makes little effort to orient public activities in infrastructure, R&D or human capital development for industrial development and value addition in this industry. Cocoa-processing firms themselves, however, invest in workers' training and education programmes, enabling them to maintain good manufacturing practices and obtain international certification.

Ghana's cocoa industry

Ghana is the world's second-largest cocoa producer, and cocoa is the country's second-biggest foreign exchange earner (after gold), accounting for 23 per cent of merchandise export earnings in 2011—the industry generated around $3.5 billion in export earnings, as the world market price gained by about 81 per cent over the previous half decade. Cocoa provides a livelihood for over 700,000 farmers, mainly in the south. The crop also accounted for 5 per cent of government revenues in 2005, through export taxes. In 2010, Ghana's strong receipts from trade taxes were mainly due to cocoa export revenues (ISSER, 2011). Cocoa was also one of the major drivers of Ghana's economic growth, increasing its share of GDP from 2.5 per cent in 2008 to 3.6 per cent in 2011.

The proportion of cocoa exports processed domestically has doubled from about 12.4 per cent in 2007 to 25.6 per cent (226,200 metric tons) in 2011. This suggests strong growth prospects for the industry as it moves up the value chain.

Role of the Ghana Cocoa Board

Unlike many other producing countries, Ghana in the 1990s did not dismantle its cocoa marketing body, the Ghana Cocoa Board (COCOBOD). While allowing private, registered buyers to control domestic marketing, Ghana retains government control over exports and, critically, over grading and quality assurance. Quality control in particular is exercised along the whole value chain in the country (figure 4.10). Ghana's cocoa beans have high fat content and rich flavour, owing partly to careful fermentation and drying processes by farmers.

The Cocoa Research Institute (an arm of COCOBOD) is responsible for research into pests and diseases; it also introduces control measures. In 2001, the Cocoa National Disease and Pest Control Committee was established to develop strategies to control capsid and blackpod through a nationally coordinated spraying programme. Under this, COCOBOD, through a network of regional offices, sprayedall cocoa fields at no cost to producers, containing the threat. Under the Cocoa Hi-technology programme, which began in 2002/03, farmers were supplied with packages of fungicides, pesticides and fertilizers to help increase their yields.

Because of its ability to guarantee higher-quality beans, COCOBOD provides more stable prices for Ghanaian producers by selling a large share of its production directly on forward markets. It also secures a price premium of around $200–250 a metric ton. COCOBOD sets pan-seasonal and pan-territorial producer prices in advance of the harvest (Fold, 2002), moves supported by the lead buyer in the value chain, Cadbury, which has sourced cocoa from Ghana for over a century. Its demand for single-origin, quality-certified cocoa means that the company has an interest in COCOBOD retaining full responsibility for quality control of all production stages.

Although quality remains high, Ghana suffers from structural constraints to productivity growth owing to an ageing farming population, poor extension services and weak infrastructure (Barrientos, 2011). In 2008, Cadbury launched the Cocoa Partnership with a view to working with stakeholders to promote sustainable livelihoods. As part of this effort, Cadbury converts some of its lead products into Fair Trade, to pass to Ghanaian producers a minimum guaranteed price and a price premium. Nestlé adopted a similar approach in 2009.

Four firms' perceptions

The cocoa-processing firms selected for Ghana's case study are a publicly owned company established in 1965, and three locally owned, recently established private companies. They employ 100–277 workers each, skilled and unskilled equally. These firms are positioned at different stages of the value chain. One firm is involved in roasting, grinding and packaging, and exports cocoa liquor. The remaining firms are further downstream, in pulverizing activities, and producing cocoa butter and powder.

The four firms export mainly to European buyers. Their main competition comes from large grinders in Ghana—Barry Callebaut and Cargill in Tema, and Archer Daniels Midland in Kumasi—and several local exporters. The only firm producing higher value added products directs 10 per cent of its output to domestic and regional markets, which are, however, difficult to supply, as they demand finished products (European buyers want intermediate products).

For the firms, quality, price and trust are the highest CSFs set by their buyers (figure 4.11). Buyers ensure high-quality supplies from their Ghanaian cocoa-processing suppliers by building trust-based relationships, which provide a premium for quality and assist in firms' upgrading. The market also has requirements, including national technical regulations: Japanese buyers are quality driven, Israeli buyers require Kosher certification, and so forth.

Linkages to buyers support these firms in various ways: European buyers buy forward, helping the firms to plan properly; Egyptian buyers supply them with labels to ensure compliance with their corporate and government standards. Buyers also assist firms by recommending materials and equipment and sometimes by providing technical support.

FIGURE 4.10: GHANA'S COCOA VALUE CHAIN

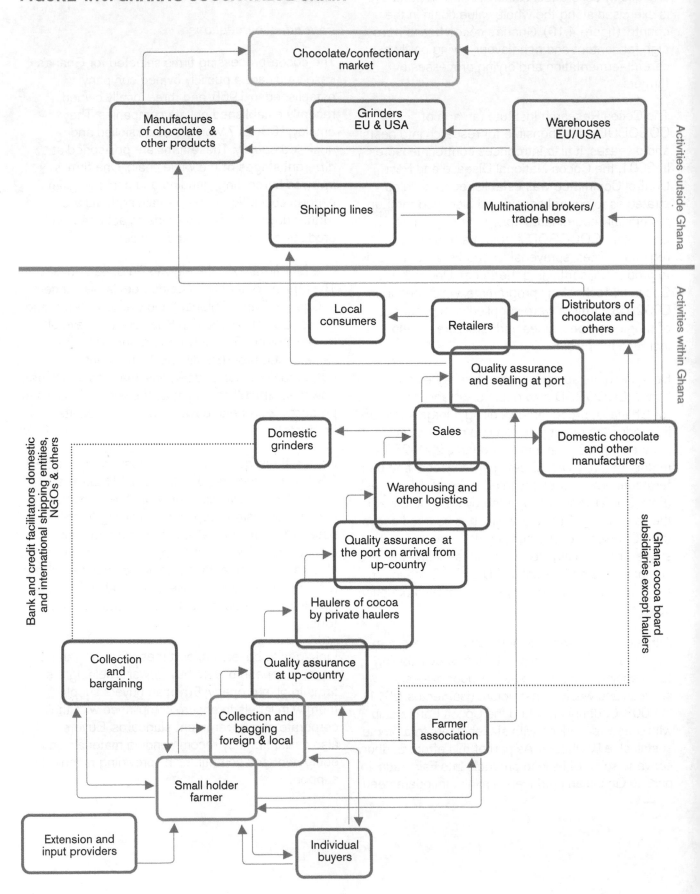

Source: ECA and AUC

FIGURE 4.11: BUYERS' CRITICAL SUCCESS FACTORS IN GHANA'S COCOA INDUSTRY

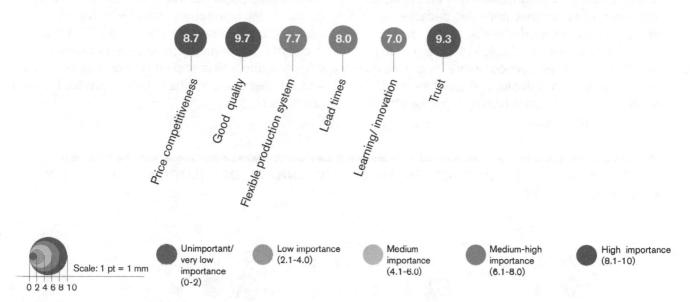

Source: Interviews with four processing firms, 2012.

The CSFs set by international buyers are passed down the value chain to cocoa bean suppliers. Quality, trust, price, learning/innovation and lead times are very important market requirements for local suppliers (figure 4.12). Cocoa-processing firms feel that foreign suppliers are more competitive than local ones, particularly on quality and trust.

FIGURE 4.12: RATING OF LOCAL AND FOREIGN SUPPLIERS RELATIVE TO LEAD-FIRM EXPECTATIONS IN GHANA'S COCOA INDUSTRY

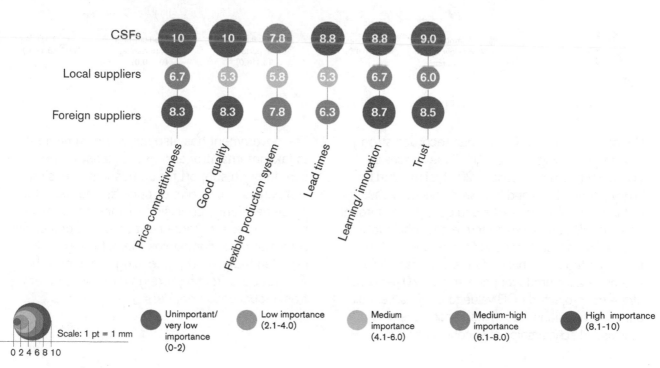

Source: Interviews with five processing firms, 2012.

Local suppliers face serious constraints in capital, skills and entrepreneurship. Poor infrastructure and unreliable electricity make it very hard to adopt just-in-time procurement strategies, because deliveries are delayed, down-time costs are high, and communication is difficult. In their relationship with suppliers, however, cocoa-processing firms go beyond monitoring activities, and assist them with quality and delivery times, helping to improve the suppliers' capabilities.

All the surveyed cocoa-processing firms identify upgrading opportunities for moving into higher value added products than their current output— cocoa butter, powder and liquor—as well as manufacturing chocolate and drinks. That move is constrained primarily by access to capital, infrastructure, costs and corruption (figure 4.13). Another key issue is small market size for finished products.

FIGURE 4.13: RATING OF FACTORS AFFECTING LINKAGE DEVELOPMENT IN GHANA'S COCOA INDUSTRY

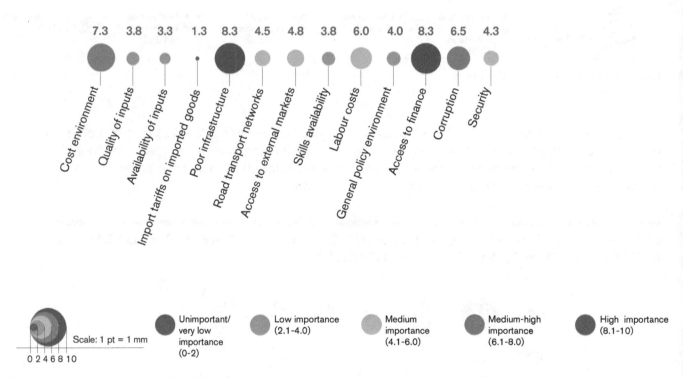

Source: Interviews with four processing firms, 2012.

Cocoa production in Ghana has recorded strong growth, increasing from 340,600 metric tons in 2001/02 to 1 million tons in 2011, stimulated by policy interventions and high world prices. Measures include controlling diseases and pests (often through COCOBOD), encouraging farmers to rehabilitate and replant old and moribund farms, and applying fertilizer. Steps to enhance farmers' welfare include a remunerative producer price at least 70 per cent of the net projected FOB value to farmers; periodic bonuses; a national health insurance scheme and clinics; and scholarships at secondary school.

The government has also made a commitment to take internal processing to at least 40 per cent through support for domestic processing companies in the form of price discounts, extended credit payment, permission to import essential machinery, and enforcement of export processing zone status for companies there. Surveyed firms reported that export processing zones have been well set up, attracting foreign direct investment from global cocoa grinders.

Cameroon's cocoa industry

The bulk of Cameroon's cocoa is exported as raw beans: in 2011 only 28,397 metric tons of the total 218,702 metric tons of cocoa was locally processed (according to the Office National du Café et du Cacao, the regulatory body)—a mere 13 per cent. In 2007–2011, less than 8 per cent was transformed locally (figure 4.14). Despite the authorities' interest in and efforts to promote local processing, integration between agriculture and the industry remains dismal.

FIGURE 4.14: CAMEROON'S VALUE-ADDED CONTENT OF COCOA EXPORT VOLUME, 2007–2011 (%)

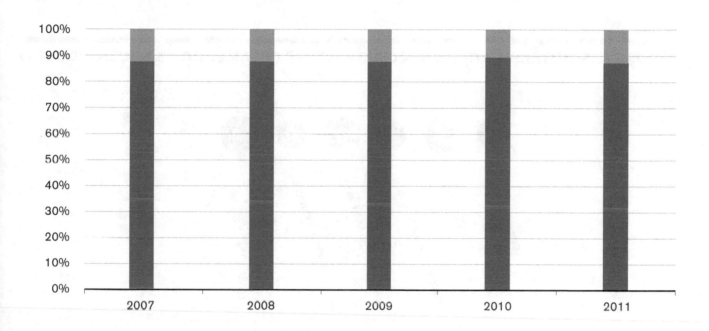

■ Processed cocoa　■ Unprocessed cocoa

Source: Office National du Café et du Cacao, 2012. http://www.freeyengo.com/services/food-amp-dinning-in-cameroon/office-national-du-cacao-et-du-cafeonce-331.htm, accessed 30 September 2012.

The processing industry is controlled by a handful of foreign and domestic companies, most of them in intermediate-product manufacturing, which has been largely dominated by Société Industrielle des Cacaos (SIC Cacaos) since it was set up in 1949. Under majority Swiss ownership (and minority public participation) the company has a processing throughput of 30,000 metric tons a year and employs around 100 workers. The firm now faces competition from other smaller domestic processing companies, employing 20–30 workers. New investment in Mbalmayo, in the centre of the country, has targeted cocoa processing, and is exporting mainly to China.

Finished cocoa products have also been dominated by one firm for several decades— Chococam, the country's sole processor. It has nearly 60 per cent of the domestic chocolate market, and exports to regional markets. But this company, too, now faces stiff competition, this time from Asia, whose finished products have an increasing share in domestic and subregional markets.

Three firms' perceptions

The case study on Cameroon cocoa-processing industry covered SIC Cacaos and two of its smaller competitors. SIC Cacaos is linked to the GVC dominated by European and US chocolate manufacturers, which absorb 95 per cent of its production.

The two domestic competitors target wholesalers in Asia, particularly China, and wholesalers and retailers in the domestic market. Both have experienced substantial sales growth.

For the Asian market, quality, trust and lead times are CSFs for the three firms. The domestic market is less demanding, allowing them to move further downstream into chocolate manufacturing. But they find it very hard to enter industrial-country GVCs because of high entry barriers related to standards and price. Trust, lead times, quality and price emerge as the key CSFs for the firms (figure 4.15).

FIGURE 4.15: BUYERS' CRITICAL SUCCESS FACTORS IN CAMEROON'S COCOA INDUSTRY

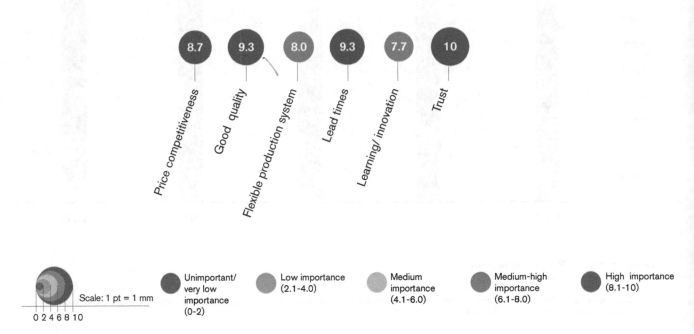

Source: Interviews with three processing firms, 2012.

The highest-ranked CSFs applied by cocoa-processing firms to their suppliers are trust, lead times, quality, flexibility, price and innovation (figure 4.16). Local suppliers underperform in two critical areas—quality and price.

The government has a strategy to revive production of major cash crops. In 2006, the Société de Développement du Cacao embarked on a vast cocoa-seedling production and distribution programme. The aim was to distribute 6 million seedlings yearly to set up 5,000 hectares of modern cocoa plantations. Surplus production stemming from these new plantations was intended to reach 50,000 metric tons by 2020. However, structural problems of access to capital, skills and infrastructure, in particular electricity, remain and have prevented cocoa growers from becoming competitive.

Growers' poor practices in cocoa-bean harvesting and drying, aggravated by poor road conditions, cause large losses of supplies and late deliveries for processors. Firms often organize awareness campaigns and workshops to train growers on best harvesting and drying practices. Some have introduced bonuses to encourage farmers to produce higher-quality beans.

The three firms show little interest in moving into higher value added activities, mainly because

FIGURE 4.16: RATING OF LOCAL AND FOREIGN SUPPLIERS RELATIVE TO LEAD-FIRM EXPECTATIONS IN CAMEROON'S COCOA INDUSTRY

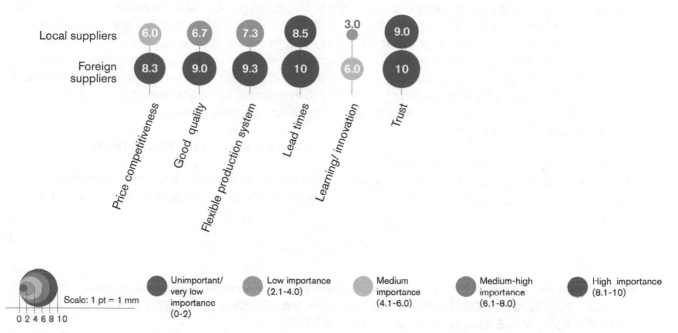

Source: Interviews with five processing firms, 2012.

of supply chain bottlenecks. SIC Cacaos has produced the same semi-finished products for several years, although the two smaller firms are diversifying into detergent, potash and biogas, and cocoa by-products (alkaloid used in wine production). Any upgrading strategy is constrained by access to skills, external markets and infrastructure (figure 4.17).

FIGURE 4.17 RATING OF FACTORS AFFECTING LINKAGE DEVELOPMENT IN CAMEROON'S COCOA INDUSTRY

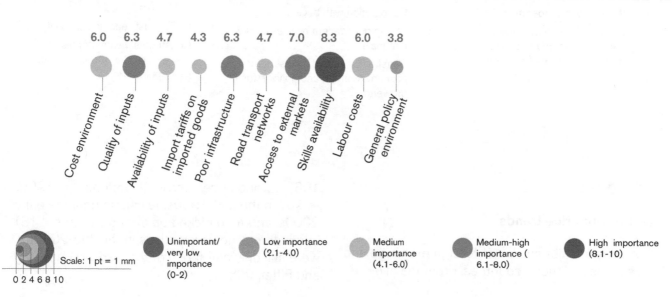

Source: Interviews with three processing firms, 2012.

Cameroon has no linkage development strategy for cocoa. The government has developed a Support Programme for the Creation and Development of Small and Medium-sized Enterprises in processing and preserving local products of mass consumption. But according to the surveyed firms, such government support has been largely ineffective. The challenge for the Cameroon policy framework lies mainly in institutional arrangements, with too many ministries, bodies and laws involved in developing small and medium-sized enterprises.

Implementation capacity is also low, and red tape is a drawback in applying laws and regulations, and in accessing finance under government schemes

(one of the companies has been waiting for financing for nearly three years). As a result, local processing activities receive very little support to expand capacity and raise their value added. This is particularly problematic because, unlike Ghana and Nigeria, Cameroon has not seen investment in its processing capabilities from international or domestic companies. Given the weakness of domestic processing, government support is critical if Cameroon is to attract investment and build domestic competitiveness.

A three-country cocoa comparison

The cocoa value chains and linkage development of the three countries are summarized in table 4.1

TABLE 4.1: SUMMARY COMPARISON OF COCOA VALUE CHAINS AND LINKAGE DEVELOPMENT: NIGERIA, GHANA AND CAMEROON

Nigeria	Ghana	Cameroon
Forward integration into final and intermediate GVC stages	*Growing forward integration into intermediate stages of the GVC*	*Static—no upgrading and no linkage development*
• Domestic/foreign capital • Intermediate/final products • Regional markets • CSFs: quality, lead times, trust • Weak buyer cooperation • Constraints: raw materials, capital, infrastructure, EU trade regime and horizontal policies for processors	• Domestic/foreign capital • Intermediate products • EU buyers • CSFs: quality, price, trust • Cooperation with buyers • Strong government policies on raw materials • Constraints: capital, infrastructure, cost environment and policies for growers	• Domestic/foreign capital • One chocolate manufacturer vs. Asian competition • Intermediate products • EU buyers • CSFs: trust, lead times, quality • Constraints: raw materials, skills, markets, cost environment and weak policies

4.2 COFFEE

Long-term price trends

Coffee is a major source of foreign exchange and jobs in many African countries. From the mid-

1980s, world prices declined, bottomed in 1992, spiked in the mid-1990s, fell again until the early 2000s, and then picked up strongly (figure 4.18). In real terms, however, prices in the mid-2000s were still only half those of the 1960s (Kaplinsky and Fitter, 2004).

FIGURE 4.18: COFFEE COMPOSITE INDICATOR PRICE OF THE INTERNATIONAL COFFEE ORGANIZATION, 1980–2011(US CENTS/LB)

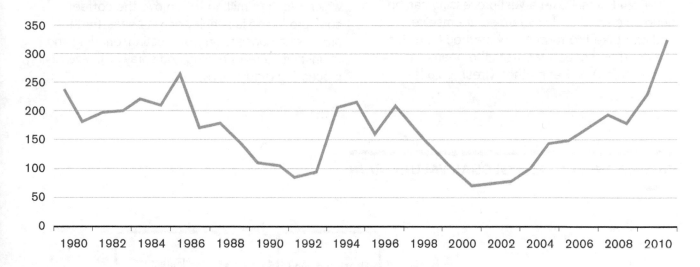

Source: UNCTADStat, retrieved from http://unctadstat.unctad.org/ReportFolders/reportFolders.aspx(accessed 20 October 2012).

Several factors underlay the declining price trend. A major factor was the end of International Coffee Agreements, which, until the 1980s, enabled producing countries to support and stabilize world prices through quota arrangements (Ponte, 2002b; Talbot, 1997b).The entry of Vietnam as a large producer of low-quality Robusta coffee contributed to an oversupply in the 1990s.

As part of structural adjustment programmes, most coffee marketing boards were dismantled, which led to higher shares of domestic income accruing to growers, but also to higher exposure to price volatility. This coincided with the substantial withdrawal of the state from extension and quality control services. As

a result, while export volumes generally increased, quality generally suffered. In Africa, institutional reforms varied widely. Whereas Uganda's liberalized market, for example, made it a large supplier of quite low-quality coffee in the 1980s and 1990s, Kenya's restrictive export regulations helped it to maintain its reputation as a supplier of fine, albeit inconsistent, coffee (Ponte, 2002a).

Coffee prices have risen strongly since the early 2000s (see figure 4.18), following agricultural commodities. They have been affected by poor harvests of high-grade Arabica producers (box 4.4), such as Brazil and Colombia, combined with sustained demand in emerging markets.

BOX 4.4: COFFEE QUALITIES

The International Coffee Organization classifies coffee as follows, by price: Mild Arabica (Colombia, Kenya, Tanzania), Brazilian Naturals, or Hard Arabica (Brazil, Ethiopia), and Robustas (Vietnam, Côte d'Ivoire, Uganda).

Some African countries are important global suppliers of specific coffees. Côte d'Ivoire and Uganda are high-volume suppliers of Robusta, and Ethiopia and Kenya are high-quality suppliers of Arabica.

Sources: Petit, 2007; Ponte, 2002a.

The global value chain

After harvesting, coffee beans need to be processed within 24 hours. Post-harvest processing can be done on a small scale by farmers themselves and can take the form of dry method (cherries are dried and separated from the beans by threshing) or wet method (fresh pulp is mechanically separated from the beans, and beans are fermented, rinsed and dried). Both dry and wet methods produce parchment coffee, which requires milling to remove the coffee coat, producing less bulky green beans. Further processing consists only of roasting/grinding and, for instant coffee, brewing and spray or freeze-drying processing (figure 4.19).

FIGURE 4.19: COFFEE GLOBAL VALUE CHAIN

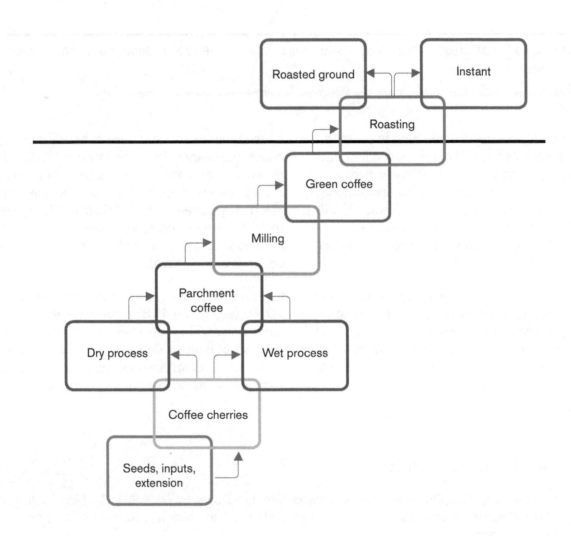

Source: ECA and AUC.

Market concentration

The demise of international and national institutional frameworks has made private firms lead players in the coffee GVC. Forward linkages are controlled by a few international traders, roasters and retailers, which during the 1990s acquired high market concentration.

Roasters are the key drivers of the GVC (Ponte, 2002b). They set the market parameters for growers, processors and domestic traders in producing countries, and for international traders. Retailing is controlled by supermarkets, but roasters command the larger profit margins. Rather than pursuing vertical integration, roasters focus on their core business: product development, R&D and marketing. In order to shed non-core activities and overheads, they have moved to supplier-managed inventory, which requires international traders to manage stocks of varying volumes, quality and origin to be supplied just in time, which has induced international traders to integrate backward into coffee-producing countries. Liberalized coffee marketing in these countries has encouraged the process, and many capital-starved domestic traders have been partly or entirely acquired by international traders.

The power of roasters has been reinforced by innovations in coffee-processing technology (Ponte, 2002b). New washing techniques enable them to blend different varieties of coffee to create a certain flavour, increasing roasters' flexibility in their sourcing strategies, reducing their dependence on specific sources and qualities, minimizing the risk of shortages and price variations, and enhancing their ability to combine supplies of varying qualities and prices (Kaplinsky and Fitter, 2004). This has weakened producers' bargaining over prices and volumes.

Coffee bar chains, such as Starbucks, have become major value chain players, revolutionizing coffee retailing (Ponte, 2002b). These retail points sell a "coffee experience" rather than just coffee, marketing coffee as a "positioning good" so that consumers pay not only for good coffee, but for the ambience and social cachet granted by being seen to drink coffee at these places. At these outlets, coffee represents less than 4 per cent of the final retail price.

Coffee demand is income elastic in that growing disposable income is associated with higher coffee consumption, but when income levels are high, it stabilizes (Ponte, 2002b). To counteract potential slumps in demand and respond to growing health, environmental and social concerns among consumers, roasters and retailers have cultivated fast-growing niche markets and created, for example, speciality, Fair Trade, organic and environmentally friendly coffees. A major retailer in the UK offered up to 96 varieties of coffee in the early 2000s (Kaplinsky and Fitter, 2004). Indeed, coffee has much potential for differentiation, and this is reflected in the price variance: in the UK market at that time, prices for 100 grams of roasted coffee varied from $0.86 for basic products to $2.40 for high-end espresso quality, to $3.30 for single-origin coffee (Kaplinsky and Fitter, 2004). Roasters and retailers are also cultivating emerging markets such as China to tap into rising income groups.

Market concentration in forward linkages has led not only to higher entry barriers for new entrants but also to unequal distribution of income between producing and consuming countries (Kaplinsky, 2004). Until the mid-2000s, while coffee growers in producing countries saw their farm gate prices collapse, retailers in consuming countries faced fairly stable revenues. Roasters and retailers may well control, respectively, up to 30 per cent and 20 per cent of total value added in the coffee GVC (Kaplinsky and Fitter, 2004).

In producing countries, declining world coffee prices in the 1990s and 2000s hurt coffee growers' income, and through that, exacerbated rural poverty, prompting calls for global interventions by, for example, re-establishing international quantitative restrictions among producing countries. This approach is complicated by its reliance on coordination among major world producers and is embedded in fraught political and economic negotiations. Another approach is generally considered more feasible because it is formulated nationally—local upgrading to increase income levels, if not shares in the GVC.

Coffee-producing countries can follow essentially two types of upgrading strategy: process and product, and functional. The first aims to produce higher-quality coffee or different types of coffee (Fair Trade, organic) in order to lift growers' prices. In other words, producing countries maximize the revenues associated with their current position in the GVC. The second aims to move beyond green bean exports, by acquiring processing, marketing and distribution capabilities that involve not only growers, but also food manufacturers and service providers.

Process and product upgrading

For roasters, quality consistency represents a key market parameter, because inconsistency forces them to adjust processing equipment and procedures (Fold and Ponte, 2008). Hence, they value consistency as much as quality. The final quality of coffee depends as much on bean types as on farming practices and primary processing (drying, washing and storage). Process upgrading therefore requires investment in extension services to farmers, capacity building for processing, transport and storage, and domestic quality control systems. Process and product upgrading underlies some companies' success in catering to the top end market, as they focus on growing practices, bean selection, handling and transport, roasting and packing (Kaplinsky and Fitter, 2004). There is ample room for African countries to develop upgrading strategies for farming and harvesting links because these links present low technological barriers to entry.

Product differentiation enables producing countries to target fast-growing niche markets, but presents some challenges as its economic benefits are not always clear-cut, and it often raises entry barriers for smallholders (box 4.5).

BOX 4.5: PRODUCT DIFFERENTIATION IN THE COFFEE GVC

Speciality coffee, in particular single-origin coffee, offers important opportunities to raise growers' revenues. For example, Jamaican Blue Mountain coffee has often sold at five times the world coffee price at some point, and has not been vulnerable to world price fluctuations (Kaplinsky and Fitter, 2004). Moving into speciality coffees requires producing countries to invest at both production and at marketing stages. The latter includes building consumer awareness on coffee quality, promoting a product image in consuming countries, and seizing the opportunity of geographical indication marks, as with wine producers (Ponte, 2002b).

For Fair Trade, organic and environmentally friendly coffee, the benefits are less straightforward. First, not all these niche markets offer market premiums. While Fair Trade enables growers to secure higher economic returns, the premiums on organic and environmental certification are more flexible, often set by market (and non-market) factors (Ponte, 2002c; Muradian and Pelupessy, 2005). Even Fair Trade coffee is hampered by inconsistent quality and excessively high prices.

Second, certification costs can throw up significant entry barriers for African producers in particular, given the proliferation of certification schemes that often differ by country and retailer, offsetting price premiums.

Third, some certifications such as Rainforest Alliance are so widespread in mainstream retailing that they are becoming "order qualifying" rather than "order winning" market requirements—a necessary, but not sufficient, condition—leading to higher production costs for coffee growers without commensurate economic benefits.

Functional upgrading

The coffee value chain offers two different opportunities in functional upgrading—roasted coffee and instant coffee.

Roasted coffee usually needs to be processed near a consumption point to preserve its flavour, which explains why international trade has traditionally taken place in green bean form. Vacuum packing enables it to preserve the flavour for a slightly longer period, but also increases transport costs (Roemer, 1979).That would also require producing companies to supply within a very short delivery time, and have access to inputs and knowledge to blend different coffee types suitable for packed roasted coffee.

Global roasters have a key competitive advantage in processed coffee products for several reasons: they can blend beans sourced from suppliers around the globe to meet their quality and price specifications, have manufacturing capabilities near the consumption point, control multiple brands and have excellent access to distribution networks.

The instant coffee value chain, however, presents issues for upgrading (box 4.6), suggesting that the opportunities for functional upgrading in speciality roasted coffee could be greater.

BOX 4.6: FUNCTIONAL UPGRADING IN THE INSTANT COFFEE GVC

Instant coffee was introduced during World War II in the US, and usually accounts for around 20 per cent of the world market by value.

This value chain is controlled by global roasters with strong market presence in both traditional and emerging markets. Similarly to the roasted ground-coffee market, global roasters differentiate their products by developing new blends and brands. Further, they have also expanded their product range by introducing coffee granules and freeze-dried coffee. The strategy's success is confirmed by large price premiums for high-quality and speciality instant coffee (Kaplinsky and Fitter, 2004).

After the war, some Latin American countries tried to move into processing and exporting instant coffee (Talbot, 1997a). These efforts were fairly successful and were usually supported by governments through financial incentives, access to lower-quality coffee beans and marketing.

Moving into instant coffee production has not, though, always translated into a revenue leap from exporting green beans (Talbot, 2002). This is because Latin American instant coffee manufacturers sold mainly in bulk to global TNCs that marketed it under their own brands. In other words, while successful in developing a manufacturing base, these countries did not secure a larger share of the overall revenues in the instant coffee GVC. Only when exporting under their own brands to emerging markets have they achieved higher profit margins.

In Africa, domestic and regional markets are very small, apart from countries where coffee consumption is part of the culture, like Ethiopia and Eritrea, or is associated with rising incomes, like South Africa. International markets therefore remain crucial, and targeting them requires access to high-quality beans (single-origin, for example) and competing with the global roasters that control brands for niche markets. Two proposals to enter the high-value coffee market at the roasted stage include deepening the level of processing of Fair Trade coffee, and moving into non-household distribution through speciality coffee bars (Muradian and Pelupessy, 2005).

Ethiopia's coffee industry

Coffee, Ethiopia's largest export, accounts for 10 per cent of GDP. Coffee production involves 1.3 million small farmers, but with dependants and employees in ancillary industries supports an estimated 15 million people (Petit, 2007).

In the 1990s, the institutional framework was partly liberalized. Private and growers' cooperatives now participate in primary processing and domestic marketing. However, vertical integration is limited and export marketing is controlled by the Ethiopian Commodity Exchange (ECX), a government body responsible for auctioning coffee. The ECX aims to retain high standards for Ethiopia's coffee, and ensures that consignments from different regions are kept separate to preserve their distinct flavours.

Since 2001, cooperative firms and some private companies have been allowed to export directly, bypassing the domestic marketing system, which nevertheless controls 80 per cent of coffee production. Coffee consignments that do not meet export standards are directed to the large domestic market, which absorbs 40 per cent of domestic coffee output. Ethiopia is the only coffee-producing country other than Brazil with a large domestic market.

Firms' perceptions

Coffee processing and exporting are very competitive, with around 200–250 firms involved. The case study covers 4 processing and exporting firms established after the 1990s' reforms. All firms are Ethiopian owned, although one of them operates in partnership with a TNC. Firm size is in the range of $4 million–8 million turnover. Firms purchase coffee beans from the ECX, apart from a cooperative of coffee growers with $46 million turnover. After receiving their beans from the ECX, exporting firms

wash, cap, sort and grade, and make logistical arrangements. Some are involved in roasting, a more labour-intensive stage. Employment consists mainly of unskilled casual workers.

Coffee-exporting firms sell 85–95 per cent of their output to international traders. For some firms, traditional markets are still prominent: the EU (60–95 per cent of total sales), where demand is growing, and to a lesser extent the US (20 per cent) and Japan (5–10 per cent), a declining market. Other firms have more differentiated markets: the Middle East, the Republic of Korea, Australia, New Zealand and South Africa. The export markets are segmented by speciality and undifferentiated coffee.

Except for the Middle East, these markets are very demanding in terms of trust, quality, price competitiveness and lead times (figure 4.20). International competition is stiff, as Ethiopian exporters are running against high-quality coffee from Brazil and Colombia. Surveyed firms report that buyers assist them to some extent with capability to monitor quality and grade coffee beans.

Coffee-exporting firms are willing to invest in developing in-house roasting capabilities, but buyers are not generally interested in semi-processed products, as it would encroach on the core business of the final industrial user, the global grinders. Coffee-exporting firms also contemplate expanding their market size and branching into new products.

At the domestic level, the challenges to local processing capabilities are twofold (figure 4.21). Access to inputs is problematic: some are unavailable, and firms would, for example, need to invest in in-house packaging if they were to export packed, roasted coffee. Also, the quality of raw materials is low. Nor is the government framework supportive: high taxes, lack of skilled labour and, to a lesser extent, corruption make it hard for firms to invest in processing facilities.

FIGURE 4.20: BUYERS' CRITICAL SUCCESS FACTORS IN ETHIOPIA'S COFFEE INDUSTRY

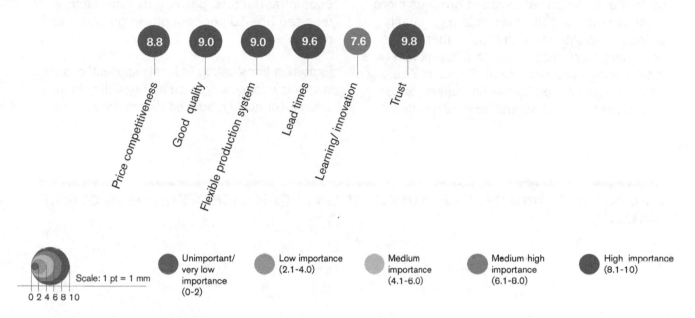

Source: Interviews with four processing and exporting firms, 2012.

FIGURE 4.21: RATING OF FACTORS AFFECTING LINKAGE DEVELOPMENT IN ETHIOPIA'S COFFEE INDUSTRY

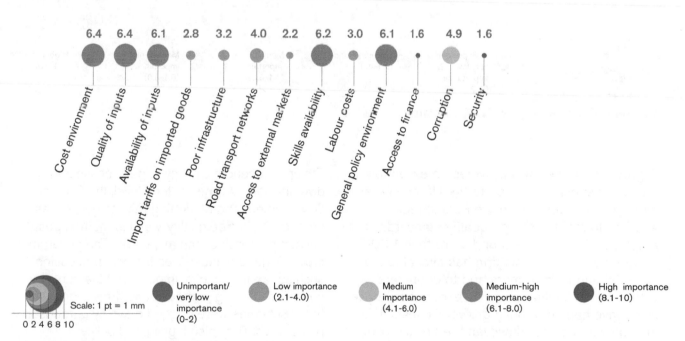

Source: Interviews with processing and exporting firms, 2012.

Exporting firms rate quality of supplies a key challenge, and are concerned at the capacity of ECX to improve the quality of beans supplied by farmers. The current system provides more incentives for fast turnover than high-quality output, although one firm argues that ECX is becoming more responsive to this problem (and is technologically advanced). But as the quality of beans is determined by the timing and handling of beans at harvesting and post-harvesting stages, and as the exporters do not work directly with farmers, they cannot assist local farmers to upgrade their capabilities. Other issues include poor infrastructure, power cuts (one factory reported 35–40 per cent power outages) and poor telecoms.

Exporting firms' rating of local suppliers' capability is very low for quality, price and flexibility to match volumes or quality required (figure 4.22).

FIGURE 4.22: RATING OF LOCAL SUPPLIERS ' PERFORMANCE IN ETHIOPIA'S COFFEE INDUSTRY

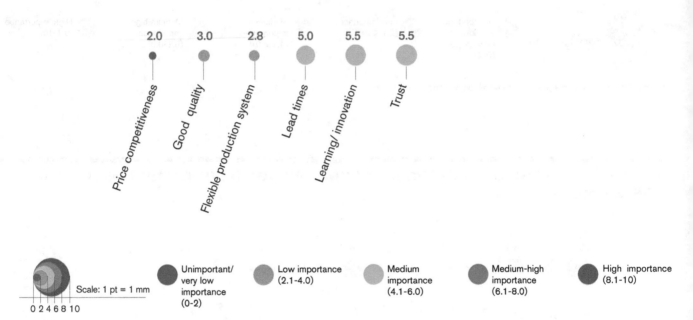

Source: Interviews with processing and exporting firms, 2012.

A growers' cooperative provides an exception. It exports speciality coffee to the US and other high-income countries in the Pacific region, and has to meet very high quality standards. It employs 113 permanent and more than 1,000 temporary workers. This firm has allocated staff to assist and train farmers and to cooperate with external facilitators. In its experience, these links have helped to build growers' capabilities in quality and costs. However, the firm's growth potential is constrained by lack of capital and weak government support.

Ethiopia's economic policy largely focuses on diversification. At the sectoral level, the Coffee Development and Marketing Plan targets farms' productivity, coffee quality, washed method post-harvest processing, and marketing. The government provides general incentives for local processing, such as tax-free capital imports, but the surveyed coffee processing and exporting firms found that these schemes were bogged down by burdensome procedures. They also highlighted policy inconsistency and scarce government willingness to cooperate with the private sector.

4.3 TEA

The global value chain

World tea prices were on a declining trend until the mid-2000s because of production expansion and productivity increases (Fold and Larsen, 2011; Ganewatta et al., 2005), but thereafter followed the general price surge of agricultural commodities (figure 4.23).

Tea requires processing within a fairly short time of harvesting. Processing into green tea (a small part of the market only) is quite easy, as tea leaves are heated, then rolled or twisted, and finally dried. Black tea requires more complex processing: tea leaves are withered (or partly dried), and rolled up or cut, fermented, dried and eventually sorted by size (figure 4.24). This processing can be done through traditional processes for higher-quality loose teas, or through cut, tear and curl for bulk teas for tea bags. The result is packet tea or tea bags.

FIGURE 4.23: WORLD TEA PRICE, MOMBASA AUCTION PRICE, JANUARY 1980– SEPTEMBER 2012 (US CENTS/KG)

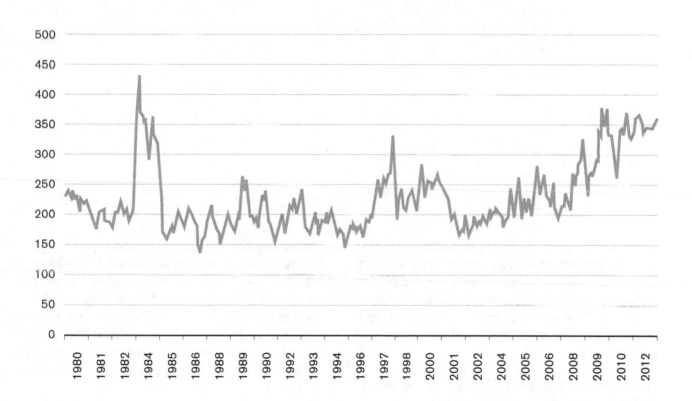

Source: IMF Primary Commodity Price monthly data, retrieved from www.imf.org/external/np/res/commod/index.aspx(accessed 18 October 2012).

Note: From July 1998, Kenya auctions, Best Pekoe Fannings. Before that: London auctions, CIF UK warehouses.

FIGURE 4.24: TEA GLOBAL VALUE CHAIN

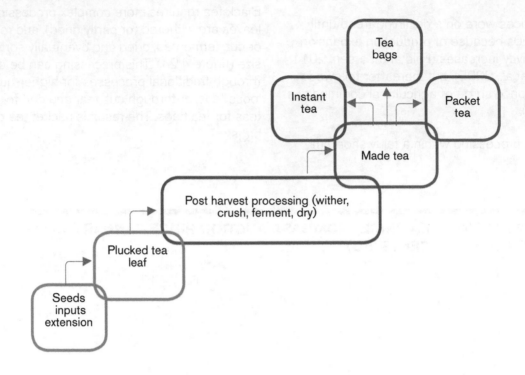

Source: ECA and AUC.

Additional value can be added by packaging into smaller, branded retail packages, or packing into tea bags, instant tea and ready-to-drink beverages. The highest growth potential is in niche markets such as organic, flavoured or green teas. Teas marketed as products with high health benefits have been particularly successful.

TNCs such as Unilever and Tetley (now owned by Tata Tea; box 4.7) dominate marketing and distribution networks in consumer markets. Three companies control more than 80 per cent of the world market (World Bank, 2008). Unlike coffee and cocoa, tea TNCs are often vertically integrated and extend upstream into tea farming, partly because tea is frequently produced on large plantations (Kenya's small production an exception). The relative capital and scale intensity required by post-harvest

processing also favours integrated companies. Similar to coffee and cocoa, however, the same tea TNCs have been under increasing pressure to comply with social sustainability standards (Fold and Larsen, 2011). The 1997 Ethical Tea Initiative brought together some of the largest TNCs in an effort to source from only approved tea producers in Kenya, Malawi, Tanzania, Zimbabwe and Asian countries.

In 2010, the world's largest exporter was Kenya, which ranked third in global tea production (10 per cent). Other African producers, together accounting for 15 per cent of world output, were in descending order Rwanda, Zimbabwe, Malawi and Tanzania. China and India accounted for 34 per cent and 25 per cent of global production, mainly for their domestic markets (table 4.2).

BOX 4.7: AN EXAMPLE OF GRADUAL UPGRADING IN DOMESTIC, REGIONAL AND GLOBAL MARKETS

After independence, India extended its control over tea production and marketing by relocating tea auction centres to the country and partly shifting plantation ownership to Indian companies (Talbot, 2002). Tata Tea started as a joint venture with a British plantation, but was later under total control of the Tata Group. After investing in tea production, the company soon moved into packaging and instant tea manufacturing. Tata consolidated its presence in the domestic market and exported to ex-communist countries and regional markets, as well as expanding production into Sri Lanka.

In the 1990s, Tata Tea partnered with UK-based Tetley to manufacture tea bags for export and domestic consumption, which allowed it to absorb sophisticated production and marketing techniques. With the acquisition in 2002 of Tetley, Tata acquired a global brand name—number one in sales in the UK and Canada, and number two in the US—making it one of the lead firms in the tea GVC.

TABLE 4.2: GLOBAL TEA PRODUCTION, CONSUMPTION AND EXPORTS BY COUNTRY, 2006–2010

	2006		2007		2008		2009		2010	
	Quantity (million kg)	Growth (%)	Quantity (million kg)	Growth (%)	Quantity (million kg)	Growth (%)	Quantity (million kg)	Growth (%)	Quantity (million kg)	Growth (%)
Production										
China	1,028	10	1,166	13	1,200	3	1,359	13	1,475	9
India	956	1	945	-1	981	4	979	-0.2	966	-1
Kenya	312	-5	370	19	346	-6	314	-9	399	27
SriLanka	311	-2	305	-2	319	5	290	-9	331	14
Indonesia	140	-10	150	7	137	-9	136	-1	129	-5
Others	833	-4	860	3	882	3	854	3	862	1
Total	3,580	4	3,796	6	3,865	2	3,932	2	4,162	6
Consumption										
World	3,491	4	3,611	3	3,717	3	3,824	3	3,980	4
Surplus										
World	89	-6	185	108	148	20	108	27	182	69
Exports										
Kenya	314	-10	344	10	383	11	342	-11	441	29
SriLanka	315	6	294	-7	297	1	280	-6	298	6
China	287	0.3	289	1	297	3	303	2	302	0
India	215	14	175	-19	200	14	195	-3	183	-6
Argentina	75	7	79	5	81	3	72	-11	106	47
Indonesia	95	-7	84	-12	96	14	92	-4	97	5
Others	277	-29	313	13	299	-4	296	-1	301	2
Total	1,578	2	1,578	0	1,653	5	1,580	-4	1,728	9

Source: Tea Board of Kenya: Annual Report 2010-2011; International Tea Committee, Annual Bulletin of Statistics, 2011 (http://www.inttea.com/publications.asp).

Note: Growth is relative to the previous year.

Kenya's tea industry

Tea has been produced on a commercial scale in Kenya for nearly 90 years. After independence, the tea strategy focused on smallholder production rather than forward linkages (Talbot, 2002).Today the sector is the largest source of foreign exchange. In 2011, almost 60 per cent of total production of 377,900 metric tons was controlled by smallholder growers (Republic of Kenya, 2012). They process and market tea through their own management body, Kenya Tea Development Agency. The sector has also attracted TNCs such as Unilever Tea (UK–Netherlands), James Finlay (UK), Williamson's Tea (UK) and Eastern Produce, Kenya (UK).

Kenya has a fairly well-developed agro-processing industry, with strong backward linkages to the agricultural sector (UNDP, 2005). These industries range from processing staple foods and fruits to producing beverages, vegetables, tea and coffee, and tobacco for the domestic and foreign markets. Most tea is exported in bulk form.

The four tea companies selected for Kenya's case study were established in the 1960s to 1980s. Formerly state-owned Kenya Tea Development Authority (KTDA) became a private company—and the largest tea firm—in 2000, and has a cooperative structure. Other tea companies interviewed are locally or East African owned, or are subsidiaries of TNCs. These subsidiaries are the main source of competition for the tea companies. All the surveyed firms are vertically integrated and grow, grade, process, blend and export tea. They import their machinery, and use local brokers and warehouses for marketing and storage. The sector is labour intensive, and each firm employs 4,200–5,700 workers. Processing is a more capital-intensive stage, and uses imported automated blending and packing equipment.

The export market is highly diversified. Supermarkets such as Tesco, Marks & Spencer and Sainsbury from the UK, and Albert Heijn from the Netherlands, are key buyers. Tea demand from the UK and the rest of Europe has been increasing, and Kenya's tea exporters have well established procedures to comply with their standards, and perceive pricing to be fair. Europe is by no means the only market, though: exports have diversified to China, India, the Middle East and North America. The domestic market takes 10–30 per cent of sales, and the regional market up to 20 per cent. Because exports are in bulk, the only variations in market requirements for exporters are quality and standards for the EU. The domestic market is easier to supply because quality is standardized and there are no trade barriers.

Firms' perceptions

The CSFs set by buyers are led by quality and price competitiveness (figure 4.25). Buyer–supplier cooperation is limited to information exchange, although some buyers send technical teams to assist exporters. KTDA operates at arm's length from its buyers.

Tea companies identify their upgrading opportunities in value-added products such as tea extracts, flavoured teas, instant tea and ready-to-drink beverages. Some firms also want to diversify into timber, flowers, nuts and vegetables. One firm is moving to tea products that follow sustainable farming practices. Import tariffs on inputs, access to inputs (in particular land), access to finance, and taxes raise production costs; poor infrastructure, fluctuating electricity prices and availability, and poor telecoms hamper tight supplier–buyer linkages (figure 4.26).

FIGURE 4.25: BUYERS' CRITICAL SUCCESS FACTORS IN KENYA'S TEA INDUSTRY

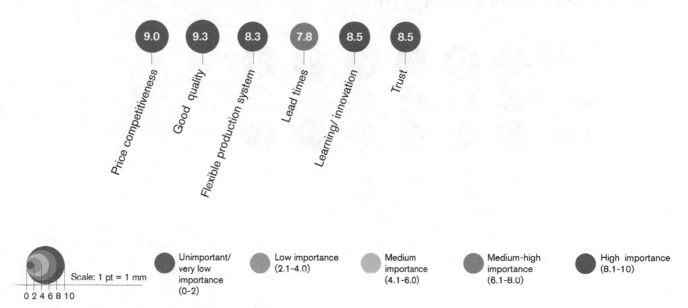

Source: Interviews with four processing firms, 2012.

FIGURE 4.26 RATING OF FACTORS AFFECTING LINKAGE DEVELOPMENT IN KENYA'S TEA INDUSTRY

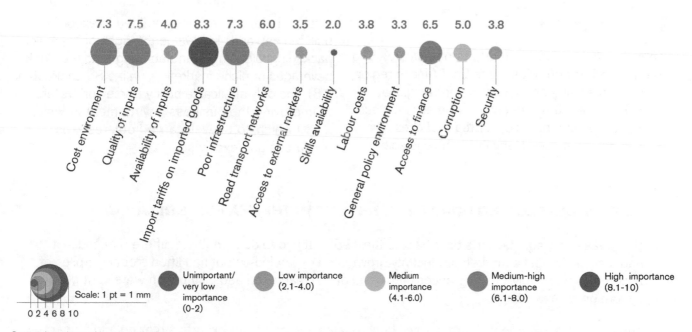

Source: Interviews with processing firms, 2012.

In addition, the supply chain has bottlenecks. Tea companies set demanding CSFs for their suppliers (figure 4.27), but local suppliers perform less well than foreign suppliers, particularly on lead times and learning/innovation, largely owing to poor infrastructure and weak skills (per the tea companies). Some firms provide farm workers with inputs and technical services (allocating staff) and, KTDA particularly, cooperate with top growers in Kenya.

FIGURE 4.27: RATING OF LOCAL AND FOREIGN SUPPLIERS RELATIVE TO LEAD FIRMS' EXPECTATIONS KENYA'S TEA INDUSTRY

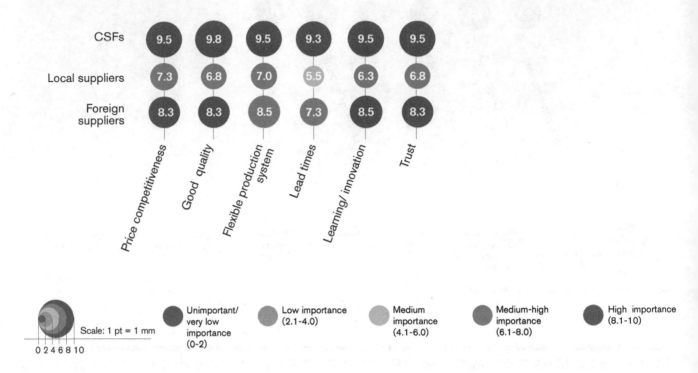

Source: Interviews with processing firms, 2012.

Limited linkage development

Kenya's auction centres market domestic tea and tea from other countries in the East African region, adding some value and facilitating intraregional trade. However, Kenya does not have an ambitious linkage development policy for tea (but does for fresh vegetables—see Kenya's fresh vegetable industry below). It remains confined to exporting bulk tea and adds little value through, for example, packaging, blending, manufacturing ready-to-drink beverages or niche marketing, unlike Sri Lanka (box 4.8). The only applicable policy framework refers to improving the business environment in Vision 2030 which, to be well carried out, requires resources and expertise.

BOX 4.8: DEVELOPING FORWARD LINKAGES IN THE TEA GVC, SRI LANKA

Sri Lanka's upgrading efforts date back to the 1980s. It had to do something different because it had a small domestic market; productivity growth and expanded output had lifted global supplies of bulk tea considerably, pushing prices down; and global marketing and distribution were controlled by foreign companies.

The Export Development Board granted duty rebates and grants for exporters moving into higher value added tea products. In the early 1990s, Sri Lanka privatized its state plantations, most of which stayed controlled by domestic companies, some receiving foreign direct investment from Tata India (Talbot, 2002). The state encouraged forward integration, and set up a domestic auction centre.

Established in 1991, the Tea Board of Sri Lanka supported exporters moving up the value chain by giving tax-free incentives based on the previous year's incremental export value of teabags and tea packets, and by paying part of the interest on loans for capital investment in processing plants (Ganewattaet al., 2005). The Tea Promotion Bureau promoted tea in export markets and provided grants to firms exporting value-added products under national brands.

By value in 2011, Sri Lanka exported almost half its tea in value-added form and almost 3 per cent as speciality tea (green value-added tea). In short, the country has developed a high-quality export sector. Kenya, in contrast, exported almost its entire tea production in bulk form (box table).

BOX TABLE: COMPOSITION OF TEA EXPORTS FROM SRI LANKA AND KENYA, 2011 (%)

	Black tea in bulk	Black tea in value-added form	Green tea in value-added form	Green tea in value-added form
Sri Lanka	50.41	46.46	2.86	2.86
Kenya	98.98	0.12	0.05	0.05

Sources: Ganewattaet al., 2005;Talbot, 2002; ITC Trademap, retrieved from www.trademap.org/SelectionMenu.aspx (accessed 30 August 2012).

4.4 AGRO-PRODUCTS

The global value chain

Agro-processing is one of the most developed manufacturing sectors in Africa, and most countries are involved to varying degrees.

This subsection focuses on fresh—and processed—fruits and vegetables. Both offer export opportunities for African producers. Some countries have already inserted themselves into fresh-produce GVCs, such as Kenya (the case-study country), Egypt, South Africa, Zambia and Zimbabwe.

Dominance of supermarkets

Africa's fresh and processed fruit and vegetable exports have traditionally gone to Europe. Supermarkets continue to play a driving role in such value chains. In the 1990s, consolidation among EU retailers led to a few large supermarkets controlling most countries (with a few exceptions such as Italy and Spain). In the UK, for example, four supermarkets have three quarters of the multiple grocery market (Barrientos and Asenso-Okyere, 2008).

EU supermarkets compete on product differentiation, advertising, investment in retail outlets and supply chain logistics (Dolan and Humphrey, 2000). Fresh fruits and vegetables are products of key strategic importance, first because supermarkets can easily sell under their own label, and second because fresh produce, with meat and wine, are determining factors in consumer choice of where to shop (Fold and Larsen, 2011). The key requirements for supermarkets are quality, consistency, variety and reliability of supplies (Dolan and Humphrey, 2000).

Much attention has focused on the role of regulatory barriers in accessing industrialized countries' GVCs for food products. Their retailers, importers and manufacturers must comply with strict food safety regulations, sanitary and phytosanitary measures, and technical regulations set nationally, regionally and globally. The UK 1990 Food and Safety Act, for example, imposes strict traceability requirements on retailers.

Supermarkets have developed firm-specific private standards to differentiate their products (Ouma, 2010). They have codes of conduct for suppliers that allow them to develop "credence goods" that meet consumers' concern for social and environmental sustainability. Some standards have become public, such as GlobalGap (formerly EuroGap), a private standard that is now a minimum requirement for the EU market.

To monitor suppliers' compliance, supermarkets, importers and exporters have set up systems of monitoring and auditing of farming practices (pesticide and fertilizer use, spraying, personal hygiene, etc.) and post-harvest practices (cold chain, handling, transport and the like).

For African smallholders it has become harder to stay in supermarket-driven value chains (Ouma, 2010), although they still find market access to lower-quality market segments driven by traditional wholesalers and catering companies. These markets are significant, though declining, in the North, but are large in Eastern Europe, Russia, Latin America and Asia, which are fast-growing importers of fruits and vegetables (Fold and Larsen, 2011). China's impact is twofold: it is becoming a large importer of fruits, but is also a major exporter of agro-processed products.

Traditionally, emerging economies have been characterized by lower requirements for quality and certification than Northern markets (Fold and Larsen, 2011). However, supermarkets from Europe and North America have expanded their market share in these economies' retail sectors, including Carrefour (France) and Walmart (US) in China and Metro (Germany) in Russia. Often they carry with them their supply chains: Walmart sources avocado, pears and grapes from Mexico and citrus fruits from South Africa for China. This trend could see higher market requirements applied to emerging economies too, including Africa.

In the value chain for fresh and processed fruits, TNCs play a major role, working alongside and in competition with supermarkets (Fold and Larsen, 2011). Branded manufacturers, such as Del Monte and Chiquita, are vertically integrated operations and focus on lowering costs and increasing margins by targeting new countries as a source of produce and as markets, and by increasing economies of scale. Supermarkets, in contrast, aim to retail a growing share of fresh and processed fruit under their own label. By doing so, they diversify their supply sources and increase profit margins.

Upgrading opportunities

All these trends offer African agro-processing industries upgrading opportunities. Local industries can add value by deepening processing activities (washing or chopping), combining products (mixed washed, peeled, and chopped vegetables, ready for cooking) and packaging (for speciality products; Dolan and Humphrey, 2000). These new products are important for supermarkets and branded manufacturers because they allow them to reformat traditional products in high-income markets (Fold and Larsen, 2011). Many retailers in Europe have favoured relocating processing to Africa because it reduces labour costs, reduces wastage and increases the value-to-volume ratio.

For fruit-processing firms in Africa, the challenge is as much about increasing competitiveness (intra-firm and in the production chain) and introducing new products as moving up the value chain (Kaplan and Kaplinsky, 1999). Movement to control global brands and access retail sectors is particularly difficult.

Another set of opportunities is linked to market differentiation. Emerging markets in Asia and Central and Eastern Europe, as well as domestic and regional markets, offer the opportunity for African agro-processing industries to supply products that meet different price and quality specifications, and to move into higher value added products. In particular, regional value chains feeding into regional African markets can play an important interim guidance role for firms as companies seek to meet the requirements of US and European consumer markets. Local firms can test their products in less demanding regional markets, establish brand names and make the changes to shift to another level.

Opportunities for regional value chains are increasing for three main reasons. The rapid economic growth of many African countries based on the commodities boom has expanded the number of middle- and high-income consumers, shifting consumption patterns and personal tastes to processed food and beverages.

In addition, the expansion of South African retail and supermarket chains into the rest of the continent is creating shelf space for these consumers to satisfy their new tastes. The supermarkets in South Africa already import processed and packaged fresh and semi-processed food from elsewhere in Southern Africa. As they move into East and West Africa they will be seeking new local sources of supply.

Finally, global retail chains are increasingly casting their eyes on African markets as a potential place to sell their wares: witness the entry of Walmart to South Africa, part of its strategy to launch into other African markets. African governments and regional trade groupings have ample opportunity to encourage local sourcing when these global players enter Africa.

Kenya's fresh vegetable industry

Until the 1960s, Kenya's fruit and vegetable industry had slow growth and was, in the main, domestically oriented. In 1967 the government established the Horticultural Crops Development Authority to expand the horticultural subsector (defined as production of fruits, vegetables and flowers), which in the following decades developed fairly free from government oversight. It has quite easy entry conditions for agribusiness enterprises, easy access to land, effective technological transfer and well-developed marketing linkages to European distributors and retailers. Today, horticulture is a major contributor to foreign exchange and employment.

Kenya's horticultural subsector employs around 4.5 million people countrywide directly in production, processing and marketing, and another 3.5 million people benefit indirectly through trade and other activities (Republic of Kenya, 2010). Cabbages, spinach, tomatoes, onions, chillies, pepper, carrots, French beans and Asian vegetables (karella, duhdi, brinjals) are some of the vegetables produced (ReSAKSS-ECA, 2010).

Opportunities for regional value chains are increasing for three main reasons. The rapid economic growth of many African countries based on the commodities boom has expanded the number of middle- and high-income consumers, shifting consumption patterns and personal tastes to processed food and beverages.

Smallholder farmers account for 70 per cent of horticultural output, but fewer than 20 per cent of them are involved in vegetable exports—75 per cent of that market is controlled by a few, large exporters (Basboga et al., 2010; Wiersinga and de Jager, 2007). This concentration of farming and exporting links reflects the organization required to meet quality standards, capital investment for post-harvest processing, and logistical capacity to supply goods just in time (Dolan and Humphrey, 2000).

The leading destinations for Kenya's horticultural exports were recently the UK (54 per cent), France (15 per cent) and Holland (11 per cent); (HCDA, 2009). Some companies have integrated with freight forwarding companies and with importing agencies in the UK, including Home grown (which accounts for 15 per cent of Kenyan horticulture exports) and Finlays Horticulture, both based in that country. Large exporters source fresh vegetables from their own farms, and their product lines are broader than small exporters. Their logistics are supported by a "pack house" next to the airport and their economies of scale help them to secure airfreight space. Home grown, for example, formed a joint venture with MK Airlines, which has a daily evening flight to the UK, ensuring reliable and timely deliveries and shipping-cost reductions (Dolan et al., 1999).

Firms' perceptions

The four companies exporting fresh vegetables in Kenya's case study were established between the 1970s and the 1980s. They are locally owned, large operations, in some cases subsidiaries of bigger groups. They have experienced strong growth in the past few years: in 2005–2011, one firm's turnover rose from $60 million to $210 million, another's from just more than $10 million to $23 million. These firms are labour intensive, with a high proportion of female workers. In one firm, of 3,300 employees, two thirds are women. Workers have received training in areas such as food safety.

Most Kenyan vegetable firms have moved to higher value added products, such as ready-to-eat foods. Firms are involved in processing the raw materials, packaging, labelling, cold storage and exporting. Most are vertically integrated with farming, but also source from outgrowers. Some have to import supplies, such as packaging material from the UK because it meets EU technical regulations. Packaging and preprinted labels/bags are one area where local firms have expressed a desire to outsource to local suppliers.

The main export markets are UK supermarkets such as Tesco, Marks & Spencer, Sainsbury and Albert Heijn of the Netherlands. Kenyan companies compete with exporters from Egypt, South Africa and Zimbabwe. Some have diversified a little into other European markets and the US, and the Middle East and East Asia are also becoming more important. Firms exported 25–40 per cent of their output to non-UK markets.

Domestic sales are low, at less than 5 per cent of output, although one firm sells 20 per cent to domestic retailers and is planning to expand this market. Diversification forces exporters to meet markets' different requirements: EU markets have strict food safety regulations, but private standards are less relevant than in the UK; exporting to Middle Eastern markets is competitive because of lower freight costs; and domestic markets have lower quality requirements.

Most UK and other European buyers have supported relocation of processing to Kenya because of strong local capabilities to meet exacting market requirements.

Indeed, buyers' have demanding requirements for Kenyan firms (figure 4.28). They expect firms to supply just-in-time, high-quality products that meet volume and product specifications with very short lead times on the basis of consumption patterns. Thus buyer–supplier cooperation aimed at compliance with private and public standards is intense, in the form of information exchange and technical teams visiting exporters' premises, although not all firms benefit from these efforts.

Proliferating private standards are a serious challenge for Kenyan exporters, which have to face up 15 different standards, such as GlobalGap, Tesco's Nature Choice, Marks &Spencer's Field to Fork and Fair Trade (Ouma, 2010). The introduction of GlobalGap alone has increased monitoring costs for exporters by 30–40 per cent, causing a restructuring of the supply chain that consolidated the supply base to exclude smaller exporters and growers and that increased linkages among farmers, exporters and importers.

Vegetable-exporting firms reflect buyers' strict market parameters in their own supply chain, including quality, lead times and flexibility, but also trust and learning/innovation, with price secondary (figure 4.29). Local suppliers, however, fared quite poorly on lead time, trust and learning/innovation.

FIGURE 4.28: CRITICAL SUCCESS FACTORS IN KENYA'S FRESH VEGETABLE INDUSTRY

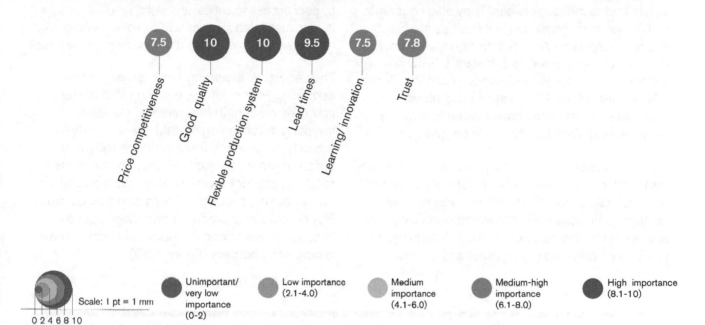

Source: Interviews with processing firms, 2012.

FIGURE 4.29: RATING OF LOCAL AND FOREIGN SUPPLIERS RELATIVE TO LEAD-FIRM EXPECTATIONS IN KENYA'S FRESH VEGETABLE INDUSTRY

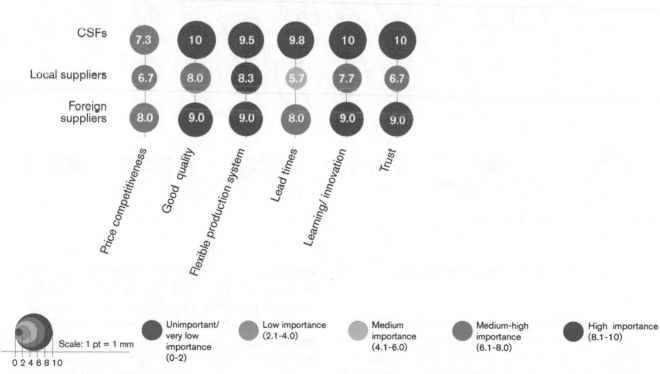

Source: Interviews with five processing firms, 2012.

To build capabilities, processing firms allocate dedicated staff to farmers and provide them with inputs and technical services. They also cooperate with external domestic parties such as the Fresh Produce Exporters Association of Kenya, Kenya Plant Health Inspectorate Services, USAID and Techno serve, as well as GlobalGap and the British Retail Consortium. All surveyed firms report that these programmes have helped to improve suppliers' capabilities, especially on quality.

The main constraints to local procurement are poor transport infrastructure (which hampers movement of perishable products and delays consignments for flights); fluctuations, costs and availability of electricity; and access to finance. Security issues lead to higher production costs (security services) and farmers cannot always work after dark. Corruption also raises production costs. Farmers in particular are affected by poor access to capital and skills, which makes it hard to meet standards as well as volume and quality requirements, which has a direct bearing on their sales.

The vegetable-exporting firms target process upgrading—for example, ensuring that labour practices meet high international standards or investing in technologies that give them the flexibility to process fresh produce following different product specifications. The firms also focus on product diversification, such as chillies, runner beans, avocados, herbs and tropical fruits. But process and product upgrading requires access to capital and economies of scale—the critical entry barriers (figure 4.30).

FIGURE 4.30: RATING OF FACTORS AFFECTING LINKAGE DEVELOPMENT IN KENYA'S FRESH VEGETABLE INDUSTRY

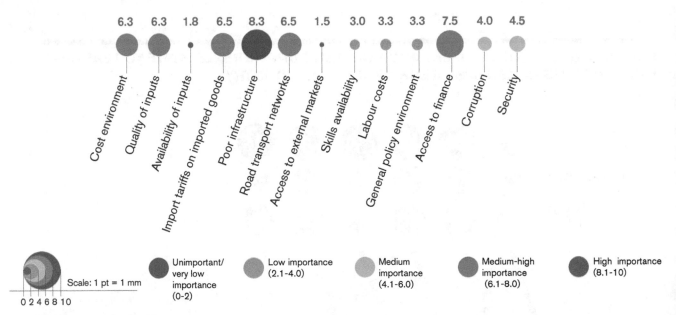

Source: Interviews with four processing firms, 2012.

Government policies and public–private cooperation

Several policies recognize value addition through processing. The Policy on Agro-industry for 2008–2012 aimed to scale up the operations of agro-processing firms by encouraging consolidation and establishing special zones and parks providing improved, targeted export services. The Agriculture Sector Development Strategy 2010–2020 also supports processing industries, and the Ministry of Agriculture has targeted barriers to rural agro-processing, including licences, product standards, entrepreneurial skills, and high costs of equipment and packaging. The National Industrial Policy includes agro-processing among the sectors to be supported through investment incentives and technical information, and supports farm research and clustering around specific agricultural resources.

Regulatory and facilitative roles in agro-industry are played by government bodies like the Horticultural Crops Development Authority, the Ministry of Trade and Industry and the Export Promotion Council, and by the private sector through the Kenya Association of Manufacturers and Fresh Produce Exporters Association of Kenya (which liaises with public and private sectors and with international organizations). It also provides export marketing information, post-harvest handling and packaging, and ensures adherence to established codes of practice.

Public–private collaboration has been critical for designing and implementing strategies to support local upgrading. Government support has been manifold: provision of subsidies has enabled firms to expand production, investment in infrastructure has reduced lead times of supplies, and support to farmers has enabled firms to reduce costs. Interviewed firms considered government assistance positive in having helped supply chain efficiency and compliance with standards.

However, the processing firms suggested that efforts should target non-EU market requirements, that the current interventions are too selective and fail to involve farmers in remote areas, and that the government should be more consistent in policy implementation. Most of these firms would respond to initiatives to work with the government or international bodies to support local processing.

However, processing firms surveyed suggested that efforts should target requirements of non-EU markets, that the current interventions are selective and do not involve farmers in remote areas, and that the government should be more consistent in policy implementation. Most of these firms would respond to initiatives to work with the government or international bodies to support local processing.

4.5 A VALUE CHAIN COMPARISON: ETHIOPIA AND KENYA

Table 4.3 outlines a country and value chain comparative overview between Ethiopia and Kenya

TABLE 4.3: SUMMARY COMPARISON: ETHIOPIA AND KENYA

Ethiopia (coffee)	Kenya (tea)	Kenya (fresh vegetables)
Opportunity for upgrading: linkages seen but not grasped	*No upgrading in forward linkages*	*Forward linkage development, significant local upgrading*
• High competition between exporters and processors • Large domestic market/EU • Marketing board inefficient • CSFs: price, quality, trust, lead times • Lead firms: some assistance, but not support for functional upgrading • Constraints: access to inputs, skills	• Dual structure • Vertical integration • Supermarkets, regional traders • CSFs: price, quality • Weak buyer cooperation • Intense supplier cooperation • Constraints: import tariffs, cost environment, land, finance	• Large firms dominate • Increased integration backward and forward • EU supermarkets • CSFs: Quality, product differentiation, lead times • Strong buyer cooperation • Good private–public cooperation • Constraints: infrastructure, access to finance, sectoral policy
No specific policy on forward linkages	*No specific policy on forward linkages*	

4.6 CONCLUSIONS

The case studies highlight that efforts to develop backward and forward linkages to soft commodities need to take into account the technical characteristics of the GVCs and the structure of the industry. These are important in determining the best strategies for local upgrading and for African firms to move into more profitable and more sustainable activities.

Government policies and local domestic capabilities are critical determinants. Policies need to target the processing industries as well as the natural resource sectors. Improved coordination is also important in the private sector between farmers, growers, processors and exporters. Only such systemic competitiveness along the entire local value chain will enable firms to meet the requirements imposed by end markets for price, quality, standards and so forth. As domestic and regional markets are encouraging firms to move up the value chain in countries with higher capabilities, Africa's regional integration is therefore important to support and deepen such upgrading.

REFERENCES

Basboga, K., L. Cramer, S. Eden, K. Nakamura, E. Omondi, and R. Ullman. 2010. "Growth in a Globalized Industry: The Case of Hillside Green Growers and Exporters Ltd." Cornell University, Cornell International Institute for Food, Agriculture and Development, Ithaca, NY.

Barrientos, S. 2011. "Beyond Fair Trade: Why Are Mainstream Chocolate Companies Pursuing Social and Economic Sustainability in Cocoa Sourcing?" Paper to International Labour Organization/International Finance Corporation Better Work Conference, 26–28 October, Washington, DC.

Barrientos, S., and K. Asenso-Okyere. 2008. *Mapping Sustainable Production in Ghanaian Cocoa*. Report to Cadbury. Retrieved from www.bwpi.manchester.ac.uk/research/ResearchProgrammes/businessfordevelopment/mappping_sustainable_production_in_ghanaian_cocoa.pdf (accessed 30 September 2012).

COPAN (Cocoa Processors Association of Nigeria). 2010. "Cocoa Processors Association of Nigeria." Memorandum/Presentation to the NEPC Stakeholders Meeting, 21 July, Lagos.

Dolan, C., and J. Humphrey. 2000. "Governance and Trade in Fresh Vegetables: The Impact of UK Supermarkets on the African Horticulture Industry." *Journal of Development Studies* 37(2): 147–76.

Dolan, C., J. Humphrey, and C. Harris-Pascal. 1999. "Horticultural Commodity Chains: The Impact of the UK Market on the African Fresh Vegetable Industry." IDS Working Paper 96, Institute for Development Studies, Sussex, UK.

FAO (Food and Agriculture Organization of the United Nations). 2009. *The State of Agricultural Commodity Markets 2009*. Rome.

———. 2011. *State of Food and Agriculture 2010–11*. Rome.

Fold, N. 2002. "Lead Firms and Competition in 'Bi-polar' Commodity Chains: Grinders and Branders in the Global Cocoa-Chocolate Industry." *Journal of Agrarian Change* 2(2): 228–47.

Fold, N., and M. N. Larsen. 2011. "Upgrading of Smallholder Agro-food Production in Africa: The Role of Lead Firm Strategies and New Markets." *International Journal of Technological Learning, Innovation and Development* 4 (1): 39–66.

Fold, N., and S. Ponte. 2008. "Are (Market) Stimulants Injurious to Quality? Liberalization, Quality Changes, and the Reputation of African Coffee and Cocoa Exports." In *Globalization and Restructuring of African Commodity Flows*, ed. N. Fold and, M. N. Larsen, 129–55. Uppsala: Nordiska Afrikainstitutet.

Ganewatta, G., R. Waschik, S. Jayasuriya, and G. Edwards. 2005. "Moving Up the Processing Ladder in Primary Product Exports: Sri Lanka's 'Value-added' Tea Industry." *Agricultural Economics* 33(3): 341–50.

HCDA (Horticultural Crops Development Authority). 2009. "Horticulture Data Report 2009." Retrieved from www.hcda.or.ke/tech/cat_pages.php?cat_ID=24.

Iyama, V. H. 2007. "Action by Private Sector Bodies in the Cocoa Value Chain: The Nigerian Experience." Presented at the First Roundtable for A Sustainable Cocoa Economy, Cocoa Association of Nigeria, October 2007, Accra.

ICCO (International Cocoa Organization). 2012. "Quarterly Bulletin of Cocoa Statistics, Vol. XXXVIII, No. 2, Cocoa year 2011/12." London.

ISSER (Institute of Statistical Social and Economic Research). 2011. *The State of the Ghanaian Economy 2010*. Accra: University of Ghana.

Kaplan, D., and R. Kaplinsky. 1999. "Trade and Industrial Policy on an Uneven Playing Field: The Case of the Deciduous Fruit Canning Industry in South Africa." *World Development* 27(10): 1787–801.

Kaplinsky, R. 2004. *Competitions Policy and the Global Coffee and Cocoa Value Chains*. Geneva: United Nations Conference on Trade and Development.

Kaplinsky, R., and R. Fitter. 2004. "Technology and Globalisation: Who Gains When Commodities Are De-commodified?"

International Journal of Technology and Globalisation 1 (1): 5–28.

Kjöllerström, M., and K. Dallto. 2007. "Natural Resource-based Industries: Prospects for Africa's Agriculture." In *Industrial development for the 21st century: Sustainable Development Perspectives*, ed. United Nations Department of Economic and Social Affairs, 119–81. New York: United Nations.

Muradian, R., and W. Pelupessy. 2005. "Governing the Coffee Chain: The Role of Voluntary Regulatory Systems." *World Development* 33(12): 2029–44.

Mwanma, V. 2011."Nigerian Cocoa Processors Want a Regulatory Board, COPAN Says." *Bloomberg News*, 13 July. Retrieved from www.bloomberg.com/news/2011-07-13/nigerian-cocoa-processors-want-a-regulatory-board-copan-says.html.

Ouma, S. 2010. "Global Standards, Local Realities: Private Agrifood Governance and the Restructuring of the Kenyan Horticulture Industry." *Economic Geography* 86(2): 197–222.

Petit, N. 2007. "Ethiopia's Coffee Sector: A Bitter or Better Future?" *Journal of Agrarian Change* 7(2): 225–63.

Ponte, S. 2002a. "Brewing a Bitter Cup? Deregulation, Quality and the Reorganization of Coffee Marketing in East Africa." *Journal of Agrarian Change* 2(2): 248–72.

———. 2002b. "The Latte Revolution? Regulation, Markets and Consumption in the Global Coffee Chain." *World Development* 30(7): 1099–122.

———. 2002c. *Standards, Trade and Equity: Lessons from the Speciality Coffee Industry*. Copenhagen: Centre for Development Research.

Republic of Kenya. 2010. *Economic Survey 2010*. Nairobi: Kenya National Bureau of Statistics.

———. 2012. *Economic Survey 2012*. Nairobi: Kenya National Bureau of Statistics.

ReSAKSS-ECA (Regional Strategic Analysis and Knowledge Support System–East & Central Asia). 2012. "Technologies for Enhancing Horticultural productivity in Kenya: Key Lessons and Messages for Programming and Policy Action." United States Agency for International Development, Washington, DC. Retrieved from http://kenya.usaid.gov/sites/default/files/u17/Horticulture%20Technolgies_Final%20Report.pdf.

Roemer, M. 1979. "Resource-based Industrialization in the Developing Countries: A Survey." *Journal of Development Economics* 6(2): 163–202.

Talbot, J. M. 1997a. "The Struggle for Control of a Commodity Chain: Instant Coffee from Latin America." *Latin American Research Review* 32(2): 117–35.

———. 1997b. "Where Does Your Coffee Dollar Go?: The Division of Income and Surplus along the Coffee Commodity Chain." *Studies in Comparative International Development (SCID)* 32(1): 56–91.

———. 2002. "Tropical Commodity Chains, Forward Integration Strategies and International Inequality: Coffee, Cocoa and Tea." R*eview of International Political Economy* 9(4): 701–34.

UNDP (United Nations Development Programme). 2005. *4th Kenya Human Development Report: Linking Industrialisation with Human Development*. Nairobi. Retrieved from http://mirror.undp.org/kenya/UNDP_4thKHDR.pdf.

Wiersinga, R., andA. de Jager. 2007. "Development of Commercial Field Vegetable Production, Distribution and Marketing for the East African Market." Working Paper, Literature Review Kenya, The Hague, Netherlands.

World Bank. 2008. *World Development Report 2008: Agriculture for Development*. Washington, DC.

NOTES

[1] The small sample size of some of the value chains in this and the next chapter requires us to be cautious when interpreting the data. However, we believe that we present a representative snapshot of the extent of backward and forward linkages and their determinants.

[2] Unlike output from the mineral and oil sectors, output from food commodity sectors can vary enormously in quality, price and specifications. This implies that the productivity, skills and technological capabilities at the commodity production stage have a critical impact on the volume, quality and price of inputs supplied to the processing industries.

[3] These include Multitrex Plc, FTN Cocoa Processing Plc, Cadbury Nigeria Plc and Nestlé Plc.

[4] Price competitiveness, good quality, flexible production system, lead times, capacity to learn and keep up with innovation ("Learning/innovation" in the charts) and trust.

[5] Others are the Manufacture-In-Bond Scheme, Export Development Fund Scheme, Currency Retention Scheme, Tax Relief on Interest Income, Pioneer Status Scheme, Export Processing Zone, Buyback Arrangement and Capital Asset Depreciation Allowance.

Making the Most of Linkages in Industrial Commodities

LOCAL CONTENT POLICIES HAVE PROBABLY BEEN THE SINGLE MOST IMPORTANT POLICY DRIVER OF LINKAGES FROM THE COMMODITY SECTOR.

Outsourcing to local suppliers by lead commodity firms in the mining and oil sectors creates an opportunity for capacity building in local content requirements.

Maintaining competitiveness of local firms in the international global chain markets require government intervention and effort.

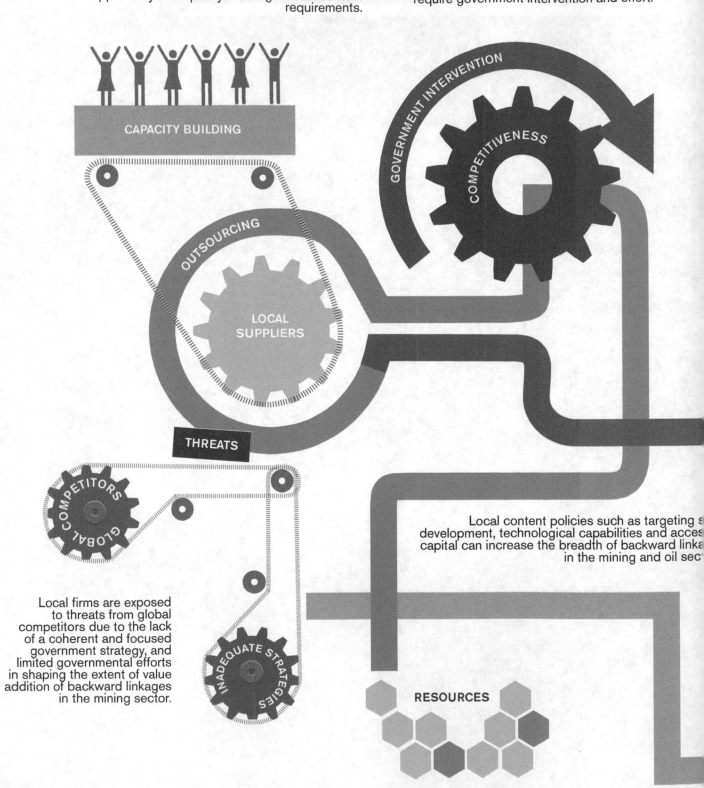

CAPACITY BUILDING

GOVERNMENT INTERVENTION

COMPETITIVENESS

OUTSOURCING

LOCAL SUPPLIERS

THREATS

GLOBAL COMPETITORS

Local content policies such as targeting s development, technological capabilities and acces capital can increase the breadth of backward linka in the mining and oil sec

Local firms are exposed to threats from global competitors due to the lack of a coherent and focused government strategy, and limited governmental efforts in shaping the extent of value addition of backward linkages in the mining sector.

INADEQUATE STRATEGIES

RESOURCES

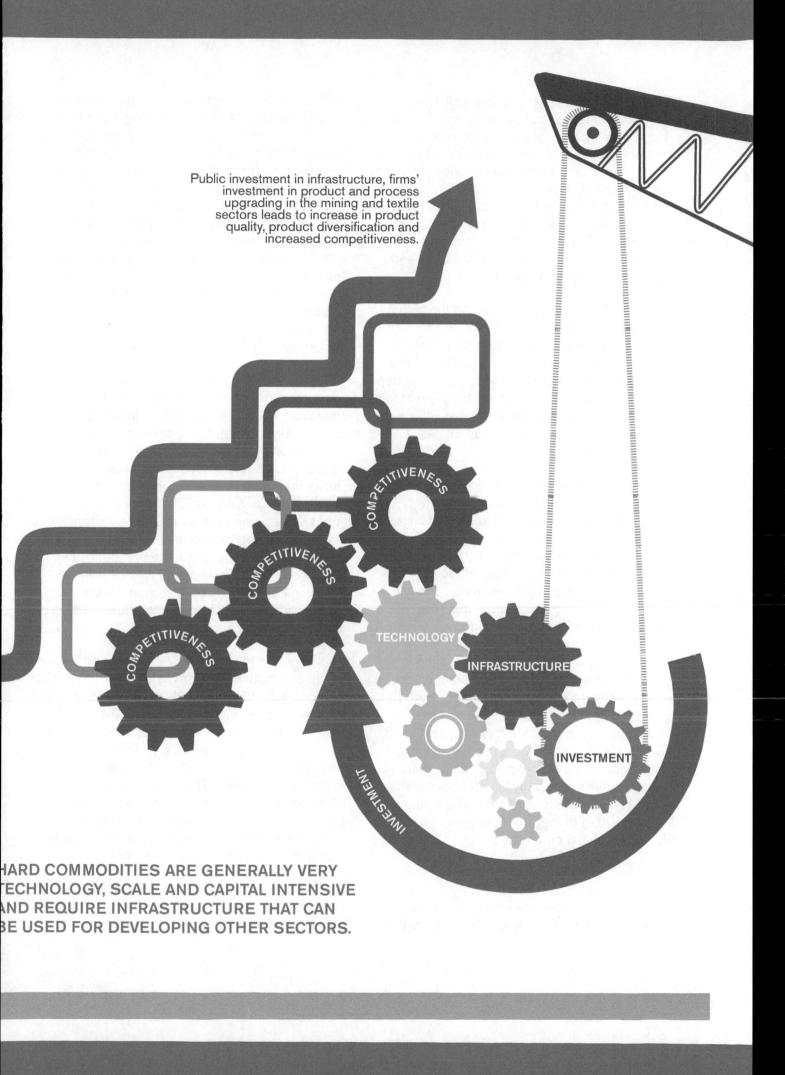

Public investment in infrastructure, firms' investment in product and process upgrading in the mining and textile sectors leads to increase in product quality, product diversification and increased competitiveness.

COMPETITIVENESS

COMPETITIVENESS

COMPETITIVENESS

TECHNOLOGY

INFRASTRUCTURE

INVESTMENT

INVESTMENT

HARD COMMODITIES ARE GENERALLY VERY
TECHNOLOGY, SCALE AND CAPITAL INTENSIVE
AND REQUIRE INFRASTRUCTURE THAT CAN
BE USED FOR DEVELOPING OTHER SECTORS.

This chapter focuses on how well Africa is making the most of primary commodities to develop linkages for its industrial commodities and to drive its industrialization. It deals primarily with backward linkages to local suppliers, but also discusses some forward processing and marketing linkages. The industrial commodity sectors discussed are cotton, textiles and clothing (Egypt); leather (Ethiopia); oil (Nigeria); copper (Zambia); gold (Ghana); and mining supplies (South Africa).

The analysis focuses on links along the global value chains (GVCs) driving these sectors and connecting local producers to export markets. It reviews how the lead firms controlling these value chains help or hinder the breadth and depth of forward linkages, the factors that prevent local firms from shifting into valued-added activities, and how government policies can influence domestic industrialization.

The case studies highlight the role of buyers and policies in developing backward and forward linkages. Ethiopia's leather industry and Nigeria's oil supply industry provide examples of countries where linkages are not only developing but also deepening into high value added activities. Nigeria's local content policies date back a few decades, and with time created opportunities seized by domestic businesses and encouraged by policies for developing business and creating skills. Ethiopia is at an earlier stage, although its export tax is accompanied by programmes to build technologies, capital and a trained workforce into which domestic firms can tap. In both cases, buyers have had an incentive to cooperate with local firms and have supported firms' product and process upgrading. Value addition is not necessarily linked to ownership of national firms, but some at least of the linkage development in these two industries has been driven by national companies.

Ghana and Zambia are in the middle of the spectrum. Mining has a long history in both countries, which have seen investment booms— Ghana since the 1980s and Zambia since the

2000s. Governments there have done little to shape backward linkages to mining, such that they have been populated by many domestic and foreign suppliers, which absorb a large share of the mining companies' local operational spending, leading to doubts over how deeply rooted these local supply chains are. It is hard to gauge the extent of value added, but it is clear, at least in Zambia, that most of the local firms surveyed are importing goods with little technological, skills or knowledge content. In Ghana, the local supply chain may well be developing more dynamic capabilities, albeit from a low base. In both cases, little is also known about the extent of domestic ownership.

The Ghanaian and Zambian case studies provide some grounds for optimism, however. First, employment linkages are very significant in size and skills content. The chances of these skills migrating to the supply chain should not be discounted, and indeed some evidence shows that this has already been happening in the oil and mining sectors. Second, skills-intensive services such as engineering, repair and maintenance services have localized because of spatial requirements. Third, the breadth of skills, technology, capital and economies of scale in supply links to mining creates real opportunities for supply firms and countries at different stages of economic development.

South Africa's mining supply industry and Egypt's textile and clothing industry show well-developed linkages with the commodity sectors, which are struggling to remain competitive. Growth in the South African industry was underlined by deep government cooperation with the mining houses and by heavy public investment in the national system of innovation. The industry acquired areas of knowledge that were specific to the deposit type and extraction techniques of local mines, and this enabled it over time to become a global leader in some products and services.

As South African mining houses internationalize, their trust-based relationships with their suppliers could give these suppliers an advantage: if the houses are confident of their suppliers' quality and competence, they are more likely to continue working with them in operations abroad. However, South African firms are still exposed to global competition and ultimately a South African mining house in Africa or Latin America will decide on the basis of the most competitive—all things considered—offer.

Egyptian cotton is world renowned for its quality. On this basis, the country integrated forward from raw cotton to fabrics to clothing and manufacturing of home textiles (such as carpets, rugs, bed linen and towels).Egypt continues to export successfully, partly through preferential agreements with the US and Europe. Moreover, the textile and clothing firms produce very high value added products. The companies invest heavily in product and process upgrading, which enables them to be strong in product quality and diversification. The most supportive government policy has been infrastructure investment; others had mixed results, largely owing to poor implementation.

Egypt's textile and clothing firms and South Africa's mining supply companies are under increasing threat from global competition. In Egypt, the textile stage of the cotton value chain has been eroded by Asian fabric manufacturers and by poor domestic capabilities. Further downstream, clothing and home textile manufacturers struggle to compete with low-cost Asian exporters in third-country markets, especially after the end of the Multifibre Arrangement.

In South Africa, the mining supply industry struggles to compete at the bottom of the technological spectrum with low-cost, low-tech Asian producers, and at the top of that spectrum with advanced economies such as Australia. In both cases, the lack of a coherent and focused government strategy to help the sectors is to blame. China is a particular threat to manufacturing activities, while Australia is to research and development (R&D)–type activities. The South African experience shows particularly

that linkage development is a cumulative process, and continuous investment is required in technologies, R&D and skills.

Egyptian firms exporting to European and US buyers have to meet stringent requirements and are assisted by global brands and retailers in meeting them. This approach is completely different from firms selling to traders in domestic and regional markets. South African mining companies had intensive linkages with suppliers that helped to jointly develop products that were highly location specific. Nigerian oil companies are cooperating with local suppliers to help upgrade local capabilities.

Similar to the soft commodities analysed in the previous chapter, Ethiopia's leather and Egypt's textile and clothing industries also rely on the quality, volume and consistency of supplies from the commodity sector to be competitive. Again, a strategy targeting the processing industries must be integrated with interventions for commodity producers and primary processors.

Finally, another finding of the case studies is that mining and oil companies see it in their own interest to outsource to local suppliers. Outsourcing has reduced transaction costs, lead times and the need for large stocks, but they only outsource if it is economically efficient, and do so in partnership with other stakeholders. The lead commodity producers' interest in outsourcing is important from a policy point of view because local content requirements coupled with capacity building could be aligned with corporate strategies of lead commodity producers. In a similar vein, Egyptian textile and clothing firms are vertically integrated because they need to internalize market failures in the weaving, dyeing and knitting stages of the value chain—but to perform at optimal capacity, they need to operate in a textile cluster that allows them to outsource these activities. Linkage development policies could therefore be instrumental in supporting broader industrialization strategies and increasing the competitiveness of existing industries.

5.1 COTTON, TEXTILES AND CLOTHING

The global value chain

The cotton to clothing GVC can be divided into several stages (box 5.1 and figure 5.1): raw material supply, including natural and synthetic fibres; yarns, including spun cotton and filament; textile fabric production and finishing; conversion and assembly of clothing and other textile-based products; distribution and sales at wholesale level; and final distribution at retail level.

BOX 5.1: SOME ELEMENTS IN THE COTTON, TEXTILE AND CLOTHING GVC

Fibres are processed from plant or chemical-based raw materials and are spun into yarn that is used to produce woven or knitted fabric. The fabric is then finished, dyed or printed, and cut into pieces to produce clothing or products for other end markets (home furnishings, industrial or technical consumer products).

Much clothing production remains labour intensive, has low start-up and fixed costs and requires simple technology—characteristics that have encouraged clothing production to relocate to low-cost areas, mainly in developing countries. Textile production is more capital and scale intensive and demands higher workers' skills. Some has stayed in developed countries or shifted towards middle-income countries.

A series of intangible activities add value to clothing products—product development, design, textile sourcing, distribution, branding and retailing. These are controlled primarily by four main types of lead firm (and by some intermediaries and suppliers): mass-merchant retailers, speciality retailers, brand marketers and brand manufacturers.

Source: Interviews with textile firms, 2012.

FIGURE 5.1: COTTON, TEXTILE AND CLOTHING GLOBAL VALUE CHAIN

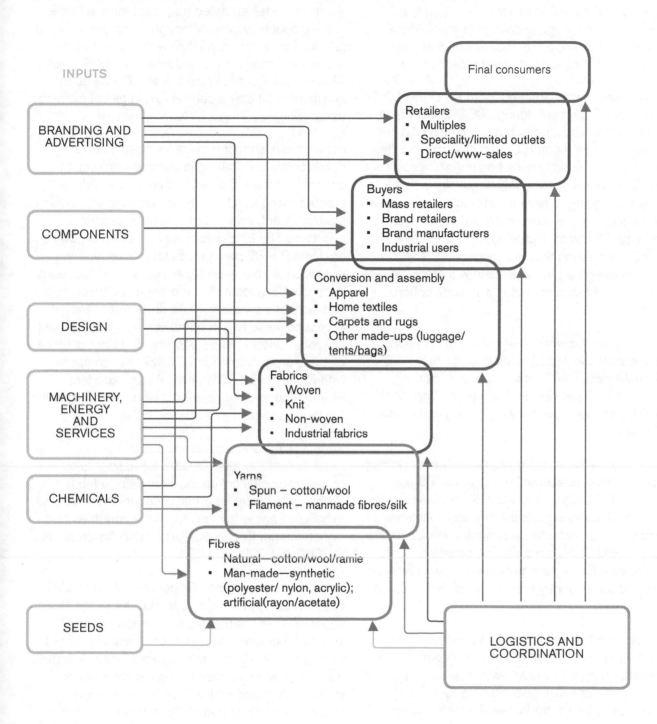

Source: ECA and AUC.

Global trends

The US, China and India dominate global cotton production, with around two thirds. Cotton is a major earner of foreign exchange in many African countries and an important means of generating cash income for millions of smallholder farmers.

World cotton yields stagnated for much of the 1990s but rose by 35 per cent during 2004–2006, primarily on technological advances, but these gains did not increase growers' income. Cotton has had very little share in the commodity price boom. As one source put it: "The consensus within the industry is that 'growers are going to have to learn to adjust to lower cotton prices' for the foreseeable future, as a result of more rapid growth in productivity" (Tschirley et al., 2010: 2). Increasing the value added in this sector through moving up the value chain is therefore a necessity for African countries with large cotton sectors.

China is by far the world's largest clothing exporter. Over the past two decades the country has continually increased its export share in clothing trade from 21.5 per cent in 1995 to 28.3 per cent in 2004, and then dramatically jumping to 42.9 per cent in 2010.

The EU-15 and the US are easily the largest clothing importing markets, accounting for above 65 per cent of global clothing imports in 2010. Developing countries' clothing exports are strongly concentrated in those two markets. African countries that produce textiles and clothing are therefore faced with Chinese exports as their most serious competition in home and third-country markets such as the EU and US.

Chinese exports have, however, a positive (complementary) impact as well as a negative (competitive) one. This is an issue that has important policy implications. Cheaper clothing for local consumers has an important welfare-enhancing effect while hurting the local manufacturers who cannot compete at these prices. Similarly, cheaper textiles provide valuable inputs to local clothing production but also threaten the long-term sustainability of regional and local textile–clothing links.

Trade regimes

The clothing (and textile) industry has been one of the most trade-regulated manufacturing activities in the global economy. Although many quotas were removed on 1 January 2005 with the end of the Multifibre Arrangement, and totally in 2009 when Chinese safeguards in the US and EU came to an end, tariffs still play a central role in global clothing trade.

For example, although average most-favoured-nation tariffs on clothing imports are around 11 per cent for the US and EU, they vary widely by product category. US tariffs on clothing products are significant, with duties on cotton products averaging 13–17 per cent and those on synthetic products 25–32 per cent. EU tariffs on clothing products vary between 0 per cent and 12 per cent, but show no systematic differences between cotton and synthetic products. Thus preferential market access to these two economies has a huge impact on global clothing trade patterns and boosts African clothing-producing countries' ability to compete with Chinese and South-east Asian exporters. Preferential trade agreements with the EU and US are thus becoming increasingly critical.

Preferential market access to the EU usually requires fulfilling "double-transformation" rules of origin—regional conversion from yarn to fabric to clothing—but rules of origin requirements changed to "single transformation" for those countries that signed interim Economic Partnership Agreements in 2008 and 2009.

The African Growth and Opportunity Act (AGOA) offers trade preferences to the US for many African countries (see chapter 2). It has been extended several times over the last decade and is now set to expire in 2015, but its temporary nature creates uncertainties for current and potential investors in the clothing industry. AGOA rules of origin requirements state that clothing has to be made 85 per cent from yarns, fabrics and threads from the US or produced in AGOA beneficiary countries. However, a special rule—the Third Country Fabric derogation—applies to less developed countries, allowing them duty-free access for clothing made from fabrics originating anywhere in the world.

Although Egypt is ineligible for AGOA, in 2005 it was accorded preferential trade access to the US through membership of the Qualifying Industrial Zone agreement linking it to clothing and textile production with Jordan and Israel.[1]

Excluding North Africa, clothing exports jumped from $2.1 billion in 2000 to $3.2 billion in 2004, but after the ending of the Multifibre Arrangement dropped back to $2.0 billion. Africa's exports to the US as a direct result of AGOA followed a similar pattern, increasing from $748 million in 2000 to $1.7 billion in 2004 and then decreasing to $904 million in 2010.

Developing countries have increasingly negotiated their own regional trade agreements. For Africa the most important are the Southern African Development Community (SADC), the East African Community, the Common Market for Eastern and Southern Africa, the Economic Community of West African States and the Southern African Customs Union (SACU), although negotiations and implementation drag out, and textiles and clothing are often put on negative lists.

Since 2006, regional preferential trade access through SACU and SADC to the South African clothing market has emerged as an important growth pole for producers in Lesotho and Swaziland, and Mauritius and Madagascar, respectively. It has increased jobs and reduced poverty, often among women. Mauritius and Madagascar's combined clothing exports to South Africa jumped from $4 million in 2004 to $63 million in 2010, and Lesotho and Swaziland's together rose from $3 million in 2005 to $105 million in 2010. Yet despite this growth, South Africa's regional clothing imports have remained almost marginal, reaching only 7.7 per cent in 2010, pointing to still-large potential.

Egypt's textile and clothing industry

The industry is one of Egypt's most dynamic (figure 5.2). In 2008, it accounted for 5 per cent of GDP, 26.4 per cent of industrial production and close to 10 per cent of exports. Textile and clothing enterprises account for a fifth of all industrial firms, and are the largest single employer with more than 400,000 workers, almost a quarter of the industrial labour force in 2008.

FIGURE 5.2: EGYPT'S TEXTILE AND CLOTHING EXPORTS, 1995–2011 ($ MILLION)

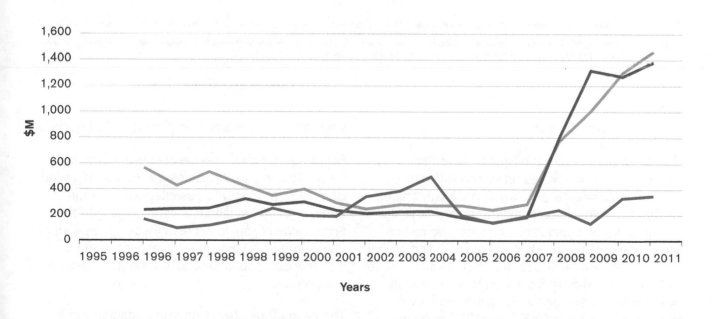

— Textile Fibres (SITC 26)   — Textile Yarn and Fabric (SITC 65)   — Apparel, Clothing and Accessories (SITC 84)

Source: UN Comtrade, retrieved from http://comtrade.un.org/ (accessed 20 October 2012).

More than 6,000 textile-related companies are registered with the Industrial Development Authority. Ready-made garment manufacturers represent 75 per cent of the textile and clothing industry (Egyptian Commercial Service, 2012), home textiles 12 per cent, cotton yarn 8 per cent, and other cotton fabrics and textiles 5 per cent. The bulk of investment in textiles and clothing comes from domestic sources ($1.3 billion out of $1.6 billion in 2012).

The end of the quota system in January 2005 had severe consequences for Egypt's textile exports to third countries, as it brought them into direct competition with those from Bangladesh, China, India, Indonesia, Pakistan and Turkey. This has been partly offset by the 2004 Qualifying Industrial Zone[2] and by the Euro-Mediterranean Partnership agreement (2005) with the EU. These two markets account for more than three quarters of Egypt's textile and clothing exports. Investment in the sector rose strongly in 1995–2007 (table 5.1).

TABLE 5.1: EGYPTIAN INVESTMENT IN TEXTILES AND CLOTHING BY SOURCE, 1995–2007 ($ MILLION)

Source	1995	2007	Change between 1995 and 2007 (%)
Domestic	76	227	199
Arab	2	49	2,350
Foreign	11	75	582
Total investment	89	351	294

Source: General Authority for Investment and Free Zones Information Center, Cairo, retrieved from www.ameinfo.com/db-3315336.html (accessed 25 July 2012).

Note: Data are converted from Egyptian pounds to US dollars using the year-average official exchange rate, published 31 December 2011. Data cover companies operating under Law 8 of 1997,inland and free zones, and companies organized by Company Law 159 of 1981.

Four firms' perceptions

The firms selected for the Egyptian case study are domestic privately owned firms, two with publicly held minority shares, and two with minority shares owned by regional companies. They are vertically integrated, with subsidiaries or sister companies involved in upstream activities (spinning and dyeing) and downstream activities (trading). Annual turnover in 2011 ranged from $7 million to $140 million, and the firms have generally registered growth in the past five years (2007–2012), hampered more recently by political instability and rising raw material costs. The firms are fairly labour-intensive

operations, with one firm employing 7,000 workers.

Egypt's labour market presents severe problems for textile companies, including shortage of skilled labour, low productivity, absenteeism and high turnover. Egyptian labour laws, according to the firms surveyed, fail to address these issues. Firms find it hard to develop human resources and, with few exceptions (box 5.2), struggle to remain competitive.

The case study covers one firm specializing in ready-made garments under a client's licence, two in home textiles (one in carpets, rugs and mats, and one in bed linen and towels) and one in yarn and synthetic fabric manufacturing and trading, which allows a raft of issues affecting different types of player to be reviewed.

Two of the firms are involved in high value added activities (table 5.2). The ready-made garment manufacturer goes beyond cut, make and trim

operations, which require shallow capabilities, to supply-chain management, knitting, dyeing and embroidery; and the carpet manufacturer adds value through hand-carving by very highly skilled workers, and through designs that include cutting irregular shapes, which creates unique products in a market where product differentiation is essential.

BOX 5.2: PROCESS UPGRADING THROUGH INVESTMENT IN SKILLS

The upgrading of MAC Carpet, a domestically owned textile manufacturer, has been impressive. It increased turnover from $101 million in 2005 to $140 million in 2011.

Part of its success is due to investing in human resources. It offers its employees training to enhance their technical and personal skills. The company views that as a main motivator for them, boosting their job satisfaction and loyalty to the company. It offers two types of training: general (functional, technical or vocational) and self-development. The company allocates 1.5 per cent of the annual remuneration budget to training and development.

MAC Carpet applies kaizen—the Japanese concept of continuous improvement—and allows workers at every level to take part. Through teamwork and openness to suggestions, it has improved productivity, raised product quality and secured higher customer satisfaction. Employees learn to spot and eliminate waste during the production stage. The approach creates a framework for a well-organized, disciplined and clean shop floor. The firm has set up 25 suggestion boxes, developed a communication plan, targeted 1,000 ideas and aims to carry out 100, and established a reward system.

TABLE 5.2: PROCESSING ACTIVITIES OF FOUR SURVEYED FIRMS, EGYPT

Firm 1 (ready-made garments)	Firm 2 (carpets, rugs and mats)	Firm 3 (bed linen and towels)	Firm 4 (yarn and synthetic fabric)
Knitting	Product design	Cutting	Yarn spinning
Dyeing	Tufting	Embroidery	Preparations
Cutting	Backing	Sewing	Warping
Sawing	Cutting	Assembly	Processing into fabric
Printing	Sewing	Finishing	
Embroidery	Carving		
Packaging	Finishing		
	Packaging		

Source: ECA and AUC.

The firms are in three GVCs (high-end domestic and regional markets, EU/US buyers, and low-end domestic market), which have varying critical success factors, or CSFs (figure 5.3). The carpet and ready-made garment manufacturers export mainly to Europe, less so to the US. The global buyers for carpets are retailers and wholesalers, and for clothing, retailers and global brands such as Levi's, Macy's, Calvin Klein, and Marks &Spencer. These firms are inserted into buyer-driven GVCs where global buyers outsource labour-intensive stages of their value chains.

FIGURE 5.3: BUYERS' CRITICAL SUCCESS FACTORS IN EGYPT'S TEXTILE INDUSTRY

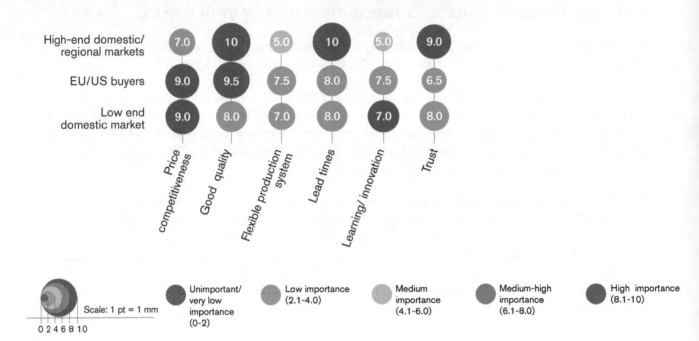

Source: Interviews with four firms, 2012.

The four firms' CSFs are very demanding (see figure 5.3). Their EU and US retailers and global brands cater to middle-income markets, and so price competitiveness and quality are important. Because price is important, Egyptian firms compete with South-east Asian and Turkish companies. Moreover, these buyers rely on just-in-time delivery, which requires their suppliers in Egypt to supply, on very short lead times, large volumes of highly differentiated products. Innovation and adjusting production to different product lines within short lead times are therefore crucial competencies for Egyptian firms.

Moreover, European and US buyers require compliance with demanding technical standards. To comply, Egyptian suppliers have to ensure consistency of quality, and to run integrated quality control systems from the yarn warehouse to inspection of final products before packing and shipping. Final quality control takes place in a mini control room, where compliance with American 2.5 Acceptance Quality Limit (AQL) and European 1.5 AQL quality standards is monitored for each order.

Beyond technical regulations, global buyers apply private standards.[3] These standards, with technical ones, require traceability. Firms have to monitor their own supply chains to ensure that standards are adhered to further along the value chain.

One the four firms specializes in small volume, high-quality home textile products (it has fewer than 70 employees). Because this firm supplies niche markets, product quality is the key CSF, which with fast lead times and trust is sufficient to maintain links to domestic and regional traders. Competition is limited to other Egyptian quality producers. One of the other three firms sells synthetic yarn and fibre to the lower end of the domestic market. In this market, price is paramount and competition from Asian manufacturers stiff.

The variance in CSFs is reflected in different upgrading trajectories by the firms. In domestic and regional markets, incentives to innovation and product quality upgrading are weak. Firms exporting to retailers and global branders have to meet demanding requirements on product differentiation, standards compliance and quality/volume consistency. Hence they invest heavily in product and process upgrading (box 5.3).

BOX 5.3: UPGRADING TO COMPETE—CARPETS AND YARN

The carpet manufacturer surveyed has invested in the latest generation of a highly versatile printing technology known as "JET printing", which results in the shortest minimum production runs in the industry today (as low as 500 square metres), maximum dye penetration into the highest and most dense piles, and the highest printing resolutions.

The firm applies more than 10 different types of backing, which allows it to produce a wide range of colour designs. This is complemented by various combinations of finishing techniques: surging, tape binding, wide webbing, and cotton or nylon fringes. Packing is tailor made for wholesale and retail markets, and includes bar coding.

The yarn exporter has adopted highly automated fabric-processing operations. Using sophisticated circular and flat-knitting machines, the firm manufactures high value added fabrics, such as single jersey, rib, pique, interlock, drop needle and mini-jacquards. This is backed up by close quality inspection during and after knitting.

Long-term relationships with European and US buyers have enabled the firms to invest in product and process upgrading, and in expanding capacity. In one firm, European buyers have assisted in complying with private standards. Conversely, firms supplying traders in domestic and regional markets operate on market-based arm's-length relationships.

The firms are demanding on their suppliers for quality, price, flexibility, lead times and trust. Local suppliers can match foreign suppliers on price, but underperform on quality, flexibility and trust. Compliance with technical and private standards requires first- and second-tier suppliers to meet not only Egyptian manufacturers' product specifications but also final buyers' public and private standards. Quality includes requirements for product characteristics and production

processes that are essential for staying in the value chain.

One firm cooperates with its suppliers to address their bottlenecks. It joined the National Supplier Development Plan run by the Industrial Modernization Centre, an independent body set up in 2000 to help build global competitiveness of Egypt's manufacturing. In one exercise, the firm selected 12 of its key suppliers for "gap analysis" on their quality, production, health and safety, and management systems. A gap closure strategy was formulated and an action plan developed, which helped in building the suppliers' capability to meet required standards. But the other firms rarely if at all assist suppliers—indeed, one reported that the procedures of the Industrial Modernization Centre are too burdensome and bureaucratic.

The firms are highly vertically integrated, because this allows them to internalize market failures and minimize transaction costs, but it is not always efficient—for example, one firm's dyeing unit operates at 50 per cent capacity. Ideally, they should outsource labour-intensive activities such as packaging, embroidery and marketing support, which would allow them to focus on their core business. Small and medium-sized enterprises and cluster development strategies could support their competitiveness.

Opportunities lie both in backward linkages (high-quality cotton fabrics) and forward linkages (new products such as carpet tiles), but these are constrained by several factors (figure 5.4). Interestingly, "soft" infrastructure issues—notably corruption and security—are more prominent than hard infrastructure matters.

FIGURE 5.4: RATING OF FACTORS AFFECTING LINKAGE DEVELOPMENT IN EGYPT'S TEXTILE INDUSTRY

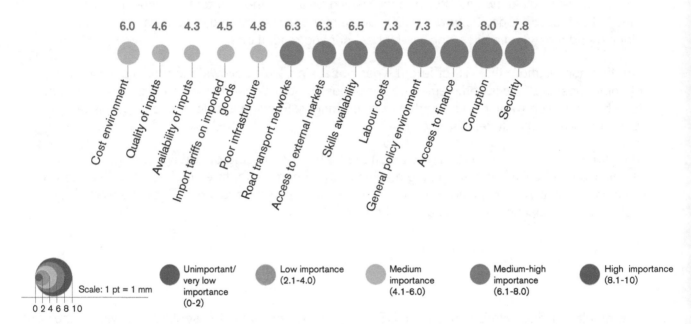

Source: Interviews with four firms, 2012.

Challenges and policies

The Egyptian textile and clothing value chain faces a twin challenge: for intermediate stages,[4] relocation to Asia; for final product manufacturers, competition from low-cost Asian producers in low and middle domestic and third-country markets. Building competitiveness in manufacturing fabric is particularly important because Egypt needs to specialize in processing its highly prized extra-long staple cotton for market niches, rather than compete on price with Asia.

Around 70 per cent of locally produced yarn is controlled by the public sector. Spinning, weaving and hemming industries have been slow to privatize because of the high cost of investment and long payback periods on investment. Dyeing and finishing are the weakest stages in the value chain, as they have received the lowest investment. Domestic capabilities in dyeing local cotton are also weak, so too in spinning and weaving where machinery in public companies has not been replaced for more than25 years (box 5.4). Management in all these stages is underperforming, and deliveries unreliable. In contrast, private companies control 99 per cent of clothing and home textile manufacturing capacity, the result of privatization over the last 15 years.

The 2008 Industrial Development Strategy aims to develop exports and deepen the country's integration

BOX 5.3: THROWING MONEY DOWN THE DRAIN

The quality of spinning, weaving and dyeing is low, often forcing local manufacturers to import yarn and finished fabrics—manufactured in Asia using high-quality Egyptian cotton—from Bangladesh, India, Pakistan, Turkey and Turkmenistan.

Egypt is therefore throwing away substantial added value in a chain where it has a unique commodity—its globally renowned raw cotton. This added value is Egypt's for the taking. The government is, however, aware that these are the least competitive stages of the value chain.

with the global economy, and proposes promotion of medium- and high-tech subsectors to ensure long-run competitiveness of the whole industrial sector (without discarding resource-based and low-tech activities). Yet the government has no coherent strategy for textiles and clothing, largely because of conflicting interests between domestic and export producers. Rather, it has used presidential decrees on cotton growing and three final product groups—textiles (yarn and fabrics), home textiles and ready-made garments.

The government is looking to attract private investment upstream in order to sharpen the country's competitive advantage, while the Textiles Development Center at the Ministry of Industry and Foreign Trade is considering promoting "Technical Textiles", which can support a broad range of industries. The Textile Development Strategy—Vision 2020 was launched in 2007, and aims to expand exports to $10 billion and create more than 5 million jobs.

The Industrial Development Authority focuses on attracting new investment to strengthen the upstream supply chain; shortening lead times for clothing exports to the EU; enabling entry to higher-value segments; and diversifying into denim mills and laundries, intimate apparel, premium knitters and premium fabric. Since 2007, Egypt has invested in free economic zones. But investment in the zones is not planned in an integrated way, and political instability has further hampered the effort. Nor is there any cluster development, and the cost of capital is high for local firms.

The firms surveyed believe that the policy framework does not promote technological upgrading. Importing new machinery, for example, is expensive because of burdensome procedures and import duties.

The vertical integration observed in the survey is unsustainable, and integrated clusters need to be developed. To increase local content, the government provides export incentives, depending on the type of product and area of production, among other factors. Firms selling to the domestic market, however, seem unaware of incentives report that they are disbursed inconsistently (depending on funding), or that procedures to claim them are unclear.

5.2 LEATHER

The global value chain

Aside from the early stage of animal husbandry, the leather GVC starts with supply of hides and culminates with finished leather products for the final market. The principal hides are bovine, sheep and goat. They are processed in tanneries before being manufactured into leather footwear, garments and accessories like travel bags and belts, technical products, or household and automotive upholstery.

The leather value chain has five stages: hide supply, semi-processed hides, finished leather, finished products, and the market. To show exactly where these two streams separate, it is necessary to separate the tanning or semi-processed hides process into two streams (figure 5.5).

FIGURE 5.5: KEY ELEMENTS OF LEATHER GLOBAL VALUE CHAIN

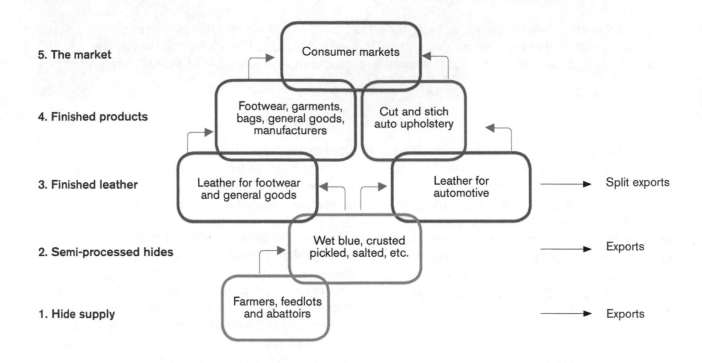

Source: ECA and AUC, 2012.

Five stages

The first processing part of the value chain takes raw hides from suppliers and tans them into semi-processed leather. This is a peculiarity of the chain since it depends on the processes and activities in another value chain—animal production and slaughter for meat. The animal production and slaughter industry has a major impact on the quality of the hides.

The main exporters of bovine and sheep hides are the US, Australia, Spain, France, UK, New Zealand and South Africa. Developing countries are the main producers of bovine hides, sheepskins and goatskins, but are not the dominant exporters of bovine hides. Their share of global exports is increasing, owing partly to improving husbandry and tanning skills. Because hides are a global commodity, the price of hides is determined on the world market.

Average global hide prices stayed fairly constant in 1988–2001, dipped to a slightly lower base, fell rapidly as the global crisis kicked in and then recovered (figure 5.6). The weak global economic situation affected consumer confidence, with a consequent decline in demand for leather and leather products. Tanners, as well as shoe and leather-goods manufacturers, face increased costs of production also from higher chemicals, energy and freight costs. The lower margins have led to tanners' unwillingness to offer higher prices for hides.

FIGURE 5.6: WORLD HIDES PRICE, JANUARY 1980–SEPTEMBER 2012 (US CENTS/LB)

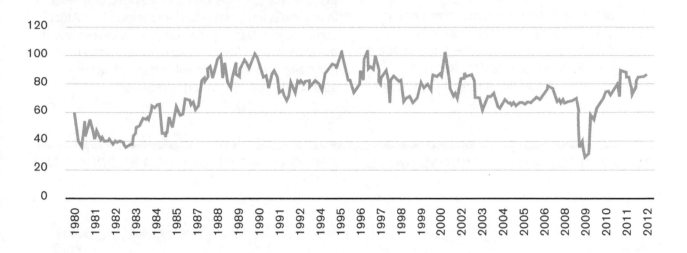

Source: International Monetary Fund Primary Commodity Price monthly data, retrieved from www.imf.org/external/data.htm (accessed 20 October 2012).

Note: Heavy native steers, more than53 pounds, wholesale dealer's price, FOB Chicago.

The next step takes semi-processed hides and re-tans them into finished leather ready for use by manufacturers. The type of finished leather depends entirely on the product that it will become part of, which is why leathers tend to be separated at this stage.

After this stage, hides can travel in one of three directions: footwear tanning, automotive tanning or exports. The orientation of finishing tanneries has altered over the last few decades. Whereas they used only to produce leather for footwear, general goods and furniture manufacturers, many are now also producing leather for automotive upholstery manufacturers.

The final production stage is the manufacture of leather products. This is undertaken by a variety of firms ranging from large, capital-intensive factories to small, labour-intensive enterprises. The GVC is ultimately driven by global marketing agents who sell intermediate and end products, operating at different stages in the chain.

These agents have market knowledge, design capability and a wide network of sales channels, which allows them to control the value chain and derive the greatest rents. They manage the complex

supplier stages of the chain, contract production by enterprises, set the quality standards, sometimes provide the necessary finance and serve the customers in the final markets.

Upgrading activities in developing countries is hence tied to meeting these knowledge-intensive and technical standards, which imposes a major burden on producers in low-income countries, as they often lack the knowledge, managerial capabilities and design skills to identify their own end markets.

Upgrading opportunities and challenges

The importance of the leather industry stems from the fact that it can flourish both in low- and high-wage economies so that, although it offers scope for exploiting natural comparative advantages in commodities, it also offers potential for low-wage economies to follow an upgrade path based on dynamic specialization.

A well-developed hide production and tanning industry is the starting point for upgrading leather-product manufacturing, which cannot develop without local supplies of material. By improving hide and tanning quality, local footwear and leather-product manufacturers in Africa can upgrade their product quality.

Quality problems are the main factor constraining African suppliers from sustaining exports. The upgrading challenge facing suppliers is demonstrated by a benchmarking exercise undertaken by the United Nations Industrial Development Organization that compared Kenya, Ethiopia and Italy (table 5.3). Although a decade old, there is little reason to assume that the relationships will have changed dramatically. In any case, the point is to demonstrate that Africa's competitive advantage lies only in the lowest link in the chain where the accruable rents are the lowest. If the aim is to move into value-added linkages, a sustained upgrading effort is required.

TABLE 5.3: QUALITATIVE BENCHMARKING OF FACTORS IN THE LEATHER SUPPLY CHAIN

Factors	Africa		Developed country
	Kenya	Ethiopia	Italy
Availability of raw hides and skins	Abundant	Abundant	Low
Quality of raw hides and skins	Generally poor	Low–high	High
Access to and cost of raw materials	Generally easy	Generally easy	Difficult
Access to financial resources	Difficult	Difficult	Easy
Sustained capital investment	Low	Low	High
Technological sophistication of facilities and equipment	Low–medium	Low–medium	Very high
Process skills	Limited	Limited	Very high
R&D	Limited	Limited	Very high
Product development	Limited	Limited	Very high
Tradition in the industry	Fairly recent	Fairly recent	Early
Unique skills within the sector	Rare	Rare	High
Degree of vertical integration	Low	Low	High
Product perception by the global market	Poor	Poor (high for sheepskin)	Very high

Source: Kiruthu (2002).

Upgrading by developing countries requires enhanced knowledge, improved technology and access to finance (Memedovic and Mattila, 2008).

To achieve business success the public sector needs to assist with productivity and technology centres, training facilities, cleaner production centres and investment and export promotion bodies to provide information and advice on technical and trading issues. These outfits need to offer practical advice for enterprises so that they can upgrade their manufacturing methods. The main objective of such support is to make enterprises competitive and attractive to the rest of the leather GVC through improving their quality, production methods and productivity. In Africa this also opens up opportunities for intraregional trade of intermediate and final products—leather manufactured products including fashion accessories, as well as inputs to the furniture and automotive industries.

Ethiopia's leather industry

Bati goatskin produces the softest, finest suede.[5] Ethiopian herders receive about $10 for the skins that will produce a Bati coat. After tanning and processing to "wet blue" or better levels for export, the exporter collects about $40–50 for the leather to be manufactured into a coat outside Ethiopia. An importing wholesaler/ manufacturer will then make the coat with a final retail price of at least $400.

Most animals are slaughtered on individual homesteads, not necessarily by people thinking of transforming hides and skins into high-quality leather, which throws up several issues, especially on defects. Thus the value chain suffers from mis-coordination from the start—animal husbandry—and continues to the delivery of hides and skins to a tannery where the real value-added stages start. That is why for many decades before the turn of the century Ethiopia exported huge quantities of raw and semi-processed hides.

The government has attempted to address this wastage at the bottom end to drive upgrading through the links in the chain. It started in 2002 by restricting exports of low value added hides and semi-processed leather, expanding into new export markets and encouraging higher-value products (Government of Ethiopia, 2002). One of the main measures used to restrict exports of low value added hides included an export tax of 150 per cent on the hides exported. These measures had a notable impact on the composition of the leather industry's exports, helping to shift the leather industry to finished products (figure 5.7).They provide the basis for engaging international lead firms to assist local tanning and manufacturing firms to upgrade their production activities. Still, the overall impact in reducing poverty and expanding the economy also has to consider income reductions for hide suppliers due to lower domestic prices.

FIGURE 5.7: VALUE-ADDED CONTENT OF LEATHER/HIDE EXPORTS FROM ETHIOPIA, 2004–2011 (%)

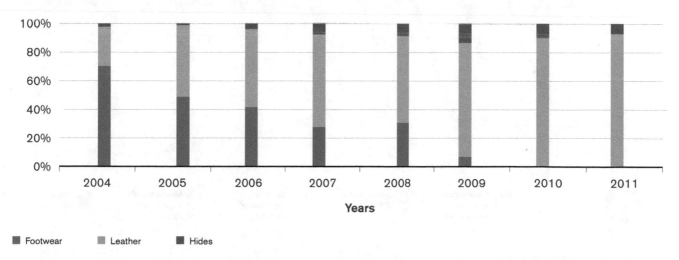

Source: UN Comtrade data, retrieved from http://comtrade.un.org/ (accessed 15 October 2012).

Note: Standard International Trade Classification 21, 61 and 85.

It is now beginning to suit the interests of foreign buyers to provide support to local tanners for process (but not product) upgrading in, for example, shortening lead times and increasing production reliability. Bini (2002) noted that local tanneries were helped to produce what they were already manufacturing, but faster and at better quality. Local footwear manufacturers have also upgraded processes (and products). Large firms have installed new machinery, changed the organization of production and raised quality, pulled by export opportunities and pushed so as to lock into GVCs and meet their global buyers' technical requirements (Tegegne and Tilahun, 2009).

The institutional environment (government and agencies) has also facilitated upgrading. The government has supported exports by providing industry zones and assisting large firms to partner international actors. The Leather and Leather Products Technology Institute, established in July 1999, has helped firms to innovate and upgrade

through training in design and shoe production skills for employees of large and medium-sized firms.

The four firms surveyed in this case study are domestic, private companies of varying ages, employing around 300 workers each. (Around 10,000 Ethiopians work in the leather sector, which is characterized by increasing domestic competition.) The firms process hides into wet blue, crust and finished leather. One firm is vertically integrated into shoe manufacturing.

Firms' perceptions

The four firms export to foreign garment buyers and to local traders. The export market used to be dominated by Europe, but is shifting to China and India. Global buyers set a high bar for the CSFs (figure 5.8). US, Italian and other European buyers are particularly demanding, partly because they have to comply with strict technical standards on chemical use and processing techniques.

FIGURE 5.8: BUYERS' CRITICAL SUCCESS FACTORS IN ETHIOPIA'S LEATHER INDUSTRY

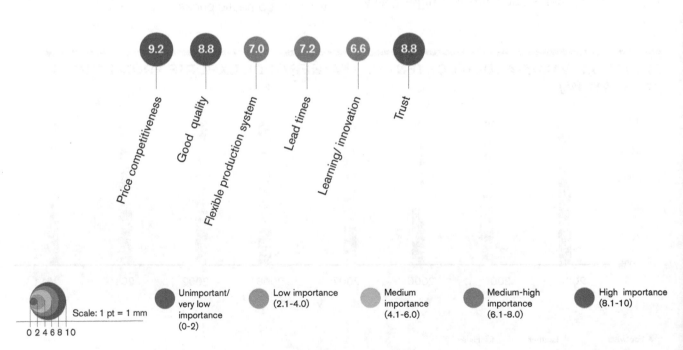

Source: Interviews with four firms, 2012

Because of demanding global buyers, tanneries set equally stiff conditions for their suppliers (figure 5.9), although local suppliers struggle to deliver high-quality skins to tanneries. Moreover, because skins easily deteriorate, poor infrastructure and weak treatment skills often cause unusable inputs. Trust remains important, and all tanneries support suppliers by providing credit and salt to preserve the skins, but the surveyed firms expressed the need for more support for the upstream stages.

FIGURE 5.9: RATING OF LOCAL SUPPLIERS RELATIVE TO LEAD-FIRMS' EXPECTATIONS IN ETHIOPIA'S LEATHER INDUSTRY

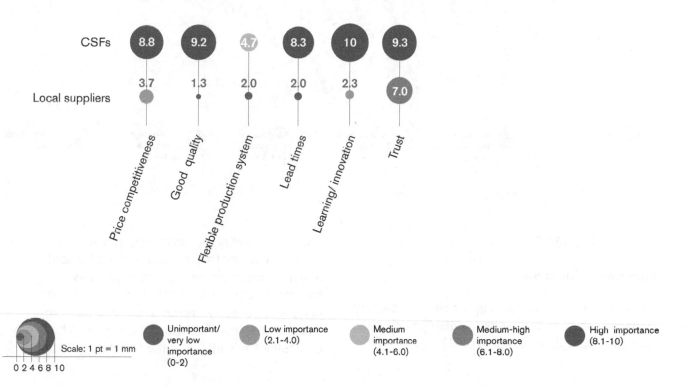

Source: Interviews with four firms, 2012

The surveyed firms believe that further upgrading opportunities lie in diversifying (colour and types of leather) and functionally upgrading into shoe manufacturing (those not already in that market). Ethiopia therefore needs to address key constraints: the cost environment, quality of inputs, availability of inputs, access to finance and infrastructure (figure 5.10).

On access to finance, the Ethiopian Competitiveness Facility, funded by the World Bank and the government, has provided matching grants to exporting companies engaged in, among other areas, the leather and shoe sectors. The International Finance Corporation (the World Bank's private sector investment arm) provides loans and capital to private investors in manufacturing, but this is not used as much owing to lack of awareness. Finally, the Ethiopian Leather and Leather Products Technology Institute plays a critical role in providing skills to the industry.

FIGURE 5.10: RATING OF FACTORS AFFECTING LINKAGE DEVELOPMENT IN ETHIOPIA'S LEATHER INDUSTRY

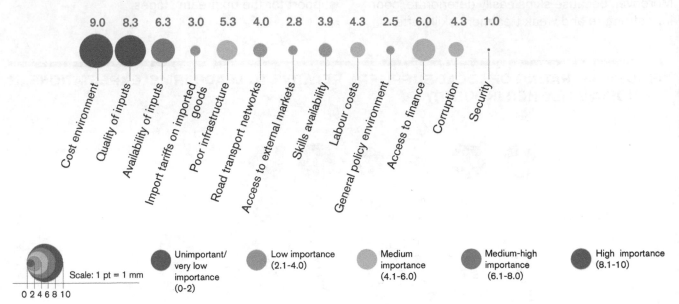

Scale: 1 pt = 1 mm
0 2 4 6 8 10

Unimportant/very low importance (0-2)

Low importance (2.1-4.0)

Medium importance (4.1-6.0)

Medium-high importance (6.1-8.0)

High importance (8.1-10)

Source: Interviews with four firms, 2012.

5.3 OIL INDUSTRY

Nigeria's value chain

Nigeria is the world's 10th-largest oil producer and depends heavily on the sector for GDP growth, taxes and, particularly, exports (figure 5.11).

The oil value chain is structured into an upstream sector (exploration and production) and a downstream sector (crude processing and marketing; figure 5.12). The key upstream players are (mainly) multinational and (less so) local companies. Multinational companies have a competitive advantage in the technology required

FIGURE 5.11: CONTRIBUTION OF OIL TO THE NIGERIAN ECONOMY, 1980–2010 (%)

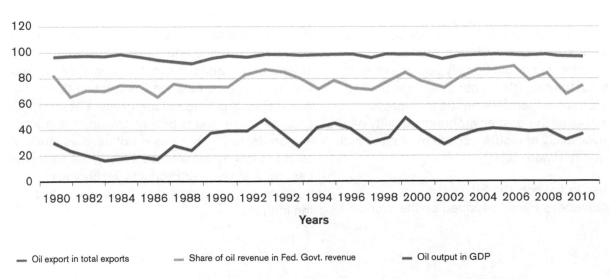

Years

— Oil export in total exports   — Share of oil revenue in Fed. Govt. revenue   — Oil output in GDP

Source: Computed from Central Bank of Nigeria Statistical Bulletin (2011), retrieved from www.cenbank.org/documents/Statbulletin.asp (accessed 15 December 2012).

for prospecting and exploration. Given that oil extraction is intensive in capital, technology and skills, the country has made real efforts to increase local content in skills in the oil industry (box 5.5). The largest oil producers are Shell Petroleum Development Company Limited, Mobil Producing Nigeria Unlimited, Chevron Nigeria Limited, and Texaco Overseas Nigeria Petroleum Company Unlimited.

FIGURE 5.12: OIL VALUE CHAIN

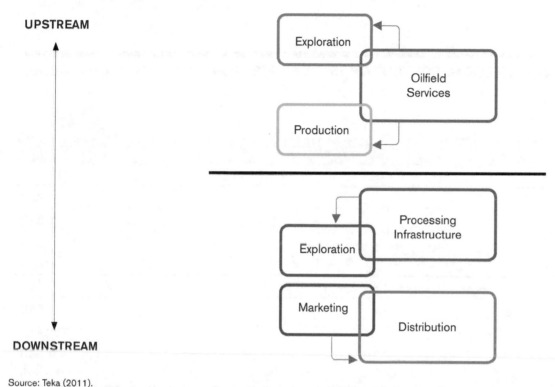

Source: Teka (2011).

BOX 5.4: UPSKILLING LOCAL WORKERS IN NIGERIA'S OIL INDUSTRY

Efforts include:

- Establishing the Petroleum Technology Development Fund in 1973 for developing, promoting and implementing petroleum technology and human resource development policies via research and training for Nigerians.

- Setting up the Petroleum Training Institute in Delta State in 1973 to train lower- and mid-level personnel to meet indigenous labour requirements.

- Founding the National College of Petroleum Studies in Kaduna in 1995 for high-level staff.

- Making heavy investments in research and education (by oil firms). Shell, for instance, introduced an Intensive Training Programme in 1998 to prepare young graduates for work in the industry.

Source: Oyejide and Adewuyi (2011).

Upstream industries

Nigeria has gradually localized some important upstream industries (Oyejide and Adewuyi, 2011). Focusing on three supply links to the oil and natural gas value chain (fabrication and construction, well construction and completion, and control systems and information and communications technology), Oyejide and Adewuyi (2011) found that local sourcing by oil companies is broad across goods and services.

The findings of a survey of 15 oil companies based in Port Harcourt and Warri (a third of the total firms based there) point to substantial local linkages: 11 of these oil companies sourced more than half their goods from local firms (table 5.4).

TABLE 5.4: SURVEY ON LOCAL CONTENT OF 15 OIL FIRMS, PORT HARCOURT AND WARRI, 2011

Local shares	%
Input share in the value of final product	
Up to 50%	33.3
Above 50%	33.3
Not indicated	33.3
Total	100.0
Share of local procurement of goods purchased from local firms	
Up to 50%	25.0
51–75%	41.7
Above 75%	33.3
Total	100.0
Share of local service done by local firms	
Up to 50%	25.0
Above 50%	75.0
Total	100.0
Share of final product purchase by local business	
Up to 25%	41.7
26–50%	33.3
Above 50%	25.0
Total	100.0

Source: Oyejide and Adewuyi (2011).

The local supply chain is not only broad but also deep, as shown by the high local content of first-tier suppliers (table 5.5). About 55 per cent of such firms indicate that their output has more than 50 per cent local content, particularly for suppliers in fabrication and construction, and in well construction and completion. Functional upgrading is also more likely in this segment.

TABLE 5.5: LOCAL CONTENT OF 45 FIRST-TIER OIL-SUPPLY FIRMS, PORT HARCOURT AND WARRI, 2011

Supplier type	Local content			
	0–25%	26–50%	51–75%	76–100%
Control system and ICT	31.6	21.1	21.1	26.3
Fabrication and construction	13.6	22.7	18.2	45.5
Well construction and completion	20.6	20.6	17.6	41.1
Others	40	40	20	–
Total	22.5	22.5	18.8	36.3

Source: Oyejide and Adewuyi (2011).

Buyer–supplier vertical cooperation is tight in oil production, in negotiations and information exchange, as well as in deeper forms of cooperation aimed at improving quality, delivery times and supply reliability, developing quality assurance systems, and ensuring technical upgrades and labour training (Oyejide and Adewuyi, 2011).

Downstream supply firms

Building on previous research, the Nigerian case study covers five downstream firms. Their core business is processing and marketing petroleum products (diesel, kerosene, lubricants, motor oil and jet fuel). All the firms are part of larger groups quoted on the Nigerian Stock Exchange, and two of the five are foreign owned. Foreign ownership is concentrated in manufacturing, which is capital and technology intensive. The firms' annual turnover ranges between $29 million and $1.1 billion, and they employ 115–503 workers, mainly with a tertiary education.

Nigeria's oil processing and marketing companies rely on a combination of imports by local agents and locally produced goods and services, the latter group accounting for 40–45 per cent of total procurement (table 5.6). Only for one smaller, local firm, did locally manufactured goods account for a hefty 65 per cent of total supplies, including food, equipment, spare parts and consumables. This figure on local procurement is consistent with that found upstream.

TABLE 5.6: LOCAL SOURCING BY OIL PROCESSING AND MARKETING COMPANIES, 2011

Supply typology	% of total procurement
Goods imported by agents	40–45
Locally manufactured goods	30
Local service providers	21–30

Source: Interviews with five downstream firms, 2012.

Of the parameters set by these five firms for their suppliers, trust is the most important when they select suppliers (figure 5.13). Trust refers both to contractual trust (meeting contractual obligations) and to competence trust (suppliers' ability to deliver).

The firms report that local companies tend to underperform (figure 5.14), although trust and price competitiveness are almost as good.

FIGURE 5.13: PROCESSING AND MARKETING FIRMS' VIEWS ON CRITICAL SUCCESS FACTORS IN NIGERIA'S OIL INDUSTRY

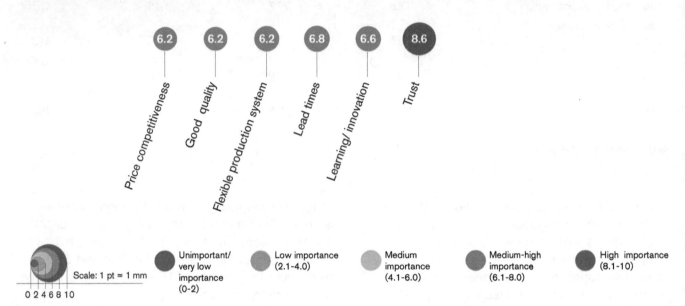

Source: Interviews with five downstream firms, 2012.

FIGURE 5.14: RATING OF LOCAL SUPPLIERS RELATIVE TO LEAD-FIRMS' EXPECTATIONS IN NIGERIA'S OIL INDUSTRY

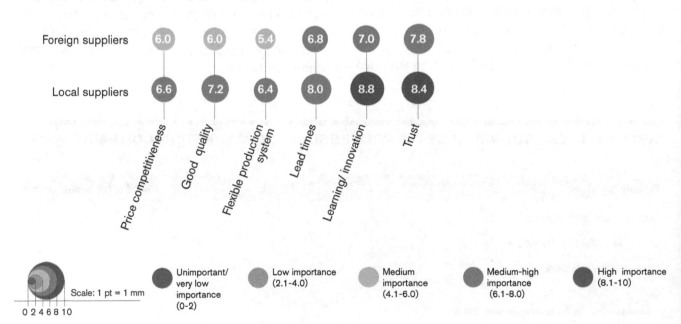

Source: Interviews with five downstream firms, 2012.

To address weak local capabilities, the five firms work with suppliers in a range of areas (table 5.7). They regard cooperation as closer for information exchange, monitoring production efficiency, facilitating access to finance, improving technical capabilities, and reducing delivery times. Two firms have set up supply-chain management departments to identify issues and assist local suppliers.

Supply-chain issues are important, but key constraints to deepening local value addition reside elsewhere: poor infrastructure, corruption and security, as well as poor access to finance (figure 5.15).

TABLE 5.7: CORPORATE VISION AND SUPPLY-CHAIN DEVELOPMENT STRATEGY

Question	Firm 1	Firm 2	Firm 3	Firm 4	Firm 5
Information exchange	Consistently	Sometimes	Sometimes	Consistently	Consistently
Monitor production efficiency	Consistently	Sometimes	Often	Consistently	Often
Upgrade production efficiency	Consistently	Sometimes	Often	Often	Sometimes
Upgrade product quality	Often	Often	Often	Often	Consistently
Reduce cost of production	Sometimes	Rarely	Sometimes	Sometimes	Sometimes
Reduce the cost of inventory	Often	Rarely	Sometimes	Rarely	Sometimes
Improve delivery time	Consistently	Sometimes	Consistently	Consistently	Consistently
Improve access to working capital/finance/equity capital	Consistently	Sometimes	Consistently	Consistently	Consistently
Provide skills training	Often	Sometimes	Often	Often	Consistently
Improve technical capabilities	Consistently	Sometimes	Consistently	Consistently	Consistently
Developing internal quality assurance system	Sometimes	Often	Sometimes	Often	Consistently
Joint new product design/ development	Consistently	Sometimes	Consistently	Sometimes	Rarely
Financing pre-investment studies i.e. business plan, market studies or feasibility studies	Consistently	Often	Consistently	Sometimes	Sometimes

Source: Interviews with five downstream firms, 2012.

FIGURE 5.15: RATING OF FACTORS AFFECTING LINKAGE DEVELOPMENT IN NIGERIA'S OIL INDUSTRY

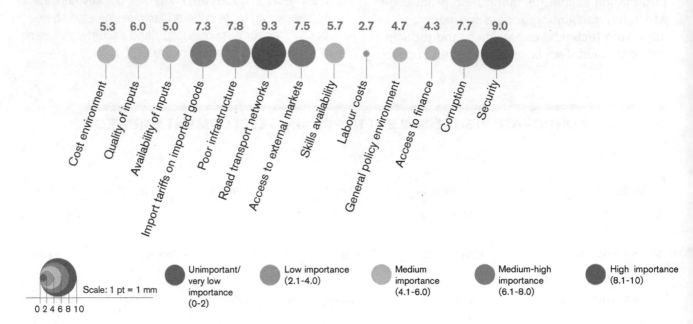

Source: Interviews with five downstream firms, 2012.

Policies

Nigeria has deployed linkage development strategies since the 1970s:

- The Petroleum Act of 1969 included a section on protecting indigenous Nigerian firms.

- The NNPC (set up in 1971) and its joint ventures with oil multinationals aimed to raise local participation in oil extraction.

- The Joint Operating Agreement of 1991 and the Production Sharing Contract of 1993 with multinational oil companies aim to have local procurement provisions. Such stipulations also apply to the Niger Delta Development Commission, set up in 2000.

- The Nigerian Content Policy of 2005 has directives on domiciliation of services, award of low-tech onshore supply of goods and services to indigenous firms, and support for domestic procurement.

In 2010, the country enacted a new Nigerian Content Policy to promote local value addition, build local capacity and improve linkages between the oil and gas industry and other sectors of the economy. This policy gives first consideration to Nigerian independent operators in awarding oil blocks, oilfield licences, oil-lifting licences and contracts. The policy has set a minimum local content target of 70 per cent for all works and contracts to be undertaken in, or on behalf of all oil and gas companies operating in, Nigeria.

Nigeria's local content strategy has had mixed success. Local content has indeed increased but not as fast as hoped for. It is estimated that local content ranged from 3–5 per cent in the 1970s to 1990s, 14 per cent in 2003 and about 20 per cent in 2004 (UNCTAD and Calag, 2006). This should be compared with 45–75 per cent recorded in, for example, Brazil, Malaysia, Norway and Venezuela (UNCTAD and Calag, 2006). By 2009, Nigeria had reached 39 per cent (Oyejide and Adewuyi, 2011).

Local content policy has suffered from poor monitoring and supervision capacity by the NNPC, and lack of comprehensive legislation (Oyejide and Adewuyi, 2011). Low funding for the NNPC is an important part of the problem (EIU, 2009), aggravated by the crisis in the Niger Delta region, where instability and violence make business difficult. The views of the firms surveyed confirm these points: they are all aware of government policy to increase local content, but think it would be more effective if coupled with implementation capacity.

5.4 COPPER

The global value chain

From 2002, copper has seen a price boom (figure 5.16). Demand has been driven by China's

investment in infrastructure and housing, and by household consumer-goods manufacturing (Farooki and Kaplinsky, 2012). The supply response to the boom has been slow owing to the long gestation periods involved in mining. Exploration and mine development—the initial stages of the value chain(figure 5.17)—require large capital investment (usually sunk costs) and involve very high risks of exploration failure. Exploration and mining have also been hit by falling ore grades in developed areas (such as the US and Chile), high cost of capital, exchange rate risks, political instability and labour disputes in producing countries, and increasing costs of exploring and mining new areas (ICSG, 2010). The combined effect has been to add upward pressure on prices.

FIGURE 5.16: COPPER, LONDON METAL EXCHANGE SPOT PRICES, JANUARY 1980–SEPTEMBER 2012 ($ PER METRIC TON)

Source: International Monetary Fund Primary Commodity Price Data, retrieved from www.imf.org/external/data.htm (accessed 20 October 2012).

Note: Grade A cathode, CIF European ports.

FIGURE 5.17: COPPER GLOBAL VALUE CHAIN

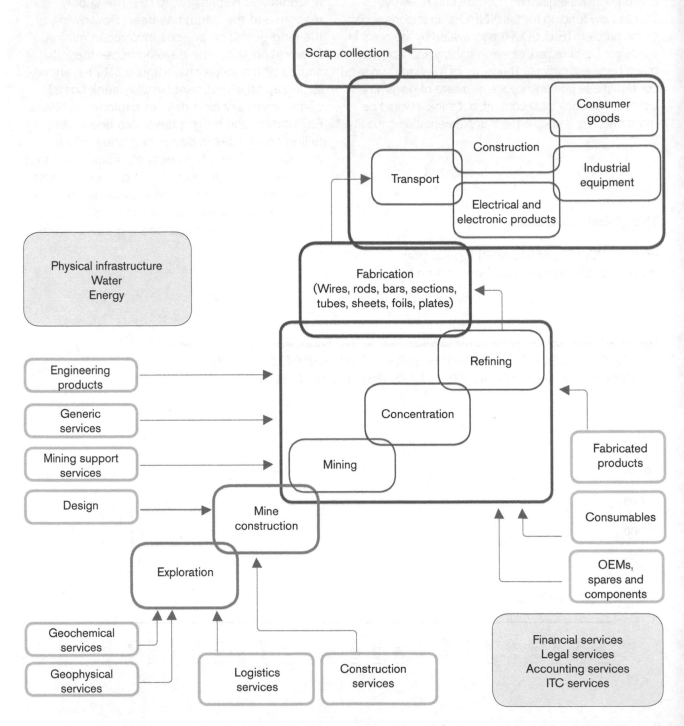

Source: ECA and AUC.

Mining, smelting and refining are the activities in the copper value chain associated with higher returns. In light of the above supply-side constraints, and given high profitability of exploration and mining in the last decade, mining companies responded with huge mergers and acquisitions around the globe (Farooki and Kaplinsky, 2012). Acquiring existing production facilities became the fastest avenue for TNCs to control production, facilitated by the privatizing wave in many developing countries from the 1990s.

An important feature of the copper mining industry is the shift in ownership. By 2009, half the top 30 mining companies came from emerging economies (Humphreys, 2009), including Brazil, Chile, India, Indonesia, Kazakhstan, Mexico, Poland, Russia and South Africa. Eight of those 15 produced copper. The leading copper commodity producers are now huge international concerns, in both industrialized and emerging economies, relying on global networks of suppliers.

The supply chain for copper mining, smelting and refining—the focus of the case study—involves a wide range of goods and services (table 5.8). These include sophisticated and capital-intensive manufactured goods, such as drilling equipment, conveyors, locomotives, and scrapers. As highly sophisticated services consist of specialized transport services and of engineering services such as mining, electrical, mechanical and civil engineering. (These goods and services tend to be imported, with little local value added.) Mid-range in technology and skills intensity are supplies such as explosives, detonators, process control services and fabrication. Low-tech, low-skills services such as cleaning, catering, security and personnel transport are the supply links often locally outsourced in African producing countries (Morris et al., 2012).

TABLE 5.8: SUPPLIES TO THE COPPER GLOBAL VALUE CHAIN

Stage	Supply
Open-pit mining and underground mining	Explosives, detonators, drilling equipment and parts, conveyors, haulage and excavators and their parts, tyres, consumables (fuel and lubricants), bulk materials handling (conveyors, locomotives, scrapers), pumps and valves, vehicles, head gear (motors, chains, cables), ventilation equipment, services.
Minerals processing	Crushing and grinding equipment, storage tanks, chemicals and reagents, liquid-solid separation equipment, materials handling (conveyors, pumps)
Smelting	Furnaces, dryers, refractories, tapping equipment
Solvent extraction and electrowinning	Reagents, chemicals, lime, handling equipment, vessels
General supplies and services	Personnel protective equipment, health services, electrical equipment, electrical and mechanical engineering services, security services, catering, cleaning, administration, process control, civil engineering services, fabrication products, construction material, rubber products, transport, power, laboratory testing services, pneumatic and hydraulic equipment and services

Source: Fessehaie (2012a).

A strategy aimed at building localized backward linkages to mining can offer opportunities for Africa to develop its manufacturing and services—particularly as investment in copper mining increases—ensuring the soundness of this strategy for some years. Because these backward linkages entail a wide range of technology, skills, capital and minimum scales, African countries at different stages of economic development have a wealth of linkage opportunities.

Zambia's copper industry

Zambia is Africa's largest copper producer, exporting $6.8 billion of copper in 2011. It contributes around 10 per cent of formal employment, and its share of GDP increased from 6.2 per cent in 2000 to 9.9 per cent in 2010. With a reserve base of 35 million metric tons of copper, even without new discoveries, copper mining could continue at current rates for 60 years (ICSG, 2007).

Copper mining was opened to private investors in the 1990s, after structural adjustment. In 1997–2004, all the mines had been privatized and sold to a heterogeneous group of investors. Alongside mining companies from Europe, North America, Australia and South Africa—most of them listed on stock exchanges—Zambia's copper attracted Vedanta

Resources from India (although listed in London) and the Non-Ferrous Metals Corporation from China.

Most copper is exported refined, reflecting heavy investment in smelting prompted by the copper price boom, as exemplified by the Chinese mining company in a $310 million smelter.

Forward linkages are few, with one main semi-fabricates manufacturers (Metal Fabricators of Zambia) producing copper wire, copper rods and power cables for the local market and for export (South Africa and other regional markets). Downstream processing capacity may come from a Chinese investment in the Chambishi Zambia–China Economic and Trade Cooperation Zone, worth $800 million.[6] This investment has the potential to transform Zambia's copper sector into a platform for industrializing the Copperbelt.

Zambia has a long history of supply linkages for Copperbelt mines (Fessehaie, 2012b). During mining nationalization in the 1970s and 1980s, backward linkage development to copper mining was used to promote local manufacturing, but after the subsequent privatization, most manufacturing capabilities were lost, and the local supply chain became populated by service providers, which may be grouped into several subcategories (box 5.6).

BOX 5.6: SERVICE PROVIDERS FOR ZAMBIA'S COPPER

Agents and distributors supply the mining sector with capital goods, spares, components and consumables (engineering products, electrical equipment, reagents). These firms often provide services with very little value added, especially another subcategory of suppliers—small importers. This is a large group of micro-businesses importing goods from South Africa irregularly, adding very little value. With no overheads and operating largely outside the tax regime, these small traders have pushed more established suppliers out of the value chain. Their lack of technical expertise, facilities or capital often translates into failure to meet delivery times, and in poor advisory and after-sale services. Because of this, after the 2008–2009 copper price collapse, many mining companies squeezed them out of their supply chains.

A small group of agents have higher capabilities. They have managed to upgrade and provide value-added services such as stockholding and stock management, and repair and maintenance services. Some have also developed backward linkages to foreign manufacturers. By becoming sole distributors and operating under technology agreements, they have addressed two key constraints facing Zambian suppliers—access to capital and to knowledge.

Another group of suppliers is highly specialized, and operates in skilled and sometimes capital-intensive supply links. These services include drilling, engineering, specialized transport, and pneumatic and hydraulic systems. Zambian-owned firms have been fairly successful in entering this subsector (as well as the above subcategories, especially when entry barriers were skills related, such as mechanical engineering, rather than capital related, such as specialized transport).

Mining equipment is generally bought through local subsidiaries of original equipment manufacturers. These subsidiaries undertake little or no manufacturing locally, but focus on after-sales services, such as provision of spares and components, repair and maintenance. They invest heavily in skills development, through continuous upskilling, local training centres and sending personnel to South Africa for further training.

Finally are the manufacturing companies supplying inputs such as metallurgical, plastic, rubber, painting and engineering products. Apart from one large steel foundry, they are quite small. This group includes companies established after privatization, mainly by South African and Asian investors, as well as firms established before the 1990s. Of the latter, very few managed to compete with imports from South Africa and Asia, and most closed. The firms that survived include Zambian, European and Asian firms.

Source: Fessehaie (2012b).

Previous research has shown that ownership of the mining companies has important consequences for local supplier upgrading (Fessehaie, 2012a). In particular, supply firms in the supply chains of industrialized countries or South African mining companies were more likely to receive direct and indirect cooperation in product and process upgrading, unlike supply firms in the supply chains of Chinese or Indian mining companies, which had arm's-length, market-based relationships. While at least the Chinese supply chain offered substantial market opportunities and lower entry barriers, neither Chinese nor Indian companies supported local upgrading (Fessehaie, 2012b). The only supply firms that could escape these dynamics were those with strong backward linkages to original equipment manufacturers as subsidiaries or sole distributors.

Two firms' employment, spending and perceptions

The case study looked at the two largest copper producers in the country, both headquartered abroad, which together account for more than half total copper output. Employment is substantial (table 5.9). The interviews found that one company had 8,656 permanent employees in 2012, the other 2843. Around 90 per cent of them are involved in mining operations, and around 10 per cent in management. Of the permanent staff, 22–26 per cent are unskilled, and 35–62 per cent have a school-leaving certificate. In one of the companies almost 38 per cent of staff have a tertiary education.

TABLE 5.9: STRUCTURE OF EMPLOYMENT IN TWO ZAMBIAN COPPER MINERS, 2012 (NUMBER OF REGULAR JOBS)

	Firm 1			Firm 2
	Female	*Male*	*Female*	*Male*
Management level				
Higher	2	19	1	2
Middle	11	55	0	51
Lower	104	831	22	140
Qualifications				
Tertiary education	527	2,731	33	428
School-leaving certificate	150	2,881	90	1,668
Unskilled	32	2,333	6	608
Nationality				
Foreign	3	105	10	148
Local	706	7,842	119	2,566
Total	**709**	**7,947**	**129**	**2,714**

Source: Interviews with five downstream firms, 2012.

The companies also employ thousands of largely unskilled contract workers (one firm reported employing 14,000). Female workers are largely represented in the tertiary-educated, lower-management sections of the labour structure. Increasing copper prices and investment have led to growing employment—in one company by as much as 20 per cent in 2005–2011.

The companies invest in human resources at different levels—funding primary, secondary and technical education in the local community, scholarship programmes at tertiary education institutions abroad, and executive business management training for senior management.

The two firms' procurement decisions are made in Zambia, although headquarters abroad are involved in big-ticket items. The structure of local procurement differs, but at first sight local operational spending appears significant in 2012 (table 5.10), at $400 million–$800 million, or more than 80 per cent of the total.

TABLE 5.10: SOURCING BY TWO COPPER FIRMS, 2012

	Suppliers				Operational spending ($ million)			
	Local		Foreign		Local		Foreign	
	Number	*%*	*Number*	*%*	*Amount*	*%*	*Amount*	*%*
Firm 1	448	58	319	42	801[a]	83	160	17
Firm 2	926	83	185	17	396[b]	84	74	16

Source: Interviews with two firms, 2012.

a. Including contract labour; excluding such labour: $584 million(77% local and 23% foreign); b. Excluding contract labour.

Note: Expenditures exclude fuel, heavy fuel oil, electricity, wages, social expenditures, certain service costs and capital costs.

A discussion of these figures requires qualification, however. First, these figures do not reflect the value-added content of the local supply chain. These values are often expenditures on local importing agents, whose operations are characterized by low levels of technology, skills, management and labour. They merely import and add a mark-up, which means that, besides some logistical capabilities, they develop very few capabilities. Second, these figures refer to locally registered suppliers, without distinguishing between Zambian- and foreign-owned businesses. Unfortunately therefore, the data tell us little about value addition and local embeddedness of Zambia's copper supply chain.

The structure of local spending also varies, the result of different procurement strategies (see table 5.10). One of the firms sources from over 900 local suppliers (more than 80 per cent of total suppliers). The average order size is

$428,000. The other relies on about half that number of local suppliers (only 58 per cent of suppliers), but places average orders of $1.3 million. The second firm has a procurement strategy that aims to consolidate and rationalize the supply base. By identifying the most capable suppliers and cooperating with them to build their competitiveness, it intends to outsource more, and better, to local suppliers. (The first mining company is not reorganizing.)

Mining companies in Zambia are often certified by the International Organization for Standardization and are required to produce consistently high-quality copper, reflected in the CSFs, along with price competitiveness and trust (figure 5.18). Poor quality or lead times could have onerous financial implications if, for example, mining ceased or if workers' safety was compromised. For these reasons, mining companies set very demanding parameters.

FIGURE 5.18: CRITICAL SUPPLY-CHAIN FACTORS IN ZAMBIA'S COPPER INDUSRTY

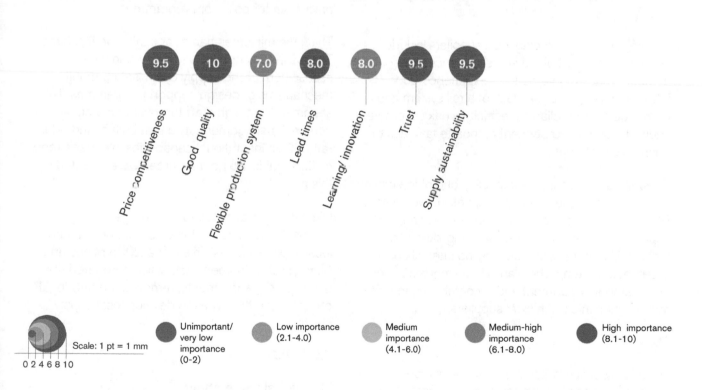

Source: Interviews with two firms, 2012

Local manufacturers often lack the technological capabilities, financial resources and economies of scale to enter the most capital- and technology-intensive links of the supply chain. Hence, the two firms report that expenditures on locally manufactured goods tend to be very low.

For local manufacturers to produce mining equipment, there are also significant barriers in terms of patents, standards compliance, R&D requirements and warranty systems enforced by original equipment manufacturers, which ensure that the latter also largely control the supply of spare parts. According to the two firms, local manufacturers could enter manufacturing of mill balls, core trays and protective personal equipment, and assemble light vehicles.

Most of the local expenditures are for local services or imports through local agents, the former mainly drilling, transport, construction, explosive blending, mechanical and electric engineering; the latter mainly mining equipment, spares and materials, largely from South Africa. For one of the firms, the major sources of imports are South Africa (58 per cent), Europe (17 per cent), India and the Middle East (12 per cent each).

The key constraints facing local suppliers include lack of technically trained and experienced personnel, managers' lack of international experience, poor infrastructure (particularly lack of a rail system and border delays), unreliable electricity, weak government support (such as 35 per cent corporate tax), lack of finance and corruption.

To address weak supplier capability, one of the mining companies designed a Local Business Development Plan, which focuses on improving delivery time, improving access to finance, providing skills and technical know-how, and developing internal quality assurance systems. The plan is implemented by the procurement department and is contributing to long-term relationships with local suppliers.

Policy

Historically, policy in Zambia played a key role in the extent and nature of local linkages (Fessehaie, 2012a,b). After privatization, the policy framework for upstream linkages to the mining sector was set by development agreements between the government and mining companies, which included provisions

on local procurement. The companies were to grant local firms adequate opportunities to bid for tenders and to ensure no unfair discrimination. They also had to submit a local business development programme, monitored by a cabinet-appointed, interministerial committee drawn from the Ministry of Mines and Mineral Development and the Ministry of Commerce, Trade and Industry.

The development agreements' provisions on local suppliers were, however, largely disregarded by both the mines and the government, for three reasons.[8]

First, the years after privatization were focused on recapitalizing the mines. Later, policymakers and the public focused on revenue and miners' wages (Mutesa, 2010). Also, until 2007, the contents of the agreements were largely unknown to the public, hamstringing civil society's efforts to lobby for enforcement (Haglund, 2010).

Second, policymakers failed to see the potential for private sector development in localizing upstream linkages. In 2012, they were not included in the Commercial, Trade and Industrial Policy nor in any private sector policy or programme.

Third, the ministries had poor institutional capacity. They failed to conduct any comprehensive assessment of the supply chain, set up monitoring mechanisms or design support programmes. This stemmed from high staff turnover and a highly personal management style that built on individual rather than institutional capabilities. Neither strong political guidance nor resources were invested in this area.

Ultimately, policy failed to encourage mining companies to increase local content or to upgrade local suppliers' capabilities. The 2008 Mines and Minerals Development Act, which abrogated the development agreements, removed the only legal obligation on the mines to develop local supply clusters.

5.5 GOLD

The global value chain

World prices for gold have soared in the last decade (figure 5.19), driven by demand, especially from emerging economies such as China. In 2009, central banks, notably those of China, India, the Philippines and Russia, used considerable amounts of their liquid reserves to buy gold as a means of diversifying their reserves assets in the aftermath of the global financial crisis (Bloch and Owusu, 2011). At the same time, new products have been devised for investment, notably exchange-traded funds.

FIGURE 5.19: WORLD GOLD PRICE, JANUARY 1970–AUGUST 2012 ($ PER TROY OUNCE)

Source: UNCTADStat, retrieved fromhttp://unctadstat.unctad.org/ReportFolders/reportFolders.aspx (accessed 18 October 2012).

Note: Gold 99.5 per cent fine, afternoon fixing, London.

Historically gold production has been dominated by a few countries, namely South Africa, the US, Canada, Australia and the former Soviet Union. South Africa has been the leading producer of gold, accounting at peak levels for 60 per cent of world mine production (Mjimba, 2011). Declining levels of production in South Africa have been offset by increasing production in smaller producing countries, including Ghana and some other countries in West Africa (Bloch and Owusu, 2011). West Africa's output (Mali, Guinea, Burkina Faso, Mauritania and Côte d'Ivoire) rose by 65 per cent in 2006–2011, to 8 per cent of global output. A total of 55 companies are involved in 123 projects in 10 West African countries, including Ghana.

The gold GVC is divided into four stages: exploration, mine development, production, and refining and beneficiation (figure 5.20). Final destinations include jewellery and industry (electronics and dentistry), as well as financial investment. The supply chain for gold production, similar to copper production, includes drilling equipment, conveyors, locomotives, scrapers, specialized transport services, engineering services, fabrication and low-tech services (cleaning, catering, and security and transport personnel).

FIGURE 5.20: THE GOLD GLOBAL VALUE CHAIN

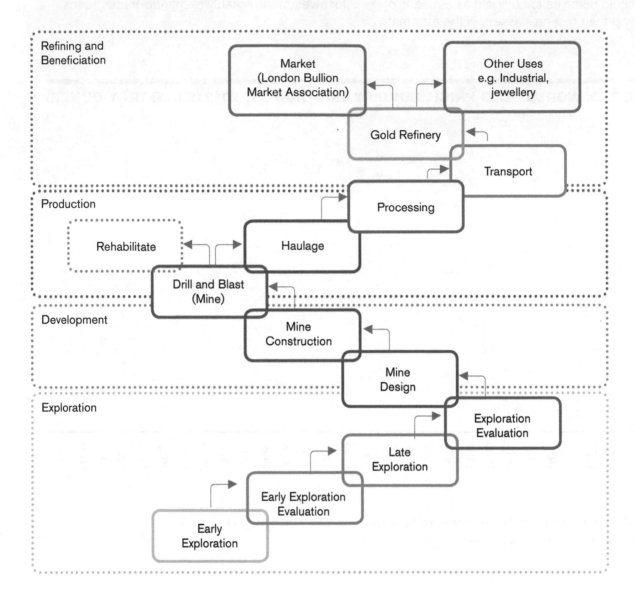

Source: Mjimba (2011).

Ghana's gold industry

Gold mining has for long been an important element of Ghana's economy (the colonizers after all called it the Gold Coast) and more recently of social development. Ghana now ranks 10th in worldwide production and second in Africa, after South Africa.[7]

Mining's contributions are manifold. The sector was the largest source of corporate tax revenue in 2010 and accounted for $5.0 billion in exports in 2011, or 40 per cent of merchandise exports. The industry accounts for more than50 per cent of foreign direct investment inflows and, with oil, accounted for 8.5 per cent of GDP in 2011. Mining showed growth of 18.8 per cent in 2010, and the extractive industry 206.5 per cent in 2011, when commercial oil production began, taking GDP growth to 14 per cent that year. Estimates from the Ghana Mineral Commission indicate that total gold production rose from 2.0 million ounces in 2004 to 3.7 million ounces in 2011. Mining and quarrying account for about 1 per cent of jobs, employing some 20,000

Ghanaians directly in large mining, 6,000 in mine support services and about 500,000 in small gold, diamond and quarry production.

Ghana has 13 large mining companies producing gold, diamonds, manganese and bauxite, and more than300 registered small mining groups and 90 mine-support service companies. Large mining is dominated by foreign multinationals from South Africa, Canada, Australia, US, UK and Norway. Small mining is dominated by Ghanaians, largely as a result of the Minerals and Mining Act of 2006 that keeps it for locals. (It is an increasingly important source of direct and indirect employment to young Ghanaians.) A worrying trend is the growing antagonism between small and large mining companies, as they compete for concessions and their operations encroach on each other.

Three firms' spending and perceptions

The case study involves three large, foreign-owned gold mining firms established in 1993–2004. They employ 2,100–5,500 workers, and appear to make substantial investments in developing human resources.

Their local sourcing is heavy, at 67–79 percent of total operational spending, or $254 million–$300 million in 2011 (table 5.11). They relied on 1,062–1,324 local firms (66–71 per cent of the total number of suppliers). Yet as with Zambia's copper mines, these figures are not indicative of local value addition or of domestic ownership of local businesses.

TABLE 5.11: SOURCING BY THREE GOLD MINING COMPANIES, 2011

| | Number of suppliers | | Value of operational expenditures ($ million) | |
	Local	Foreign	Local	Foreign
Firm 1	1,062 (68)	497 (32)	254(77)	74(23)
Firm 2	1,324 (71)	530 (29)	300(67)	150(33)
Firm 2	1,142 (66)	578 (34)	271(79)	79(21)

Source: Interviews with three firms

Note: Expenditures exclude fuel, electricity and wages capital costs. Figures in parentheses are percentages.

Local firms are involved in providing smaller equipment, components, simpler and basic manufactured products (bolts, protective equipment, fans, etc.), consumables, as well as maintenance and repair services. The problem is that those produced locally rarely meet industry requirements, so that local suppliers also import these items. According to a senior officer at the Minerals Commission, it is encouraging foreign companies that supply these local suppliers to relocate and operate in Ghana.

The firms have strict standards on occupational safety, health and the environment, which are passed down the value chain. Suppliers need to comply with them in order to enter the supply chain. In terms of CSFs, the chain is quality driven: quality is the most important criterion in selecting suppliers, followed by learning/innovation and trust (figure 5.21).

FIGURE 5.21: RATING OF LOCAL SUPPLIERS RELATIVE TO LEAD-FIRMS' EXPECTATIONS IN GHANA'S GOLD INDUSTRY

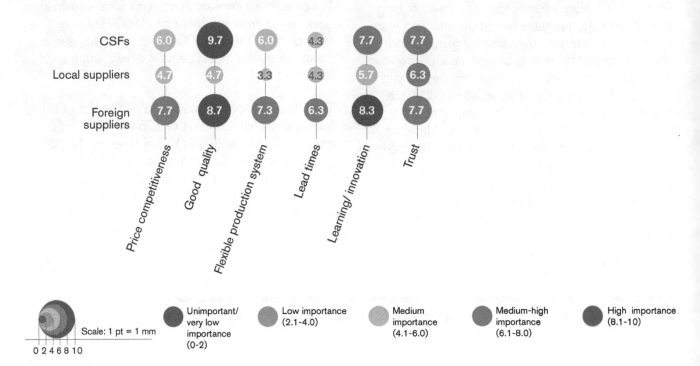

Source: Interviews with three firms, 2012

The firms have found that local suppliers (relative to foreigners) underperform on quality particularly, and that they have weaker production flexibility and learning/innovation. Their competitiveness is affected by bad roads, lack of a rail system, power shortages, limited access to finance, corruption and poor security, and a weak local business culture (for example, in respecting agreed lead times). Mobile communication has been helpful in improving supplier performance, however.

To address supply-chain bottlenecks, buyers cooperate with suppliers. They allocate staff to identify local suppliers and build capacity. Information exchange takes place through annual suppliers' summits and buyer–seller forums, and has seen local suppliers' capabilities improve on increased competition and technological capacity. Finance, skills and technological competency are other areas of cooperation.

The firms also identify challenges to increasing local processing (figure 5.22). Gold refining and further manufacturing into jewellery, medals, and industrial uses are hampered primarily by poor infrastructure, the single most important hindrance in developing forward and backward linkages.

Policy

The policy framework (encapsulated in the Minerals and Mining Act of 2006) reflects the government's effort to manage Ghana's mineral resources along the lines of sustainability and broad-based development. It focuses on skills creation, workers' safety and health.

Arising from the recent discovery and exploitation of oil and gas reserves, the issue of local-content backward linkages has taken on a new importance. A new draft policy, to be placed before the cabinet,

FIGURE 5.22: RATING OF FACTORS AFFECTING LINKAGE DEVELOPMENT IN GHANA'S GOLD INDUSTRY

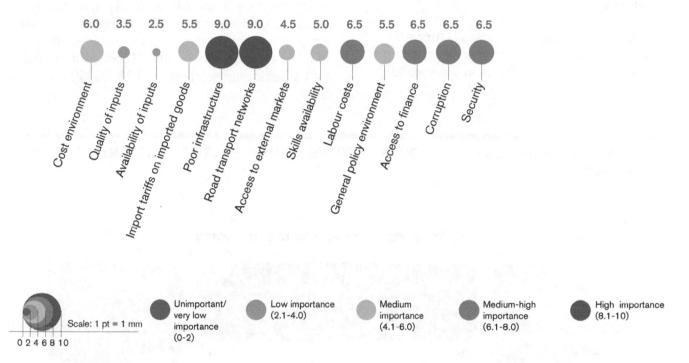

Source: Interviews with three firms, 2012.

aims to establish a more comprehensive and forward-looking framework for mining. It highlights local content to facilitate backward linkage and community development, as well as regional economic integration.

5.6 A THREE-COUNTRY COMPARISON: NIGERIA, ZAMBIA AND GHANA

These three countries' linkage development is summarized in table 5.12.

TABLE 5.12: SUMMARY COMPARISON: NIGERIA, ZAMBIA AND GHANA

Nigeria (oil)	Zambia (copper)	Ghana (gold)
Deep linkages and upgrading	*Broad but shallow linkages and no real upgrading*	*Growing linkages, but from a low basis*
• Buyer cooperation • Local content policy • CSFs: trust, lead times • Constraints: poor infrastructure, safety, corruption	• Buyer cooperation varies • Employment linkages are more important • CSFs: trust, lead times, price, consistency • Constraints: skills, finance, infrastructure	• Buyer cooperation • Skills development • CSFs: quality, technical standards, innovation • Constraints: infrastructure, finance, corruption
Strong local content policies	**No policy framework**	**New local content policy**

5.7 SOUTH AFRICA'S MINING SUPPLY INDUSTRY

Features

Mining plays a major role in South African history and economic performance, including industrialization (figure 5.23). In the second quarter of 2012, for example, mining and quarrying contributed R 66 billion to nominal GDP, which stood at R 768 billion, or a little more than 8 per cent (Statistics South Africa, 2011). The mining industry's own assessment (including the induced impact on other sectors) is close to 19 per cent of GDP, and a little more than16 per cent of total formal sector employment (CMSA, 2012).

FIGURE 5.23: LINKAGES FROM SOUTH AFRICA'S MINING SECTOR TO THE REST OF THE ECONOMY

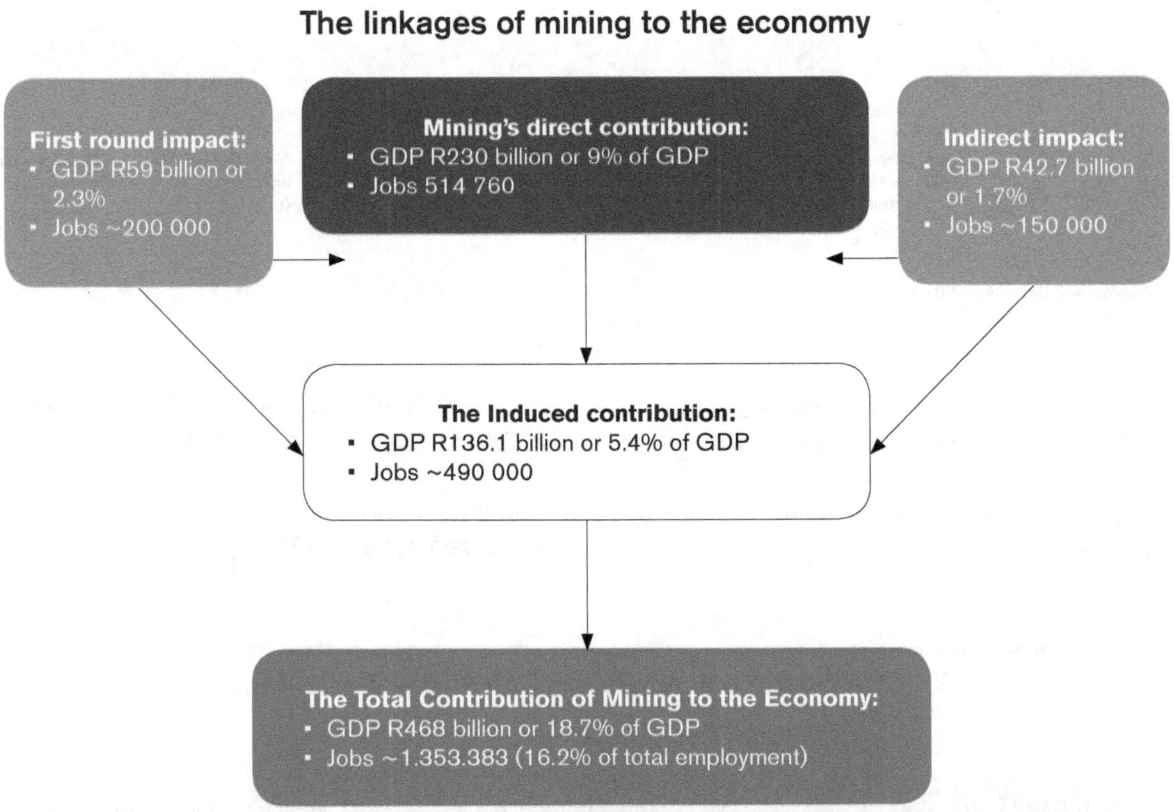

The linkages of mining to the economy

First round impact:
- GDP R59 billion or 2.3%
- Jobs ~200 000

Mining's direct contribution:
- GDP R230 billion or 9% of GDP
- Jobs 514 760

Indirect impact:
- GDP R42.7 billion or 1.7%
- Jobs ~150 000

The Induced contribution:
- GDP R136.1 billion or 5.4% of GDP
- Jobs ~490 000

The Total Contribution of Mining to the Economy:
- GDP R468 billion or 18.7% of GDP
- Jobs ~1.353.383 (16.2% of total employment)

Source: Quantec and IDC, 2010 data, retrieved from www.quantec.co.za/data (accessed 20 November 2012).

Total income of the mining industry (after depreciation and impairments) were R447 billion in 2011, and total expenditures (on the same basis) came to R437 billion. Purchasing and operating costs account for the largest share of income, followed by labour costs and capital spending (figure 5.24).

FIGURE 5.24: SOUTH AFRICA'S MINING SECTOR EXPENDITURE, 2011 (RAND)

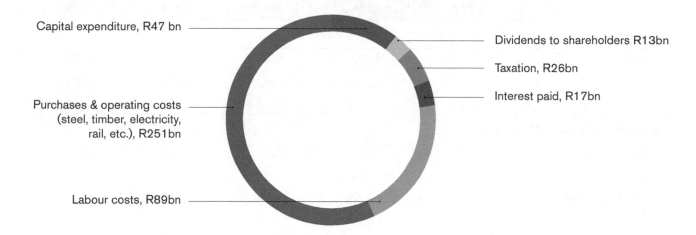

Capital expenditure, R47 bn

Dividends to shareholders R13bn

Taxation, R26bn

Interest paid, R17bn

Purchases & operating costs (steel, timber, electricity, rail, etc.), R251bn

Labour costs, R89bn

Source: Statistics South Africa (2011).

Although no precise data are available, a very large share of spending is local—of the R437 billion, an estimated 89 per cent in the country. This is why mining has such a big impact on the rest of the national economy—the money from mining circulates throughout the economy, affecting sectors as diverse as financial services and housing. Some of the spending goes towards importing equipment (such as drag-lines) that is not made in South Africa but that helps to improve mining's capital stock and the economy's productive base.

The export performance of the mining equipment and specialist services sector is indicative of its global position. Using the classification of the South African Capital Equipment Export Council (SACEEC), mining equipment is one of South Africa's largest exports, constituting 8.5 per cent of the total in 2005–2009 and 55 per cent of capital equipment exports. South Africa's global export share of the SACEEC categories over the same period averaged 0.9 per cent, which compares with South Africa's share of all global exports of 0.4 per cent. The revealed comparative advantage for mining equipment is therefore 2.25 (0.9/0.4), which is substantial.

Exports of mining equipment were put at R29 billion in 2011, having increased by 20 per cent from the previous year (SACEEC). To this figure one should add around a third, representing exports of specialist mining services in areas such as geology, exploration, mining and refining.

The local content of exports of mining equipment and specialist services is very high—estimated at 90 per cent largely explained by the country's dense network of supplier industries and the raw materials and skills required. In terms of manufacturing value added, these exports are particularly significant. Furthermore, this industry does not enjoy tariff protection (with few exceptions), nor does it receive much in the way of government subsidies. In short, it is an internationally competitive industry.

South Africa has a strong trade surplus in mining equipment with the rest of Africa (table 5.13). The share of Africa (excluding North Africa) in mining exports has risen in recent years, improving the overall trade balance, although the fastest-growing market for South African mining equipment is Latin America, according to the SACEEC. Latin America has many new mining projects, and South African exporters have a strong presence there.

TABLE 5.13: SOUTH AFRICA'S TRADE IN MINING EQUIPMENT, 2005–2009 ($ MILLION)

	2005	2006	2007	2008	2009
With the world					
Exports	3,292	4,722	6,201	6,743	4,130
Imports	3,174	4,286	5,988	6,175	3,669
Surplus	119	436	213	568	461
With Africa(excluding North Africa)					
Exports	787	1,026	1,494	1,936	1,543
Imports	11	13	15	24	32
Share of total exports (%)	24	22	24	29	37

Source: UN Comtrade, retrieved from http://comtrade.un.org/(accessed through the World Integrated Trade Solutions, 25 February 2011).

Before 1994, South African mining houses were very largely domestically focused, but the ending of apartheid allowed them to greatly expand operations abroad, a trend generally accelerating as they find that investments abroad are more attractive than those in South Africa.

It is important to analyse how much this expansion abroad boosts exports of South African mining equipment and specialist services—in other words, whether South African mining houses "take with them" South African suppliers. Interviews with mining houses and key suppliers provided differing perspectives as to whether locally known and trusted suppliers were at a competitive advantage.

The overall assessment was that this was a factor, but only to a limited extent. Most of the work is done on an open tender basis and, while knowledge and trust of local suppliers are of some consequence, tendering is highly competitive. The view of a major mining house is probably representative: "Almost all that we procure is on open tender. Sole source is a real exception. Trust is some advantage. It may also bring synergies with existent businesses. The South African supplier advantage is there, but it is on the margin."

A key marketing issue is that, once a product has been tried and tested and seen to work in South African conditions, it is recognized that it will work anywhere. South African mining houses are known to be very sophisticated and knowledgeable on what is available, and so firms that succeed with them and in South African conditions have the capacity and "pedigree" to succeed in global markets.

When operating abroad, mining houses and suppliers use very little local input, unless domestic supply firms are highly capable. Local sourcing is usually confined to labour and basic goods. There is no hostility on the part of South African mining firms to procuring products and services locally, indeed this is seen as advantageous, saving logistical costs and reducing delays and uncertainties. However, local procurement needs to be cost effective and reliable. The mining industry is also becoming more willing to procure locally, if this happens within a framework of economic sustainability and partnership with other stakeholders.

A regional hub

South Africa's role as a regional hub in the mining industry deserves particular attention. A first dimension is that some multinational firms use South Africa as a base from which they service and adapt their offerings to the rest of Africa. This was seen in interviews with some of the Scandinavian (Finnish and Swedish) companies. They have large operations in South Africa—among the largest of their operations outside their home country.

What attracts these firms to South Africa is large domestic demand for their products, a very dense network of competent supply industries and high-level skills, more especially experiential skills. South Africa is a regional hub for TNC mining companies that service and support continental operations, although some mining companies are said to have moved their research outside South Africa.

A second dimension is that some firms there provide a full-scale service in mining engineering, procurement and construction management. These firms can undertake the full gamut of tasks to bring a mine into operation, providing turnkey solutions from exploration to a working mining operation. They also undertake contract mining.

These firms are important to the industry because they provide a market for other local input providers. In an industry where trust is some advantage and with much tacit knowledge, experience with trusted suppliers is also very important. These firms are in a highly competitive market with global players (generally much larger players) and there is little room for any "local charity." So, domestic firms have to meet the requirements and have to be cost effective. This use of local inputs is also encouraged by domestic policy. Where South African firms get export credit finance, they must use at least 65 per cent local product.

A third dimension is that mining projects are administered and directed from South African head offices.[9] Sasol's operation in Mozambique, for example, produces liquid natural gas, which also entails a plant to process and compress the gas and pipe it to South Africa under a local company manager for on-site operations, but with ultimate control from South Africa.

Still, the advantages of directing global activities from South Africa may be declining. This is partly a function of a growing exposure to activities abroad—South Africa tends to be a declining share of group output. But it is also a function of the greater perceived risks in South Africa and declining relative advantages of support infrastructure. On the latter, the infrastructure is regarded as improving elsewhere (often from a low

base) whereas it is generally declining in South Africa.

The absence of government policy is also important. South Africa is not positioning itself as a hub and has no policies to encourage hub activity. By contrast, Botswana and Mauritius provide incentives for such activities and are very easy on work permits for skilled persons.

Competitiveness issues and policy implications

South African suppliers are global leaders in areas such as washing spirals, underground locomotives, submersible pumps, hydropower equipment and mining fans. The country's firms are also leaders in a raft of mining services—prospecting; geological services; shaft sinking and turnkey new mine design and operation services, as well as many others. They have a global competitive advantage in the following four main areas.

Mine safety is particularly strong and growing very fast. A third of members of the export council make safety equipment or safety-oriented equipment. This subsector includes many smaller companies, and is a very dynamic product area with new-firm entry and new products. Tracked mining—especially rail-based track mining and the use of underground locomotives—is dominated by one major company. Another company is also active and has developed fuel cell technology and associated products using platinum. In the area of shaft sinking, especially vertical shaft sinking, South Africa is the global leader. This subsector is dominated by large companies but there are many small companies managed by larger companies headquartered abroad. Finally, ventilation has been an area of considerable expertise for a very long time with a well-established society, journal and multiple companies.

Development in these areas is strong and considered much greater than in comparable mining countries such as Chile or Australia, although at least some of these areas have limited applicability to Africa, which has very little deep mining. South African capacity is generally well developed where there is considerable local demand, but in oil and gas, for example, the country has limited capacity outside ancillary services such as environmental evaluation and the generic construction and plant-maintenance skills of technicians, plumbers and welders, etc.

Several factors contribute to South Africa's competitive advantage. The most important are skills, especially experiential skills; well-established companies with leading-edge products and competencies; public research linked to firms; highly sophisticated customers; well-developed and dense networks of local supply industries and services; and geographical clustering—mining houses are clustered around Johannesburg, supply industries around East Rand. However, some of these advantages are declining or are not being further developed.

There are skills shortages at every level, particularly engineers and artisans, and many firms believe that standards are declining. Publicly funded research has fallen significantly. Mining and mining-related activities are ignored in South Africa's innovation policies. There is less research in the universities and declining links between firms and science councils. Companies increasingly see their major areas of operation outside the country, and regard South Africa as a less attractive place from which to direct and administer mining projects. The decline of South African mining output and lack of new investments is reducing the overall size, holding back the technological advance for local suppliers. Lastly, the sector is under increased competition from China at the lower end, especially equipment production, and from Australia at the upper end, especially R&D. The result is growth well below the optimum—although the industry is still very technologically sophisticated with global reach and high local content.

Mining equipment and specialist services have not received any explicit government subsidy at any stage in their development, although mining supply firms benefit from government programmes on loans, and support for studies in SADC countries and Export Marketing and Investment assistance. But some public support remains highly problematic: beyond the need to boost publicly funded R&D in research institutions and universities, university training needs to be expanded (particularly engineers) and weak artisanal training improved and recognized in other countries.

Addressing these problems is particularly urgent in the light of growing manufacturing competition (principally from East and South-east Asia) and of rising knowledge and innovation competition (mainly from Australia).

A further policy challenge is to support the spread of mining-input technologies and companies into non-mining products and markets (to some limited extent this is already happening). Some firms fail to see potential applications outside known areas and customers. But the South African capital equipment sector is highly organized with an active export association, which lets the government investigate, with the industry and association, how firms could apply their technological capacities to new products and new markets.

Precise policy modalities will differ, but South Africa can learn from Finland's experience (box 5.7). The emphasis on diversification through promoting linkages and spillovers between industries, a systemic approach to an integrated industrial and technology policy, and the development of policy in close collaboration with firms, industry associations and research bodies, provide a guideline for encouraging the lateral movement of technological competencies (Kaplan, 2012).

BOX 5.7: A NORDIC APPROACH

Finland is a paradigmatic example of successful diversification from natural resource–based industries. Its governments adopted a systems approach to industrial and technology policies, emphasizing linkages and spillovers among industries, research organizations and universities. They promoted knowledge production and formulated policy through public–private partnerships involving economic research bodies, industry federations and firms (Dahlman et al., 2006).

That firms who move into new areas take risks while much of the benefit of success falls to follower firms (second movers) constitutes a market failure, and this potentially provides a space for public policy.

One possible direct mechanism to encourage the spread of frontier technologies into new products and markets would be a "challenge fund", which would support firms to use their mining-related technological capacities in this way. The fund would meet part of the costs incurred by the firm. Qualifying items would be public goods such as training and infrastructure. Applications for support should be judged on competitiveness and by an arm's-length group composed principally of business people with industry knowledge. Such a fund could signal to firms the government's commitment to enhance new product and market development.

5.8 CONCLUSIONS

The case studies convey an important message for any African country interested in developing linkage industries: policies such as local content measures can be successful in increasing the breadth of backward linkages—the range of goods and services sourced locally by mining and oil companies. However, to increase the depth of such linkages— the value added of local activities—measures are

When backward and forward linkages have been developed successfully, government effort is required to maintain the international competitiveness of local industries.

essential to target skills development, technological capabilities, access to capital and so forth. Buyer–supplier cooperation is also critical at every stage of the value chain.

The same holds for forward linkage policies, such as export taxes or incentives to processing industries. These need to be supported by complementary policies targeting competencies of processing industries and of local suppliers.

If governments wish to embed linkages by promoting domestic ownership of the targeted supply or processing firm, the focus of policy should still be on increasing local value-added activities, as these have the most potential to create positive spillovers and to build firms' competencies in new areas.

When backward and forward linkages have been developed successfully, government effort is required to maintain the international competitiveness of local industries. Local upgrading is a continuous process. Industrial policies, ideally coordinated with other sectoral policies, should identify competitiveness bottlenecks in the local value chain, and address them.

REFERENCES

Bini, A. 2002. "Upgrading in the Leather Value Chain: The Learning Experience of Ethiopian Tanneries." M. Phil. Development Studies dissertation, Institute of Development Studies, University of Sussex.

Bloch, R., and G. Owusu. 2011. "Linkages in Ghana's Gold Mining Industry: Challenging the Enclave Thesis." MMCP Discussion Paper 1, Open University, Milton Keynes, UK.

CMSA (Chamber of Mines of South Africa). 2012. *Annual Report: Putting South Africa First.* Johannesburg.

Dahlman, C.J., J. Routti, and P. Yla-Anttila. 2006. *Finland as a Knowledge Economy. Elements of Success and Lessons Learned: Overview.* Washington, DC: World Bank Institute.

Egyptian Commercial Service. 2012. "Egytrade -Embassy of the A. R. of Egypt in Brussels - Economic and Commercial Bureau."Retrieved from www.egytrade.be/286(accessed 14 August 2012).

EIU (Economist Intelligence Unit). 2009. "Country Profile 2009: Nigeria." London. Retrieved from http://portal.eiu.com/report_dl.asp?issue_id= 544096039&mode=pdf (accessed 13 May 2009).

Farooki, M., and R. Kaplinsky. 2012.*The Impact of China on Global Commodity Prices: The Global Reshaping of the Resource Sector.* London: Routledge.

Fessehaie, J. 2012a. "The Dynamics of Zambia's Copper Value Chain." Unpublished PhD Thesis, University of Cape Town, South Africa.

———. 2012b. "What Determines the Breadth and Depth of Zambia's Backward Linkages to Copper Mining? The Role of Public Policy and Value Chain Dynamics." *Resources Policy* 37(4): 434–51.

GFMS Group. 2010. *Gold Survey* 2010. London.

Government of Ethiopia. 2002. "Industrial Development Strategy of Ethiopia, August 2002." Ministry of Trade and Industry, Addis Ababa.

Haglund, D. 2010. "Policy Evolution and Organisational Learning in Zambia's Mining Sector." Unpublished PhD Thesis, University of Bath, UK.

Humphreys, D. 2009. *Emerging Players in Global Mining.* Extractive Industries for Development Series Working Paper 5. Washington, DC: World Bank.

IDEA(International Institute for Democracy and Electoral Assistance).2001.Democracy inNigeria: *Continuing Dialogue(s) for Nation-building.* Capacity-building Series 10. Stockholm.

ICSG (International Copper Study Group). 2007. *Zambia Country Profile.* ICSG Insight 2. Lisbon.

———. 2010. *World Copper Factbook* 2010. Lisbon.

Kaplan, D. 2012. "South African Mining Equipment and Specialist Services: Technological Capacity, Export Performance and Policy." *Resources Policy* 37(4):425–33.

Kiruthu, S. 2002. *Benchmarking the African Leather Sector.* Vienna: United Nations Industrial Development Organization.

Mähler, A. 2010.*Nigeria: APrime Example of the Resource Curse? Revisiting the Oil-Violence Link in the Niger Delta.* GIGA Working Paper 120, German Institute of Global and Area, Hamburg.

Memedovic, O., and H. Mattila. 2008. "The Global Leather Value Chain: The Industries, the Main Actors and Prospects for Upgrading in LDCs." *International Journal of Technological Learning, Innovation and Development* 1(4): 482–519.

Mjimba, V. 2011. "The Nature and Determinants of Linkages in Emerging Minerals Commodity Sectors: A Case Study of

Gold Mining in Tanzania." MMCP Discussion Paper 7, Open University, Milton Keynes, UK.

Morris, M., R. Kaplinsky, andD. Kaplan. 2012.*One Thing Leads to Another: Promoting Industrialisation by Making the Most of the Commodity Boom in sub-Saharan Africa*. Published online by M.Morris, R. Kaplinsky, and D.Kaplan. Available at: http://oro.open.ac.uk/30047/7/MMCP_Paper_12.pdf

Mutesa, F. 2010. "China and Zambia: Between Development and Politics." In *The Rise of China and India in Africa: Challenges, Opportunities and Critical Interventions*, ed. F. Cheru and C. Obi, 167–78. Uppsala, Sweden: Zed Books.

Oyejide, T.A., and A. O. Adewuyi. 2011. "Enhancing Linkages of Oil and Gas Industry in the Nigerian Economy." MMCP Discussion Paper 8, Open University, Milton Keynes, UK.

Statistics South Africa.2011. "Quarterly Financial Statistics, December 2011." Pretoria.

Tegegne, G., and T. Tilahun. 2009. "Innovation in the Footwear Sector and Some Effects on Employment and Poverty in Ethiopia: A Case Study Approach." Addis Ababa University, African Clothing and Footwear Research Network.

Teka, Z. 2011. "Backward Linkages in the Manufacturing Sector in the Oil and Gas Value Chain in Angola." MMCP Discussion Paper 11, Open University, Milton Keynes, UK.

Tschirley, D., C. Poulton, N. Gergely, P. Labaste, J. Baffes, D. Boughton, and D. Estur. 2010. "Institutional Diversity and Performance in African Cotton Sectors." *Development Policy Review* 28(3): 295–323.

Ukiwo, U. 2008. "Nationalization versus Indigenization of the Rentier Space: Oil and Conflicts in Nigeria." In *Extractive Economies and Conflicts in the Global South: Multiregional Perspectives on Rentier Politics*, ed. K. Omeje, 75–91. Aldershot, UK: Ashgate.

UNCTAD (United Nations Conference on Trade and Development) and Calag. 2006.Creating Local *Linkages by Empowering Indigenous Entrepreneurs. African Oil and Gas Services Sector Survey*, Vol 1–Nigeria. Geneva: United Nations.

NOTES

[1] Qualifying Industrial Zones are designated geographical areas in Egypt that enjoy duty-free status with the US. Companies in such zones are granted quota- and duty-free access to the US, provided that they satisfy predefined rules of origin, that is, 35 per cent of the commodity is manufactured in a qualifying zone, and a minimum of 10.5 per cent of the product is from Israeli inputs.

[2] Clothing exports from Egypt to the US through the Qualifying Industrial Zone increased from $288.3 million in 2005 to $924.1 million by December 2011.

[3] Such as Walmart Ethical Standard, Kohl's Terms of Engagement, Target Standard for Vendor Engagement, SEARS Code of Vendor Conduct and the Disney Code of Conduct for Manufacturers.

[4] In which cotton lint is transformed into fabrics.

[5] "Ethiopian Leather," Light Years IP, retrieved from www.lightyearsip.net/scopingstudy/ethiopian_leather.aspx (accessed 15 November 2012).

[6] Including Chambishi Copper Smelter, acid plants, as well as a copper semi-fabricates manufacturing plant.

[7] The International Finance Corporation Suppliers' Development Programme was relatively well observed.

[8] The country also commercially exploits diamonds, manganese, bauxite and aluminium.

[9] These activities often also include financial and business services.

Making the Most of Policy Linkages in Commodities

THE BIG DIFFERENCES IN SOFT, HARD AND ENERGY COMMODITY SECTORS AFFECT HOW LINKAGES DEVELOP

COMMODITIES SPAN HIGH- AND LOW-TECHNOLOGY INDUSTRIES, LARGE AND SMALL ENTERPRISES, AND CAPITAL- AND LABOUR-INTENSIVE SECTORS. THEY ALSO DEPEND ON DIFFERENT TYPES OF INFRASTRUCTURE.

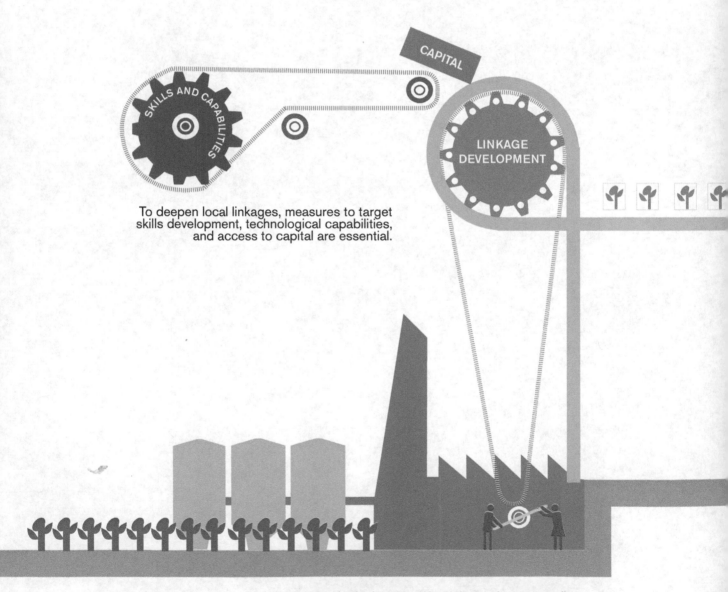

To deepen local linkages, measures to target skills development, technological capabilities, and access to capital are essential.

Most soft commodities have little technological content, lend themselves to small production, are labour intensive, require diffused infrastructure and rarely stay fresh in their natural state, requiring early processing.

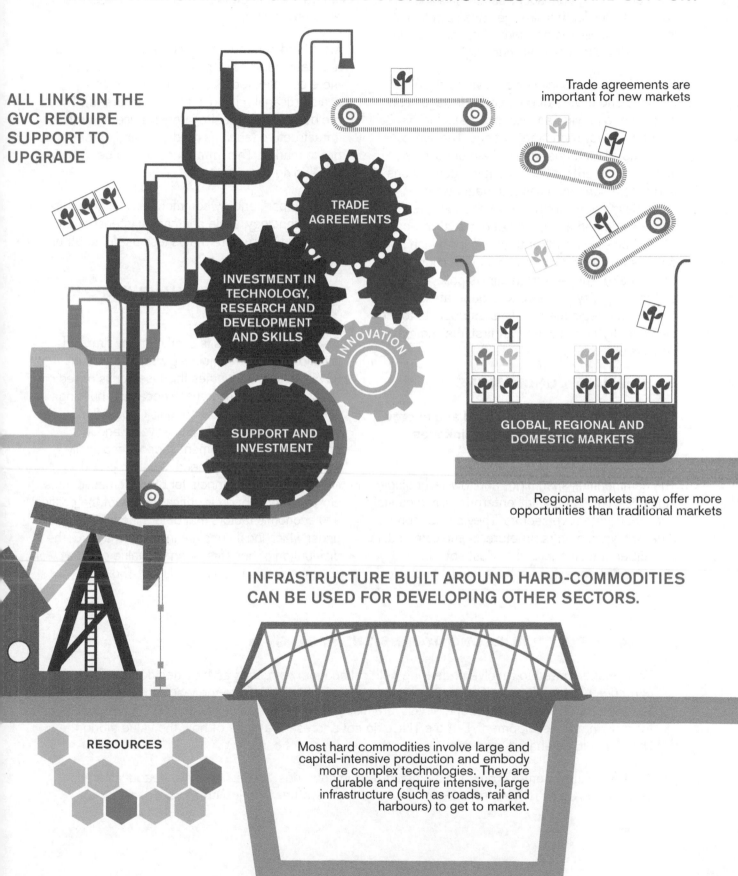

FINDING INTERNATIONAL BUYERS IS CRUCIAL …

… AND THEN STAYING IN GVCS NEEDS SYSTEMATIC INVESTMENT AND SUPPORT

ALL LINKS IN THE GVC REQUIRE SUPPORT TO UPGRADE

Trade agreements are important for new markets

TRADE AGREEMENTS

INVESTMENT IN TECHNOLOGY, RESEARCH AND DEVELOPMENT AND SKILLS

INNOVATION

SUPPORT AND INVESTMENT

GLOBAL, REGIONAL AND DOMESTIC MARKETS

Regional markets may offer more opportunities than traditional markets

INFRASTRUCTURE BUILT AROUND HARD-COMMODITIES CAN BE USED FOR DEVELOPING OTHER SECTORS.

RESOURCES

Most hard commodities involve large and capital-intensive production and embody more complex technologies. They are durable and require intensive, large infrastructure (such as roads, rail and harbours) to get to market.

The earlier chapters suggest that backward and forward linkages are developing in the soft, hard and energy commodity sectors in some African countries. The depth of linkages (the accretion of local value added) varies more by country than the breadth (the share of local spending).

Some summary conclusions on value chain linkages and drivers of commodity linkages can be drawn to provide an evidence base for this chapter's policy recommendations. The aim is not to detail individual value-chain or country issues, but to present cross-cutting conclusions and recommendations as foundations for ministries to apply to their own economic reality. The recommendations are set out in a nine-part policy framework (rather than in a long wish list of policies that may not apply to a given country or value chain). This approach allows policymakers to use the policy framework to generate more detailed strategic mechanisms appropriate to their own country's conditions. But first, the summary conclusions.

6.1 SUMMARY CONCLUSIONS

The big differences in soft, hard and energy commodity sectors affect how linkages develop

The commodities span high- and low-technology industries, large and small enterprises, and capital- and labour-intensive sectors. They also depend on different types of infrastructure. Some commodities also differ in their shelf lives. Most soft commodities, for example, have low technological

content, lend themselves to small production, are labour intensive, require diffused infrastructure, and rarely stay fresh in their natural state, requiring early processing.

Most hard commodities by contrast involve large and capital-intensive production and embody more complex technologies (although small-scale artisanal mining is fairly widespread). They are durable and require intensive use of large infrastructure (such as roads, rail and harbours) to get to market. This infrastructure can be used for developing other sectors.

For their part, energy commodities are generally very technology, scale and capital intensive and require infrastructure that is less useful to other sectors.

FINDING INTERNATIONAL BUYERS IS CRUCIAL …

Searching for buyers is costly for any firm, but is critical for a firm to join a global value chain (GVC). In some countries this insertion is based on relationships built over many decades—building linkages is neither easy nor quick. Local firms attempting to move into higher value added products need government support, especially as those firms that succeed can then provide information and channels for other domestic firms. Government support is critical in view of the political and economic factors that determine the conditions under which local firms are inserted in a GVC, the distribution of benefits along the value chain as well as resolution of trade policy issues (box 6.1).

BOX 6.1: POLITICAL ECONOMY TENSIONS FROM GVCs

Policymakers need to resolve underlying political economy stresses as they decide how their countries will benefit from GVCs. Transnational corporations (TNCs)—the lead firms—are at the forefront of advocating for deeper GVCs, premising their policy advocacy that GVCs are good for growth and development. But the TNCs do not address the issue of how the value along the chain should be shared (and this is where the policymakers come in).

Another anxiety comes from jobs. Some citizens in countries where TNCs are headquartered perceive GVCs as job destroyers—for their countries—rather than job creators.

Yet the most critical tension relates to multilateral trading rules. As discussed in chapter 2, the Doha Round has made little progress, and moves to liberalize non-agricultural goods and services are two areas with divergent views not only between developed and developing countries but even among developing countries. There are those, including the African Group, who argue that these chains are being promoted, mainly by industrial countries, as an indirect route to more deeply liberalizing trade in industrial goods (as well as services). For GVCs to be efficient, any barriers along the chain must be eliminated. This means that an export tax, for instance cannot be employed as a negative subsidy, neither can an import tariff be higher in say a given developing country, for as long as the export tax or the import tariff relate to a given GVC.

... and then staying in GVCs needs systematic investment and support

Once firms are in the GVC they are subject to very demanding market requirements. Lead firms require their suppliers to be globally competitive on critical success factors (CSFs) such as price, quality, delivery times and innovation for these companies to ward off other competitors seeking to become GVC suppliers. Firms in those value chains also have to meet technical, private, health and environmental standards set by global governance regulators.

Linkage development is thus a progressive and cumulative process, one that requires continuous investment in technology, research and development (R&D) and skills, to help firms upgrade their capabilities. This requires assistance from three sources—the lead firms, domestic skills training bodies and local innovation institutions.

All links in the value chain require support to upgrade

This may require trade-offs between various links. For example, adding value in agro-processing and making the most of soft-commodity endowments through building forward linkages has its own specific issues and constraints. Output from food commodity sectors can vary enormously in terms of meeting quality, price and technical specifications. These all relate back to the first stage of agricultural production where productivity, skills and technological capabilities have a critical impact on the volume, quality and price of inputs supplied to the processing industries. Failure to tackle these

issues through appropriate policies and strategic interventions severely constrains attempts to add value in the agro-processing stage and to shift the focal point of local industrialization.

Regional markets may offer more opportunities than traditional markets

Africa's markets may be less demanding than GVCs, allowing local firms to build the production capabilities needed to move into more demanding chains. Regional markets are particularly important for countries without large domestic markets, which underlines the importance of streamlining regional integration in Africa. Some GVCs of course offer more opportunities than others for intraregional trade, notably agro-processing chains, because Africa is fairly rich in supplies and their products tap into final markets among the continent's rising middle class.

Trade agreements are important for new markets and products

African countries could improve market access for their value-added products through agreements with traditional and emerging partners. Their strategy should aim to reduce high tariffs (on cocoa to India for example), remove tariff escalation (in the EU for instance) and remove non-tariff barriers. Tariffs have generally declined, but while several proposals were made to overcome tariff escalation, non-tariff barriers (especially technical barriers for manufactures) have escalated. For example, non-tariff barrier proposals have recently been made in the non-agricultural market access negotiations by several economies including the EU, US, Argentina, China, Cuba and Japan. African countries therefore need to adopt a unified continental negotiation framework to maximize the development impact of economic and trade agreements.

6.2 FACTORS DRIVING LOCAL LINKAGES

The unevenness of backward and forward linkage development is a function of two primary sets of linkage drivers—structural and country specific—in

a distinction that has major implications for policy (Morris et al., 2012).

Structural drivers refer to the age of the commodity-exploiting sector and sectoral factors such as the requirement for just-in-time and flexible logistics, the type of individual commodity deposits, and the technological complexity of the sector. By their nature these structural drivers are hard for policy interventions to influence. Country-specific drivers refer to more contingent factors that are dependent on national contexts, and are much easier to influence by policy (box 6.2).

BOX 6.2: COUNTRY-SPECIFIC LINKAGE DRIVERS

Examples of these contingent drivers are:

- The nationality of the lead commodity firms, and their approach to developing linkages.

- The end markets and their CSF requirements.

- The nature and quality of hard and soft infrastructure (including poor access to credit institutions), which help (or hinder) linkage development.

- Skills and institutional capabilities, at firm and country level.

- Social and political factors, such as corruption and security.

- Government policies and effectiveness of implementation.

In other words, policymakers must analyse how multiple factors influence the economic terrain of each country. A country-specific industrialization strategy to facilitate local production linkages would depend on the sector, commodity characteristics (linkage possibilities vary), characteristics of particular value chains, CSFs in different value chains, firms' and institutions' capabilities, stakeholders, and state capacity to make the necessary institutional arrangements.

As country-specific drivers are more easily open to influence from industrial policy measures, they are the areas that policymakers should focus on.

Policymakers cannot, however, make simple, generic solutions for CSFs, which differ widely by country, sector and value chain (figures 6.1 and 6.2) and which have no easily identifiable uniformity.

FIGURE 6.1: VARIATION OF FACTORS AFECTING LINKAGE DEVELOPMENT BY SECTOR AND COUNTRY

	Nigeria Cocoa	Nigeria Oil	Egypt Textile	Kenya Tea	Kenya Vegetable	Ethiopia Coffee	Ethiopia Leather	Ghana Cocoa	Cameroon Cocoa	Ghana Gold
Cost environment	6.0	5.3	6.0	7.3	6.3	6.4	9.0	7.3	6.0	6.0
Quality of inputs	5.4	6.0	4.6	7.5	6.3	6.4	8.3	3.8	6.3	3.5
Availability of inputs	7.4	5.0	4.3	4.0	1.8	6.1	6.3	3.3	4.7	2.5
Import tariffs on imported goods	6.6	7.3	4.5	8.3	6.5	2.8	3.0	1.3	4.3	5.5
Poor infrastructure	8.4	7.8	4.8	7.3	8.3	3.2	5.3	8.3	6.3	9.0
Road transport networks	8.4	9.3	6.3	6.0	6.5	4.0	4.0	4.5	4.7	9.0
Access to external markets	8.4	7.5	6.3	3.5	1.5	2.2	2.8	4.8	7.0	4.5
Skills availability	1.6	5.7	6.5	2.0	3.0	6.2	3.9	3.8	8.3	5.0
Labour costs	6.2	2.7	7.3	3.8	3.3	3.0	4.3	6.0	6.0	6.5
General policy environment	6.2	4.7	7.3	3.3	3.3	6.1	2.5	4.0	3.8	5.5
Access to finance	9.0	4.3	7.3	6.5	7.5	1.6	6.0	8.3		5.5
Corruption	6.6	7.7	8.0	5.0	4.0	4.9	4.3	6.5		6.5
Security	7.6	9.0	7.8	3.8	4.5	1.6	1.0	4.3		6.5

Scale: 1 pt = 1 mm
0 2 4 6 8 10

Unimportant/very low importance (0-2) Low importance (2.1-4.0) Medium importance (4.1-6.0) Medium-high importance (6.1-8.0) High importance (8.1-10)

Source: Firm surveys in chapters 4 and 5.

FIGURE 6.2: VARIATION OF CSFs BY SECTOR AND VALUE CHAIN

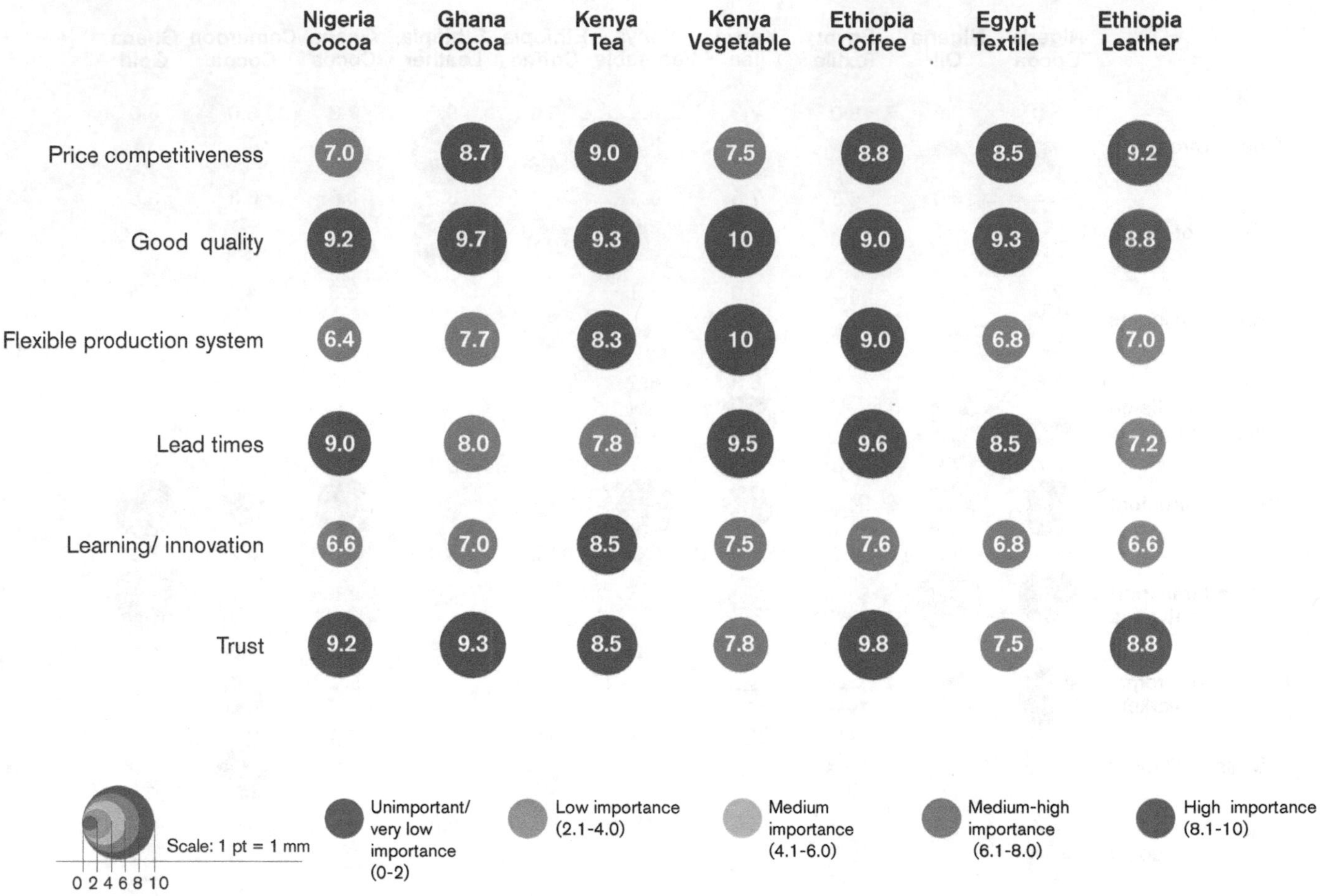

	Nigeria Cocoa	Ghana Cocoa	Kenya Tea	Kenya Vegetable	Ethiopia Coffee	Egypt Textile	Ethiopia Leather
Price competitiveness	7.0	8.7	9.0	7.5	8.8	8.5	9.2
Good quality	9.2	9.7	9.3	10	9.0	9.3	8.8
Flexible production system	6.4	7.7	8.3	10	9.0	6.8	7.0
Lead times	9.0	8.0	7.8	9.5	9.6	8.5	7.2
Learning/ innovation	6.6	7.0	8.5	7.5	7.6	6.8	6.6
Trust	9.2	9.3	8.5	7.8	9.8	7.5	8.8

Scale: 1 pt = 1 mm
0 2 4 6 8 10

Unimportant/ very low importance (0-2) | Low importance (2.1-4.0) | Medium importance (4.1-6.0) | Medium-high importance (6.1-8.0) | High importance (8.1-10)

Source: Firm surveys in chapters 4 and 5.

These figures underline the fact that a "one size fits all" approach would be a mistake. Instead, policymakers need to push through with policies on the basis of evidence for their country, and the sector and value chain under consideration. Policies will also require focused and institutionally grounded implementation strategies, with responsibilities clearly demarcated. And they need to be listed by priority so as to avoid politically driven non-implementable wish lists—given that in the real world, policy decisions revolve around trade-offs and resource availability. Policies must also be backed by transparent budgets to ensure that resources are available and results are achievable. Finally, national governments should take into account that some steps are better carried out at lower tiers, such as state, provincial or local government, to ensure the necessary institutional intimacy and knowledge-flows between civil servants and firms.

Lead commodity firms are the major drivers of GVCs and hence of linkage development. Many lead firms have structured programmes for supplier development in their global operations. These lead commodity firms embody routines for supply chain development, which hold considerable potential for local linkage development, given appropriate government policy interventions (Morris et al., 2012).

Moreover, foreign-owned lead firms, with roots in the economies of the Organisation for Economic Co-operation and Development, are vulnerable to pressures from civil society organizations in their home countries as well as from local communities in the host country to foster local industrialization, and so can be pressured by host governments to help develop local linkages.

The governance environment and engagement of local communities living near lead firms' commodity production can play a key role in enhancing local linkage development. Often this is played out in corporate social responsibility projects to ensure buy-in from local communities. In addition, many lead commodity firms have signed—often independently monitored—agreements with governments, designed to enhance local procurement. National governments must, though, use the opportunities available in their policy armoury.

This pattern of supply chain development is, however, less evident in new entrants from China. A number of African countries have had considerable success in negotiating bilateral agreements with China on infrastructure construction, industrial training, and supplier development, all of which are conducive to local linkages (although implementation is not always in line with the agreements—this ultimately is an issue for the local state).

Hard infrastructure is a significant country-specific driver: poor transport undermines the capacity of local suppliers to feed into value chains; power utility breakdowns short-circuit operational efficiency and increase costs; and slow telecoms stop local firms from taking advantage of the rapid communication that is necessary to access knowledge-intensive markets. The lead firms have some capacity to cover their own infrastructure needs and to solve their own problems, but less so their suppliers'.

The upshot is that, although lead commodity producers may wish to increase outsourcing, weak infrastructure forces them to either internalize these non-core value-added activities or import from stable foreign suppliers. Logistical efficiency also has a bearing on linkage development, as does soft infrastructure such as business support and trade facilitation.

Solid human resources are a precondition for building linkages. The skill and capability constraint in Africa is a critical determinant of linkages both by lead firms and their suppliers and downstream firms. The main gaps are usually in vocational areas (welders, fitters and turners, drivers of specialist equipment), more advanced engineering skills, and management skills for world-class manufacturing techniques. Although African governments recognize this skills gap, their ability to launch institutionally driven programmes to upgrade suppliers, processors and manufacturers is severely limited. Nearly all African countries depend on international bodies and programmes to build capabilities. As countries attempt to move up the value chain—especially for inputs to the lead commodity producers—demand for skills will necessarily increase. Any successful industrial development process will therefore soon encounter the binding constraint of skills development.

Three broad, overlapping strands are apparent on how African governments view the promotion of linkages from commodities. Many governments express a stated wish to make the most of commodities through linkages but show little strategic thinking beyond that. Others articulate a vision but they interpret "localization" as greater participation by citizens as owners rather than as a deepening of domestic value added.

Only a few put forward some sort of coherent vision, yet because most policies that exist only on paper are very poorly implemented, it is precisely these markers of progress that are needed to turn vision to reality—they should include timetables and benchmarks, positive and negative sanctions, inter-ministerial coherence, human resource capacity and political will.

6.3 A POLICY FRAMEWORK

The ultimate goal of the following nine-point policy framework is to avoid a commodity linkage template, but to help African governments in developing policies and implementation mechanisms to drive their own commodity-based industrialization. A more specific objective is to accelerate the broadening and deepening of production linkages to the particular commodity endowments of each African country—as discussed in chapter 3—and hence to shift the industrialization curve to the left (see figure 3.5).

1. Adopting a coherent industrial policy

Many high-income countries started industrializing on the basis of their natural resources, gradually developing backward and forward linkages—"one thing leads to another," per Hirschman (1981). So, the process can be left to the market and the vagaries of time, but for these precursors it was slow and the results hit and miss, and for Africa today the process may (or may not) broaden and deepen linkages

over long decades of commodity extraction (Morris et al., 2012).

So to speed up and deepen the process of value addition and linkage development, African governments need to respond strategically— working closely with other stakeholders—through formulating and implementing industrial policy along the priorities of the Accelerated Industrial Development of Africa (AIDA) Action Plan (see chapter 3). Three broad families of linkage development, where governments can hope to influence the trajectory of local supply, may be identified (box 6.3).

BOX 6.3: INFLUENCING THE TRAJECTORY OF LOCAL SUPPLY

Below are three families of industrial policy interventions to boost local linkages, depending on the ease with which linkages can be developed (box figure).

Low-hanging fruit

The first set of interventions aims to gather the "low-hanging fruit," where domestic capabilities are such that local firms can produce competitively, and these linkages provide short-term returns to major commodity firms.

Capabilities may be among labour-intensive sectors where low wages are a competitive advantage, or in sectors with high natural protection. (This protection may reflect sectors with rapid degradation of the product, where there is extensive processing loss and where transport-to-value ratios are high.) Suppliers can produce high-quality products reliably at prices that are near the global price frontier.

The priority focus in the short term should be on these low-hanging (or easily graspable) linkages. Examples are capable and competitive local suppliers whose existence is unknown to lead commodity buyers because their purchasing eyes are locked on habitual imports from their home country or other regular suppliers from other countries.

This may simply be an information problem and require buyers to be given information to help match them with potential suppliers. Or it may require government and service institutions to target support at local suppliers to reach the frontier of a buyer's CSF. Lead commodity chief executives, governments and local industry associations can play a critical role here.

Blossoms

Next are linkages where embryonic capabilities exist and where there is some prospect, with reasonable time-bound support, that local producers will "blossom" and be able to compete with foreign producers in the medium term. The primary barrier is technological, and hence various forms of government innovation and skill-enhancing support are a priority.

Another obstacle is where inputs are critical to the lead firms, such as the refluting of rollers and grinders in the Zambian copper mine production chain. The various country case studies identified the existence of local suppliers who, with some assistance, could rapidly escalate their competitiveness and meet the CSF market requirements of lead commodity firms. Development of local capabilities needs to be approached with realistic and appropriate time frames.

Seedlings

The final area consists of high profile linkages that are beyond feasible reach in the short to medium term. These linkages are ambitious "seedlings," which government can aim at in the long term. Indeed, those linkages seemingly beyond feasible reach should only be considered as part of innovative long-term industrial strategies with strong R&D support that can help break new ground. Several resource-poor countries such as Japan and Singapore provide good lessons on how well-designed industrial strategies can help such countries to develop industries and products, especially the cars and electronics that were beyond feasible reach at one point.

BOX FIGURE TRAJECTORY OF LOCAL SUPPLY

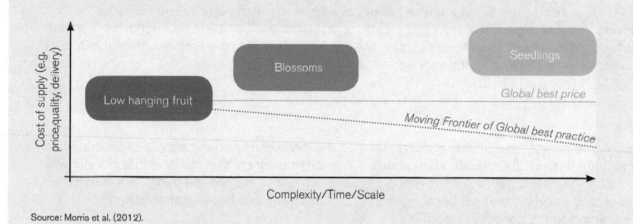

Source: Morris et al. (2012).

Some recommendations include:

- Design policies to grasp the low-hanging fruit. They may often combine very simple inputs (food, water and accommodation for workers) and more technology- and scale-intensive inputs.

- For embryonic linkages, develop targeted interventions that enable local producers to compete gradually with foreign producers. Many interventions are likely to be on building the national system of innovation, enhancing management capabilities, upgrading workforce skills and focusing on very specific and realistic technology/R&D support activities.

- Give priority to linkages that are within easy grasp or that require embryonic capabilities, policy for linkages beyond feasible reach should focus on long-term R&D that can help countries break new ground and develop new products.

2. Creating institutional industrial policy mechanisms

Best-practice industrial policy, and the mechanisms to effectively implement it, are usually country specific and optimally produced when governments work with key producer stakeholders—lead commodity producers and local suppliers. Such partnerships are all the more necessary because of the pervasive misalignment between policy and implementation that often occurs in developing countries (box 6.4).

BOX 6.4: THE GAP BETWEEN RHETORIC AND PERFORMANCE

This gap arises from three misalignments. The pervasive failure of governments, lead-commodity firms and other actors in the commodity value chain to work with suppliers and processors is perhaps the most important.

Next, within value chains, lead firms often fail to back up their strategic commitment to broadening and deepening linkages with appropriate structures. With a mine, for example, the potential for misalignment starts early in commissioning and construction where site procurement managers establish sourcing patterns based on what they regarded as best practice (what is familiar to them) from their past activities.

A final, but similar, misalignment is between governments' stated objectives on linkage development and the institutions and structures to promote it. For example, support is often the duty of the ministry that oversees commodities rather than where it belongs—with the ministry responsible for developing industry and services related to commodities.

Governments do not have all the answers—and have to learn. Hence their "leadership" entails not directing the participants but brokering meetings and ensuring that sectional interests are redirected to the collective good. They therefore need an informed picture of the strengths and vulnerabilities of the major lead commodity firms in the sector. Such knowledge will enable them to make sure that these firms actively promote local linkages, and encourage other local and foreign investors to broaden and deepen their forward and backward linkages.

Although these coalitions will inevitably reflect country context (the characteristics of the sector and the existing value chains), they should include all the main corporate participants (the dominant lead commodity firms, first-tier and some second-tier suppliers), governments, and (if possible without being overloaded) representatives of research and innovation institutions.

Experts and specialist service providers within an industry are likely to have insights into what is required and may be particularly helpful in designing and implementing policies.

Such multi-stakeholder coalitions are important for three reasons. First, each party has specific knowledge that it can contribute. Second, they will create an institutional dynamic, build public awareness and a "moral momentum" among private actors, especially lead commodity firms, focusing attention on the importance of local sourcing, local processing and general linkage development. Third, because successful implementation requires key stakeholders to take part, they are better involved in developing the linkage strategy.

Some recommendations include:

- Set up a multi-stakeholder institutional council focused on developing linkages to the commodity sector, led by the most appropriate government department (usually the ministry of industry).

- Charge the council with developing a joint, strategic vision for industrialization, garnering the most reliable and important information, and developing under its supervision an appropriate step-by-step linkage strategy specifying activities, outputs, responsibilities and milestones.

- Commission the council to oversee consultancy research and strategy development plans.

3. Developing local content policy

Local content policies have probably been the single most important policy driver of linkages from the commodity sector. World Trade Organization rules provide some legal leeway to least-developed economies—and many countries find real-life mechanisms to implement such policies.

It is crucial for such policies to be evidence based and well informed rather than ideologically driven. Local content policies to promote domestic value added have often in Africa been conflated with indigenization policies designed to transfer ownership of linkage firms, confusing two issues. The first is the need to expand local value added economic activities, and this may require attracting foreign investment, skills and technologies. The second, equally important, is to develop domestic entrepreneurship—including recognizing specific constraints that women face—and to facilitate its access to value chains. This latter goal requires instruments that range from access to capital to programmes that develop small and medium-sized enterprises.

Any local content policy should be based on the following principles: first, work with the private sector; second, engage the major commodity firms to voluntarily facilitate local sourcing; third, when necessary, use regulations to compel them to increase the breadth and depth of linkages; and finally, ensure that industrial policy has detailed step-by-step implementation measures, including monitoring and evaluation as well as sanctions.

Critical for developing domestic entrepreneurship is to provide access to finance, especially for firms willing to undertake the risks involved in moving beyond importing into more knowledge- and capital-intensive activities. Concessionary finance should therefore be part of any local content policy.

Some recommendations include:

- Ensure that local content policies are concerned with adding value locally rather than satisfying sectional political interest groups.

- Make sure that local content policies address inequality—including gender inequality—in the participation and benefit from the value, rather than perpetuating them.

- Facilitate access to finance by local women entrepreneurs.

- Identify, specify and favour subsectors that are embryonic or within easy grasp rather than beyond feasible reach.

- Remove red tape on local businesses and streamline regulations to allow new enterprises to set up.

- Ensure that policies aimed at building local content are supported by access to suitable concessionary finance through development finance institutions.

4. Raising lead-firm procurement, sourcing and processing

Major commodity firms have the potential to deliver a major impact on local (backward and forward) production linkages. They also have a major responsibility to facilitate them, but even though it is in their interest to procure locally, foster local sourcing and develop local linkages, they rarely see these steps as part of their core business. Procurement managers, struggling to meet externally imposed targets, are often driven by other factors than finding competent local firms to source from. Unless managers receive direction from the top, they will follow sourcing patterns that are most familiar to them. Governments can, though, play a persuasive and regulatory role in ensuring that lead commodity firms facilitate local sourcing.

Some recommendations include:

- Engage with major commodity firms' chief executives to ensure that they develop and publicize a strategic vision committing their company to developing local linkages.

- Require foreign lead firms to report on local sourcing by number of such enterprises, and the degree of local value added, including a clear roll-out plan for future local sourcing. Such a mechanism is likely to focus the minds of their chief executives, engender a climate of moral enforceability and help to encourage local linkages.

- Require lead commodity firms to internalize local procurement practices that should be stipulated and institutionalized as a necessary part of the activities of the company.

- Ensure that contracts with lead commodity firms to extract minerals and energy do not restrict local supply in favour of foreign suppliers as part of any aid package.

5. Running supply-chain development programmes among major commodity firms

It is in the interests of lead commodity firms to outsource many of their supplies and services. Some of them can only be imported but many can be provided locally, and as time goes by, with appropriate domestic policies, local provision can widen greatly. Although lead assemblers in the automotive industry have substantial resources to assist component suppliers upgrade their operations through internal supply-chain development programmes, such practices are extremely rare in energy, hard and soft commodity sectors. The lead firms, especially in mining, have skills that are not aligned to building such capabilities among their suppliers. Some agro-processors such as Nestlé have, though, brought in such skills and capabilities to assist farmer-suppliers.

This creates a major policy gap between interests, intentions, needs and supply-chain capabilities for African governments to fill, in three main ways. First, through a regulatory framework requiring major commodity firms to have supply-chain development reporting mechanisms, creating a moral imperative for them to focus their attention in this area. Second, public-private matching funds to facilitate supply-chain development can make a real impact on local firms' upgrading. Third, private specialist service providers can be encouraged and even subsidized if the government formulates sectoral implementation strategies.

Some recommendations include:

- Liaise with lead commodity firms through industrial policy councils to set up customized and appropriate supply chain development programmes.

- Encourage and assist lead firms in soft commodities to provide large and resource-intensive interventions to expand and upgrade agricultural producers, especially in outputs meeting the necessary quality standards, feeding into selected value chains.

- Focus on target niche markets and ensure quality certification, whether environmental sustainability, speciality products, Fair Trade and so on.

- Set up public-private commodity funding mechanisms to bring in private sector service providers skilled in developing firms' capabilities in backward and forward linkages.

6. Boosting local skills and technologies

Many potential local suppliers and processors are well behind the international competition. They lack adequate skills, technological capacities and the supportive institutions that would enable them to close the gap. Firms' spending to close the gap is often suboptimal, a result of extensive market failure. Hence, public provision can potentially play an important role in meeting these market failures. Skill shortages in many African countries represent often a binding constraint on developing industrial linkages. Lack of sufficient (and appropriate) skills hamstrings local suppliers in upgrading competitiveness, meeting technical requirements, innovating, or adopting world-class manufacturing practices and customer management programmes.

These capability gaps pervade all levels of the local economy. Among managers these gaps are often in operational and financial skills, knowledge of world-class manufacturing and manufacturing excellence, and specialist technical and engineering capability. Gaps in the general workforce refer to artisanal, basic engineering, maintenance, machinist and operator skills.

Closing these gaps requires coordinated firm, government and donor programmes to upgrade training facilities. Suppliers are often caught in a classic coordination problem—they cannot get into supply chains until they exhibit the necessary skills, technology and management capabilities, but they have great difficulty in acquiring these without being involved in supply chain programmes.

Developing backward linkages to hard commodities is particularly demanding of technological capabilities, and so government support is crucial. The case study on South Africa highlights the importance of prioritizing engineering, maintenance and technical skills at all levels, as such skills are more easily portable and play an important role in spinning off horizontal linkages into other ancillary linkage industries. Training programmes aimed at building engineering capabilities at all levels should be undertaken incrementally so as to build and spread the general corpus of these skills throughout the economy. The South African case also demonstrates that even with very high technological skills, declining investment in education, research and specialist mining and engineering institutions can lower a country's competitiveness. Building and maintaining these skills requires a partnership between private and public institutions, such as universities and specialist research centres.

Some recommendations include:

- Create matching-grant programmes for skills development and capability building that can be accessed by local firms.

- Attract international agencies to run skills-building programmes for local commodity firms.

- Create technical training institutions and upgrade curricula to expand the number of technical personnel, artisans and basic maintenance workers, as well as general engineering capabilities ranging from basic maintenance to tertiary skills.

- Offer tax incentives towards promoting R&D expenditures in the private sector. The structure would be left to individual countries—whether tax expenditures or allowable expenses. But the targeted policy outcome would be for firms to invest in R&D, including linking with local academic and research institutions (including polytechnics).

- Make it easier for firms to hire foreign workers with scarce skills, following the examples of Botswana and Mauritius.

7. Addressing infrastructure bottlenecks

The pervasive inadequacy of infrastructure in Africa is a major constraint on industrial development. It affects not only inter-country infrastructure but also feeder roads between agricultural producers and processing centres. With electricity, water, telecoms, information and communications technology and the like, administered prices can hinder expansion of services and affordability of access, undermining the competitiveness—and thus sustainability—of many businesses. Addressing this issue is often the most important factor in aiding the development of both the commodity sector itself and its linkages.

Focusing on infrastructure development has additional employment spin-offs for unskilled and semi-skilled jobs as well as training those with higher artisanal skills.

Some recommendations include:

- Avoid enclave infrastructure interventions aimed only at satisfying commodity producers' needs.

- Use commodity access to leverage favourable financing of infrastructure in bilateral agreements. In some cases transnational corporations in extractive industries can provide infrastructure for their own purposes, which, with government intervention, can be leveraged for use by other enterprises. When the government has financial resources, public-private partnerships can be set up to abet infrastructure provision.

- Make the regulatory framework effective, efficient and business friendly.

8. Coordinating ministries to improve policy implementation

Value chains are cross-cutting; government ministries are not. Ministries normally guard their own mandates, rendering policy coherence and inter-departmental cooperation difficult, despite its critical importance for implementing a commodity-based industrial strategy. Soft commodities tend to fall under the ministry of agriculture, and hard commodities under the mining and oil ministries—but an industrial policy requires input and direction from the ministry of industry.

Industrial policy requires well-targeted use of resources, which are controlled by the ministry of finance. It is therefore critical that national budgets include resources for commodity-based industrial strategies.

Even with the financing, linkage development strategies often stumble at implementation. For example, the ministry responsible for the commodity sector may be charged with designing and adopting the local-content or local-processing requirements, but building firms' capabilities requires interventions under the ministry responsible for industrial development. Similarly, linkage development may require technical and vocational training investment to prioritize certain skills, but the education ministry may have other urgencies. This often happens with technology, as linkage development requires industrial capabilities while public research institutes target innovation in agriculture or health.

In soft commodities, any policy to increase local processing needs to build on agricultural policies aimed at expanding production, improving product quality and developing infrastructure between rural and industrial areas.

Lastly, an important source of misalignment exists between ministries of trade and of industry. Trade negotiating strategies should support national industrial policy goals, but what they secure in multilateral or bilateral trade forums often fails to meet the strategic interests of local processing or supplier industries, so that trade measures on local content or export taxes may actually constrain policy space for developing linkages.

Some recommendations include:

- Secure a mandate at the highest political level to ensure that the interventions of relevant ministries and agencies are aligned to the national linkage development strategy.

- Create coherence within the government system to ensure that ministries have a local linkage development vision and make institutional arrangements to aid policy implementation and overcome coordination problems.

- Target the agricultural sector in order to raise productivity and quality (through grading and standardizing services) and to help companies specialize in niche markets (such as speciality coffees and high-quality cotton).

- Ensure that trade negotiations are aligned to industrial strategies.

9. Negotiating regional trade arrangements and fostering intra-African trade

Regional markets can play an important role in facilitating local production linkages within and between African countries, partly because they provide learning opportunities and allow domestic firms to build their production capabilities in a staged, step-by-step process. Also, local suppliers providing inputs and services to lead firms are in effect servicing a bounded, easier-to-satisfy market and can use this to build their capabilities. Finally, regional markets allow companies to build economies of scale, specialize a little between countries, and upgrade functionally through building regional "country of origin" branding and thus higher returns. Particularly for soft commodities and speciality products, however, this requires a regional perspective and a realization that not all countries in a region can occupy the same branding space.

Some recommendations include:

- Speed up launch of regional trade arrangements on important areas such as non-tariff barriers, sanitary and phytosanitary measures, technical barriers to trade, harmonization of customs procedures, and so forth.

- Ensure that country members that have not yet done so sign and implement the tariff-reduction schedules envisaged by the Continental Free Trade Area agreement.

- Remove cross-border impediments and facilitate rapid movement of goods and services within a regional trade area through physical infrastructure development and regulatory harmonization.

- Tackle the specific constraints that women face in regional markets in cross-border trade, including violence, corruption and confiscation of goods.

6.4 FINAL WORDS

African governments' adoption of these policy recommendations is only a first, albeit important, step for them to take advantage of the industrialization opportunities provided by the commodity boom. Governments also need to put their own house in order, in the sense of developing their own departments' attitudes and capacity. Most government officials dealing with enterprises have never been inside a factory and have no hands-on knowledge of what firms do—let alone their competitiveness.

Governments therefore have to run training programs to enhance the capabilities and knowledge of their own civil servants, for without skilled human resources in state bodies it will be hard to convince lead commodity producers and local firms that they are serious. And without political will and capacity, these recommendations will probably remain—no doubt compelling— words on paper, but will have little impact on the trajectory and speed of industrialization. In which case, Africa will have lost the chance of "making the most of its commodities."

REFERENCES

Hirschman, A. O. 1981. *Essays in Trespassing: Economics to Politics and Beyond.* New York: Cambridge University Press.

Kaplinsky, R., and M. Farooki. 2012. *Promoting Industrial Diversification in Resource Intensive Economies—The Examples of sub-Saharan Africa and Central Asia Regions.* Vienna: United Nations Industrial Development Organization.

Morris, M., R. Kaplinsky, and D. Kaplan. 2012. *One Thing Leads to Another: Promoting Industrialisation by Making the Most of the Commodity Boom in sub-Saharan Africa.* Published online by M. Morris, R. Kaplinsky, and D. Kaplan. Available at: http://oro.open.ac.uk/30047/7/MMCP_Paper_12.pdf

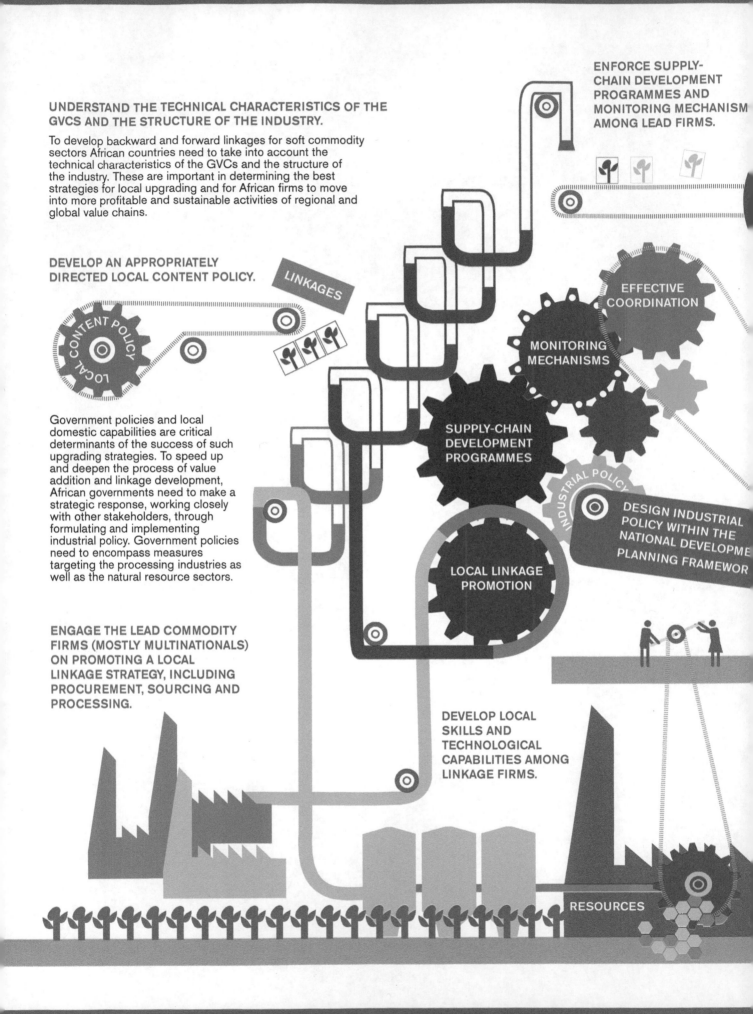

UNDERSTAND THE TECHNICAL CHARACTERISTICS OF THE GVCS AND THE STRUCTURE OF THE INDUSTRY.

To develop backward and forward linkages for soft commodity sectors African countries need to take into account the technical characteristics of the GVCs and the structure of the industry. These are important in determining the best strategies for local upgrading and for African firms to move into more profitable and sustainable activities of regional and global value chains.

DEVELOP AN APPROPRIATELY DIRECTED LOCAL CONTENT POLICY.

Government policies and local domestic capabilities are critical determinants of the success of such upgrading strategies. To speed up and deepen the process of value addition and linkage development, African governments need to make a strategic response, working closely with other stakeholders, through formulating and implementing industrial policy. Government policies need to encompass measures targeting the processing industries as well as the natural resource sectors.

ENGAGE THE LEAD COMMODITY FIRMS (MOSTLY MULTINATIONALS) ON PROMOTING A LOCAL LINKAGE STRATEGY, INCLUDING PROCUREMENT, SOURCING AND PROCESSING.

ENFORCE SUPPLY-CHAIN DEVELOPMENT PROGRAMMES AND MONITORING MECHANISM AMONG LEAD FIRMS.

LINKAGES

LOCAL CONTENT POLICY

EFFECTIVE COORDINATION

MONITORING MECHANISMS

SUPPLY-CHAIN DEVELOPMENT PROGRAMMES

INDUSTRIAL POLICY

DESIGN INDUSTRIAL POLICY WITHIN THE NATIONAL DEVELOPME PLANNING FRAMEWOR

LOCAL LINKAGE PROMOTION

DEVELOP LOCAL SKILLS AND TECHNOLOGICAL CAPABILITIES AMONG LINKAGE FIRMS.

RESOURCES

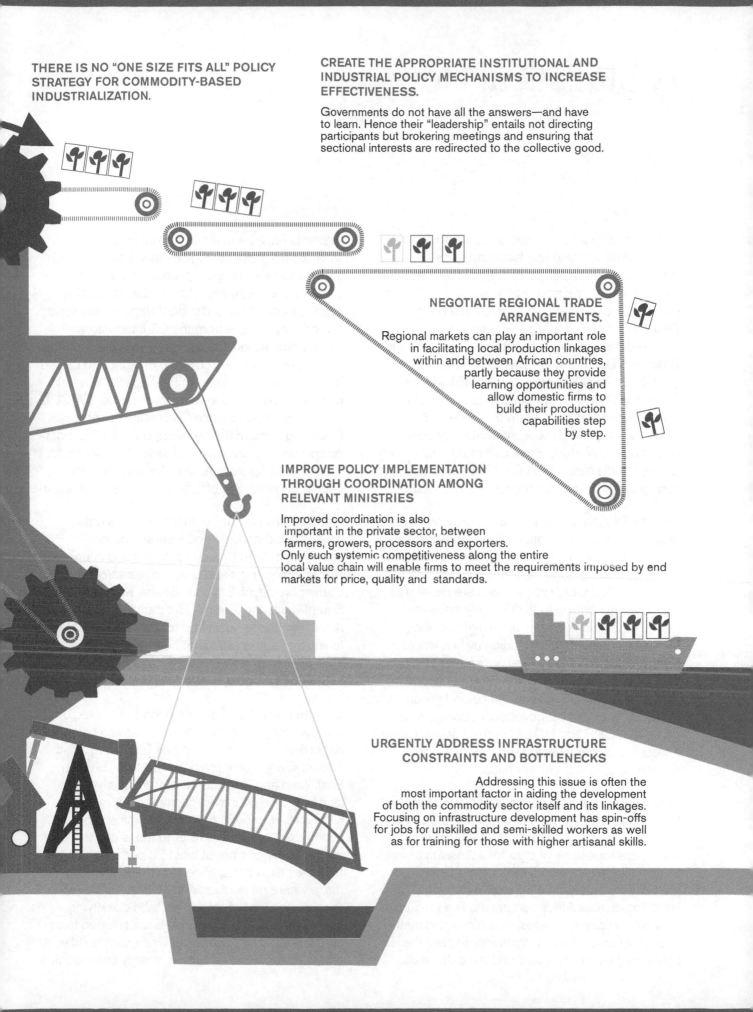

THERE IS NO "ONE SIZE FITS ALL" POLICY STRATEGY FOR COMMODITY-BASED INDUSTRIALIZATION.

CREATE THE APPROPRIATE INSTITUTIONAL AND INDUSTRIAL POLICY MECHANISMS TO INCREASE EFFECTIVENESS.

Governments do not have all the answers—and have to learn. Hence their "leadership" entails not directing participants but brokering meetings and ensuring that sectional interests are redirected to the collective good.

NEGOTIATE REGIONAL TRADE ARRANGEMENTS.

Regional markets can play an important role in facilitating local production linkages within and between African countries, partly because they provide learning opportunities and allow domestic firms to build their production capabilities step by step.

IMPROVE POLICY IMPLEMENTATION THROUGH COORDINATION AMONG RELEVANT MINISTRIES

Improved coordination is also important in the private sector, between farmers, growers, processors and exporters. Only such systemic competitiveness along the entire local value chain will enable firms to meet the requirements imposed by end markets for price, quality and standards.

URGENTLY ADDRESS INFRASTRUCTURE CONSTRAINTS AND BOTTLENECKS

Addressing this issue is often the most important factor in aiding the development of both the commodity sector itself and its linkages. Focusing on infrastructure development has spin-offs for jobs for unskilled and semi-skilled workers as well as for training for those with higher artisanal skills.

A Statistical Note

This year's *Economic Report on Africa* is based on the latest updated and harmonized data from various sources, including questionnaires developed by the authors. The main economic and social data variables are obtained from the United Nations Department of Economic and Social Affairs (UN-DESA) database and the United Nations Statistical Database. Data from the statistical databases of the International Monetary Fund (IMF), African Economic Outlook, Economist Intelligence Unit (EIU), United Nations Centre for Trade and Development, World Bank, International Labour Organization, World Trade Organization and United States International Trade Centre are also used in connection with various economic indicators.

The UN-DESA's Global Economic Outlook database provides comparable data on GDP growth for all African countries, except Seychelles and Swaziland for which data are obtained from the IMF and EIU databank. Real GDP growth rates are generated using country data with 2005 as the base year. Subregional inflation rates are weighted using individual consumption spending by household in billions of US dollars. Central government fiscal balances are calculated using GDP at current market prices in US dollars, and central government receipts minus central government outlays as a percent of GDP and GDP at current prices. Current account balances are calculated from national income accounts at current prices.

Social data are based on the latest data from United Nations Agencies deposited in the United Nations Statistical Database (UNSD). The UNSD, the official repository of data for assessing progress towards the Millennium Development Goals, provides accurate and comparable data on Goal indicators across African countries. The irregularity of surveys/censuses, ages, definitions and methods of production of the indicators may explain the lag between the reporting year and the data years.

Attempts have been made to source all trade statistics from United Nations data sources. Trade data (exports and imports) are from the online UNCTADstat database. The US data on textile imports from Africa under the African Growth and Opportunity Act are from the US International Trade Commission. Commodity prices are from the World Bank's Global Economic Prospect 2012. Aid for trade statistics are from the Organization for Economic Cooperation and Development (OECD)/ Development Assistance Committee's Creditor Reporting System (CRS), which provides the most comprehensive and updated data on aid for trade. Employment figures are from the International Labour Organization official employment database.

The thematic part of the report employs data collected, harmonized and analysed by local consultants through questionnaires and interviews with selected firms and policy makers from Algeria, Cameroon, Egypt, Ethiopia, Ghana, Kenya, Nigeria, South Africa and Zambia. But data in the report may differ from those published for reasons including timing and aggregation methods. Historical data may differ from previous editions of this report due to availability, recent revisions and timing.

Countries are classified into geographical regions and country groupings. Unless otherwise noted, the data cover 53 African countries (excluding South Sudan). Geographic regions are: North, Southern, East, West and Central. Parts of the analysis are also based on country groupings of oil importers, oil exporters, mineral rich and non-mineral rich countries. Oil exporters refer to those countries whose oil exports are at least 20 per cent higher than their oil imports. Mineral rich countries are those where mineral exports account for more than 20 per cent of total exports. In classifying commodities, ores and minerals are referred to as hard commodities, agricultural raw commodities as soft commodities and fuel as energy commodities.

Acronyms

AAF-SAP	African Alternative Framework for Structural Adjustment Programmes
ADI	Agro-industry Development Initiative
AERC	African Economic Research Consortium
AfDB	African Development Bank
AGOA	Africa Growth and Opportunity Act
AIDA	Accelerated Industrial Development of Africa
AIDS	Acquired Immune Deficiency Syndrome
AMU	Arab Maghreb Union
AMV	African Mining Vision
APCI	African Productive Capacity Initiative
APRM	African Peer Review Mechanism
ATF	African Trade Forum
AU	African Union
AUC	African Union Commission
BRIC	Brazil, Russia, India and China
CAADP	Comprehensive African Agricultural Development Programme
CAMI	Conference of African Ministers of Industry
CEN-SAD	Community of Sahel-Saharan States
CEPR	Centre for Economic Policy Research
CFA	African Financial Community
CFTA	Continental Free Trade Area
CIF	Cost Insurance and Freight
CMT	Cut, Make and Trim
CNRC	Centre National du Registre du Commerce
COCAN	Cocoa Association of Nigeria
COCOBOD	Cocoa Board
CODESRIA	Council for the Development of Social Science Research in Africa
COMESA	Common Market for Eastern and Southern Africa
COPAN	Cocoa Processors Association of Nigeria
CSF	Critical Success Factor
DAC	Development Assistance Committee
DFQF	Duty-Free and Quota-Free
DOTS	Directly Observed Treatment Short Course
EAC	East African Community
EBC	Everything But Arms
ECA	United Nations Economic Commission for Africa
ECCAS	Economic Community of Central Africa
ECF	Ethiopian Competitiveness Facility
ECOWAS	Economic Community of West African States
ECX	Ethiopian Commodity Exchange
EEG	Export Expansion Grant
EIU	Economist Intelligence Unit
EMIA	Export Marketing and Investment Assistance
EPAs	Economic Partnership Agreements

EPC	Export Promotion Council
EPCI	Engineering, Procurement, Construction and Installation
EPZ	Export Processing Zone
ESM	European Stability Mechanism
ETF	Exchange-Traded Fund
EU	European Union
FAO	Food and Agriculture Organisation
FDI	Foreign Direct Investment
FOCAC	Forum on China-Africa Cooperation
FPEAK	Fresh Produce Exporters Association of Kenya
GDF	Global Development Finance
GDP	Gross Domestic Product
GHI	Global Hunger Index
GNI	Gross National Income
GRI	Global Reporting Initiative
GRIPS	Graduate Institute for Policy Studies
GSP	Generalised System of Preferences
GVC	global value chains
HCDA	Horticultural Crops Development Authority
HIPC	Heavily Indebted Poor Countries
HIV	Human Immunodeficiency Virus
HSRC	Human Sciences Research Council
ICCO	International Cocoa Organisation
ICO	International Coffee Organisation
ICSG	increasing costs of exploring and mining new areas
ICT	Information and Communication Technology
IDC	Industrial Development Corporation
IDS	Institute of Development Studies
IEA	International Energy Agency
IFAD	International Fund for Agricultural Development
IFPRI	International Food Policy Research Institute
IGAD	Intergovernmental Authority on Development
ILO	International Labour Organisation
IMC	Industrial Modernisation Centre
IMF	International Monetary Fund
IPRCC	International Poverty Reduction Centre in China
ITNs	Insecticide-Treated Mosquito Nets
JIT	Just In Time
JOA	Joint Operating Agreements
KAM	Kenya Association of Manufacturers
KTDA	Kenya Tea Development Agency
LAC	Latin America and the Caribbean
LDCs	Least-Developed Countries
LICs	Low Income Countries
LLPTI	leather and leather product training institute
LME	London Metal Exchange
LTRO	Long-Term Refinancing Operations
MDGs	Millennium Development Goals
MDRI	Multilateral Debt Relief Initiative
MENA	Middle East and North Africa
MFA	Multi Fibre Agreement
MFN	Most Favoured Nation
MMR	Maternal Mortality Ratio
NDDC	Niger Delta Development Commission
NEPAD	New Partnership for Africa's Development

NNPC	Nigeria National Petroleum Corporation
NSDP	National Supplier Development Plan
NSE	Nigerian Stock Exchange
ODA	Official Development Assistance
OECD	Organisation for Economic Co-operation and Development
OMT	Outright Monetary Transactions
ONCC	Office National du Café et du Cacao
OPEC	Organisation of the Petroleum Exporting Countries
OSBP	One-Stop-Border-Post
PCRD	Post Conflict Reconstruction and Development
PIB	Petroleum Industry Bill
PIDA	Programme for Infrastructure Development in Africa
PPE	Personal protective equipment
PPIAF	Public-Private Infrastructure Advisory Facility
PPP	Public-Private Partnerships
PSC	Production Sharing Contract
PTDF	Petroleum Technology Development Fund
PTI	Petroleum Training Institute
QIZ	Qualifying Industrial Zone
RECs	Regional Economic Communities
RMG	Ready Made Garments
ROO	Rules of Origin
SACEEC	South African Capital Equipment Export Council
SACU	South African Customs Union
SADC	Southern African Development Community
SAP	Structural Adjustment Programme
SAR	Special Administration Region
SCID	Studies in Comparative International Development
SIC Cacaos	Societé Industrielle des Cacaos
SODECAO	Societé de Development du Cacao
SPS	Sanitary and phyto-sanitary measures
SSM	Special Safeguard Mechanism
SURF	sub-sea umbilicals, risers and flow line
SWF	Sovereign Wealth Funds
TBT	Technical barriers to trade
TCF	Third Country Fabric
UN	United Nations
UNCTAD	United Nations Conference on Trade and Development
UN-DESA	United Nations Department of Economic and Social Affairs
UNDP	United Nations Development Programme
UNIDO	United Nations Industrial Development Organisation
UNOSAA	United Nations Office of the Special Advisor for Africa
UNRISD	United Nations Research Institute for Social Development
UNU-WIDER	United Nations University World Institute for Development Economics Research
US	United States
USA	United States of America
US-GSP	United States-Generalized System of Preferences
USITC	United States International Trade Commission
WB	World Bank
WDI	World Development Indicators
WEF	World Economic Forum
WHO	World Health Organisation
WTO	World Trade Organisation

Acknowledgements

The Economic Report on Africa 2013, a joint publication of the United Nations Economic Commission for Africa (ECA) and the African Union Commission (AUC), was prepared under the leadership of Carlos Lopes, ECA's Executive Secretary, and Nkosazana Dlamini Zuma, Chairperson of AUC, with the active involvement of Abdalla Hamdok, Deputy Executive Secretary of ECA, and Maxwell Mkwezalamba, Commissioner for Economic Affairs, AUC. The report team benefited from the guidance and supervision of Emmanuel Nnadozie, ECA's Director of Economic Development and NEPAD Division, and René Kouassi N'Guettia, Director of the Economic Affairs Department, AUC.

The report's substantive team comprised Adam B. Elhiraika (Coordinator), Souleymane Abdallah, Bartholomew Armah, Chigozirim Bodart, Julianne Deitch, Adrian Gauci, Aissatou Gueye, Zheng Jian, Mama Keita, Samson Kwalingana, Ahamada Marie, Michael Mbate, Simon Mevel, Siope Ofa, John Sloan and Giovanni Valensisi, from ECA; Ndinaye Charumbira, Dauda Suma, and Hailu Kinfe, from AUC; and Tariq Haq, Michael Mwasikakata and Irmgard Nubler, from ILO.

Background papers were commissioned from Prof. Mike Morris and Dr. Judith Fessehaie, both of the University of Cape Town and nine country studies were undertaken by Dr. Youcef Benabdallah (Algeria), Dr. Désiré Avom (Cameroon), Mr. Rami Waguih Lofty Hanna (Egypt), Dr. Ahmed A. Kellow (Ethiopia), Dr. William Baah–Boateng (Ghana), Dr. Rosemary Atieno (Kenya), Prof. David Olusanya Ajakaiye (Nigeria), Prof. David Kaplan (South Africa) and Dr. Caleb Mailoni Fundanga (Zambia).

Useful comments were received from Stephen Karingi, Laura Páez and Gonzague Rosalie of ECA, Mr. Wilson Atta Krofah, Pan African Chamber of Commerce and Industry; Dr. Winford Masanjala, Ministry of Energy and Mining, Malawi; Ms. Khethiwe Mhlanga, Ministry of Commerce Industry and Trade, Swaziland; Ms. Wakap Tchagang Ariane, Ministry of Economy, Planning and Regional Development, Cameroon; Ms. Sampa Kangwa Wilkie, SRO-SA; Ms. Manisha Dookhony, Rwanda Development Board, Kigali; Prof. Yash Tandon, Independent Consultant, London; Prof. Benjamin Turok, Member of Parliament, South Africa; Prof. Ammon Mbelle, University of Dar es Salaam; Mr. Jean Bakole, UNIDO Regional Office, Addis Ababa; and Ms. Candide Leguede, FEFA CEDEAO, Lome.

We are particularly grateful for the expert advice provided by Dr. Ha-Joon Chang, University of Cambridge, UK; Dr. Yilmaz Akyüz, South Centre, Geneva; and Prof. Raphael Kaplinsky, Open University, UK.

This report would not have been possible without the contribution of the following: Doreen Bongoy-Mawalla, Hazel Scott, Etienne Kabou, Marcel Ngoma-Mouaya, Charles Ndungu, Teshome Yohannes, Ferdos Isa, Adeyinka Adeyemi, Mercy Wambui, Aloysius Fomenky, Tsitsi Mtetwa, Uzumma Erume, Agare Kassahun, Yetinayet Mengistu, Azeb Moguesse, Shewaye Woldeyes, Ariam Abraham, Solomon Wedere, Bekele Demissie of ECA; Bruce Ross-Larson and Jack Harlow of Communications Development Incorporated (CDI); Carolina Rodriguez, Giacomo Frigerio and Valentina Frigerio of Factblink; and Eunice Mafundikwa, Communication Consultant.